Handbook of the Money and Capital Markets

Handbook
of the Money
and Capital Markets

Alan Gart

Quorum Books
New York · Westport, Connecticut · London

HG
181
.G367
1988

Library of Congress Cataloging-in-Publication Data

Gart, Alan.
    Handbook of the money and capital markets / Alan Gart.
        p.   cm.
    Includes index.
    ISBN 0-89930-270-X (lib. bdg. : alk. paper)
    1. Money market—United States.   2. Capital market—United States.
3. Stock-market—United States.   4. Financial institutions—United
States.   I. Title.
HG181.G367 1988
332.63'2'0973—dc19   87-24938

British Library Cataloguing in Publication Data is available.

Library of Congress Catalog Card Number: 87-24938
ISBN: 0-89930-270-X

First published in 1988 by Quorum Books

Greenwood Press, Inc.
88 Post Road West, Westport, Connecticut   06881

Printed in the United States of America

The paper used in this book complies with the
Permanent Paper Standard issued by the National
Information Standards Organization (Z39.48-1984).

10   9   8   7   6   5   4   3   2   1

Contents

Contents

Tables and Figures

TABLES

FIGURES

Preface

In the last decade we have experienced many new instruments in the money and capital markets, deregulation, dramatic changes in our financial institutions and in our tax laws. Personal income tax rates have declined from a maximum of 50 percent in 1986 to 33 percent in 1988; corporate tax rates have experienced a commensurate decline from a maximum rate of 46 percent in 1986 to a rate of 34 percent in 1988. Accordingly, the investment tax credit and numerous tax deductions have been abolished.

During the 1980s we have seen an enormous growth of financial conglomerates and supermarkets such as American Express and Sears. Retailers and automobile companies have joined the traditional players in the financial services industry. Many of the older firms within the financial services industry have been forced to merge or have failed. For example, close to 260 commercial banks failed during 1985 and 1986. These failures were related to poor management, fraud, poor credit quality controls in lending practices, and a lack of diversification of the loan portfolio. This has been particularly true in the troubled energy, agriculture, and commercial real estate sectors.

Many thrift institutions have had difficulty in adjusting to the postderegulation era. Following a period where savings and loans failed because of balance sheet mismatches of long-term fixed rate mortgages with short-term variable rate deposits, many savings and loans adjusted suboptimally to the deregulation of thrift assets. In reaching for higher yields, some thrifts have sacrificed loan quality, while others have made loans in areas where the lending institution has had limited credit expertise. The failure of many banks and thrifts led to changes in interstate merger and acquisition legislation. The Garn–St Germain Bill (1982) permitted state banks and thrifts to acquire failing depository institutions regardless of where the bank is domiciled. In addition, some states passed legislation allowing out-of-state bank mergers in either regional compacts or in reciprocal interstate agreements between states. This has led to the formation of a number of "super regional" banks such as Sun Trust, Wachovia, NCNB, First Union, and Fleet Financial Group. These laws have also cleared the way for the merger of the Chemical Bank of New York with the Texas Commerce Bank and the merger of Security Pacific Bank with Washington's Ranier Bank. The "nonbank" bank, an institution that cannot make both demand deposits and commercial loans, has also brought about the equivalent of limited interstate banking as many insurance companies, brokerage firms, and bank holding companies set them up in key locations throughout the United States. These nonbank banks were formed when Congress could not agree to ban them.

High and volatile interest rates in the 1970s and early 1980s led to the development of a variety of new mortgage instruments that included variable rate, adjustable rate, renegotiated rate, reverse annuity, graduated payment, and shared or equity participation mortgages. Many of the new mortgage instruments shorten the effective length of time for which the mortgage lender is locked into a specific interest rate. Consequently, mortgage lenders tend to bear less interest rate risk and mortgage holders tend to bear more interest rate risk.

We have also seen the development and popularization of mortgage pass-through securities, mortgage-backed bonds, and collateralized mortgage obligations. Germane to collateralized securities, we have also seen the collateralization of automobile and credit card loans, lease-backed loans, multifamily pass-through securities, and commercial real estate pass-through securities.

There is a growing tendency for corporate borrowing to take the form of negotiable securities issued in the public capital markets rather than in the form of nonmarketable loans (for example, private placements) negotiated with life insurance companies and other financial intermediaries. For example, commercial paper has become increasingly competitive with bank loans in the short-term credit market. By year-end 1985, bank loans constituted only 24 percent of short-term debt at large manufacturing companies, compared with 59 percent in early 1974. In addition, large corporations and governments are often bypassing syndicated loans in the Eurodollar market in favor of financing arrangements that allow them to issue debt under their own names. By year-end 1985, financing in the form of securities had an 80 percent share of total funds raised in international financial markets compared with 33 percent in 1980.[1]

This shift toward borrowing in the form of securities reduces the role of the traditional intermediary that just makes loans and issues deposits. The traditional intermediary provides all forms of financial intermediation under one roof by pooling the funds of many savers and lending the funds in a different form to a diverse set of borrowers. The new growth of securities markets implies an "unbundling" of this process with many of these services being provided by different intermediaries. Although a bank or savings association may originate the loan, an investment bank may package it into a security and distribute it, for example, the aforementioned securitization of home mortgages, car loans, and credit card loans. An insurance company may even insure the security and a pension or mutual fund may end up financing it as a portfolio investment. The traditional intermediaries will still help link ultimate savers and borrowers, but the way in which they do business may change substantially.[2]

Other relatively new financial instruments that are competing for the attention of short-term corporate investors are money market preferred funds, adjustable rate and convertible adjustable rate preferred stock, daily adjustable tax-exempt securities, municipal option put securities, and universal commercial paper. On the other hand, zero-coupon bonds and junk bonds have become popular investment instruments for those interested in longer-term investments. Also, in 1986, Citicorp issued the first perpetual American bank holding company notes.

The large U.S. banks, facing overseas competition and the loss of their best corporate borrowers to alternative financing methods, wish to expand into fields such as real estate, insurance, investment advisory, underwriting mortgage-backed securities, commercial paper, municipal revenue bonds, and consumer-related receivables. Some of these large banks have threatened to give up their banking charters in order to expand into potentially more lucrative activities.

The Federal Reserve has already granted some banks permission to find buyers for corporate commercial paper and to underwrite municipal revenue bonds and mortgage-backed securities. The Fed decided that selling commercial paper did not violate the ban on commercial bank underwriting because the bank does not make a public offering of the paper, which has a maturity of under 270 days. In addition, the Fed twice denied banks authority to underwrite first-mortgage life insurance, but recently gave the go-ahead. At the same time, the FDIC (Federal Deposit Insurance Corporation) is preparing to let banks invest in real estate and to ease a proposed rule on sharing facilities with insurance companies. The new activity contrasts with the regulators' previous stand that banks should look to Congress for the authority to move into insurance sales and limited corporate underwriting, as well as for interstate banking privileges. The restrictions come primarily from the Glass-Steagall Act and from the Bank Holding Company Acts. In particular, Glass-Steagall separated commercial banking from securities underwriting. However, during the 1980s, Congress has not been able to agree on comprehensive changes, partly because of strong competitive lobbying efforts by commercial banks, insurance companies, and investment banking interests.[3]

The commercial banks contend that what is at stake is whether they can remain profitable and maintain market share when they are being challenged by nonbank rivals in this country and by foreign banks that are not bound by the same regulations. Year-end 1986 data show that commercial banks hold approximately one-half of the deposits and money market holdings of households, businesses, and governments, compared with 64 percent at the beginning of 1975. The regulators appear willing to compromise or even liberalize their restrictive covenants, in part, so as not to lose the large banks that have threatened to give up their bank charters from their regulatory preserve.

DEBT EXPANSION

Debt expansion has grown more rapidly than gross national product (GNP) in the United States. Credit market debt outstanding at the end of 1986 exceeded nominal GNP by more than 2 to 1, while in 1980 it was 70 percent higher than GNP. In both 1960 and 1970, it was roughly 50 percent higher than GNP. At the end of 1986, total credit market debt approximated $9 trillion, compared with $4.6 trillion at the start of the decade and $1.6 trillion in 1970. A deterioration in the quality of credit has accompanied this swift debt growth, which averaged 12 percent per year so far in the 1980s and 11 percent in the 1970s.[4]

This credit deterioration has been most noticeable in the U.S. business sector, where more credit ratings have been downgraded than upgraded during the 1980s. The universe of AAA-rated industrial and utility corporations has declined to just over two dozen companies from 56 in the mid-1970s. The percentage of new corporate bond issues composed of junk bonds has grown substantially during the 1980s. A major contribution to this erosion in quality has been the simultaneous increase in debt and the actual decline in the equity positions of business corporations. "Event risks," such as takeovers, have resulted in a sudden collapse in credit quality. Shortly after Beatrice Foods was acquired in a leveraged buyout, the credit rating declined from AAA to junk bond status. The credit quality deterioration is also evident in other sectors such as agriculture (where prices have plummeted) and commercial real estate (where there has been an excess of new office buildings in some parts of the country). Large real estate loan losses have been reported at a number of banks, thrifts and insurance companies, reflecting the fact that rental income is insufficient to support the debt service of many office projects.[5]

The attitude toward debt has been transformed from a hesitancy to borrow in the early post–World War II period to an intense use of credit during the 1970s and 1980s. This is true for individuals as well as for corporations. In addition, financial deregulation has facilitated the creation of debt because it spurs competition, reinforcing the drive for new markets and enlarged market standing. Financial innovation has either facilitated a credit that could not have been financed at all using earlier techniques or was utilized to reduce financing costs. With the advent of the passing through of interest rate risk to the ultimate borrower through floating rate loans and notes, financial institutions became aggressively more entrepreneurial and growth oriented than in the past. Securitization and the internationalization of finance have also encouraged debt creation. Major corporations, governments, and institutions seek the best terms in the United States, Europe, or Japan. Advances in communication and technology, together with financial deregulation, have intensified competition among the key financial centers, institutions, and markets.[6]

CONTENTS OF THE BOOK

Dynamic changes in the money and capital markets and a prolonged bull market in which the Dow Jones Industrial average climbed from 777 in August 1982 to

2,700 in August 1987, while bond rates declined substantially, have helped intensify the interest of investors in both fixed income securities and the stock market. With short-term money market rates in the 5.5 to 7.5 percent range and with U.S. Government bond rates offering between 8.5 to 9.8 percent in 1987, the achievement of an extra 5 to 10 basis points in yield is more important in this environment than it was when rates were at double digit levels.

This book was written with the goal of helping the investor achieve that extra yield, while at the same time understanding the additional risk associated with reaching for higher interest rates. The book also attempts to relate the dynamics of the financial markets by providing both a basic primer and a more complete understanding of the following:

1. Money and capital market instruments
2. Recent developments in the money and capital markets
3. Selected debt and equity market relationships and concepts
4. The underpinnings of basic valuation theory
5. Interest rate spreads and differentials
6. Basic bond portfolio strategies
7. The determinants of the level of interest rates
8. Credit ratings for debt instruments
9. Signals or ''red flags'' that investors might follow to minimize default risk
10. The new mortgage instruments
11. Tax-exempt securities
12. Securitization, junk bonds, and insured bonds
13. Interest rate swaps
14. Foreign exchange options

The handbook provides an overview of contemporary financial markets with particular emphasis on instruments, their markets, innovations, and changes. These new instruments include collateralized mortgage obligations, real estate development conduits, securitized automobile and credit card loans, credit enhanced and universal commercial paper, variable coupon renewable notes, money market preferred funds, adjustable rate and auction preferred stock, taxable municipals, interest rate swaps, and CDs (certificates of deposit) that are indexed to stock market performance.

The money and capital markets have been subjected to severe inflation followed by deflation in one decade, volatile interest rate and energy price swings, drastic changes in both individual and corporate taxes, and a shift in the way in which the Federal Reserve operates. In addition, rapid developments in computer and communications technology and the trend toward internationalization and deregulation have stimulated large-scale innovation in financial markets and institutions. The computer revolution has provided the capacity to process and communicate massive amounts of data quickly and efficiently. This has encouraged the expansion and development of financial services and the entry of nontraditional players into the financial services industry. It has also led to the development of alternative distribution systems and ways in which financial services are sold to the public.

NOTES

1. J. Loeys, "Low-Grade Bonds: A Growing Source of Corporate Funding," *Economic Review,* Federal Reserve Bank of Philadelphia, November/December 1986, pp. 9–12.

2. J. J. O'Leary, "How Life Insurance Companies Shifted Investment Focus," *Bankers Monthly Magazine,* June 15, 1982, pp. 2–28.

3. T. Curry and M. Warshawsky, "Life Insurance Companies in a Changing Environment," *Federal Reserve Bulletin,* June 1986, pp. 449–459.

4. H. Kaufman, "Debt: The Threat to Economic and Financial Stability," *Economic Review,* Federal Reserve Bank of Kansas City, December 1986, pp. 3–4.

5. Ibid., pp. 4–7.

6. Ibid.

Acknowledgments

I would like to thank Jerry Belloit (University of North Florida) for writing the chapter on the mortgage market, John B. Guerard (Lehigh University and O'Connor Associates) for writing the chapter on foreign exchange options, and David Leahigh (Lehigh University) for editing some of the chapters and making valuable suggestions. I would also like to thank Tom Druitt (Goldman Sachs) for inviting me to attend seminars on the money and capital markets sponsored by Goldman Sachs, and Debbie McNaulty (Federal Reserve Bank of Philadelphia) for her invaluable assistance. Amée Pollack (Franklin and Marshall College) deserves special praise for drawing many of the graphs and figures. I would also like to thank Lehman College for a Schuster Fellowship Grant to help defray typing and copying costs.

My family members, Deedy, Lisa, Steven, Zelda, and Herman Gart, each contributed by typing, editing, and proofreading, as well as by providing understanding and moral support. I owe much to my family for their support and tolerance over the long period required to write the book.

1

Introduction to Financial Markets and Institutions

A highly developed economy such as that of the United States relies on financial markets and institutions to transfer funds efficiently from savers to borrowers. There are many different financial markets in a developed economy. Each market deals with a somewhat different type of security, serves a different customer, or operates in a different geographical area.

Financial markets perform both a financial and economic function. They facilitate the transfer of real economic resources from lenders to borrowers while providing borrowers with funds to carry out their plans. At the same time, financial markets provide lenders with earning assets so that a lender's wealth may be held in a productive form without having the direct ownership of real assets.

The complex of financial markets and institutions is referred to as the financial sector of the economy. The financial system encompasses the instruments, institutions, markets, and rules governing the conduct of trade that expedite the flow of funds from buyers to sellers and from savers to lenders. The part of the financial system involving those institutions that are involved in the creation and distribution of money are referred to as the monetary system. A financial system makes possible the highly complex, specialized, and efficient methods of production that create much of the wealth of the economy. Without finance, trade would be sharply reduced while businesses and individuals would be severely restricted in what, how, and when they produce and consume.

There are numerous interrelated markets for loanable funds and securities. Loan markets also differ geographically. For example, local loans are usually made for mortgages and consumer loans by banks, thrifts, finance companies, and retail firms, while securities of the largest corporations are traded nationally or even internationally. These financial markets are diverse, with many different types of loans and securities for a variety of purposes. However, these markets are closely interconnected. Security price and yield information flow rapidly and freely throughout financial markets. When markets are closely linked, interest rates in the linked markets fluctuate together as supply and demand conditions change.

In an efficient market, funds flow freely and quickly among various sources and uses. Since financial instruments are often substitutable for each other, changes in supply and demand in one sector often have a spillover effect into another sector. Transactions move easily from one market segment to another with relatively low transfer costs compared to those attached to a change of real commodities.

The government and central bank try to promote conditions conducive to the sound and efficient operation of the financial sector through fiscal and monetary policy. The central bank uses monetary policy to make changes in the financial sector intended to affect conditions in the real (goods) sector of the economy. These policies are undertaken to help the economy attain economic growth, generate employment, and keep inflation at a moderate rate.

FINANCIAL MARKETS

Financial markets are where financial assets and liabilities are exchanged. These markets represent the channels through which savings are allocated to investment. In addition, they provide a variety of assets for savers and various forms in which governments, companies, and other potential borrowers can raise funds at relatively reasonable cost. Financial markets always change in response to shifting demands from the public, changing technological developments, and changes in laws and regulations.

MONEY AND CAPITAL MARKETS

The financial markets are often subdivided into two categories: money markets and capital markets. By convention, a security evidencing a loan that matures within a year is considered a money market instrument, while those instruments that have original maturities of more than one year are considered to be capital market instruments. Because of their short terms to maturity, the debt instruments traded in the money markets undergo the least price fluctuations. Capital market instruments have far wider price fluctuations than money market instruments and are therefore considered to be riskier investments (see chapter 4).

The capital markets are designed to finance long-term investments such as homes, schools, highways, shopping centers, industrial plants, and office buildings. The best known segment of the capital markets is the market for common stocks that are traded on the major stock exchanges. Since stocks have no maturity date and are claims in perpetuity, the stock market is a subset of the capital market. The residential mortgage market is the biggest of the debt markets (see Table 1.1). Although the size of the corporate debt market is considerably smaller than the stock market, with the amount of corporate debt outstand-

Table 1.1
The Leading Capital Market Instruments: Amount Outstanding ($ billions)

Type of Instrument	1960	1970	1980	1985
Corporate Stocks (Market Value)	451	906	1636	2868
Residential Mortgages	160	353	1108	1684
Corporate Bonds	75	188	447	714
U.S. Government Securities	NA	301	743	1600
State and Local Government(Tax-Exempt)	71	144	350	674
U.S.Government Sponsored Agencies	10	44	160	258
Bank Loans	118	162	461	683
Consumer Loans	65	143	399	665
Commercial and Farm Mortgages	46	115	350	582

Sources: Federal Reserve Flow of Funds Accounts, Federal Reserve Bulletin, and Banking and Monetary Statistics, 1941–1986.

Table 1.2
The Principal Money Market Instruments: Amount Outstanding ($ billions)

Type of Instrument	1960	1970	1984	1985
Negotiable CDs(Large Denomination)	0	25	410	427
U.S. Treasury Bills	32	81	374	381
Commercial Paper	4	33	246	273
Bankers' Acceptances	2	7	75	68
Repurchase Agreements	0	3	118	141
Eurodollars	1	2	95	92
Federal Funds	1	20	70	84

Sources: Federal Reserve Flow of Funds Accounts, Federal Reserve Bulletin, and Banking and Monetary Statistics, 1941–1986.

Note that the figures for Federal Funds are approximate.

ing being less than one-quarter that of stocks, the volume of new corporate bonds issues each year is much larger than the volume of new stock issues.

In contrast, the money market is designed for the making of short-term loans to finance such things as the working capital needs of corporations and to provide governments with short-term funds. Large denomination bank certificates of deposit and U.S. Treasury bills are the most widely issued money market instruments (see Table 1.2).

Futures, Options, and Foreign Exchange Markets

The spot market, often referred to as the cash market, is the market in which securities are traded for immediate delivery and payment. The futures market is the market in which securities are traded for future delivery and payment. The instrument traded is called a futures contract. If a futures contract is traded over the counter by negotiations, it is called a forward contract and the market is referred to as a forward market.

The options market is the market in which securities are traded for conditional future delivery. The instrument traded is an options contract of which the most popular types are put and call options. A put option permits the owner to sell a given security to the writer of the option at a predetermined price before a certain date, while a call option permits the owner to purchase a particular security from the seller or the writer of the option at a particular price before a certain date. These option contracts do not have to be executed and may be permitted to lapse at maturity.

Another important market is the foreign exchange market, where foreign currencies are traded either against domestic currencies or against each other. Trading takes place for either spot or future delivery on organized exchanges like the Chicago Board of Trade of the International Monetary Market or over the counter between foreign currency dealers or commercial banks. The U.S. dollar, the British pound, the Japanese yen, the German mark, the Swiss franc, and the French franc are among the most popularly traded currencies. Their exchange rates are determined in the foreign exchange market. The value of some currencies can be quite volatile. For example, from the beginning of 1973 to the beginning of 1980, the dollar declined 60 percent against the German mark, and 20 percent against the French franc. However, from early 1980 to the beginning of 1985, the dollar strengthened by 140 percent against the French franc, 80 percent against the German mark, and 60 percent against the Swiss franc before the dollar plummeted in 1986 and early 1987. The relative prices of these currencies affect the cost of overseas travel and influence the volume of goods that are imported and exported, as well as relative inflation rates in the respective countries.

Primary and Secondary Markets

The primary financial market is for the sale and trading of new securities never before issued, while the secondary market deals in securities previously issued.

The principal function of the primary market is the raising of financial capital to support new investment in equipment, the stock of inventories, and buildings. Primary markets are those in which the seller of the securities is also the issuer of the securities and receives the proceeds from the sale. When you sell common stocks or bonds that you have been holding in portfolio or place an order to buy shares currently being traded on the New York Stock Exchange, you are participating in a secondary market transaction. These secondary markets provide "liquidity" for financial assets. Liquidity refers to the ease with which an asset may be converted into money upon short notice without loss of principal. Of course, money has the advantage of being perfectly liquid; it can be spent to purchase goods and services without having to be converted into some other form. Because money earns the lowest return of all assets, savers usually minimize their holdings of money (kept in the form of cash or demand deposits) and tend to hold money market instruments, stocks, bonds, and other financial assets until they need spendable funds. While demand as well as most passbook and

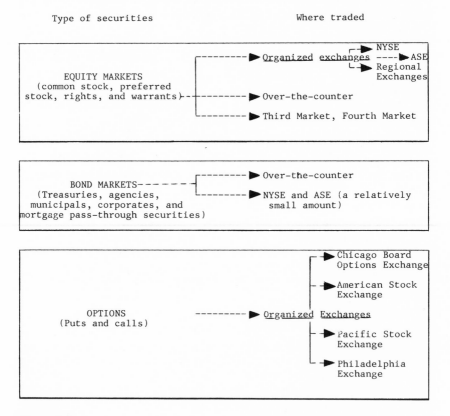

Figure 1.1
Secondary Markets

money market deposits at banks normally have complete liquidity, holdings of individual mortgages and other financial assets are not easy to convert into cash. While common and preferred stocks, bonds, bills, and CDs are commonly referred to as financial assets, tangible assets like homes, equipment, inventories, and oil- and gas-producing wells are referred to as real assets.

An active secondary market has always existed for U.S. government securities and stocks listed on major exchanges. During the 1970s and 1980s, the secondary markets for corporate, municipal bonds, and mortgage instruments have expanded significantly. In addition, secondary markets have developed for consumer credit and bank business loans in the mid 1980s.

Stocks and bonds that have already been sold to the public are often traded in the formal secondary markets (for example, the New York Stock Exchange) or over the counter (see Figure 1.1). If the security exchanges comprise the first market and the over-the-counter market (OTC) the second market, then the third market refers to an OTC transaction in a security that is traded on an organized exchange. Trading typically takes place between large institutional investors, such as insurance companies and pension funds, who often hold large blocks of stock and negotiate a price directly between the buyer and the seller. The growth of the third market in the 1960s and early 1970s was related to the growth of institutional trading in large blocks of stock and minimum commission fees charged at the time by exchange members. Since the SEC (Securities and Exchange Commission) fixed commissions on May Day 1975, activity in the third market has declined significantly. The fourth market refers to transactions made directly between a buyer and a seller of a large block. The Instinct system is a wire network that provides up-to-date information on the number of shares subscribers are willing to buy or sell at specified prices. Dealers and brokers are totally eliminated.

SUPPLY AND DEMAND FOR CREDIT

Four market sectors are the primary users of funds: business, household, government, and foreign. Their demand for funds takes the form of mortgages, corporate and foreign bonds, common and preferred stock, short-term business borrowing, and federal, foreign, and state and local government debt, as well as consumer installment debt. The supply of funds comes primarily from households, insurance companies, pension, retirement and profit-sharing plans, savings and loan associations, investment companies, savings banks, commercial banks, trust departments, foreigners, and business corporations (see Table 1.3).

Financial markets are subjected to a constantly changing set of counteracting forces—the forces of supply and demand, which can tend to move relative interest rates apart—and to a set of equalizing forces, which tend to keep the expected returns from different securities in a relationship that often reflects only their relative risks and not their supplies. Also, changes in the business cycle,

Table 1.3
Summary of Supply and Demand for Credit
(Annual Net Increases in Amounts Outstanding. Dollars in Billions)

	1981	1982	1983	1984	1985	1986E	1987P	Amt. Out. 31 Dec 86E
Net Demand								
Privately Held Mortgages	$68.8	$13.9	$95.4	$139.7	$127.4	$98.9	$92.6	$1,699.7
Corporate and Foreign Bonds	35.8	60.4	52.9	93.3	118.7	121.7	112.7	941.3
Total Long-Term Private	104.6	74.3	148.2	233.0	246.1	220.5	205.4	2,641.0
Short-Term Business Borrowing	118.4	55.8	55.4	152.2	112.0	102.2	78.8	1,236.6
Short-Term Other Borrowing	28.1	22.1	63.2	88.7	114.0	68.8	60.8	838.1
Total Short-Term Private	46.5	77.9	118.5	240.9	226.0	171.0	139.7	2,074.7
Privately Held Federal Debt	123.2	214.3	242.7	261.1	277.7	357.4	332.8	2,359.3
Tax-Exempt Notes and Bonds	18.2	54.4	42.2	67.0	124.4	54.4	54.5	796.7
Total Government Debt	141.4	268.7	284.9	328.0	402.1	411.7	387.3	3,156.0
Total Net Demand for Credit	**$392.5**	**$421.0**	**$551.7**	**$801.9**	**$874.3**	**$803.2**	**$732.4**	**$7,871.7**
Net Supply[a]								
Thrift Institutions	$26.4	$21.2	$133.8	$149.9	$84.1	$86.9	$92.5	$1,265.2
Insurance and Pensions	86.2	82.0	98.3	125.3	135.7	152.6	161.8	1,452.7
Investment Companies	71.3	52.3	6.1	82.9	114.4	184.6	144.2	597.6
Other Nonbank Finance	27.3	9.7	20.8	46.7	56.8	60.1	59.7	436.7
Total Nonbank Finance	211.3	165.1	259.0	404.8	391.0	484.2	458.2	3,752.3
Commercial Banks	100.5	102.4	139.9	170.8	207.2	137.7	121.0	2,102.0
Domestic Nonfinancials[b]	8.0	22.8	54.3	52.9	72.5	66.3	60.3	425.0
Foreign Investors	10.7	12.5	18.3	27.9	29.8	75.9	79.0	407.5
Subtotal	330.5	302.9	471.5	656.3	700.5	764.1	718.5	6,686.9
Residual: Households Direct	62.0	118.1	80.2	145.5	173.8	39.1	13.9	1,184.9
Total Net Supply of Credit	**$392.5**	**$421.0**	**$551.7**	**$801.9**	**$874.3**	**$803.2**	**$732.4**	**$7,871.7**
Memo								
Net Issuance Corporate Stock	$-23.5	$-20.3	$25.8	$-81.7	$-61.4	$-62.6	$-69.4	$2,990.0
Total Credit and Stock	368.9	400.7	577.5	720.2	812.8	740.6	663.0	10,861.7
Percentage of Total Absorbed by								
Households	42.5%	28.8%	43.5%	41.9%	41.9%	40.6%	43.8%	
Nonfinancial Business	23.9	17.5	15.3	5.2	9.5	5.6	5.8	
Financial Institutions	11.0	3.8	6.6	1.6	13.3	16.5	13.2	
Government	16.4	44.6	34.3	31.7	35.0	37.4	36.0	
Foreigners	6.1	5.3	0.3	-0.4	0.3	1.0	1.2	

[a] Excludes funds for equities and other demands not tabulated above.
[b] Corporations and non-Federal governments.

Source: Prospects for Financial Markets in 1987. Salomon Brothers Inc., December 1986.

economic activity, and inflation are key factors influencing the supply and demand for funds in the business, household, and government sector.

TYPES OF FINANCIAL TRANSACTIONS

In addition to facilitating the flow of savings into investments, the financial markets furnish credit in many forms to consumers and businesses. Financial systems move scarce funds from surplus budget units (SBUs) to those who wish to borrow and invest; money is exchanged for financial assets. Money can be directed to those deficit budget units (DBUs) that can use funds most efficiently and can afford to pay an appropriate return to the lender. Also, financial markets provide marketability and liquidity, enabling SBUs and DBUs to make portfolio changes quickly and at low cost.

The transfer of funds from savers to borrowers can be accomplished by (1) direct financing, (2) semidirect financing, and (3) indirect financing.[1] Although the marketplace does accommodate some suppliers and demanders of funds directly, financial intermediaries play the most important role of channeling the funds of the large number of suppliers to the various users of funds (indirect financing) (see Figure 1.2).

Direct financing is the simplest method of carrying out financial transactions because borrower and lender meet each other and exchange funds in return for financial assets. However, it has a number of limitations.[2]

1. Both borrower and lender must want to exchange the same amount of funds at the same time.
2. The lender must be willing to accept the risk, liquidity, and maturity characteristics of the borrower's IOU.
3. Both lender and borrower must often incur substantial search or information costs to find each other; for example, the borrower may have to contact numerous potential

(a) Direct Transfer of Funds

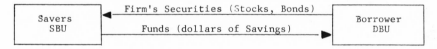

(b) Semidirect Transfer Using Brokers and Dealers

(c) Indirect Transfer Using Financial Intermediary

Figure 1.2
Ways to Transfer Financial Capital in the Economy

lenders before finding one with just the right amount of funds and a willingness to accept the borrower's IOU.

An example of direct financing stems from a new business that may go directly to a saver or group of savers called "venture capitalists." The venture capitalist will lend funds to the firm and/or take an equity position in the firm if they feel that the new firm will be successful.

In order to facilitate financial transactions and minimize search costs, securities brokers and dealers bring surplus and deficit budget units together with respect to compatibility in denomination, maturity, credit risk, and so forth (see Figure 1.2). This form of financing is called *semidirect finance* and is an improvement over direct finance because it lowers the search costs for financial markets participants. In addition, a dealer will often split up a large issue of securities into smaller units that are affordable to buyers of more modest means. This broadens the flow of savings into investment. Also, brokers and dealers will often provide a secondary market where the securities can be offered for resale. This secondary market give those securities a measure of liquidity and marketability.

Financial brokers generate fee income by charging a commission for introducing the borrower to the lender or for selling the firm's securities. Dealers differ from brokers in that they purchase the security from the DBU to resell to the SBU, maintaining an inventory of securities for customers to purchase. Dealer profits are generated from being able to sell the securities at a higher price than that at which they were purchased. The possibility of losses make the risks of a dealer considerably higher than those of a broker. It is possible for a firm to be both a broker and a dealer, depending on the securities trades. Brokers and dealers are also called investment bankers. In semidirect financing, the securities being issued just pass through the investment banking firm. They are not transferred into a different type of security.

Even with the contribution of brokers and dealers, the semidirect approach is not without its limitations, as the lender must be willing to accept the borrower's IOU, which may be quite risky, illiquid, or slow to mature. There must be fundamental coincidence of wants and needs between the borrower and saver for semidirect financial transactions to take place. The limitations of both direct and semidirect finance led to the development of indirect financial transactions that are carried out with the help of financial intermediaries such as depository institutions like banks or contractual institutions like insurance companies or pension funds. The key role of these financial institutions is to serve as intermediaries between ultimate lenders and borrowers, but in a completely different and more involved way than the role played by brokers and dealers. The financial intermediary collects the savings of individuals and other SBUs and issues its own (indirect) securities in exchange for these savings (for example, a bank CD or passbook). The intermediary then uses the funds collected from individual savers to acquire the business firm's (direct) securities, like stocks and bonds.

Financial intermediaries tend to acquire the IOUs issued by borrowers and at the same time sell their own IOUs to savers. For example, banks and thrifts accept consumer deposits, which become institutional liabilities, and use the funds to make investments and loans by accepting IOUs from borrowers. Although security brokers and dealers, investment bankers, and mortgage bankers

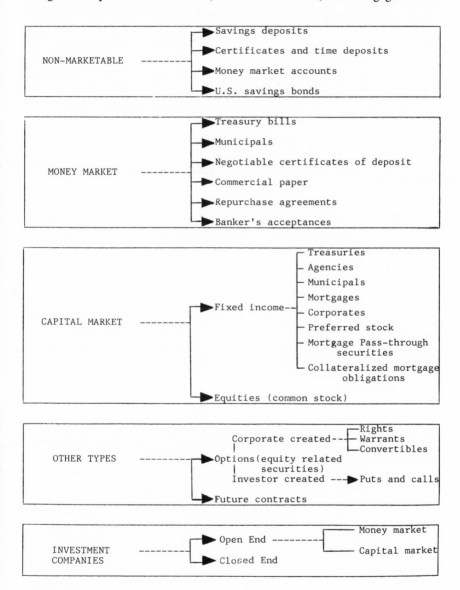

Figure 1.3
Major Types of Financial Assets

are financial institutions, they are different from the other financial intermediaries. These institutions do not create their own IOUs. Instead, they tend to pass securities issued by other institutions along to other investors. For example, mortgage bankers acquire mortgage securities arising from the construction of homes, apartments, and businesses and place these mortgages with long-term lenders such as pension funds, life insurance companies, and thrift institutions.

The financial markets facilitate the creation of financial securities and their transfer from issuers to investors. Financial securities are essentially IOUs, is-

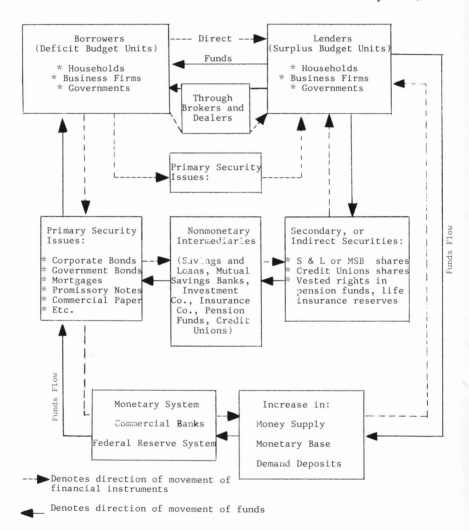

Figure 1.4
The Relationship of Intermediaries and Money and Credit Instruments to Borrowing and Lending

sued by those budget units that spend more than their current income (borrowers), while financial securities are purchased by budget units (savers), who spend less than their current income on consumption and investment.

Budget units are neither permament DBUs nor permanent SBUs, but instead alternate between the two as their income and tastes change and as interest rates fluctuate. However, most people follow a reasonably predictable pattern over their lives. Most people are born DBUs, financed by their parents until they leave school. After obtaining permanent employment, most people become SBUs for a while. After marriage and the purchase of their first home, they become DBUs again. After that, they slowly regain SBU status and their children enter college, at which time they again become DBUs. After graduation of the last child, people usually become SBUs until retirement. During the retirement period, they generally return to DBU status. However, they usually consume their own savings. At death, remaining savings are usually transferred to their heirs. The pattern may become different with changes in interest rates and the development of unforeseen events. For example, higher interest rates in any one period are likely to induce these units to be SBUs rather than DBUs at that time.[3] An important consequence of the process of financial intermediation is that capital formation and economic wealth are greater than they would be in the absence of this financial market system. Also, another positive consequence of this process is the formation of a lower level of interest rates in financial markets. This is because of the existence of financial intermediaries that help reduce the demand to hold money and increase the incentive to save out of current income.

Figure 1.3 shows the major types of financial assets available to investors, while Figure 1.4 shows the relationship of intermediaries and money and credit instruments to borrowers and lenders.

COMPARISON OF ASSET HOLDINGS

Table 1.4 shows a breakdown of the asset composition of the major financial intermediaries. It shows the commercial banks as the dominant holders of government securities, municipal bonds, and business and consumer loans. However, with recent changes in the tax laws, banks are not likely to expand their holdings of municipal bonds. Savings and loans were the dominant holder of mortgages, while households and pension funds were the major investors in corporate equities. Insurance companies and mutual funds were also large holders of common stocks. Finance companies, credit unions, and nonfinancial corporations were right behind commercial banks in loans to consumers. The property-casualty companies are major investors in municipal bonds, particularly during periods when the underwriting cycle is favorable. Households are also large investors in tax-free municipal bonds, government securities, and corporate equities.

Table 1.5 shows the total assets of the most important financial intermediaries. Commercial banks are the largest of these intermediaries, followed by savings

Table 1.4
Earning Asset Composition of Major Financial Institutions (Year-end 1985, billions of $)

	Total Financial Assets	Government Securities	Municipal Securities	Foreign & Corporate Bonds	Business Loans[1]	Mortgages	Consumer Loans[2]	Corporate Equities
Commercial Banks	1984	257	231	17	576	422	295	—
Savings & Loans	1072	154	1	—	17	657	45	—
Life Insurance Companies[3]	780	90	10	274	31	171	54	77
Private Pension Funds	757	107	—	119	—	5	—	383
Public Pension Funds	432	129	1	123	—	15	—	145
Finance Companies	358	—	—	—	153	54	146	—
Property-Casualty Companies	290	56	87	34	—	3	—	57
Mutual Funds	283	65	76	20	4	—	—	114
Credit Unions	137	13	—	—	—	9	76	—
Money-Market Funds	208	43	—	—	99	—	—	—

[1]Includes open market paper
[2]Includes life insurance policy loans
[3]Includes pension funds managed by life insurance companies

Source: Board of Governors of the Federal Reserve System, Flow of Funds Accounts.

Table 1.5

Total Assets of Financial Intermediaries at Year-End (Billions of Dollars)

Financial Intermediary	1960	1965	1970	1975	1980	1985*
Commercial Banks	$257.6	$377.3	$ 576.2	$ 964.9	$1,703.7	$2,460.3
Savings Institutions:						
Savings Associations . . .	71.5	129.6	176.2	338.2	630.7	952.2
Savings Banks	40.6	58.2	79.0	121.1	171.6	325.7
Total	112.1	187.8	255.2	459.3	802.3	1,277.9
Life Insurance Companies .	119.6	158.9	207.3	289.3	479.2	812.0
Private Pension Funds	38.1	73.6	110.4	186.6	412.5	655.2
State and Local						
Pension Funds	19.7	34.1	60.3	104.8	198.1	397.2
Finance Companies	27.6	44.7	64.0	98.8	191.3	331.7
Money Market Funds	. . .	. . .	. . .	3.7	74.4	207.5
Investment Companies . . .	17.0	35.2	47.6	42.2	58.4	251.5
Credit Unions	6.3	11.0	18.0	36.9	71.6	135.3
Total	$598.0	$922.6	$1,339.0	$2,186.5	$3,991.5	$6,528.6

*Preliminary.
Sources: CUNA International, Inc.; Federal Home Loan Bank Board; Federal Reserve Board; Institute of Life Insurance; Investment Company Institute; National Council of Savings Institutions; United States League of Savings Institutions.

and loan associations and life insurance companies. Private pension funds and state and local government pension funds are also quite large and play a key role in supplying funds to the money and capital markets. Since Table 1.5 was constructed, open-end investment companies have exhibited rapid growth in total assets, reaching approximately $425 billion at year-end 1986. This can be attributed to the sustained bull market for both stocks and bonds during the 1985–1986 period. In June 1986, the Federal Reserve ruled that bank holding companies could sell mutual fund shares through their brokerage subsidiaries. With bank holding companies acting as distributors, mutual funds should continue as one of the most important financial intermediaries.

NOTES

1. P. S. Rose, *Money and Capital Markets,* Special Edition (Plano, Texas: Business Publications, 1984), pp. 33–39.

2. Ibid.

3. G. C. Kaufman, *The U.S. Financial System: Money Markets and Institutions.*

Money Markets

The term *money market* refers to the marketplace where borrowers and lenders exchange short-term funds. There is no unique location; the money market is a complex of thousands of locations throughout the world, each trading distinctly different financial instruments. In current usage, money markets refer to the markets for short-term credit investments such as Treasury bills, federal funds, commercial paper, bankers' acceptances, repurchase agreements, loans to security dealers, and negotiable certificates of deposit. Money market instruments are generally financial claims that have low default risk, maturities under one year, and high marketability.

A key function of the money markets is to provide a vehicle that enables economic units to adjust their liquidity positions. Money market instruments permit these units to bridge the gap between cash receipts and cash expenditures, solving their liquidity needs. An efficiently functioning money market provides liquidity to the economy, which eventually channels the flow of funds to the most important use throughout the country. The money market provides a source of short-term funds for many borrowers. By providing a continuous flow of loan funds through the market it is possible for borrowers through renewals or rollovers of loans to obtain funds on a more or less continuous basis. Both institutions and individuals supply funds to the money markets.

The money market is particularly important to commercial banks in managing their money positions. Banks in the aggregate are large-scale buyers and sellers of most money market instruments, especially federal funds and CDs. The money market permits a more intensive use of bank reserves and enhances the ability of the commercial banking system to allocate funds efficiently. By allowing depository institutions, particularly banks, to operate with lower excess reserves, the banking system is more sensitive to central bank policy actions.[1] With the exception of commercial paper, which does not have a broad secondary market, all of these instruments are liabilities of a commercial bank, the government, or a quasi-government agency.

Although the term *market* may suggest trading of assets, some investments and loans are seldom traded or not traded at all after their purchase in the primary market. There is a secondary market where financial assets representing short-term claims are traded at rates determined by supply and demand. The secondary market is largely an over-the-phone market with over three dozen government security dealers (some of which are banks) and about two dozen large commercial banks that trade heavily in money market instruments.

Money market obligations traded in the secondary market have a low risk of either capital loss or default because interest rate risk is minimized with assets that have a maturity under one year. There is a high degree of safety or low default risk because the financial instruments are issued by borrowers of extremely high credit standing such as the government, government agencies, and commercial banks.

The Federal Reserve is the most important buyer and seller of Treasury and agency securities, influencing daily money market conditions with its open market operations. The New York Federal Reserve Bank is the dominant player, conducting open market operations with recognized U.S. securities dealers. The New York Federal Reserve Bank implements Federal Open Market Committee policy directives by targeting reserve availability, money growth, and interest rates on federal funds. Changes in the federal funds rate ultimately affect other interest rates.

The money market is the main focus of central bank activities in implementing monetary policy. The daily operations of the Federal Open Market Trading Desk occupy an important place in the money markets, conducting transactions in U.S. government securities, bankers' acceptances, and in federal agency issues. The Federal Reserve enters the market frequently to provide new depository institution reserves through sales. Federal Reserve operations are also undertaken to compensate for changes in float, Treasury balances, currency in circulation, and to achieve its economic and financial objectives. Since the early 1970s these objectives have concentrated on achieving targeted ranges of growth rates of the money supply.[2]

FEDERAL FUNDS MARKET

Prior to the formation of the Federal Reserve System, the short-term markets included only commercial paper and call and time loans on security collateral at the New York Stock Exchange. The big New York banks were large lenders in security collateral, while the smaller banks throughout the country usually placed most of their short-term liquid funds in the open market for commercial paper or in interest-bearing deposits with the New York banks. For many of these banks, the interbank deposits served some of the purposes that sales of federal funds later came to serve.

The financing of World War I inaugurated a market for short-term U.S. government securities. The Federal Reserve System, which was started in 1914, encouraged and supported the organization of an acceptance market. The federal funds market emerged as an informal by-product of the organization of the reserve system. It began with the trading of reserves by several of the New York City banks as a means of adjusting their reserve positions. By the early 1920s, it became a "new market" within the money market.

Federal funds represent monies bought and sold by banks among themselves to meet reserve requirements against deposits. They are considered the most liquid, interest-bearing, near-cash asset. Although those funds are usually bought and sold for one night, term federal funds may be purchased for periods of up to about one year.

Federal funds are essentially short-term loans of immediately available funds. Such immediately available funds include deposits at Federal Reserves and collected liabilities of commercial banks and other depository institutions. Since Federal Reserve member banks are required to hold cash reserves at the Reserve Bank or in vault cash equal to a specified percentage of their deposits, the banks can lend out reserves in excess of the required amount. In the federal funds market, lending is referred to as sales and borrowing as purchases. The credit quality of the participating banks is well known to all other banks, permitting the transactions to be consummated quickly by telephone on an unsecured basis. The interest rate on federal funds transactions is determined by market conditions and the reputation of the borrowing bank. An essential feature of both federal funds and repurchase agreements is that transactions are settled in "immediately available funds." In addition, commercial banks that are members of the Federal Reserve System can acquire funds not subject to reserve requirements in both markets. The rapid growth of the markets for federal funds and for repurchase agreements might be considered as part of a trend in financial markets toward more aggressive portfolio management by holders of financial assets.

In selling federal funds, banks are making unsecured loans to other banks at one of the lowest money market rates. Some banks carefully monitor the credit risks they assume. They will only sell federal funds to banks with established credit lines. In establishing a credit line, the lending bank considers the borrowing bank's reputation in the market, its capital structure and size, and other factors that may affect the bank's creditworthiness.

If there were only one commercial bank in the United States, there would be no need for a market in federal funds. The rate on overnight borrowing would be the rate on repurchase agreements between the bank and its customers. Since there are many deposit institutions in the economy, a bank can obtain credit by borrowing from another bank or through a repurchase agreement with a bank customer. The federal funds market provides a mechanism for the efficient distribution of reserve balances among commercial banks and thrift institutions.

From its origin as a market limited to the purchase and sale of excess reserve deposits among member banks, the market has undergone enormous expansion. Active liability management practices of the last three decades created new demand for federal funds, while less restrictive regulations brought the funds market to a new group of financial institutions. Federal funds are an important purchased liability for large banks, a profitable liquid investment for a wide range of market participants, and a valuable reserve adjustment.[3]

TREASURY SECURITIES

One of the responsibilities of the U.S. Treasury Department is to provide financing for the U.S. government. Most of the funds are raised by publicly selling marketable securities such as Treasury bonds, bills, and notes. The Federal Reserve Banks act as agents for the Treasury in the selling of these securities. An individual or company may purchase these without any fee. These securities also may be purchased through financial institutions for a fee on a registered or book entry basis. Purchase of a registered security means that the buyer receives a certificate verifying ownership, while in the book entry method a purchaser receives a receipt rather than a certificate as evidence of purchase.

Treasury bills are short-term securities with original maturities of 13, 26, and 52 weeks. They are sold in minimum amounts of $10,000 and in multiples of $5,000 above the minimum. Currently, Treasury bills are sold on a book entry basis, protecting the purchaser from loss, theft, or counterfeiting and reducing Treasury processing costs. The 13- and 26-week Treasury bills are offered each week as follows: the offering is announced on Tuesday, auctioned the following Monday, and issued the following Thursday. The 52-week bills offering is announced every fourth Friday, auctioned the following Thursday, and issued one week later on Thursday. When purchasing a bill, the discount value is paid by 2:30 p.m. on the auction day through the federal wire system, while the full face value is paid at maturity. The auction determines the average selling price for the bills. The difference between the actual price of the bills and their face value is called the "discount." In noncompetitive tenders at the Federal Reserve Bank, the face value is paid at purchase with a check from the buyer, while a check for the discount as set by the auction is sent immediately by the central bank to the buyers. There is a highly liquid and active secondary market for Treasury bills. Buyers and sellers can trade in large quantities without affecting the market price. The bills are traded on a discount basis and redeemed at maturity for par value. Treasury bills do not bear what is conventionally known as credit or default risk, the risk that a debtor will not pay at the maturity of the security. Unlike other money market investments, the income earned on Treasury bills is exempt from state and local taxes.

There are two ways of participating in a Treasury bill auction. Investors can submit a competitive tender stating the amount they are willing to pay for the bills and the quantity desired at that price. The auction process relies on the participation of the primary government securities dealers (see chapter 7).

The Treasury also accepts noncompetitive tenders stating the face value of bills desired. A noncompetitive tender sacrifices certainty of prices in return for certainty of delivery. The Treasury guarantees to meet fully all noncompetitive demand up to a maximum of $1 million per bidder, per auction, but at a price that

INTEREST RATES

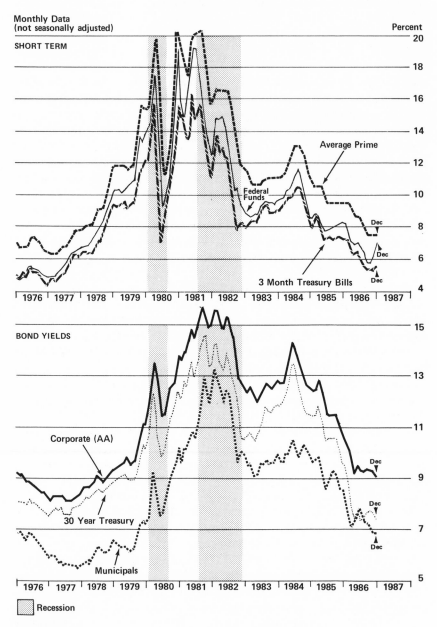

Source: *Charts on the Economic Outlook.* Brown Brothers Harriman and Co., March 1987.

Figure 2.1
Bond Yields

is equal to the average of the accepted competitive prices for the bills. Large dealer banks and broker-dealer firms submit the bulk of the competitive bids, while small banks, small companies, and individuals account for most of the noncompetitive demand for bills.

Figure 2.1 shows the relationship between the Treasury bill rate, the federal funds rate, and the prime rate from 1976 to 1986.

The mechanics of the auction require the U.S. Treasury first to subtract the amount of noncompetitive bids from the total amount of the bills to be sold. For example, if T-bills totaling $2 billion in face value are to be auctioned and noncompetitive bids total $500 million, that means that $1.5 billion is available to competitive bidders in the order of their bids—highest buys first. If there are $2.5 billion worth of competitive bids, only $1.5 billion will be available to the highest bidders, while $1 billion of competitive bids will be denied. This process assures the Treasury of receiving the highest possible revenues from the sale of the bills. The lowest accepted bid is commonly referred to as the "stop-out" price. Although the noncompetitive bid ensures that the bidder will get to buy T-bills on the day of the auction, the exact price is not known in advance.

Generally speaking, the auction method is simpler and less time consuming than the subscription method because the market establishes a yield, making it unnecessary for the Treasury to second guess market conditions and thereby eliminating the problems associated with oversubscription or undersubscription. The Treasury just chooses the amount of the offerings and allows the market to do the rest. Bill auctions provide the Treasury with a flexible debt financing tool.

Although commercial banks are still among the largest holders of Treasury bills outstanding, their holdings of bills vary cyclically and in the opposite direction of the holdings of individuals. The commercial banking systems' investments in bills tend to increase substantially during periods of slack economic activity and tend to decline in periods of strong economic activity when loan demand and interest rates are usually rising. Money market funds and foreign investors join individuals and banks as the largest holders of Treasury bills.

Calculating the Discount Rate Investment Yield on Treasury Bills

Since Treasury bills are sold at a discount below face value, they are redeemed at face value at maturity. In calculating the investment yield to maturity, we use the following formula:

$$\text{Investment Yield} = \frac{(\$100 - p) \times 365}{p \times \text{days to maturity}}$$

p = price of your T-bill in dollars per $100 of face amount

Example:
Supp⟩se you buy a 91-day Treasury bill for $96.562 per $100 of face amount.

Since bills are sold in minimum $10,000 denominations, you would pay $9,650.20 and receive $10,000 at maturity. Using the above formula, the yield would be 14.28 percent, calculated as follows:

$$\frac{(\$100 - 96.562) \times 365}{\$96.562 \times 91} = .1428 \text{ or } 14.28\%$$

Special Issues of Bills

The Anticipation Bills (TABs). TABS were first introduced in 1951 to bridge temporary cash flow problems. They typically have a maturity date one week after corporate profit tax payment dates. They are acceptable at face value in payment of such taxes when presented by a corporation, allowing several days of "free interest" on TABS.

Strip Issues. Introduced in 1961, strip issues are blocks of bills that mature on sequential maturity dates. They are used when the Treasury needs cash and desires to spread its borrowings out over several bill maturities rather than adding a large amount to a single maturity. They are also used by the Treasury if interest rates are quite low in one segment of maturities, providing the government with an opportunity to borrow inexpensively.

Cash Management Bills. Introduced in 1975, cash management bills are aimed at the institutional rather than retail investors and have extremely short maturities. Cash management bills, like strip issues, are reopenings of existing maturities.

Coupon Issues. Coupon issues are entitlements to a stream of multiple Treasury payments in the form of returned principal at maturity and a regular sequence of coupons or semiannual interest payments. The coupon rate is the ratio of the coupon payments made in a single year to the principal value of the issue.

SECURITIES DEALERS AND BROKERS

The market for U.S. government securities centers on the dealers who report daily activity, inventory, and financing to the Federal Reserve Bank of New York. Of the total, 13 are commercial banks and 27 are nonbank dealers (see Table 2.1). The dealers buy and sell securities for their own account, arranging transactions with both their customers and other dealers. They also purchase debt directly from the Treasury for resale to investors. A primary dealer is allowed to buy government securities directly from the Fed in return for maintaining constant markets in Treasury debt. In addition to meeting financial and management criteria, primary dealers must also maintain average customer trading volume in government securities of at least three-quarters of 1 percent of total primary dealer customer volume. In addition to the dealers, there are brokers who specialize in the matching of buyers and sellers among the dealers in the government securities market. Dealers trade actively with customers as well as among them-

Table 2.1
The Primary Dealers of U.S. Government Securities

Banks

Bank of America NT & SA, New York
Bankers Trust Co., New York
Chase Manhattan Government Securities Inc., New York
Chemical Bank, New York
Citibank NA, New York
Continental Illinois National Bank and Trust Co., Chicago
Crocker National Bank, San Francisco
First Interstate Bank of California, Los Angeles
First National Bank, Chicago
Harris Trust and Savings Bank, Chicago
Manufacturers Hanover Trust Co., New York
Morgan Guaranty Trust Co., Inc., New York
Security Pacific National Bank

NonBanks

Bear, Stearns & Co., New York
Briggs, Schaedle & Co. Inc., New York
Carroll McEntee & McGinley Inc., New York
Daiwa Securities America
Dean Witter Reynolds Inc., New York
Discount Corp. of New York
Donaldson, Lufkin & Jenrette Securities Corp. New York
Drexel Burnham Lambert Government Securities Corp., New York
First Boston Corp., New York
Greenwich Capital Markets Inc., Greenwich, Conn.
Goldman, Sachs & Co., New York
E.F. Hutton & Co. Inc. New York
Kidder, Peabody & Co. Inc., New York
Kleinwort Benson Government Securities Inc., New York
Aubrey G. Lanston & Co. Inc., New York
Lehman Government Securities Inc., New York
Merrill Lynch Government Securities Inc., New York
Morgan Stanley & Co. Inc., New York
Nomura Securities International
Paine Webber Inc., New York
Wm. E. Pollock Government Securities Inc., New York
Prudential-Bache Securities Inc., New York
Refco Partners, New York
L.F. Rothschild, Unterberg, Towbin
Salomon Brothers Inc., New York
Smith Barney Government Securities Inc., New York
Thomson McKinnon Securities

selves. Brokers facilitate this interdealer trading because they bring buyers and sellers together; the interdealer brokers themselves do not make markets or hold securities for their own account. Bankers charge a commission on each transaction, amounting to about $78 per $1 million of Treasury coupon issues sold. In some cases, brokers provide their services by displaying participating dealers' bids and offers on closed circuit TV screens located in the dealers' trading rooms. In the dealer market, just about all trading is transacted on the phone as there is no formal centralized marketplace.[4]

The dealers make markets by purchasing and selling securities for their own account. Dealers do not charge commissions on their trades, but hope to sell securities at prices above the ones at which they were bought. Dealers seek to have a positive carry on the securities that they have in inventory, that is, they try to earn more interest on their positioned securities than they must pay on the funds raised to finance that inventory.[5]

A dealer is a principal in a transaction. Dealers purchase and sell bids for their own inventory and at their own risk. When a dealer is asked for its purchase and sales prices on a particular bill, he quotes bid and offers discount rates. Suppose that a bill has n days to go until maturity and the dealer quotes bid discount rate B and offers rate S. The bid and offer prices at which the dealer is willing to buy and sell, denoted PB and PS, respectively, are then:

$$PS = 100 \left(1 - \frac{nS}{360}\right); PB = 100 \left(1 - \frac{nB}{360}\right)$$

For example, suppose a dealer quotes a market of 8.45 bid and 8.40 offered on a 90-day bill. Then its bid and offer prices are:

$$PS = 100 \left(1 - \frac{90(.0840)}{360}\right) = 97.9000$$

$$PB = 100 \left(1 - \frac{90(.0845)}{360}\right) = 97.8875$$

The dealer's spread is $125 per $1 million face value of the bills. Note that $97.9000 - 97.8875 = .0125$ percent of face value.

The bill market is probably the most liquid market in the world because the size of a conventional transaction can run to as much as $25 million and because the difference between a dealer's bid and ask price could be as low as 1 basis point. This would mean only a $25 difference per $1 million face value on a 90-day bill.

Dealers position themselves in the various maturities of Treasury securities based upon their expectations about interest rates. Management relies on their trader's skill to enable the firm to change its position in various maturities whenever the outlook changes. The spread between bid and offered prices usually depends upon the outlook for interest rates and the current state of market activity. Spreads are narrow for Treasury bills because (after as small as 2 basis points) they are actively traded and involve less risk of price loss than longer-term securities. The longer the term to maturity and the smaller the size of the requested transaction, the wider the spread becomes.[6]

The Treasury market is the world's largest securities market with more than five times the dollar volume of the New York Stock Exchange. According to the Federal Reserve Bank of New York, the major dealers in government securities trade about $40 billion of Treasury securities a day with about half the business going through brokers. Because there is no central trading floor for Treasury issues, a handful of little known broker firms have evolved to execute trades between securities firms. These brokers provide the Treasury bond market with the same services that the New York Stock Exchange provides to the equity market and make trades as agent, not principal.

Another factor enhancing the integration of the Treasury market is the existence of an extremely well organized system of interdealer trading. Firms such as Fundamental Brokers Incorporated, R.M.J. Securities, Garban Limited, Chaperdaine & Company, Cantor Fitzgerald, and Newcomb Securities can help a trader completely canvass the quotations of his competitors in a matter of minutes. A direct wire telephone system links traders in different dealer markets, while Garban, Fundamental, and Newcomb provide electronic brokerage screens with fast quote bids and offerings on active issues showing. The screen brokers have helped change the structure of the Treasury securities market from a dealer market to something close to a centralized auction market.

Interdealer trading smoothes out random inventory imbalances among dealers and dampens quotations and transaction price fluctuations that might arise out of such imbalances. A key reason dealers place orders with brokers is because brokers conceal the identities of the ultimate buyers and sellers in a trade.

The liquidity service of immediate execution cannot be supplied without some cost because supplying immediately exposes the supplier to risk of capital loss brought about by potential price fluctuations of the securities held in inventory. This implies that securities cannot be sold quickly except at a discount to their current "equilibrium" price and that they cannot be purchased quickly except at a premium to their current "equilibrium" price. The sizes of the discount and the premium represent the cost of supplying immediacy in sales and purchases. Therefore, the size of the bid-ask spread reflects the cost of supplying liquidity service, essentially related to the frequency of trading in that security. More active securities trade on smaller spreads because liquidity services are both less costly and less valuable to provide for such issue. Also, the relation between the price of liquidity services and the cost of those services is enforced by competition.[7]

REPURCHASE AGREEMENTS

A repurchase agreement, commonly called a repo or RP, is an acquisition of funds through the sale of securities, with a simultaneous agreement by the seller to repurchase them at a later date. Essentially, RPs are a secured means of borrowing and lending short-term funds. Repos are usually made for one business day (overnight), although longer maturities and continuing contracts are not uncommon. The continuing contract consists of a series of RPs that are automatically renewed each day unless terminated by either party to the transaction. Most repurchase agreements involve U.S. government or federal agency securities.

In an RP contract, the borrower pays interest on the funds acquired at a rate negotiated with the lender. This interest rate is not determined by yields on the government securities bought and sold. The interest rate on RPs approximates the federal funds rate but frequently is slightly lower because RPs are collateralized borrowings and federal funds are not.

The term *reverse repurchase agreement* signifies the same transaction viewed from the perspective of the lender. In an RP the borrower sells a security to receive funds and repurchases the security on an agreed upon date. In a reverse RP the lender buys a security and resells it at maturity. Money center banks and government securities dealers frequently arrange reverse RPs in order to obtain government securities with which to engage in an RP.[8]

Even though the majority of repurchase agreements are conducted with commercial banks, repos do not have deposit insurance. However, they are backed by high quality securities. Most RPs are in amounts well in excess of $5 million, but there are retail RPs in amounts less than $100,000. As long as possession of the purchased security is obtained in an RP transaction, there is little default risk since securities generally involve federal government or agency issues. However, there is an interest rate risk in regard to market interest rate movements, should one of the parties default on the repo contract. In order to avoid this default possibility, it is necessary that the proper legal language be used in the repo contract and that the repurchase agreement occur only between institutions and individuals with the highest credit standards. RP transactions are negotiated by telephone, either on a direct basis between parties supplying and acquiring funds or through U.S. government securities dealers. These transactions must be settled in immediately available federal funds. Securities that are purchased and sold under RPs are transferred through the Commissioner of Public Debt wire transfer system operated by the Federal Reserve.[9]

Government securities dealers such as Drysdale, Lombard-Wall, EMS, and BBS failed during the period from 1982 to 1985, leaving many RP players with losses because of their failure to have "proper" RP contracts and because of failure to take possession of the purchased securities (see Table 2.2). For example, Drysdale traded on an extremely large scale relative to its capital so that its failure jeopardized the smooth functioning of the repurchase agreement market as well as the government securities market. Drysdale raised working capital by exploiting a market practice germane to the pricing of RPs. Under an RP, securities are sold with an agreement to buy them back at a specified price and future date. The investor earns the difference between the repurchase price and the original sale price. Prior to the Drysdale default, the provider of coupon-

Table 2.2
Major Failures of Government Securities Dealers

Dealer	Date
Drysdale Government Securities,Inc.	May 1982
Comark	June 1982
Lombard-Wall,Inc.	August 1982
Lion Capital Group	May 1984
RTD Securities Inc.	May 1984
E.S.M. Government Securities	March 1985
Bevill,Bresler & Schulman Asset Management Corp.	April 1985

bearing securities was usually not paid the value of the interest that had accrued since the last coupon payment. When a payment date was near, the securities were worth more to the buyer than the price realized by the seller.

On the other hand, when securities are sold outright, accrued interest is paid to the seller. The asymmetry of the pricing conventions for the two types of transactions allowed dealers to raise capital temporarily by buying securities through an RP, without paying for the accrued interest. The dealer could then sell the securities outright and realize the accrued interest. Drysdale relied on "blind" brokering, a market practice of not disclosing the names of the participants in a transaction. A number of banks had built up a large volume of blind brokering business with Drysdale. Even though these banks viewed themselves merely as agents between Drysdale and their customers, these banks provided anonymity to Drysdale, enabling the firm to raise funds on a huge scale. Drysdale escaped the normal tendency for market participants to limit their volume of financing transactions with any one firm because its identity was screened from its counterparties.

Drysdale used its working capital to build up positions on which it incurred sizable trading losses. The extent of these losses was first revealed in mid-May 1982, when the firm failed to meet a liability for interest payments on securities that it had borrowed. Drysdale was forced to stop trading when market participants became unwilling to deal with Drysdale.

The Federal Reserve acted promptly to maintain an orderly market and met with the commercial banks and the government securities dealers who were involved in the problem on the day of the default. Federal Reserve officials informed commercial banks that the discount window would remain open to assist them should there be unusual liquidity problems and indicated that the Fed would lend out $2 billion worth of securities from its portfolio. Positions generated as a result of Drysdale's activities could be unwound in an orderly fashion.

An immediate effect of the Drysdale collapse was a widespread review and tightening of credit purchases. This contributed to the failure of another dealer firm, Lombard-Wall, Inc., which opened up a new question: the legal status of an RP. During the bankruptcy proceeding, some Lombard customers were temporarily unable to liquidate holdings obtained from the firm under RPs, while others were delayed in reobtaining securities that had been provided to the firm under RP arrangements. For a few weeks after the Drysdale default, these developments had a detrimental effect on confidence in the market for RPs, with RP activity declining and the spread between overnight dealer loans and RP rates narrowing as market attention to risks increased.

After the Drysdale, Bevill, Bresler, & Schulman Lombard, and E.M.S. failures, further steps to improve trading practices and to strengthen monitoring of market development were implemented by the Federal Reserve Bank. The Fed strengthened its procedures for examining the securities activities of banks and government securities dealers. The market practice of not including accrued interest when valuing RPs came to an end.

Repurchase agreements are effectively collateralized short-term loans by corporations, money market funds, and individuals that earn interest rates that are usually just under the federal funds rate. Collateral in book entry form at the Fed commands a lower repo rate than collateral that is issued in definitive form. This is partially related to the higher operational cost associated with physical delivery of securities. Repo transactions are treated for accounting purposes as a borrowing on the books of banks and dealers. No gain or loss is recognized on the sale of the security while the coupon payment on the underlying security continues to be accrued to the owner during the term of the transaction.

The creditworthiness and liquidity of the underlying collateral in a repo, as well as the creditworthiness of the bank or dealer and their need for funds and general market conditions, determine the interest rate earned on RP agreements. Consequently, institutions that hold the most creditworthy and liquid instruments in their portfolio can often use these securities to borrow money and arbitrage into a less creditworthy and/or less liquid instrument that has a higher yield than is paid in the repo agreement.

Prior to the establishment of money market funds the repo was an important overnight ''depository'' for corporations. Corporations invested short-term funds by buying a security from a bank or dealer who would repurchase the security at a higher price. The difference between the purchase and sale price essentially becomes the interest earned. Initially, the repo became important to corporations with excess funds because corporations had no other bank vehicle on which they could earn interest on maturities under 30 days. It was also a good source of funds for banks because the rate paid for these funds was usually below the federal funds rate.

The one-day repo is a major source of financing by securities dealers to fund trading positions. The dealer repo rate is generally higher than the bank repo rate.

A lengthy period of uncertainty for the repo market ended when Congress passed a bill that was signed by the president on July 10, 1984, which permits an investor the right to liquidate the collateral without waiting for a bankruptcy order. The uncertainty surrounding this multibillion dollar market first appeared when a judge issued a 1982 ruling on the treatment of repo collateral in the bankruptcy filing of Lombard-Wall. That ruling had classified repurchase agreements as secured loans and not as separate purchase and sale transactions. By characterizing a repo as a secured loan, the court then ruled that the automatic stay provision of the code, applicable to the creditor action, prevented the holder of securities acquired as collateral in a repo from liquidating them and closing out the transaction.[10]

A House subcommittee approved a bill setting up a board to regulate all government securities dealers, the "Government Securities Rulemaking Board," which would set requirements and standards for government securities trading. The measure would also require the estimated 100 to 200 unregistered dealers to register with the SEC (Securities and Exchange Commission). The Federal Reserve Board would enforce regulation established by the new board. The lawmakers took the action in response to the failures of E.S.M. Government Securities Service, which touched off the Ohio thrift crisis and the later collapse of Bevill, Bresler and Schulman Asset Management Corp.

BANKERS' ACCEPTANCES

Bankers' acceptances (BAs) are orders to pay special amounts at a given time that are usually related to international trade but are now used domestically as well. BAs acknowledge an obligation to pay for goods in transit. Banks usually finance these instruments under a letter of credit agreement, making the customer and the bank obligated to honor the liability. The banker's acceptance is essentially a negotiable time draft drawn on a bank that is "accepted" by the bank on the issue date. For example, suppose an exporter sells goods that will not be delivered for three months and goes to his bank to draw a draft payable in three months. As soon as the bank stamps the draft accepted, the BA can be sold as a money market instrument at a discount from face value. The bank or the customer may provide this discounting service. The rate at which the BA traded is a function of the bank on which it is drawn. As with CDs, the larger banks typically offer the lowest rates. The secondary market is similar to that for CDs. Transactions are typically for at least $1 million with settlement in federal funds. Bankers' acceptances trade on a discount basis with interest payments on an actual day, 360-day basis. They closely resemble commercial paper in form since they are short-term, non–interest-bearing notes sold at a discount and redeemed by the accepting bank at maturity for full face value. Bankers' acceptances carry the issuers pledge to pay, carry the guarantee of the accepting bank, and are backed by the underlying goods being financed. They are extremely liquid instruments. Many banks keep a portion of the acceptances they create as investments, selling the rest to other banks, dealers, money market funds, central banks, corporations, and foreign and domestic institutional investors. The discount rate paid on BAs is always above the discount rate on Treasury bills because of the increased credit risk and is usually comparable in yield to commercial paper of similar quality and maturity.

The draft underlying an acceptance sometimes is preauthorized by a "letter of credit" issued by the importer's home bank (see Figure 2.2). The largest bankers' acceptances are "outright" or "clean acceptances," often arising from an agreement between a foreign bank (for their customer and the accepting U.S. bank). Bankers' acceptances are used for two principal types of financing—for domestic trade and storage and international trade. The 10-fold increase in world trade over the past 12 years has been accompanied by the rapid growth of short-term credit to finance the international movement of goods. The U.S. bankers' acceptance market has played an important part in providing this expansion credit financing for both U.S. and worldwide trade.

As an investment instrument BAs are discounted notes in bearer form with

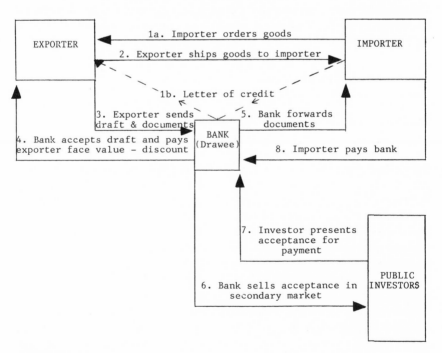

Figure 2.2
A Typical Trade Transaction

interest calculated on a 360-day basis and paid at maturity. The effective bond equivalent yield is among the highest of all the money market instruments. BAs are negotiable through many specialized dealers who make secondary market transactions. The most common maturities are between 30 and 180 days. The main buyers of BAs in the primary market are banks, money market funds, commercial companies, and other financial institutions that need high-grade, short-term debt instruments for their portfolios (see Table 2.3). Bankers' acceptances are actively traded in the secondary market. Their marketability compares

Table 2.3

Commercial Paper and Bankers Dollar Acceptances Outstanding (Millions of dollars, end of period)

Instrument	1982 Dec.	1983 Dec.	1984 Dec.	1985 Dec.	1986 Dec.
	Commercial paper (seasonally adjusted unless noted otherwise)				
1 All issuers	**166,436**	**187,658**	**237,586**	**300,899**	**332,330**
Financial companies[3]					
Dealer-placed paper[4]					
2 Total	34,605	44,455	56,485	78,443	100,942
3 Bank-related (not seasonally adjusted)	2,516	2,441	2,035	1,602	2,265
Directly placed paper[5]					
4 Total	84,393	97,042	110,543	135,504	152,159
5 Bank-related (not seasonally adjusted)	32,034	35,566	42,105	44,778	40,860
6 Nonfinancial companies[6]	47,437	46,161	70,558	86,952	79,229
	Bankers dollar acceptances (not seasonally adjusted)[7]				
7 Total...............................	**79,543**	**78,309**	**78,364**r	**68,413**r	**64,974**r
Holder					
8 Accepting banks	10,910	9,355	9,811	11,197r	13,423r
9 Own bills......................	9,471	8,125	8,621	9,471r	11,707r
10 Bills bought	1,439	1,230	1,191	1,726	1,716
Federal Reserve Banks					
11 Own account	1,480	418	0	0	0
12 Foreign correspondents	949	729	671	937	1,317
13 Others	66,204	67,807	67,881r	56,279r	50,234r
Basis					
14 Imports into United States	17,683	15,649	17,845r	15,147	14,670r
15 Exports from United States	16,328	16,880	16,305r	13,204	12,940r
16 All other	45,531	45,781	44,214r	40,062r	37,364r

1. Effective Dec. 1, 1982, there was a break in the commercial paper series. The key changes in the content of the data involved additions to the reporting panel, the exclusion of broker or dealer placed borrowings under any master note agreements from the reported data, and the reclassification of a large portion of bank–related paper from dealer–placed to directly placed.

2. Correction of a previous misclassification of paper by a reporter has created a break in the series beginning December 1983. The correction adds some paper to nonfinancial and to dealer-placed financial paper.

3. Institutions engaged primarily in activities such as, but not limited to, commercial, savings, and mortgage banking; sales, personal, and mortgage financing; factoring, finance leasing, and other business lending; insurance underwriting; and other investment activities.

4. Includes all financial company paper sold by dealers in the open market.

5. As reported by financial companies that place their paper directly with investors.

6. Includes public utilities and firms engaged primarily in such activities as communications, construction, manufacturing, mining, wholesale and retail trade, transportation, and services.

7. Beginning October 1984, the number of respondents in the bankers acceptance survey were reduced from 340 to 160 institutions—those with $50 million or more in total acceptances. The new reporting group accounts for over 95 percent of total acceptances activity.

Source: Federal Reserve Bulletin, April 1986.

favorably with that of prime name bank CDs and the highest quality dealer-placed commercial paper. An investor can easily liquidate high quality BAs at a dealer's posted bid price.

Bankers' acceptances are a secure form of investment since they carry the irrevocable guarantee of the issuing bank, regardless of any difficulty the bank may face in obtaining payment from its customer. In the highly unlikely event that the bank might default, the investment is self-liquidating in that revenue can be generated from the sale of the imported good.

COMMERCIAL PAPER MARKET

Commercial paper can be traced to the early 1800s when tobacco companies, textile mills, and railroads were among the early issuers. The early paper was usually placed by dealers, and the principal buyers were the commercial banks. The introduction of the car and other consumer durables created a demand by consumers for short-term personal loans. This led to the growth of consumer finance companies such as General Motors Acceptance Corporation (GMAC) that issued commercial paper to finance the purchase of General Motors' automobiles. GMAC was the first to sell commercial paper directly to the public rather than have the paper sold through dealers.

At present, about 80 companies sell their commercial paper through direct placements and their volume accounts for approximately 60 percent of all commercial paper sold. The major incentive for direct placement is that the issuer can save the 5 to 15 basis point dealer's commission.

The major investors in commercial paper are banks, money market funds, mutual funds, insurance companies, pension funds, bank trust departments, and nonfinancial business firms (see Table 2.4). Commercial banks also play a key role in the operation of the market, as they act as agents in issuing paper, hold it for safekeeping, and facilitate payment in federal funds. Although commercial banks cannot issue commercial paper, bank holding companies are among the leading issuers of this paper.

There are close to 800 firms that issue significant quantities of commercial paper and another 400 that issue smaller quantities of paper (see Table 2.5). The amount issued varies, depending upon economic conditions, alternative sources of funds, and current and future expectations of interest rates.

Commercial paper is an unsecured promissory note of a corporation to meet short-term credit needs. Like Treasury bills, commercial paper is characterized by a single payment at maturity and has a price prior to maturity that is at a discount from its face value (discounted paper). Commercial paper typically carries a higher yield than Treasury bills, reflecting greater risk and reduced liquidity. Also, the maturity of commercial paper may be tailored precisely to the needs of the investor.

Issuers must have a good credit rating so that their IOUs are accepted for trading in the money market. There are about 1,200 issuers of commercial paper

Table 2.4
Holdings of Open Market Paper, Including Bankers' Acceptances

($ in Billions)	1985	1984	1983	1982	1981	1980
Commercial Banks	$15.3	16.6	16.7	18.1	17.7	16.9
Thrift Institutions	28.5	22.6	18.5	13.8	10.0	7.4
Life Insurance	34.0	29.3	25.3	21.7	17.6	10.1
Private Pension Funds	33.0	30.4	26.7	22.3	23.7	22.5
Mutual Funds	6.5	6.4	4.0	3.0	3.6	3.8
Money Market Funds	99.1	98.0	66.2	69.1	70.4	31.6
Households	26.2	0.0	10.1	14.2	16.5	23.8
Nonfinancial Corps.	66.3	63.3	52.9	42.2	34.3	24.4
Foreign	53.0	43.4	40.4	35.0	35.5	34.7
Federal Reserve & Agencies	0.1	0.7	1.2	1.8	0.9	1.2

Source: Salomon Brothers Inc.

Table 2.5
Survey of Industry Groups Issuing Commercial Paper

Industry Grouping	Percentage of Total
Industrial	42.0
Public Utilities	21.9
Finance	17.6
Bank Holding	13.6
Mortgage Finance	1.0
Insurance	2.8
Transportation	1.1
Total	100.0

Source: Moody's.

in the U.S.; about 40 issuers are foreign based. There exist both directly placed and dealer placed paper of both financial (bank and nonbank related) companies and nonfinancial companies. Rates paid differ by maturity (up to 270 days) and by the credit rating of the issuer. Notes with maturities greater than the 270 days are rare because they would have to be registered with the SEC. Commercial paper is usually rated by Moody's, Standard and Poor's, or Fitch. A rating of at least P2/A2 is usually necessary to issue commercial paper actively. Commercial paper has a usual minimum of $100,000, but some direct issuers sell notes as small as $25,000. Most direct issuers offer some form of prepayment option, while liquidity for dealer issued papers is often provided by the dealer's willingness to repurchase the paper at prevailing rates. Commercial paper is generally sold on a discount basis in bearer form, although paper is also available that is interest bearing.

In addition to issuing commercial paper in the United States, there are some U.S. finance companies and industrial firms operating in Canada that issue commercial paper in Canada. Also, a number of U.S. multinationals issue dollar-denominated commercial paper through dealers in London. The return on commercial paper is fully taxable to the investor at all levels of government.

There were five defaults that occurred during the 1960s, the largest of which amounted to $35 million. However, the commercial paper market was traumatized by Penn Central's default of $82 million of its commercial paper outstanding in 1970. In the aftermath of the Penn Central default, many corporations experienced difficulty refinancing their maturing commercial paper as investors became concerned with the creditworthiness of borrowers. Although some paper had been rated long before the Penn Central crisis, commercial paper was now rated on a widespread basis. Following the failure of Franklin National Bank in 1974, many bank holding companies experienced difficulty in issuing commercial paper.

Companies selling commercial paper expect to roll over their paper as it matures; that is, firms plan to issue new paper to pay off maturing paper. There always exists the danger that an adverse turn in the paper market might make rolling over paper difficult or expensive. Therefore, most firms that issue paper back their outstanding paper with bank lines of credit by obtaining a promise from a bank to lend them an amount equal to their outstanding paper at any time. This credit line is paid for by a small fee, a compensating deposit balance or through a combination of fees and balances. Backup lines of credit ensure a source of funds in the event that the issuing company experiences a cash flow problem, if credit markets become tight, or if the entire commercial paper market runs into difficulty.

The rapid growth in the commercial paper market in the late 1970s and early 1980s, in part related to the secular substitution of short-term for long-term debt, was related to the high inflation rates of that period. On the demand side, investors also became wary of long-term, fixed-rate securities because of the uncertainty of the real rate of return over time and funds tended to flow away from the capital market into the money markets.[11]

Commercial paper is issued directly by companies such as GMAC and Beneficial Finance and through dealers such as Goldman Sachs, Salomon Brothers, First Boston, and Merrill Lynch. Dealers typically charge a fee of one-eighth of 1 percent. The dealer assumes a fiduciary responsibility to check out thoroughly the credit of each firm that sells paper through the firm.

Credit Enhanced Commercial Paper

Bank supported commercial paper generally refers to that paper issued by a corporation that has the underlying "irrevocable" support of a well-known commercial bank(s) with the highest credit ratings. While the investor still attaches some value to the basic creditworthiness of the operating company, in effect such commercial paper notes actually become "two name" paper and therefore constitute a stronger credit than bank-name paper alone. The irrevocable nature of the support distinguishes it from the standard "revocable" backup lines of credit and represents the means by which rating agencies and investors may shift the focus of their credit judgment from the actual issuer of commercial paper to the underlying support bank(s).

Irrevocable support has taken the form of either an irrevocable standby letter of credit (LOC) or an irrevocable revolving credit loan commitment (IRC). Under an LOC arrangement, the bank agrees to make letter of credit disbursements directly to the holder of the commercial paper or to a paying agent acting on their behalf; the IRC represents an irrevocable commitment to make loans for the account of the issuer for the exclusive purposes of repaying maturing notes by advancing such loans directly to the issuing agent acting on behalf of the holders of commercial paper.

Regardless of whether the underlying support is in the form of an irrevocable LOC or IRC, each mechanism provides for the immediate payment of each commercial paper note upon presentation at maturity. Thus, in case the funds are not made available at maturity, the paying agent is obligated and empowered to draw under the LOC or to create loans under the IRC in order to provide the investor with payment in full.

For a fee, commercial banks sell letters of credit to a municipality or local agency that issues bonds or notes. In effect, the banks lend their high credit rating to the local issuer, which enhances the issuer's credit. The higher the credit rating the lower the borrowing costs to the issuer of the bond. For example, banks wrote letters of credit on more than $60 billion of municipal bonds and notes during 1985. The cost of a letter of credit to the bond issuer is between 9 and 35 basis points. It is a function of competitive market conditions and the credit quality of the bond issuer. The enhanced credit rating can save the bond issuer between 50 and 100 basis points in borrowing costs. Although the market was originally dominated by U.S. money center banks, foreign banks have offered considerably lower rates and have begun to capture a large share of this letter of credit business in the municipal bond market. It is the Japanese banks that have been anxious to capture market share and to penetrate the U.S. banking and money and capital markets.

Variable Rate Commercial Paper

Many corporate issuers use commercial paper borrowings as a "quasi-permanent" part of their capitalizations. Similarly, many investors, particularly money market funds, have a continuous supply of short-term funds that they must invest. In addition, a substantial number of issuers and investors maintain constant outstandings and investments on a large scale. Consequently, a substantial portion of the short-term market is continually refinanced. Dealers become accustomed to selling a specific issuer's commercial paper to a particular investor, while investors become accustomed to buying a particular issuer's paper. However, because the terms of the transaction are reviewed at the maturity of the paper, both investors and issuers retain the liquidity and low interest rate risk characteristics of short maturity securities. However, the market has retained some cumbersome operational procedures. For example, even though both parties may agree to renew on the same terms, each rollover transaction must be renegotiated among the issuer, the dealer, and investor. A renewal entails the repaying of one note with the proceeds from the subsequent note. This process involves the expense of retiring old notes and issuing new notes, as well as the moving of funds back and forth. An instrument has been developed that eliminates the time and cost associated with continuous rollovers in the commercial paper market. It also stabilizes the availability of the paper for the investor and funds for the issuer with no loss of liquidity. This security is called *floating rate commercial paper*. The participants usually agree to participate in an arrangement for periods of up to nine months with the interest rate negotiated and expressed as a spread above or below a publicly available index such as the T-bill rate or LIBOR (London Interbank Offered Rate). The most typical resetting of interest rates is monthly or daily. These instruments often contain put and call features. However, it is understood among participants that these options will not be exercised under normal circumstances.

Universal Commercial Paper

As investors have diversified their portfolios internationally, there has been a growing interest in money market instruments denominated in foreign currencies. Although foreign instruments offer the investor currency risk (depreciation, should relevant exchange rates move unfavorably, or appreciation, should relevant exchange rates move favorably), these debt instruments typically offer high interest rates in certain currencies. For example, in December 1986, yields on domestic commercial paper were in the neighborhood of 5 percent, while yields on commercial paper issued by Australian companies were close to 15 percent.

For most currencies, liquid money markets do not exist. If they do exist, the instruments may be subject to local withholding taxes and may be subject to seasoning and settlement concerns. Universal commercial paper was introduced in 1986. It is a short-term liquid currency instrument that offers investors the foreign currency yield, settles in the United States, needs no seasoning, and has no foreign withholding taxes. Universal commercial paper is issued by a U.S. corporation in the United States. The paper is denominated and payable in non-U.S. currencies. Just like dollar denominated commercial paper, universal commercial paper is exempt from registration under U.S. securities laws.

Asset-Based Commercial Paper

The phenomenon of the securitization of assets has come to the commercial paper market. Generally, an entity is established whose purpose is to purchase assets with the proceeds from borrowing activity in the commercial paper market. The purchased assets are usually high quality securities or receivables that generate a return and are either liquid or have short maturities. Investors in asset-based commercial paper are repaid by the cash flows generated by the assets and are protected by the relatively liquid nature of these underlying assets. For corporate issuers, asset-backed commercial paper provides a mechanism for the low cost financing of an institution's or a firm's high quality assets, increased liquidity through asset sales, funding diversity, and balance sheet management.

Moody's Commercial Paper Ratings

Issuers rated Prime-1 (or related supporting institutions) have a superior capacity for repayment of short-term promissory obligations. Prime-1 repayment capacity will normally be evidenced by the following characteristics:

- Leading market positions in well-established industries.
- High rates of return on funds employed.
- Conservative capitalization structures with moderate reliance on debt and ample asset protection.
- Broad margins in earnings coverage of fixed financial charges and high internal cash generation.
- Well-established access to a range of financial markets and assured sources of alternate liquidity.

Issuers rated Prime-2 (or related supporting institutions) have a strong capacity for repayment of short-term promissory obligations. This will normally be evidenced by many of the characteristics cited above but to a lesser degree. Earnings trends and coverage ratios, while sound, will be more subject to variation.

Capitalization characteristics, while still appropriate, may be more affected by external conditions. Ample alternate liquidity is maintained.

Issuers rated Prime-3 (or related supporting institutions) have an acceptable capacity for repayment of short-term promissory obligations. The effect of industry characteristics and market composition may be more pronounced. Variability in earnings and profitability may result in changes in the level of debt protection measurements and the requirement for relatively high financial leverage. Adequate alternate liquidity is maintained.

Issuers rated Not Prime do not fall within any of the Prime rating categories. Standard & Poor's has similar ratings for commercial paper (A1, A2, A3) that are comparable to Moody's ratings (P1, P2, and P3).

CERTIFICATES OF DEPOSIT

As corporations became more adept at cash management during the 1950s, they attempted to economize on their holdings of interest-free demand deposits. Since few commercial banks offered corporations interest bearing deposits as an alternative to demand deposit accounts, there was a precipitous drop in the importance of corporate deposits in the banking system's balance sheet as corporate treasurers made more active use of Treasury bills, repurchase agreements, and commercial paper. This situation prompted First National City Bank of New York to introduce negotiable certificates of deposits (CDs) to the bank's foreign customers in 1960 and to domestic customers in 1961. An announcement by the Discount Corporation of New York to make a secondary market in CDs was crucial to the success of the new instrument.

Negotiable certificates of deposit are uncollateralized bank liabilities of $100,000 or more. These instruments were initially subject to Regulation Q rate ceilings, but ceilings were abolished for CDs in June 1970. As a matter of fact, banks substituted Eurodollar CDs for domestic CDs in 1969–1970, when market interest rates exceeded the ceilings that banks were permitted to pay on domestic CDs. There is an active secondary market in the top bank names in round lots of $5 million but trades of $1 million and less can be negotiated at a 5 to 10 basis point concession. Once again, credit quality of the issuer and size and maturity of the issue, as well as general market conditions, determine the interest rate level. Regional banks used to sell CDs at rates about 5 to 35 basis points higher than rates paid by the top 10 banks. However, the perceived risks associated with Latin American loans and the lower return on assets of the large money center banks have taken away the interest rate advantages of some money center banks over regional banks. CD rates are generally in line with bond equivalent commercial paper rates of comparable quality and maturity. Moody's now assigns credit quality ratings to CDs of most banks. The income received from an investment in CDs is fully taxable at all levels of government. CDs are not sold at a discount.

Although most CDs are sold directly by the bank to the customer, CDs are also sold for the banks by dealers for a small commission. CDs are issued at face value, pay interest at maturity and have maturities between 14 days and about 10 years. (Most CDs have an original maturity of one to six months with 70 to 87 percent of outstanding CDs having maturities of four months or less.) Yields on CDs exceed those on Treasury bills because there is an additional element of credit risk and they are less liquid. In addition to fixed CDs there are also variable rate CDs, for example, or six-month CDs with a 30-day rollover and a one-year CD with a three-month rollover. On each rollover date, accrued interest is paid and a new coupon is set. The major buyer of variable rate CDs are money market funds that treat the maturity date of the CD as the rollover date and that obtain a rate 10 to 30 basis points above the average rate that banks are paying on new CDs with an original maturity equal to the length of the roll period. Banks tend to offer variable rate CDs if they expect rates to decline. Discount CDs have also been introduced to the market. Even though the secondary market for CDs of large well-known banks is well organized, it does not operate as smoothly as the secondary market in Treasury securities. Among other factors, this is because CDs are more heterogeneous than Treasury securities and offer varying degrees of credit risk.

Negotiable CDs are a much more liquid form of investment than a time deposit. Yields on CDs for top name banks are lower than rates available on comparable time deposits because of their marketability. Yields on CDs issued by prime banks may be up to 100 basis points higher than Treasury bill rates during normal times. A difference of between 10 and 50 basis points may exist between prime CDs of first class banks and those lesser known or lower rated banks. The CD market is dominated by institutional and corporate investors who require a secure, short-term liquid investment.

Floating rate CDs differ from fixed rate CDs in that interest rates float off a publicly verifiable rate index and typically have maturities in the 18 to 30 month range. Trading values on both fixed-rate and variable rate CDs are dictated by the relative creditworthiness of the issuing bank.

Banks issue floating rate CDs because lower interest rate risk characteristics are combined with the absence of reserve requirements on CDs that have final maturities in excess of 18 months. These CDs are actively used by commercial banks to enhance their interest rate risk management capability and because of the existence of a swap market. Banks have been able to reduce net funding costs by issuing floating rate CDs and swapping into fixed rate liabilities.

The Chase Manhattan Bank has developed a revolutionary new bank deposit that gives the depositor the opportunity to earn interest based upon the performance of the S&P (Standard & Poors) 500 stock index with no risk to the initial principal. The depositor can elect to have a guaranteed return of 4 percent regardless of the performance of the S&P index plus a percentage of any increase in the S&P index. The depositor can choose another option that offers no guaranteed return but gives the depositor a higher portion of any gain in the S&P 500 index. These time deposits are insured up to $100,000 by the FDIC and are available in minimum deposits of $1,000 for periods of 3, 6, 9 or 12 months. The Chase Manhattan Market Index Investment is essentially a bank time deposit, which features the safety of a fixed-term CD, but is keyed to stock market performance.

MASTER NOTES

A master note is a variation of a commercial paper program negotiated between a direct paper issuer and a large short-term investor. The major advantage to the issuer is stability of funds, while the major advantage to the investor is a higher rate and added flexibility. The interest rate on a master note typically is about 25 basis points over the rate the issuer is paying others in the commercial paper market for comparable maturities. The arrangement calls for the investor to maintain some minimum level of investment, but is permitted to make investment level adjustments of up to some agreed upon maximum. The rate paid is generally for a 90- to 180-day instrument, even though the investment may be for as little as one day.

EURODOLLARS

Eurodollars are deposit liabilities, denominated in U.S. dollars, at banks located outside the United States. Eurodollar deposits are not generally considered to be part of a country's money supply, except for overnight Eurodollar deposits held by U.S. residents in Caribbean branches of U.S. banks. These deposits may be owned by individuals, governments, banks, or corporations from anywhere in the world. The term *Eurodollar* dates from an earlier period when the market was located primarily in Europe. Regardless of where the dollar denominated deposits are held abroad, dollar deposits located anywhere in the world outside of the United States are still referred to as Eurodollars. The huge growth of this market has largely been the result of efforts to move dollar financial intermediation outside the regulatory jurisdiction of the U.S. monetary authorities. Eurodollar deposits of U.S. banks were originally free from reserve requirements and most other regulatory burdens imposed by the Federal Reserve. Host countries have competed for Eurodollar business by promising few regulations, low taxes, and other incentives to attract a portion of the Eurodollar banking industry.

Eurodollar certificates of deposits are U.S. dollar obligations that resemble domestic CDs except that they are the liability of the London branch of a U.S. or foreign commercial bank, typically payable in London or at an offshore branch. The minimum is usually not issued for less than $1 million to large institutions, major security dealers, or money market funds. It is primarily a wholesale market, in which large denomination deposits are sold by banks, and loans are made in rather large denominations. Much of the market is interbank in nature, that is, major multinational banks buy and sell Eurodollars among themselves. Trading of Eurodollars among banks is done at the London interbank offered rate or at LIBOR plus some premium. Rates generally float while adjustments are tied to changes in the LIBOR rate. U.S. banks borrow Eurodollar deposits regularly as a source of funds—an alternative to borrowing in the domestic market.

Interest payments are based on actual days, on a 360-day basis. Although normal settlement of directly issued paper is in London in clearinghouse funds, federal funds settlements can be negotiated on secondary transactions in round lots of $5 million. Rates on domestic Eurodollar CDs are typically higher than for domestic U.S. CDs, while foreign Eurodollar CD issuers generally pay 5 to 25 basis points more than U.S. Eurodollar issuers. Eurodollar CDs are less liquid than domestic CDs and are available through Carribean branches as well as in London. A Eurodollar time deposit, like a domestic time deposit, is an illiquid asset. The Eurodollar CD market originated in 1966 when the London branch of Citibank issued such an instrument. The incentive for U.S. banks to issue CDs abroad was provided for by regulations restricting their ability to raise funds in the domestic market. Eurodollar CD maturities run from 30 days to about five years, but terms of one month to one year are most common.

Eurodollar depositors face the risk that the host country in which the Eurodollar bank is located might prevent withdrawal of funds and their transmission of funds to depositors in other countries. Residents in other countries face this same risk in deposits held in the United States. U.S. residents will find that Eurodollar CDs are not insured, while domestic CDs are insured by the FDIC for deposits up to $100,000.

On November 1, 1980, the Federal Reserve introduced new reserve requirements of 3 percent against the issue of all dollar-denominated CDs from 14 days to four years and 364 days maturity. Previously, Eurodollar CDs were subject to no reserve requirements and were therefore cheaper for U.S. banks to issue than were domestic CDs. As a result of the reserve requirement, U.S. banks issue fewer Eurodollar CDs and the yield differential between Eurodollar and domestic CDs has narrowed.

YANKEE CERTIFICATES OF DEPOSIT

Yankee certificates of deposit are obligations of non-U.S. banks issued in the United States by the branch offices of foreign banks in minimum denominations of $1 million. They are issued in maturities of 30 to 360 days through security dealers with settlement typically in New York in federal funds. Interest is paid on an actual day, 360-day basis. For maturities of less than one year, interest is usually paid at maturity. Longer term CDs pay interest either annually or semiannually. Yankee CDs are less liquid than domestic CDs and trade at yields close to those on Eurodollar CDs. The major buyers of Yankee CDs are money market funds and corporations that wish to maximize yield and require maturities on specific dates. The foreign issuers of Yankee CDs are well-known international banks, headquartered primarily in Western Europe, England, or Japan. The market is primarily a shorter term market with maturities of three months or less. Investors in these instruments look to the creditworthiness of the parent organization in assessing their risk, since the obligation of a branch of a foreign bank is in actuality an obligation of the parent bank.

AGENCY SECURITIES

Securities of government-sponsored agencies are neither direct obligations of the U.S. government nor do they carry a guarantee. However, they are priced close to comparable government securities because the marketplace perceives these securities as being "moral obligations" of the government. Under normal conditions the yield on agency securities average 10 to 25 basis points higher than that of Treasury securities of comparable maturity.

Some agency issues are backed by the full faith and credit of the United States, while others are guaranteed by the issuing agency. Because no agency security has ever defaulted and because agency issues have higher yields than Treasury obligations, some people consider this area of the bond market the government's bargain counter. Many investors feel that the federal government would not allow a sponsored agency to default on a debt issue. Nevertheless, the confidence of investors in the quality of sponsored agency securities was shaken during 1981 and early 1982, so that interest rate spreads widened considerably. During 1985, following numerous bank failures associated with defaults on agricultural loans, the Farm Credit Banks paid a considerable premium over other agency issues.

A number of different government agencies issue bonds. Three of them are concerned with financing America's agricultural industry and are known as the Farm Credit Banks. They are the Federal Intermediate Credit Banks (FICBs), Banks for Cooperatives (B Coops), and the Federal Land Banks (FLBs). The FICBs and B Coops lend primarily (but not exclusively) for periods of one year or less, while the FLBs do more long-term lending. However, today these three agency debt issuers now save money under the FFCB (Federal Farm Credit Banks), using consolidated systemwide bonds. (See Chapter 7 for a more complete treatment of agency securities.)

VARIABLE COUPON RENEWABLE NOTES

Variable coupon renewable notes are registered securities that represent the unsecured obligations of issuers such as banks or other corporations with a sizable and consistent need for short-term funds. They are purchased by investors who are attracted by the higher yield available on these instruments compared to other money market investments. These variable notes provide investors with yields similar to those on intermediate-term notes. These investments also can be classified as money market instruments because their maturity is classified as being equal to the interest rate reset period. The attractive floating interest rate is paid to investors in return for agreeing periodically to extend the maturity of the instrument, while at the same time having the option of not extending the maturity of the instrument and fixing the final maturity (which is typically 270 days). On the other hand, it provides the issuer with longer term floating rate funds at intermediate-term rate levels. Issuers enjoy the stability provided by the likelihood that investors will choose consistently to extend the maturity of the instrument.

The interest rate paid on variable coupon renewable notes is calculated as a spread over a publicly available rate. The rate is fixed for a specified period that is shorter than the maturity of the notes. The spread from the base rate is usually reduced if the holder elects to terminate the maturity extension. However, the investor can elect to sell the security in the secondary market instead of receiving the reduced yield.

MONEY MARKET PREFERRED FUNDS

Floating rate preferred was introduced in 1982, in the form of adjustable rate preferred, which paid a dividend linked to the rate on Treasury securities. Floating rate preferred combines some of the advantages of debt and equity securities. Since dividends are reset periodically, adjustable preferred instruments offer returns that vary with market interest rates. Also, corporate investors do not have to pay taxes on 80 percent of their dividend income.

Money market preferred has given investors something they did not seem to obtain from other floating rate preferreds: confidence that they will be able to sell the stock at almost any time at the price they paid for it. Because of the 80 percent tax break, investors have been willing to accept a lower yield on equity than on debt securities.

About the only thing investors don't seem to like about money market preferred stock is that in owning equity they are more vulnerable to an issuer's financial problems then in owning debt. To resolve this potential problem, United States Steel Corporation's second issue of money market preferred was insured; they were known as "stainless steels." The first issue, known as "carbon steels" was not insured. The insured issue is costing the company 200 basis points less in dividend costs than the "carbon steel" issue.

ADJUSTABLE RATE PREFERRED STOCK

The adjustable rate preferred market began in May 1982. As of year-end 1986, there were more than 100 issues outstanding with a par value in excess of $10 billion. Virtually all of the issues are perpetual preferreds with cumulative dividends and have call or redemption provisions, as well as minimum and maximum dividend rates.

Adjustable or floating rate preferred stock is a preferred stock whose dividend rate changes on a quarterly basis. The quarterly adjustment or reset is usually indexed to U.S. Treasury securities. Adjustable rate preferred stocks are pri-

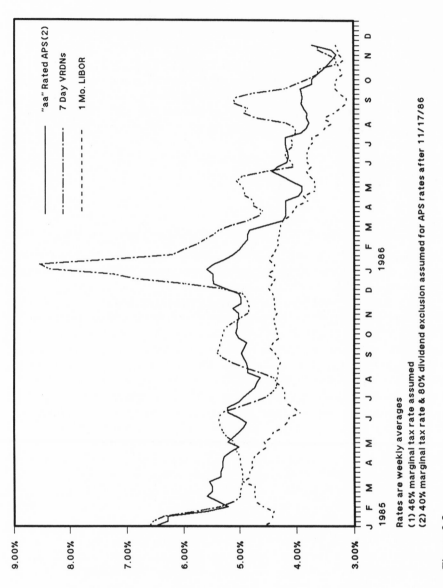

Figure 2.3
After-Tax Yield Comparison: Selected Short Term Securities

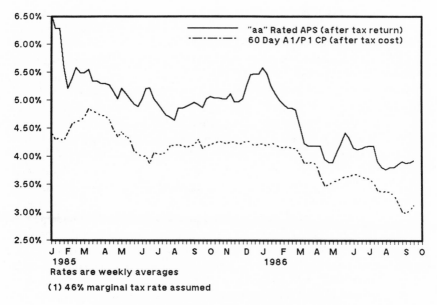

Rates are weekly averages

(1) 46% marginal tax rate assumed

After Tax Return/Cost Differential

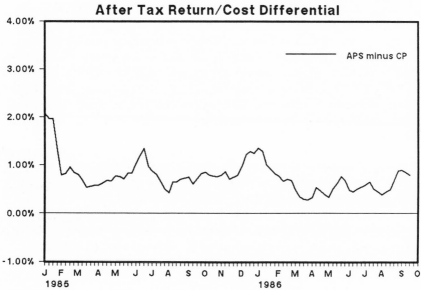

Figure 2.4
After Tax Return and Cost: APS vs. Commercial Paper

marily purchased by companies and mutual funds as substitutes for money market instruments. These companies are seeking high after-tax returns while minimizing principal risk. The after-tax yield on preferred stocks tend to be considerably higher than most other equivalently rated instruments because of the 80 percent dividend exclusion available to corporate investors. The effective tax rate on the dividend income for a corporation in the 40 percent marginal tax bracket is only 8 percent, while the effective tax rate for a corporation in the 34 percent marginal tax rate is 6.8 percent. The after-tax return to corporations is typically 300 to 500 basis points above short-term Treasury bills. The adjustable feature is designed to keep the dividend rate on the preferred competitive with other money market rates within a designated range. The presence of a minimum dividend rate provides a floor if interest rates should fall substantially. There is also an active secondary market for these issues. There are some disadvantages associated with holding these issues. The presence of a maximum dividend rate decreases the effectiveness of the adjustable rate feature if rates approach the ceiling level. In a period of declining interest rates, the stocks will underperform fixed-rate perpetual preferreds and will not provide the potential for significant capital gains. Since these instruments have no final maturity, substantial market risk exists as opposed to minimal market risk associated with money market instruments that have a final maturity.

Whereby fixed rate preferred stock is undesirable to potential investors in periods of rising interest rates, ARPs have less price risk than straight preferred stock for a company with similar risks. ARPs satisfy a corporate investor's desire to maintain principal. There are also convertible adjustable rate preferred stock issues. These securities are convertible into a fixed dollar amount of common stock equal to the original purchase price of the preferred.

Another relatively new addition to the marketplace is a convertible exchangeable preferred stock. This is preferred stock with both a convertible and exchangeable provision. The stock is exchangeable at the option of the issuer into debentures or at the option of the buyer into a specified number of shares of the issuer's common stock. The convertible provision gives the buyer protection of principal and a chance to participate in potential capital gains should the price of the common stock increase, while the exchangeable provision gives the issuer capital structure flexibility.

Figure 2.3 shows the after-tax yield comparison on aa-rated adjustable preferred stock, seven-day variable rate notes, and the one-month London interbank offered rate. Figure 2.4 shows the after-tax return on aa-rated adjustable preferred stock versus the after-tax return on high quality 60-day commercial paper.

AUCTION PREFERRED STOCK

Auction preferred stock was created in October of 1984 and as of year-end 1986 there were about 60 issuing companies with a par value of approximately $9 billion. Auction preferred stock is a money market investment instrument that offers tax-paying corporations attractive after-tax yields when compared to alternative investments. Tax-paying corporations are able to exclude 80 percent of the dividend received from their taxable income if they hold the security 46 days.

To ensure a current market rate, the dividends are reset every 49 days through a Dutch auction. In a Dutch auction, potential investors and current holders of auction preferred stock set the dividend yield through a bidding process in which the highest accepted dividend bid sets the rates for all investors. Bids are accepted from lowest yield to highest up to the point where all shares available are put for bid. Additionally, the Dutch auction provides a formalized selling process through which investors may sell their shares at par.

Par values have been either $100,000 or $500,000 per share. The auction preferred stocks offer investors low market risk because of the liquidity provided by the Dutch auction, higher after-tax yields than most other money market investments, and dividends that reset every 49 days to take care of market changes. After-tax returns for the corporate taxpayer should average 150 to 200 basis points above short-term Treasury bills.

TAX-EXEMPT MONEY MARKET INSTRUMENTS

There are three major types of tax-free, short-term instruments: tax-exempt commercial paper, tax-free anticipation notes, and obligations of local housing and project notes. Tax-exempt commercial paper is issued by tax-exempt borrowers in minimum $100,000 denominations that have an ongoing need for short-term funds. The interest rate paid is established by the issuing institution for a range of maturities from 5 to 270 days. However, most issues have a maturity of 90 days or less. This paper is quite popular with tax-free money market funds and corporations that need liquid funds and pay a full tax rate.

Tax-free anticipation notes are issued in the anticipation of a more permanent source of money by states and other public agencies. The obligations might be tax anticipation notes (TANs) or revenue anticipation notes (RANs), which are redeemed by the collection of revenues and taxes, and bond anticipation notes (BANs), which are redeemed by the issuance of longer term bonds.

These obligations provide a cash flow bridge between nonsynchronous revenues and expenditures and are basically analogous to working capital loans. Revenues, such as property taxes, tend to be realized during one or two concentrated periods of the fiscal year, while expenditures tend to be more evenly spaced over the year. Bond anticipation notes are used to finance construction work in progress by providing short-term funds for interim contract expenditures until projects are completed and final costs are estimated. BANs are normally retired through the issuance of long-term bonds. Anticipation notes are usually sold on a competitive bid basis in $5,000 units, with regular settlement in five business days in federal funds. Some issues set $25,000 minimums and are settled for cash or one-day settlement. Notes are issued in interest-bearing form with interest calculated on the basis of a 30-day month, 360-day year with

Table 2.6
Yields and Spread Relationships

MUNICIPAL YIELDS	1981	1982	1983	1984	1985 June
3-Month	7.83	6.95	5.11	5.65	4.22
As a % of Treasury Bill	55.8	65.5	59.4	59.3	60.7
6-Month	8.33	7.36	5.36	6.00	4.24
As a % of Treasury Bill	60.3	66.5	61.4	61.5	59.8

Source: Federal Reserve Bulletin.

interest at maturity. Secondary market transactions usually range from $500,000 to $5 million.

Municipal note issues are sold to investors by dealers who obtain the security through competitive bidding or through negotiation with the issuer. These dealers also make a secondary market for these notes. The yield that a municipality must pay to issue notes depends upon the general level of short-term rates, the length of time for which it borrows, and its credit rating. A high quality credit can borrow at a rate well below the yield on Treasury bills of equivalent maturity because of the value to the investor of the tax exemption on the municipal notes.[12] Table 2.6 shows the yields available on three- and six-month municipal notes and their relationship to Treasury bill yields.

PROJECT NOTES

Project notes (PNs) are obligations issued by local housing and urban renewal agencies that are sold in monthly auctions. They are administered under a U.S. Department of Housing and Urban Development program and carry the full faith and credit guarantee of the U.S. government. PNs are similar to anticipation notes germane to price, form, settlement, calculation of interest, and secondary market transactions.

Tax-Exempt Variable Rate Demand Notes

Tax-exempt variable rate demand notes are floating rate notes that usually yield 80 percent to 120 percent of an index of 30-, 60-, or 90-day tax-free rates. They generally have a put option, that is, they are putable on seven-day notice by the investor back to the issuer. Rates on these instruments usually change weekly and they are generally backed by a letter of credit. Daily demand notes are similar to the above note except for the fact that they can be put back to the issuer daily.

Tax, Revenue, and Bond Anticipation Notes

Tax anticipation notes are issued in anticipation of tax receipts and paid out of those receipts. Revenue anticipation notes are issued in anticipation of other sources of future revenue. Typically, the revenues consist of federal or state aid. Bond anticipation notes are considered the least secure of the municipality's notes. They provide a means of interim financing in anticipation of a future bond offering. Therefore, they are only as secure as the local government's ability to issue those bonds.

General Obligation Notes

Some state and local governments will issue general obligation notes for a variety of purposes with the full backing of the issuer. General obligation notes are the equivalent in credit quality of general obligation bonds. They are often used for the same purposes as TANs and BANs.

KEY TO MOODY'S SHORT-TERM LOAN RATINGS

MIG 1—Loans bearing this designation are of the best quality, enjoying strong protection from established cash flows of funds for their servicing or from established and broad-based access to the market for refinancing or both.

MIG 2—Loans bearing this designation are of high quality, with margins of protection ample, although not so large as in the preceding group.

MIG 3—Loans bearing this designation are of favorable quality, with all security elements accounted for but lacking the undeniable strength of the preceding grades. Market access for refinancing, in particular, is likely to be less well established.

MIG 4—Loans bearing this designation are of adequate quality, carrying specific risk but having protection commonly regarded as required of an investment security and not distinctly or predominantly speculative.

SHORT-TERM TAX-EXEMPT FUNDS

Short-term tax-exempt funds (STEFs) are the tax-exempt counterpart to money market funds (MMFs). STEFs invest in short-term securities issued by state and local governments that pay interest income that is exempt from federal income taxes. The first STEF was formed in 1977, and by 1985 there were 112 operating with combined assets of over $36 billion. Since STEF portfolios usually have a longer average maturity than MMF portfolios, the variation in the STEFs share price and in the investor's principal is modestly greater than for MMF shares.

MONEY MARKET DEALERS AND BROKERS

Dealers and brokers who specialize in one or more money market instruments play an important role in helping economic units adjust their liquidity positions. Economic units such as government bodies, corporations, and financial institutions all have recurring problems of liquidity management. For example, corporations use money markets to invest temporarily idle cash, while large corporations often obtain funds by selling commercial paper in the money markets. The primary function of money markets dealers is to help make markets in instruments such as Treasury bills, CDs, and commercial paper by standing ready to buy and sell securities from their inventories. Transactions are almost always conducted by telephone. The most important dealers and brokers all over the world are tied to each other and to their most important customers by direct phone lines. The money market trading rooms of the biggest brokers and dealers can be characterized by a high degree of tension and lots of activity. Traders are surrounded by a battery of phones and blinking lights on the keyboard that indicate incoming calls.

PAYMENTS AND DELIVERIES

Transactions are normally settled in federal funds, with parties instructing their bank or the Federal Reserve to transfer funds from the account of the buyer to the account of the seller or dealer. Securities are rarely shipped between buyer and seller, but physical transfer of securities does take place between the New York City banks of the seller and buyer. The large money center banks have safekeeping facilities within their trust departments that arrange for the release of funds for purchase of securities after delivery of the securities to the safekeeping window of the purchaser's bank. In the case of some securities, there is a computerized book entry system rather than physical delivery of securities.

INTEREST RATE RELATIONSHIPS

The most normal interest rate relationship is that of Treasury bill rates as the lowest, with agency securities rates, negotiable CD rates, bankers' acceptance rates, commercial paper rates, and Eurodollar rates in ascending order for securities of comparable quality and maturity. Although this rate scale is most typical, these rate rankings change as a function of perception of default, supply, and demand and other factors.

Until 1965, wide fluctuations in money market rates were unusual. Since 1965, there have been much greater fluctuations in these interest rates that have been related to economic problems, monetary policy, volatile energy prices and inflation in the 1970s and 1980s, uncertainty about the recycling of petrodollars and the international monetary system, and several crises involving foreign currencies and the dollar. Yield spreads also increased after 1965. This included

Table 2.7
Representative Money Market Investment Yields

	Rating	Pre-Tax Yield (a)	After-Tax Yield (b)(d)	Taxable Equivalent Yield (c)(d)	Liquidity
(as of 12/01/86)					
Overnight Gov Repo Rate		6.00%	3.24%	6.00%	1 Day
1 Day Variable Rate Demand Note	V-MIG 1	3.75	3.70	6.85	1 Day
VCRs	AA	6.25	3.38	6.25	7 days
7 Day Variable Rate Demand Note	V-MIG 1	3.85	3.80	7.04	7 days
30 Day Commercial Paper	A1/P1	5.98	3.23	5.98	30 Days
Tax Exempt 30 Day Com. Paper	A1/P1	4.00	4.00	7.41	30 Days
Auction Preferred Stock (APS)					
Double "A"	AA	4.50	4.19	7.76	49 Days (e)
Single "A"	A	4.65	4.33	8.02	49 Days (e)
Collateralized	AAA	4.80	4.47	8.28	49 Days (e)
60 Day Commercial Paper	A1/P1	5.93	3.20	5.93	60 Days
Tax Exempt 60 Day Com. Paper	A1/P1	4.25	4.25	7.87	60 Days
T-Bills (3mo)	-	5.45	2.94	5.45	90 Days
Domestic CD's (3mo)	AA	5.86	3.16	5.86	90 Days
Eurodollar CD's (3mo)	AA	5.90	3.19	5.90	90 Days
T-Bills (6mo)	-	5.57	3.01	5.57	180 Days
Tax Exempt Put Bond (6mos)	AAA	4.25	4.25	7.87	180 Days
Adj. Rate Preferred Stock (ARPS)	AA	5.50(f)	5.12	9.48	
Medium Term Notes (1yr)	AA	6.15	3.32	6.15	1 Year
Tax Exempt Put Bond (1yr)	AAA	4.50	4.50	8.33	1 Year
Medium Term Notes (2yr)	AA	6.65	3.59	6.65	2 Years
CMOs (2yr)	AAA	7.00	3.78	7.00	2 Years (g)
Tax Exempt Put Bond (2yr)	AAA	4.88	4.88	9.04	2 Years
Medium Term Notes (3yr)	AA	7.00	3.78	7.00	3 Years
CMOs (3yr)	AAA	7.35	3.97	7.35	3 Years (g)
Tax Exempt Put Bond (3yr)	AAA	5.13	5.13	9.50	3 Years

(a) All yields quoted on a money market (simple interest) basis, with the exception of the 1 and 7 Day Variable Rate Demand Notes, which are quoted on a bond equivalent basis.
(b) Assumes a 46% corporate tax rate and an 85% dividend exclusion on preferred stock dividends.
(c) The after-tax yield adjusted to a pre-tax basis assuming a 46% corporate tax rate.
(d) All yields quoted on a money market basis including the 1 and 7 Day Variable Rate Demand Notes.
(e) Assumes sale of preferred at successful auction as opposed to an actual maturity.
(f) Yield to call.
(g) Approximate average life. (Agency Collateralized)

yield spreads between different maturities of the same instrument and between yields on Treasury bills and other instruments with the same maturity.

Table 2.7 shows the relationship between representative money market investment yields, while Table 2.8 lists the key money market instruments and their most important features and characteristics.

Table 2.8
Instruments in the Money Market

Instruments	Typical Maturities	Principal Borrowers	Secondary Market
Federal Funds	Chiefly 1 business day	Banks	None
Negotiable Certificates of Deposit (CDs)	1,2,3 and 6 months	Banks	Active
Bankers Acceptances	90 Days	Financial & bus. enterprises	Active
Eurodollars:		Banks	
Time Deposits (non-negotiable)	Overnight, 1 week & 1 to 6 months	Banks	None
CDs (negotiable)	1 to 6 Months	Banks	Moderately active
Treasury Bills	3 to 12 Months	U.S. Government	Very active
Repurchase Agreements	1 Day, 1 week, 3-6 months	Banks, securities dealers, other owners of gov'ts	Very active primary market for short maturities
Futures Contracts (Treasury Bills, CD's, and Eurodollars)	3-18 Months	Dealers, Banks (Users)	Active arbitrage with cash market
Federal Agencies		Federally sponsored agencies:	
Discount Notes	30-360 Days	Farm Credit System Federal Home Loan Banks	Limited
Coupon Securities	6-9 Months	Federal National Mortgage Assn.	Active
Commercial Paper	30-270 Days	Financial & bus. enterprises	Limited
Municipal Notes	30 Days to 1 year	State & local gov'ts	Moderately active for large issuers

Source: Paul Meek, *U.S. Monetary Policy and Financial Markets* (New York: Federal Reserve Bank of New York, 1982). p. 57.

NOTES

1. J. Parthemos, "The Money Market," in *Instruments of the Money Market,* T. Q. Cook and J. G. Duffield, eds. (Richmond, Va.: Federal Reserve Bank of Richmond, 1981), p. 5.

2. Ibid., pp. 5–6.

3. S. I. Maerowitz, "Federal Funds," in *Instruments of the Money Market,* p. 50.

4. C. J. McCurdy, "The Dealer Market for U.S. Government Securities," in *Instruments of the Money Markets,* p. 32.

5. Ibid.

6. Ibid., pp. 32–37.

7. K. D. Garbade, *Securities Markets,* (New York: McGraw-Hill, 1982), p. 478.

8. N. N. Bowsher, "Repurchase Agreements," in *Instruments of the Money Market,* pp. 54–55.

9. Ibid., p. 54.

10. *Bond News Highlights.* (Livingston, N.J.: Bevill, Bresler and Schulman, July 1984), p. 1.

11. P. A. Abken, "Commercial Paper," in *Instruments of the Money Market,* p. 103–4.

12. T. Q. Cook and J. G. Duffield, "Short Term Investment Pools," in *Instruments of the Money Market,* pp. 136–39.

SELECTED BIBLIOGRAPHY

Abken, Peter A. "Commercial Paper." Federal Reserve Bank of Richmond, *Economic Review* (March–April 1981): 11–22.

Banks, Lois "The Market for Agency Securities." Federal Reserve Bank of New York, *Quarterly Review* (Spring 1978): 7–21.

Brick, John R. *Financial Markets: Instruments and Concepts.* Richmond, Va.: Robert F. Dame, 1981.

Cook, Timothy O., and Bruce J. Summers. *Instruments of the Money Market,* 5th ed. Richmond, Va.: Federal Reserve Bank of Richmond, 1981.

Darst, David M. *The Handbook of the Bond and Money Markets.* New York: McGraw-Hill, 1981.

Erwin, George D. "The Farm Credit System: Looking for the Proper Balance." Federal Reserve Bank of Chicago, *Economic Perspective* (November–December 1985): 8–16.

Fabozzi, Frank J., and Irving M. Pollack, eds. *The Handbook of Fixed Income Securities.* Homewood, Ill.: Dow-Jones-Irwin, 1983.

Feder, Gershon, and Knud Ross. "Risk Assessments and Risk Premiums in the Eurodollar Market." *Journal of Finance* (June 1982): 679–691.

Ferri, Michael, and James D. Caines. "A Study of the Yield Spreads in the Money Markets: 1971 to 1978," *Financial Management* (Autumn 1980): 52–59.

First Boston Corporation. *Handbook of Securities of the United States Government and Federal Agencies.* New York, 1986.

Furlong, Frederick, and Randall Puzena. Federal Reserve Bank of San Francisco, *Farm Credit System Weekly Letter* (December 20, 1985).

Goodfriend, Marvin. "Eurodollars," *Economic Review,* Federal Reserve Bank of Richmond, May/June 1981, pp. 12–18.

Goodfriend, Marvin. "Eurodollars." *Instruments of the Money Market.* 5th ed. T. C. Cook and B. J. Summers, eds. Richmond, Va.: Federal Reserve Bank of Richmond, 1981, pp. 123–133.

Hervey, Jack L. "Bankers Acceptances Revisited." Federal Reserve Bank of Chicago, *Economic Perspectives* (May/June 1983): 21–31.

Howell, Donna. "Federally Sponsored Credit Agency Securities." *Instruments of the Money Market.* 5th ed. T. C. Cook and B. J. Summers, eds. Federal Reserve Bank of Richmond, 1981; pp. 378–380.

Hurley, Evelyn M. "The Commercial Paper Market Since the Mid-Seventies." *Federal Reserve Bulletin* (June 1982): 327–344.

Jensen, Frederick, and Patrick M. Parkinson. "Recent Developments in the Bankers Acceptance Market." *Federal Reserve Bulletin* (January 1986): 1–12.

Lucas, Charles, Marcos T. Jones, and Thom B. Thurston. "Federal Funds and Repurchase Agreements." Federal Reserve Bank of New York, *Quarterly Review,* (Summer 1977): 33–48.

McCurdy, Christopher J. "The Dealer Market for U.S. Government Securities," Federal Reserve Bank of New York, *Quarterly Review,* (Winter 1978): 35–47.

Meek, Paul. *U.S. Monetary Policy and Financial Markets*. New York: Federal Reserve
    Bank of New York, 1982.
Melton, William C., and Jean M. Mahr. "Bankers' Acceptances." Federal Reserve Bank
    of New York, *Quarterly Review* (Summer 1981): 35–55.
Moran, Michael, "The Federally Sponsored Credit Agencies: An Overview." *Federal
    Reserve Bulletin* (June 1985): 373–388.
Parthemus, James. "The Money Market." *Instruments of the Money Market*. 5th ed. T.
    C. Cook and B. J. Summers, eds. Richmond, Va.: Federal Reserve Bank of
    Richmond, 1981, pp. 3–10.
Pozena, Randall J. "Risk in the Repo Market." Federal Reserve Bank of San Francisco,
    Weekly Letter (September 13, 1985): 1–2.
Summers, Bruce. "Negotiable Certificates of Deposit." Federal Reserve Bank of Rich-
    mond, *Economic Review* (July/August 1980): 8–19.
Tucker, James F. *Buying Treasury Securities at Federal Reserve Banks*. Richmond, Va.:
    Federal Reserve Bank of Richmond, 1980.
Willis, Parker B. *The Federal Funds Market—Its Origins and Development*. 3rd ed.
    Boston: Federal Reserve Bank of Boston, 1968.

3

Introduction to Foreign Currency Options

John Guerard, Jr.

The purpose of this chapter is to give a brief derivation of the traditional Black and Scholes option pricing model (OPM), the binomial model, the implications of time series modeling of exchange rates on currency options, and a survey of the empirical literature on the efficiency of the currency call option models.

BLACK AND SCHOLES OPTION PRICING MODEL

Although the organized exchange for call options on stocks began in 1973, the trading of currency call options on an organized exchange—the Philadelphia Exchange—did not begin until 1982. Option models did not begin with Black and Scholes (1973); it is well known that Sprenkel (1964) developed a similar model. However, the primary contribution of the OPM was to develop a riskless hedging strategy that led to the rapid acceptance of the Black and Scholes model by the Wall Street community. Their OPM may be developed in the following manner: Let us assume that a manager establishes a long (buy) position in a stock and is concerned about a possible decline in the market that could negate stock price upward movements or simply wants to hedge the position. The manager could (sell) write a call option to hedge the stock purchase; however, the optimal call-writing strategy would be to write one call for every 100 shares purchased. Therefore, one needs to establish and maintain a hedge ratio to reduce the risk of the stock market position. Assuming continuous trading in a stock that pays no dividends, costless transactions, the absence of taxes, a stock price series following a log normal distribution, and a European call option (exercisable only at maturity), one can replicate the Black and Scholes OPM development.

The value of the hedged portfolio, MV_H, is a function of the quantities and prices of the stock and call option positions.

$$MV_H = P_{cs}Q_s + MV_cQ_c \qquad (1)$$

where

P_{cs} is the stock price
Q_s is the quantity of stock
MV_c is the market value of the call option and
Q_c is the quantity of the call options

The change in the value of the hedged position is a function of the change in stock price and, hence, price of the call option, holding the respective quantities constant.

$$dMV_H = Q_s dP_{cs} + Q_c \, dMV_c$$

The change in the call price can be expressed as a function of the change in time and the stock price, which follows a log normal distribution. The change in the call option, using Itö calculus, may be written as:

$$dMV_c = \frac{\partial MV_c}{\partial P_{cs}} \, dP_{cs} + \frac{\partial MV_c}{\partial_t} \, dt + \frac{1}{2} \frac{\partial^2 MV_c}{\partial P_{cs}^2} \, \sigma^2 P_{cs}^2 \, dt \tag{2}$$

The first two terms of equation (2) are very familiar. The third term, incorporating the instantaneous variance of the stock price series, σ^2, necessitates the use of stochastic (Itö) calculus to solve the problem.

$$dMV_H = Q_s dP_{cs} + Q_c \left[\frac{\partial MV_c}{\partial P_{cs}} \, dP_{cs} + \left(\frac{\partial MV_c}{\partial t} + \frac{1}{2} \frac{\partial MV_c^2}{\partial P_{cs}^2} \, \sigma^2 \, P_{cs}^2 \right) dt \right] \tag{3}$$

If the quantity of stock purchased is such that the movements from writing one call option are exactly offset, that is, $Q_c = -1$, and $Q_s = \partial MV_c / \partial P_{cs}$, then (3) may be written as:

$$dMV_H = - \left(\frac{\partial MVc}{\partial t} + \frac{1}{2} \frac{\partial^2 MV_c}{\partial P_{cs}^2} \, P_{cs}^2 \sigma^2 \right) dt \tag{4}$$

In equilibrium, the stock and call option movements should offset and the manager should earn the risk-free rate, r.

$$dMV_H / MV_H = rdt \tag{5}$$

The substitution of (1) and (4) into (5) yields:

$$\frac{\partial MV_c}{\partial t} = rMV_c - rMV_c = \frac{\partial MV_c}{\partial P_{cs}} - \frac{1}{2} \frac{\partial^2 MV_c}{\partial P_{cs}^2} \, P_{cs}^2 \, \sigma^2 \tag{6}$$

The boundary condition to (6) on the expiration date of the option contract, t^*, is

$$MV_c^* = \text{Max } [P_{cs}^* - E, 0] \tag{7}$$

where E is the exercise of price of the stock option. The solution to (6) is:

$$MV_c = P_{cs}N(d_1) - \frac{E}{e^{rt}} N(d_2) \tag{8}$$

where

$$d_1 = \frac{ln(P_{cs/E}) + \left(r + \dfrac{\sigma^2}{2}\right)t}{\sigma\sqrt{t}}$$

$$d_2 = \frac{ln(P_{cs/E}) + \left(r - \dfrac{\sigma^2}{2}\right)t}{\sigma\sqrt{t}}$$

Equation (8) is the traditional Black and Scholes OPM.

The Black and Scholes OPM value of a call is a function of five variables. Of course, an increase in the stock price or decrease in the exercise price increases the value of the call. An increase in the time to maturity of the call allows the investor a greater chance for the stock price to exceed the exercise price, increasing the value of the call. As the risk-free rate rises, the discounted exercise price, E/e^{rt} falls and the value of the call rises. Last, as the variance of the stock price rises, there is a greater probability that the stock price will exceed the exercise price, hence, the value of the call option will be higher. Thus, we may summarize the functional relationships within the Black and Scholes OPM:

$$MV_c = f(\overset{+}{P}_{cs}, \overset{-}{E_x}, \overset{+}{r}, \overset{+}{t}, \overset{+}{\sigma^2})$$

The finance literature is rich with extensions of the Black and Scholes OPM to analyze many decisions: the notion of stockholder and bondholder relationships may be discussed in the OPM context (Jensen and Meckling, 1976), commodities (Black, 1976), mergers and divestitures (Galai and Masulis, 1976), convertible bond valuation (Ingersol, 1977) the term structure of interest rates (Merton, 1974), subordinated debt (Black and Cox, 1976), warrants (Smith, 1977), and foreign currency options (Garman and Kohlhagen, 1983). The Garman and Kohlhagen solution to the pricing of a foreign currency call option replicates the traditional Black and Scholes stock call option derivation with an adjustment for interest rate differentials. Interest rate differentials reflect the expected forward discounts on foreign exchange, which should reflect the interest parity theory. The call option on foreign exchange may be written as:

$$MV_c = \frac{\text{Spot}}{e^{r_f t}} \; N\left[\frac{ln(\text{Spot}/E + r_d - r_f + \left(\frac{\sigma^2}{2}\right)t}{\sigma\sqrt{t}}\right]$$

$$-\frac{E}{e^{r_d t}} \; N\left[\frac{ln(\text{Spot}/E + r_d - r_f + \left(\frac{\sigma^2}{2}\right)t}{\sigma\sqrt{t}}\right] \tag{9}$$

where r_d is the domestic interest rate and r_f is the foreign interest rate. It is assumed that the spot price of currencies followed a log normal distribution; that is, the natural logarithm of $\text{Spot}_t/\text{Spot}_{t-1}$ follows a normal probability distribution.

BINOMIAL MODEL APPROXIMATIONS

The mathematics underlying the Black and Scholes OPM may be disheartening to many readers. Perhaps an easier method of developing the OPM is to discuss the derivation of an alternative model, the binomial option pricing model. The binomial model was originally presented in Sharpe (1978) and refined in Rendleman and Bartter (1979) and Cox, Ross, and Rubinstein (1979). The binomial model assumes that the current stock price, P_{cs}, will move either upward or downward in the next period. The movement upward, u, occurs with a probability of q and the downward movement, d, occurs with a probability $(1-q)$. Let r represent one plus the risk-free rate, and the upward and downward movement rates of return will be represented by $u-1$ and $d-1$, respectively. If C is the current value of the call option, C_u is the value of the call option if the stock price rises and C_d is the value of the call if the stock price falls.

$$
\begin{array}{ccc}
 & \textit{Value of the Call} & \textit{Probability} \\
\nearrow C_u & C_u = \max[uP_{cs} - E, 0] & p \\
C & & \\
\searrow C_d & C_d = \max[dP_{cs} - E, 0] & 1 - p
\end{array}
\tag{10}
$$

A riskless hedge may be constructed by adding risk-free bonds, amount B, to the portfolio such that the portfolio contains h shares of stock and B dollars of debt.

$$
h_{cs} + B \quad
\begin{array}{l}
\nearrow -huP_{cs} + B \\
\searrow hdP_{cs} + B
\end{array}
$$

The optimal h and B values to hedge the portfolio, equal to the end of period values of the two scenarios are:

$$h = \frac{C_u - C_d}{(u - d)P_{cs}} \qquad B = \frac{UC_u - dC_d}{(u - d)r} \qquad (11)$$

Thus, h and B are optimal hedge ratios. The probability that the stock price will rise is given by:

$$q = \frac{r - d}{u - d} \qquad (12)$$

Thus, the value of the call at the end of one period is:

$$MV_c = [pCu + (1 - p)Cd]/r \qquad (13)$$

The two-period call option model may be expressed by examining the potential stock price and probability patterns.

	Value of Stock and Call	Probability

$$
\begin{array}{ccl}
 & & u^2 P_{cs} & p^2 \\
 & uP_{cs} & & \\
P_{cs} & & udP_{cs} & p(1 - p) \\
 & dP_{cs} & duP_{cs} & (1 - p)p \\
 & & d^2 P_{cs} & (1 - p)^2
\end{array}
$$

and

$$
\begin{array}{cll}
 & C_{uu} = \text{Max}[u^2 P_s - E, 0] & p^2 \\
C_u & C_{ud} = \text{Max}[udP_{cs} - E, 0] & p(1 - p) \\
MV_c & & \\
C_d & C_{du} = \text{Max}[duP_{cs} - E, 0] & (1 - p)p \\
 & C_{dd} = \text{Max}[d^2 P_{cs} - E, 0] & (1 - p)^2
\end{array}
$$

The theoretical value of the two-period option is found by:

$$MV_c = [p^2 C_{uu} + 2p(1 - p)C_{ud} + (1 - p)^2 C_{dd}]/r^2$$

$$= [p^2 \text{Max} [u^2 P_{cs} - E, 0] + 2p(1 - p) \text{Max}[udP_{cs} - E, 0]$$

$$+ (1 - p)^2 \text{Max}[d^2 P_{cs} - E, 0]/r^2 \qquad (14)$$

A generalized equation can be written for equation 14 in terms of the traditional binomial model for t time periods.

$$MV_c = \sum_{j=0}^{t} \frac{t!}{j!(t - j)!} p^j (1 - p)^{t-j} \text{Max}[0, u^j d^{t-j} P_{cs} - E] \; /r^t \qquad (15)$$

The variable j represents the number of upward stock price movements occurring in t time periods. A convenient way to rewrite the binomial model is to define a to be the number of upward movements necessary to ensure that the call option finishes "in the money" (P_{cs} exceeds E). Equation 15 may be written as:

$$MV_c = \sum_{j=a}^{t} \frac{t!}{j!(t-j)!} \, p^t (1-p)^{t-j} [u^t d^{t-j} P_{cs} - E] \; / r^t \qquad (16)$$

or

$$MV_c = P_{cs} \sum_{j=a}^{t} \frac{t!}{j!(t-j)!} \, p^t (1-p)^{t-j} \left(\frac{u^t d^{t-j}}{r^t} \right) - $$

$$\frac{E}{r^t} \sum_{j=a}^{t} \frac{t!}{j!(t-j)!} \, p^t (1-p)^{t-j} \left(\frac{u^t d^{t-j}}{r^t} \right) \qquad (16b)$$

Equation 16b may be written as:

$$MV_c = P_{cs} B \, [a, \, t, \, P] - \frac{EB}{r^t} \, [a, \, t, \, p]$$

As the number of periods, t, increases, the binomial distribution converges to the normal distribution and with continuous compounding r^t becomes e^{rt}. Continuous market operations leading the binomial model to converge to the normal distribution and the binomial options model to converge to the Black and Scholes OPM.

TIME SERIES ANALYSIS OF EXCHANGE RATES: CURRENCY OPTION IMPLICATIONS

The purpose of this section is to identify, estimate, and forecast univariate time series models of exchange rates in the tradition of Box and Jenkins. In an efficient market, one would expect currency price movements to follow a random walk (Granger, 1975). Financial economists have found slight differences from the random walk; however, these differences were generally captured by a first-order moving average operator the ARIMA (0, 1, 1) (Levich, 1979). Such a pattern is normally referred to as a random walk with drift. The general model is of the form:

$$\phi(B) \, (1 - B) \, ^d X_t = \theta(B) \epsilon_t \qquad (17)$$

where

$$\phi(B) = 1 - \phi_1 B^1 - \phi_2 B^2 - \ldots - \phi_p B^p$$
$$\theta(B) = 1 - \theta_1 B^1 - \theta_2 B^2 - \ldots - \theta_q B^q$$
$$X_t = \text{observed time series}$$
$$B = \text{backward operator}$$
$$\epsilon_t = \text{randomly distributed error term.}$$

Table 3.1
Tools for Time Series Model Identification

							Country						
	CN		FR		GY		JP		SW		UK	
lag	A	PA	A	PA	A	PA	A	PA	A	PA	A	PA
1	.147	.147	.240	.240	.255	.256	-.334	-.334	.324	.324	.394	.394
2	-.223	-.250	.099	.044	.103	.040	-.000	-.126	-.014	-.133	.103	-.062
3	-.205	-.139	.170	.146	-.002	-.040	.114	.082	-.147	-.112	.061	.050
4	-.027	-.028	-.012	-.093	-.006	-.001	-.000	.079	-.063	.027	.067	.035
5	.145	.084	.127	.146	.010	.017	.002	.045	.003	.002	.106	.079
6	-.012	-.095	.242	.178	.164	.169	-.109	-.124	.077	.060	.135	.075
7	-.212	-.179	-.038	-.142	.035	-.051	-.004	-.108	-.110	-.184	-.028	-.135
8	.052	.141	-.075	-.109	-.026	-.054	-.112	-.186	-.145	-.049	-.165	-.136
9	.111	-.002	.069	.090	.008	.041	-.112	-.228	-.113	-.040	-.082	.033
10	.203	.169	-.020	.001	.068	.077	.222	.151	.004	.015	-.013	.005
11	-.027	-.049	.046	.007	.078	.045	-.112	.086	.082	.046	.007	.008
12	-.392	-.301	-.030	-.127	-.082	-.173	-.112	-.101	.048	-.032	-.037	-.047
13	-.124	-.007	-.140	-.044	-.128	-.088	-.001	-.198	-.067	-.058	-.103	-.048
14	.174	.063	.002	.088	-.034	.077	-.001	-.195	-.059	-.003	-.124	-.035
15	.139	-.002	.075	.061	.037	.060	.111	.050	.072	.099	-.068	-.020
16	-.025	-.057	.144	.143	.152	.105	-.221	-.134	.212	-.138	.063	.091
17	-.144	.005	-.091	-.230	-.091	-.242	.111	-.015	.016	-.155	.027	-.022
18	.061	.071	-.122	-.052	-.186	-.123	-.010	-.003	-.180	-.136	.104	.158
19	.058	-.161	-.171	-.118	-.178	-.008	.001	.012	-.273	-.129	-.089	-.207
20	-.139	-.142	-.094	-.012	-.071	.020	.113	.007	-.151	-.034	-.160	-.079
21	-.034	.117	.136	.167	.128	.164	-.001	.000	.154	.199	.039	.141
22	-.143	-.144	-.046	-.135	.026	-.145	-.001	-.002	.143	-.065	.033	-.096
23	.013	-.014	-.062	.073	-.009	.041	-.001	-.016	.040	.033	-.070	-.077
24	.154	-.034	-.018	.020	-.100	-.032	.110	.072	.010	.077	-.141	-.100

The standard error is approximately .150.
A denotes autocorrelation function estimated.
PA denotes partial autocorrelation function estimates.

The polynominal $\phi(B)$ represents the autoregressive (AR) operator with which the current series value is expressed as a linear combination of the previous values of the series. The $\theta(B)$ polynominal represents the moving average (MA) operator with which the current series value may be expressed as a linear combination of the previous shock series. The backward operator, B, is employed for convenience in notation; that is,

$$BX_t = X_{t-1}$$

The $(1 - B)^d$ polynominal expresses the degree of differentiation necessary to produce a stationary series, one with a constant error variance. The reader is referred to the works of Box and Jenkins (1970) and Granger and Newbold (1977) for complete discussions of time series modeling. The model normally employed in describing the statistical function producing the exchange rates models is a random walk with drift (RWD) function in which the series is differenced ($d = 1$) to stationary, and a first order moving average term ($q = 1$) is estimated to analyze the drift function. The RWD process is quite common in economics (Granger and Newbold, 1977).

The monthly spot exchange rate series were obtained from Data Resources, Inc. (DRI) and are modeled from January 1978 to December 1981. The univariate time series models are estimated using 48 monthly observations [in keeping with the 45 to 50 observations suggested in Montgomery and Johnson (1976) and

Table 3.2
Univariate Time Series Models

Country	Constant (t)	MA (q) (t)	Variance	Ljung–Box Statistic (df)
$\overline{\text{CN}}$	−.0013 (−1.32)	(−1.17) −.173 (1)	.00007	14.5 (21)
$\overline{\text{FR}}$	−.0008 (−.82)	(1.63) −.237 (1)	.0003	18.13 (22)
$\overline{\text{GY}}$	−.0006 (−.24)	(−1.53) −.223 (1)	.0002	13.3 (22)
$\overline{\text{JP}}$	−.0001 (.34)	(2.61) .383 (1)	.0001	17.2 (22)
$\overline{\text{SW}}$	.0011 (.29)	(−2.35) −.336 (1)	.0004	18.2 (22)
$\overline{\text{UK}}$	−.0006 (−.05)	(−2.85) −.392 (1)	.0027	12.7 (22)

Granger and Newbold (1977)]. One would expect the series to require first differencing for stationarity with the autocorrelation function and partial correlation function cutting off after lag 1. This implies a first order moving average operator ($q = 1$). The RWD process is appropriate for the French, German, Swiss, and United Kingdom series; however, the Canadian series has an additional twelfth order moving order parameter that is statistically significant. Please see Table 3.1 for autocorrelation and partial autocorrelation function estimates.

The univariate time series models are estimated using the SAS system for the January 1978 to December 1981 period and are shown in Table 3.2. The Ljung-Box statistics reveal that the model error terms are random (white noise) and the models are adequately fitted.

The spot prices of currencies follow a very near random walk. This tends to support the price movements assumed in the Black and Scholes currency option model. The reader immediately notices that the first-order moving average operator is statistically significant for the French, Japanese, Swiss, and British series; these series do not follow a pure random walk, but rather a random walk with drift. The models are adequately fitted by residual plots and other diagnostic checks (Box and Jenkins, 1970). The forecasts of these models will be used in composite model building.

COMPOSITE MODEL BUILDING FOR FOREIGN EXCHANGE RATES: HOW EFFICIENT ARE CURRENCY OPTIONS?

It has been shown in the literature that composite forecasting models may produce more accurate forecasts than individual forecasts (Granger and Newbold, 1977). However, many questions have emerged in the literature. First, should the correlations among the forecast variables be taken into account? Second, should mere averages of the forecast variables be employed rather than the risk-minimizing, forecast-weighting scheme developed from traditional portfolio theory analysis? Last, are the composite model forecast coefficients stable across variables and time? These questions are quite difficult to answer and this chapter will attempt to present evidence using the exchange rate data and forecasts to develop composite forecasting models.

One might ask a seemingly naive question before proceeding to estimate composite forecasting models: What forecasting benchmark should be used as a reasonable comparison for the composite models and what is the purpose of the exercise? In an efficient market, the current future (or forward) price of the foreign exchange should equal the expected future spot rate. Therefore, the forward rate should serve as a reasonable benchmark for our forecasting models (Goodman, 1979; Levich, 1980). Moreover, Levich has further suggested that composite models might be useful in producing forecast errors that have a smaller error variance than the forecast variance implicit in the forward prices of foreign exchange. Furthermore, the improved forecasting of composite foreign exchange prices should allow firms to be able to profit by taking positions in foreign exchange markets. The implications for foreign currency options are greatest in taking foreign exchange positions. Rather than take a position in the forward market by buying or selling short currencies, one may engage in option trading and have the potential for larger gains (although enduring potentially larger risks) than traders merely taking currency positions.

One of the earliest studies of combining forecasts was developed by Bates and Granger (1969) for airline passenger data, and the weighting scheme employed was taken from the Markowitz risk-minimizing portfolio weighting scheme. That is, the combined forecast, C_t, is a weighted average of the two individual forecasts where w, the optimal weight for forecast 1, f, is found in the following manner:

$$C_t = Wf_t^1 + (1 - W)f_t^2 \qquad (18)$$

The forecast error of the actual value, X, is:

$$e_t = X_t - c_t = we_t^1 + (1 - w) e_t^1 \qquad (19)$$

$$E(e_t^j) = \sigma_j^2 \qquad (20)$$

The optimal weight, w, is found by taking the partial derivative of the forecast error variance

$$\sigma_F^2 = w^2\sigma_1^2 + (1 - w)^2\sigma_2^2 + 2(1 - w)w\rho_{12}\,\sigma_1\,\sigma_2 \qquad (21)$$

with respect to w and setting the partial derivative equal to zero. Thus,

$$w = \frac{\sigma_2(\sigma_2 - \rho_{12}\sigma_1\sigma_2)}{\sigma_1^2 + \sigma_2^2 - 2\rho_{12}\sigma_1\sigma_2} \qquad (22)$$

Of course the forecast error and error variance could be minimized by finding two forecasts perfectly inversely correlated such that the forecast errors in essence canceled themselves out. This is not an easy task in the business world, particularly given exchange rate forecasts. Bates and Granger found evidence to support the naive weighting scheme of independence among the variables. That is, Bates and Granger found that the estimation of optimal composite weights assuming the correlation coefficients among the forecast variables were zero produces as good a set of models as those models estimating the optimal weights with a calculation of ρ_{ij}, the rho factor. The optimal weight, w, may be negative, particularly if the forecast variables are quite highly correlated. Thus, one recognizes that need for estimating forecast weights in the presence of multicollinearity, the existence of highly correlated forecast variables.

The statistical literature of the 1980s is rich with empirical tests of optimal weighting analysis in composite model building. Several central themes have developed corresponding to the questions posed in the introduction to this chapter. Evidence has been developed in studies by Makridakis and Winkler (1983), Clemen and Winkler (1986), and Winkler (1981) that equally weighted composite models are more successful in producing lower postsample forecast error variance than composite models using the independence hypothesis of Bates and Granger. The equally weighted scheme is far more naive than the independence assumption because the respective forecast error variance ratios are ignored. That is, if the time series of forecast variable one is twice as volatile as the forecast variable two series, the equally weighting scheme does not assign Bates and Granger weights of .33 and .67, respectively, but rather .50 and .50, respectively. The success of the equally weighted forecast schemes offers a great challenge to statisticians to construct ''better'' forecasting. Models using the equally weighted forecast serve as another benchmark.

Econometric modeling to produce optimal estimated weights was proposed by Reinmuth and Geurts (1979) and Granger and Ramanathan (1984). The latter study proposed using ordinary least squares analysis to combine forecasts without restrictions on the weights or constant term. The unrestricted weighting scheme produces an unbiased forecast with the lowest estimated mean square error. However, one must be aware that a high degree of correlation among forecast variables is evidence of multicollinearity, which produces overinflated standard error of regression coefficients (hence, low t values) and unstable regression coefficients. The unstable optimal forecast weights in the two-forecast case was found by Kang (1986) in his reexamination of the Clemen and Winkler GNP forecasting data. The presence of multicollinearity leads researchers to analyze alternative regression models to the traditional ordinary least squares (OLS) approach. However, although the biased regression analysis produced more stable weights than did the OLS models, there was little statistical difference in forecasting efficiency when compared to the equally weighted forecasting scheme.

Let us briefly describe the regression models that may be used to estimate optimal weights in composite model building. The Granger and Kamanathan methodology obtains weights from the regression coefficient, estimated from:

$$\min (X - \delta_0 1 - F\delta)^T (X - \delta_0 1 - F\delta) \tag{23}$$

where

X = a vector $(1xn)$ of X values to be forecast
F = a matrix (nxk) of forecast values
1 = vector (of 1s) of constants, and
δ_0 = constant term

One simply runs ordinary least squares to obtain the coefficients by regressing the actual values against the forecasts produced by different methods and/or sources.

$$\hat{\delta}^- = \hat{\alpha} - \hat{\delta}_0 (F^T F)^{-1} F^{1T} 1 \text{ or } \hat{\delta} = (F^T F)^{-1} F^T \delta. \tag{24}$$

The Granger and Ramanathan does not make any adjustments for multicollinearity.

There are two primary regression alternatives to ordinary least squares analysis when confronted with the high correlations among the independent variables. One may employ ridge regression or latent root regression to alleviate the multicollinearities. If the F matrix contains forecast variables that are highly correlated, then the inverse of the forecast, F, matrix will be quite small, the regression coefficients are unstable, and the matrix is said to be ill conditioned. The standard errors of the regression coefficients tend to be overinflated and, thus, the t values of the regression coefficients are too small. Ridge regression finds an estimator in which bias is added. If the bias added to the regression estimator is small such that the mean square error of the biased regression coefficient is less than the mean square error of the unbiased regression coefficient, then the variance of the ridge estimator is smaller than the variance of the unbiased (OLS) estimator. The smaller variance of the biased estimator implies that the estimator is more stable than the OLS estimator. The reader is referred to Montgomery and Peck (1982) for a complete discussion of ridge regression. The biasing parameter, k, may be found by ridge inspection, as in Hoerl and Kennard (1970), or estimated by the Hoerl, Kennard, and Baldwin (1975) procedure.

$$\beta_{\text{RIDGE}} = (F^1 F + kI)^{-1} F^1 X \tag{25}$$

The estimated k may be found by:

$$k = \frac{p\hat{\sigma}^2}{\hat{\beta}^1 \hat{\beta}} \tag{26}$$

where p is independent variables, and β and $\hat{\sigma}^2$ are the regression coefficients and estimated mean square errors found from ordinary least squares analysis.

Latent root regression seeks to identify near singularities in the independent variables and determine the predictive value of the near singularities. It is the goal of latent root regression to eliminate the nonpredictive near singularities of the standardized dependent and independent variable, A, matrix. The correlation matrix is composed of latent roots λ_i and corresponding latent vectors, α_i, *defined as:*

$$|A^1 A - \lambda_i| = 0$$
$$(A^1 A - \lambda_i I)\alpha_i = 0$$

Values for λ_i and α_{0i} become close to zero as a nonpredictive near singularity is identified. Webster, Gunst, and Mason (1976) suggest deletion of eigen vectors when $|\lambda_i| \leq .30$ and $|\alpha_{0i}| \leq .10$. The reader is referred to the work of Webster, Gunst, and Mason (1974, 1976) for a complete description of latent root regression and a comparison with OLS analysis.

ANALYSIS OF FOREIGN EXCHANGE FORECASTS: AN APPLICATION OF COMPOSITE MODEL BUILDING

In this section, composite models are estimated using a bank forecast and univariate Box-Jenkins forecast to attempt to estimate postsample forecasting models that are superior to forward prices of foreign exchange for the Canadian dollar, pound sterling, deutsche mark, French franc, and Swiss franc. Moreover, in addition to estimating models using only a bank and time series forecasts, the forward price variable is added to the general model to analyze the incremental value of the bank and time series forecasts.

The bank forecast represents the monthly exchange rate forecast made approximately once a month for two to five forecast dates (usually at the end of each quarter) during the next 11 to 13 months. A major money center bank made its forecasts available to the authors. The univariate time series, *BJU,* model forecasts are produced to match the bank forecasts. The forward prices were obtained from Data Resources, Inc. to match the bank and time series forecasts. Furthermore, composite models are developed for medium (six months ahead) and long (one year ahead) forecasts. It is important to distinguish between the sample estimation and postsample forecasting periods. An estimation period from January 1982 to December 1983 was employed initially to estimate the composite models. The composite model estimations are shown in Table 3.1. The general form of the model is:

$$\text{Actspot}_{\ell t} = a_0 + a_1 \text{Bank}_{\ell t} + a_2 BJU_{\ell t} + a_3 \text{Forward}_{\ell t} + e_t \qquad (27)$$

where Actspot is the actual spot price of foreign exchange that will prevail at forecast period based on the current time t, Bank is the bank forecast for time ℓ prepared at time t, BJU is the univariate time series forecast prepared at time t, Forward is the forward price for time ℓ prevailing at time t, and e_t is the randomly distributed error term.

Equation 27 may be rewritten to produce the linear correction factor models estimated in equation 23.

The addition of the forward price of a foreign exchange variable to the composite model produces a case of extreme multicollinearity. In an efficient market, one would expect the forward price to be an unbiased estimate of the future spot price (Cornell, 1977). Thus, one might expect the bank or time series forecasts to add little to the forward price in the regression analysis. However, although the bank and time series variables are not statistically significant when included in the OLS regression equation with the forward price of foreign exchange, it is rather naive to conclude that these variables offer little incremental value to the forecaster (Goodman, 1979). The OLS equations (equation 12) exhibit multicollinearity and thus the linear correction technique used to examine the incremental value of the variables (equation 13) are not as efficiently estimated as one would believe (see Christie, Kennelley, and Schaefer, 1984, for a similar analysis of the incremental value of replacement cost information).

In the medium-term regression analyses, denoted with *Ms,* the OLS equation estimates reveal: (1) the time series forecast is positive and statistically significant, whereas the bank forecast is generally negative and insignificant (equation 11); (2) the time series forecast variable is statistically significant and complements the forward price variable in the Canadian, German, and United Kingdom analyses (equation 13); (3) the ridge regression time series and bank weights tend to be positive (and statistically significant in the French and United Kingdom regressions) (equation 14); (4) the time series and forward price variables are statistically significant in the medium-term ridge and latent root regression analyses (equations 15 and 16). Thus, it does not appear to be the case that the forward price of a foreign exchange variable is a sufficient variable for forecasting in an estimation period regime.

The long-run regression analyses, denoted with *Ls,* show the importance of the bank forecast variable in the composite model building process. In the Canadian long-term regressions, the bank forecast is the only statistically significant variable; the forward price is not statistically significant. In the French, German, Swiss, and British analyses, the OLS regression (equation 23) shows the statistical significance of the forward price and time series forecasts; however, the bank forecast variable is statistically significant and positive in the ridge regressions (equations 24 and 25). The forward price variable can be used as an input to a composite model with approximately equal weights as the bank and time series variable (equation 25) in the European analyses. One might expect support to be found for the Clemen and Winkler (1986) and Makridakis and Winkler (1983) positions on equal weighting of variables. Moreover, it is evident that the application of ridge regression is quite appropriate.

POSTSAMPLE FORECASTING EFFICIENCY

The models estimated in the previous section would lead one to believe that the ridge regression model using bank, time series, and forward rates would outperform the forward price variable in postsample forecasting efficiency. A postsample period of January 1984 to December 1985 (20 monthly observations) is reserved to test forecasting efficiency for short-, medium-, and long-term models. Forecasting efficiency is measured in terms of the smallest absolute error and variance of that error term. For France, the best model to forecast short-term and medium-term exchange rates is simply the forward rate; however, the ridge estimation using only the time series and bank forecasts is the best long-run model. Moreover, the estimated model outperforms the equal weighting scheme. The French results also are consistent for German and British analyses. Again, the forward variable is sufficient for short-term and medium-term German and British exchange rate forecasts while the ridge estimated time series and bank forecast models outperform the long-term forward and equal weighting models. The best long-term Swiss model is the ridge model with time series and bank forecasts; however, the equally weighted model of bank time series and forward variable forecasts outperform the forward rate in forecasting short-term and medium-term movements.

The long-run ridge regression models tend to produce variance of the absolute error terms that are less than the variance of the error terms implied in the forward price. Let us define a term, *EC*, denoting an "efficiency criterion" for postsample forecasting efficiency relative to the forward price:

$$EC = \frac{\sigma^2(|e|)\text{composite models}}{\sigma^2(|e|)\text{forward price}}$$

One would expect the *EC* to be less than 1.0 to show forecasting superiority. This is generally the case with the long-run ridge regression (of time series and bank forecasts) and equally weighted long-run forecast models. It is interesting to note that the ridge models using only bank and time series forecasts outperform the ridge models with bank, time series, and forward price variables. This is an intuitive explanation for the result.

SUMMARY AND CONCLUSIONS

It has been shown in this chapter that the high degree of correlation among bank, time series, and forward price forecasts of foreign exchange provides an excellent example for biased regression results. Moreover, although reasonable estimation models need not imply good postsample forecasting results, the ridge regression weighted and equally weighted forecasts performed very well in long-term exchange rate forecasting. The forward rate is quite difficult to beat, as one would expect in an efficient market.

Implications for Efficiency in the Foreign Currency Markets

One would expect that few opportunities should exist for abnormal returns using the Black and Scholes foreign currency option model because spot prices converge toward a normal probability distribution and the composite forecast using the bank and time series forecasts rarely "beat" the forward market by statistically significant differences. Foreign currency options have been traded only since 1982. An initial study by Bodurtha and Courtadon (1986) found few opportunities for arbitrage profits when analyzing data from the Philadelphia Stock Exchange from February 28, 1983 to September 14, 1984. They found only 31 option trades out of 52,509 violated early exercise arbitrage and only one put-call pair out of 3,998 violated put-call parity once transaction costs were taken into account. Thus, as one would have expected, the currency options market is relatively efficient.

BIBLIOGRAPHY

Bates, J. M., and C.W.J. Granger. "The Combination of Forecasts." *Operational Research Quarterly* 20 (1969): 451–68.

Begg, D.K.H. *The Rational Expectations Revolution in Macroeconomics*. Baltimore: Johns Hopkins University Press, 1982.

Black, F. "The Pricing of Commodity." *Journal of Financial Economics* 3 (1976): 167–79.

Black, F., and J. C. Cox. "Valuing Corporate Securities: Some Effects of Bond Indenture Provisions." *Journal of Finance* 31 (1976): 351–67.

Black, F., and M. Scholes. "The Pricing of Options and Corporate Liabilities." *Journal of Political Economy* 81 (1973): 637.

Bodurtha, J. R., and G. R. Courtadon. "Efficiency Tests of Foreign Currency Options Market," *Journal of Finance* 41 (1986): 151–162.

Box, G. E. P., and G. M. Jenkins. *Time Series Analysis: Forecasting and Control*. San Francisco: Holden-Day, 1970.

Christie, A. A., M. D. Kennelley, and T. F. Schaefer. "Testing for Incremental Information Content in the Presence of Multicollinearity." *Journal of Accounting and Economics* 6 (1984): 205–17.

Clemen, R. T., and R. L. Winkler. "Combining Economic Forecasts." *Journal of Business and Statistics* 4 (1986): 39–46.

Cornell, B. "Spot Rates, Forward Rates and Exchange Market Efficiency." *Journal of Financial Economics* 5 (1977): 55–65.

Cox, J. C., and S. A. Ross. "The Valuation of Options for Alternative Stochastic Processes." *Journal of Financial Economics* 3 (1976): 145–66.

Cox, J. C., S. A. Ross, and M. Rubinstein, "Option Pricing: A Simplified Approach." *Journal of Financial Economics* 7 (1979): 229–63.

Galai, D. "Tests of Market Efficiency of the Chicago Board Options Exchange." *Journal of Business* 50 (1977): 167–97.

Galai, D., and R. W. Masulis. "The Option Pricing Model and the Risk Factor of the Stock." *Journal of Financial Economics* 3 (1976): 53–81.

Garman, M. B., and S. W. Kohlhagen. "Foreign Currency Option Values." *Journal of International Money and Finance* 2 (1983): 231–37.

Goodman, S. H. "Foreign Exchange Rate Forecasting Techniques: Implications for Business and Policy." *Journal of Finance* 34 (1979): 415–27.

Granger, C.W.J. "A Survey of Empirical Studies on Capital Markets." In E. Elton and M. J. Gruber, eds., *International Capital Markets*. Amsterdam: North-Holland, 1975.

Granger, C.W.J., and R. Kamanathan. "Improved Methods of Combining Forecasts." *Journal of Forecasting* 3 (1984): 197–204.

Granger, C.W.J., and P. Newbold. *Forecasting, Economic Time Series*. New York: Academic Press, 1977.

Gunst, R. F., J. T. Webster, and R. L. Mason. "A Companion of Least Squares and Latent Root Regression Estimators." *Technometrics* 18 (1976): 75–83.

Hoerl, A. E., and R. W. Kennard. "Ridge Regression: Applications to Nonorthogonal Problems." *Technometrics* 12 (1970): 69–82.

Hoerl, A. E., R. W. Kennard, and K. F. Baldwin. "Ridge Regression: Some Simulations." *Communication in Statistics* 4 (1975): 105–23.

Ingersol, J. "A Theoretical and Empirical Investigation of the Dual Purpose Funds: An Application of Contingent Claims Analysis." *Journal of Financial Economics* 3 (1976): 83–123.

Ingersol, J. E. "A Contingent-Claims Valuation of Convertible Securities." *Journal of Financial Economics* 4 (1977): 289–322.

Jensen, M. C. and W. H. Meckling. "Theory of the Firm: Managerial Behavior, Agency Costs and Ownership Structure." *Journal of Financial Economics* 3 (1976): 350–60.

Kang, H. "Unstable Weights in the Combination of Forecasts." *Management Science* 32 (1986): 683–95.

Latane, H., and R. Rendleman. "Standard Deviations of Stock Price Ratios Implied in Option Prices." *Journal of Finance* 31 (1976): 369–81.

Levich, R. *The International Money Market: An Assessment of Forecasting Techniques and Market Efficiency.* Greenwich, Conn.: JAI Press, 1979.

Levich, R. M. "Analyzing the Accuracy of Foreign Exchange Advisory Services, Theory and Evidence." In R. Levich and G. Wihlborg, eds., *Exchange Risk and Exposure.* Lexington, Mass.: Lexington Books, 1980.

Makridakis, S., and R. L. Winkler. "Averages of Forecasts." *Management Science* 29 (1983): 987–96.

Merton, R. C. "On the Pricing of Corporate Debt: The Risk Structure of Interest Rates." *Journal of Finance* 29 (1974): 449–70.

Merton, R. C. "Option Pricing When Underlying Stock Returns Are Discontinuous." *Journal of Financial Economics* 3 (1976): 125–44.

Merton, R. C. "Theory of Rational Option Pricing." *Bell Journal of Economics and Management Science* 4 (1973): 141–83.

Mikkleson, W. "An Examination of the Agency Cost of Debt Rationale for Convertible Bonds and Warrants."

Montgomery, D. C., and L. A. Johnson. *Forecasting and Time Series Analysis.* New York: McGraw-Hill Book Company, 1976.

Montgomery, D. C., and E. A. Peck. *An Introduction to Linear Regression Analysis.* New York: John Wiley and Sons, 1982.

Myers, S. C. "Determinants of Corporate Borrowing." *Journal of Financial Economics* 5 (1977): 147–75.

Reinmuth, R. E., and M. D. Geurts. "A Multideterministic Approach to Forecasting." In S. Makridakis and S. C. Wheelright, eds., *Forecasting.* Amsterdam: North-Holland, 1979.

Rendleman, R., and B. Bartter. "Two-State Option Pricing." *Journal of Finance* 34 (1979): 1093–1110.

Smith, C. W. "Alternative Methods for Raising Capital: Rights Versus Underwritten Offerings." *Journal of Financial Economics* 5 (1977): 273–307.

Smith, C. W. "Option Pricing: A Review." *Journal of Financial Economics* 3 (1976): 3–51.

Sharpe, W. F. *Investments.* Englewood Cliffs, N.J.: Prentice-Hall, 1978.

Sprenkel, C. M. "Warrant Prices as Indicators of Expectations and Preferences." In Paul Cootner, eds., *The Random Character of Stock Market Prices,* MIT Press, Cambridge, Mass., (1964), 412–474.

Webster, J. T., R. F. Gunst, and R. L. Mason. "Latent Root Regression Analysis." *Technometrics* 16 (1974): 513–22.

Winkler, R. L. "Combining Probability Distributions from Dependent Information Sources." *Management Science* 27 (1981): 479–88.

4

Capital Markets

SOURCES AND USES OF FUNDS

While the money markets permit liquidity adjustments for lenders and borrowers, the capital market is where long-term lenders and borrowers meet. The capital market is a market for financial investments that are direct or indirect claims to real capital. These financial instruments include:

1. U.S. Treasury notes and bonds
2. Long-term securities of agencies sponsored by the federal government
3. Corporate and foreign bonds
4. Long-term tax-exempt securities of state and local governments
5. Common and preferred stocks
6. Eurobonds
7. Mortgages and mortgage-backed securities

These capital market instruments are held by households and a variety of institutional investors (see Table 1.1). The largest holders of U.S. government and agency securities are private nonbank financial institutions, households, foreign interests, and commercial banks. The biggest holders of tax-exempt state and local bonds are households, commercial banks, and insurance companies, while insurance companies are the largest holders of corporate and foreign bonds. Households, insurance companies and pension funds are the largest holders of corporate equities, while savings associations, U.S. government-sponsored agencies, mortgage pools, and commercial banks are the largest holders of mortgages.

Businesses and the federal government are the largest net borrowers of funds in the capital markets. Households are the largest supplier of funds to the markets, especially the stock market. Life insurance companies and pension funds are among the financial institutions holding large positions in the corporate bond and stock market, while savings and loans, life insurance companies, commercial banks, and mortgage pools are among the largest holders of mortgages. Households, mutual funds, commercial banks, and property-casualty companies are the dominant buyers of municipal bonds.

New issues of equity or debt securities may be sold directly to investors by the issuing corporation or underwritten and distributed by a syndicate of investment bankers. The roles of the investment banker are essentially to provide advisory, administrative, and risk-bearing (underwriting) services in the distribution or marketing of securities once they have been purchased from the issuer. Underwriting refers to the investment bankers guarantee to buy the new security issue for a fixed price. The risk involved is that the underwriter may not be able to sell the entire issue for more than the purchase price because of deterioration in market conditions.

Capital markets are markets in which long-term financial assets are bought and sold and in which lenders and investors provide long-term funds in exchange for financial assets offered by borrowers. Capital markets facilitate the financing of long-term capital goods, for example, buildings and projects for both a primary and a secondary market. The primary market includes public offerings through negotiated or competitive sales and private placements. The availability of secondary capital markets allows purchasers of long-term securities to make portfolio adjustments, making the securities liquid and more attractive for investors to hold. This feature attracts more capital flows into the markets for investment purposes then would otherwise be the case. Brokers and dealers bring securities buyers and sellers together while the formal stock and bond exchanges, as well as computerized trading mechanisms, match the needs of buyers and sellers in the secondary markets. They also provide opportunities for greater marketability than would otherwise be the case if they were not available.

Salient features differentiating fixed income securities from stocks are the amount of uncertainty of cash flows and the priority of lien position. Bonds have contractually guaranteed interest payments that usually pay a higher yield than the dividends paid on common stock. Stocks have a perpetual maturity date as opposed to a defined maturity date for bonds. As long as there is not a default on the bond issue, bond issues have relatively assured cash flows.

The total return on bonds consists of coupon payments, price changes in asset value, and reinvestment returns when coupon payments are rolled over or invested in other instruments when the original bonds mature or are sold. Stocks offer investors a less certain dividend, but the potential for dividend increases and capital gains, as well as the opportunity to reinvest dividends or the funds obtained through the sale of the stock.

NATURE, ROLE, AND EFFICIENCY OF CAPITAL MARKETS

Capital markets in which trading in secondary issues lacks considerable volume are referred to as ''thin'' markets because financial assets cannot be bought and

Table 4.1
Corporate Financing by Stocks and Bonds (millions)

| | New Stock Issues | | | New Bond Issues | | Private Placements | | |
| | Common Stock | | | | | | | |
Year	Total	Conventional	Other*	Total	Convertible	Total	Bonds	Stocks
1985	$41325	$17322	$17854	$85643	$8012	$73100	$60900	$12200
1984	26370	8669	13482	59578	3408	53100	43700	9400
1983	53021	29794	15534	50067	5871	35500	28800	6700
1982	28572	13409	10210	45398	3076	24300	20700	3600
1981	26922	14238	10988	38966	4271	18500	16000	2500
1980	22476	12670	6612	44650	4665	15800	13800	2000
1979	10780	6004	2812	26468	865	22500	19700	2800
1978	9481	5247	2477	20468	407	23500	21700	1800

* Includes limited partnership interests, voting trust certificates and condominium securities.

Private placement data for 1985 is understated due to exclusion of the second half of the Year's certificates of deposit and mortgage related activity for some firms.

Source: Federal Reserve Bulletin and Securities and Exchange Commission.

sold quickly without the possibility of substantial loss. There is generally a large spread between bid and ask prices in "thin" markets. When long-term assets can be sold quickly without much loss and when orders to buy or sell come from different groups, markets are said to have breadth. Markets are said to have depth when there are buy and sell orders below and above the current market price, while markets are characterized as resilient when new orders come into the market in volume when prices fluctuate. Markets are called efficient when they provide liquidity and allocate resources to the most productive uses at the least possible cost. The costs of issuing new securities, called flotation costs, have tended to decline over time. This decline in flotation costs has been helped by increased competition and shelf registration issues (SEC Rule 415). Although efficiency of capital markets may be improved, U.S. capital markets are generally felt to be relatively efficient.

NEW ISSUES MARKET

The cost of debt is tax advantaged because interest payments are tax deductible. The percentage of bond versus stock financing is influenced by both common stock prices and by the levels of both long- and short-term interest rates, as well as by expectations of the pattern of future interest rates. In the new issues market for corporate securities, bonds averaged 73 percent of all long-term corporate securities sold from 1970 through 1983 (see Table 4.1). In fact, bonds as a percentage of total corporate securities reached a high of 57 percent in 1983. The low point occured during a bullish stock market when many corporations took advantage of market enthusiasm for common stocks to clean up their balance sheets and remove debt. The only stock financing of any significance from 1970 through 1982 was carried out by utilities, which accounted for almost 42 percent of the stock financing during this period. Since utilities have high debt-to-equity ratios relative to manufacturing companies, they must sell stock to keep these ratios from becoming too high and having a negative impact on their credit rating. On the other hand, in the period from 1982 to 1986, when stock prices set annual highs each year, utilities accounted for under 10 percent of total stock financing. Manufacturing companies and financial service and real estate companies accounted for close to one half of the equity financing during this period.

PUBLIC VERSUS PRIVATE PLACEMENTS

There are a variety of types of corporate bonds such as long-term issues, intermediate bonds and notes, high-quality and low-quality bonds, utility and industrial bonds, callable bonds, sinking fund bonds, private placement and public issues. Publicly issued bonds are sold primarily to a rather large number of institutional purchasers through a public sale or underwriting by investment bankers. There exists a secondary market for these publicly issued bonds, which is not always the case for privately placed issues. Private placements are much less liquid and are sold to a relatively small number of large sophisticated financial institutions (mostly life insurance companies) through private negotiations. Private placements tend to have shorter average maturities and more substantial cash sinking fund provisions than publicly issued bonds. Private placements are longer term equivalents of bank loans. High quality credits tend to finance in the public markets, while weaker credits tend to finance through private placements. There are, of course, exceptions to these generalizations.

Private placements provided 31 percent of the funds for new corporate issues during the 1970s (see Figure 4.1). Life insurance companies have been the major source of capital in the private placement market while pension funds have recently shown an increased interest. The market has also taken on an international flavor as foreign investors, particularly from OPEC, have become acquainted with the market. Industrial and utility companies have been the primary issuers in the direct placement market. Credit and finance companies have also been modest users of the market. Participation in this market by pension funds has been a direct result of the increasing presence of higher rated companies issuing securities in the private market.

Raising capital in the private placement market frequently offers companies advantages such as speed, reduced fees, ability to complete complex financings, and the opportunity to sell issues in a variety of sizes that may not be available in the public market. Issuers in the private placement market do not have to register the issue with the SEC. This advantage is important during the periods of security market volatility, when attractive financing opportunities can suddenly appear and disappear.

The participation of better rated corporations in the private placement market has forced firms with lower ratings to add equity "kickers" to some of their issues. Without these added sweeteners, the lowest rated companies would find it extremely difficult to compete for funds with better rated companies. Additionally, direct placements are not terribly liquid instruments even though a secondary market does exist.

Many private placements are arranged through forward commitments at prespecified interest rates with life insurance companies who recognize the relative predictability of their future inflows. The borrower will have access to the "takedown" of this long-term debt over the period of the forward commitment, which might be from 90 days to one year. In exchange for this commitment, insurance companies charge a fee of about one-half of 1 percent of the principal of the loan and an interest rate somewhat in excess of the current long-term rate.

Private placements are often unilateral, customized loan agreements with complex contractual restrictions on the borrowers' actions. The lack of standardization of these covenants and the occasional need for renegotiation when borrowers want to transgress the covenant restrictions make it extremely costly to have a lot of lenders per issue, or to change the identity of the lenders. Therefore, there is not much of a secondary market for private placements.[1] Historically, life insurance companies, to which most private placements have been sold, had no great

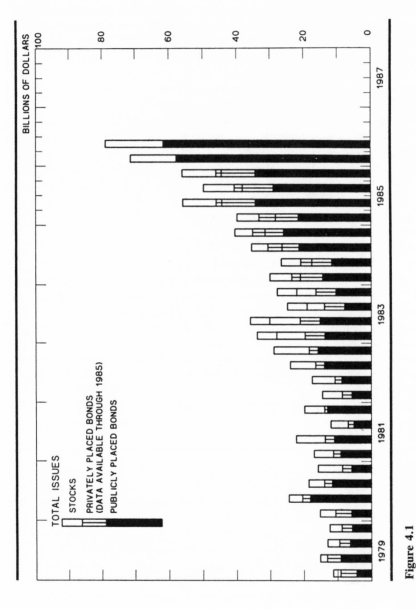

Figure 4.1
Public vs. Private Placement of Bonds

Source: Federal Reserve Chart Book. Washington, D.C.: Federal Reserve Publications Services, February 1987.

need for marketability or liquidity because they expected to hold their investments until maturity.[2] They had long-term liabilities and received predictable cash flows. During the 1980s, though, they have had to abandon their traditional buy and hold until maturity policy and become more active in managing their investment portfolios. As a result some life insurancers have shifted their investment focus away from nonmarketable, illiquid assets, such as private placements, toward publicly traded securities.[3]

THE RISKS OF INVESTMENT

The risks facing an investment are numerous and vary according to the type of investment security. There is always purchasing power risk which is related to inflation, but this is a problem independent of the type of securities held. The risks associated with securities investment include the business risk and the market risk, default (credit) risk, and interest rate risk associated with fixed income securities. There is also a marketability or liquidity risk (see Table 4.2).

Business risk reflects the variability of earnings per share of common stock, particularly if the changes in earnings are vastly different from what was expected by Wall Street analysts. All companies are susceptible to changes in earnings brought about by a change in their business. This is a risk that investors assume in buying equity securities, bonds, and preferred stocks that rely on the profitability of the firm for making interest or dividend payments.

Market risk is the risk of loss caused by changes in the market price of equities unrelated to the normal or intrinsic value of the company. It is quite difficult to predict the short-term price movement of common stocks. It is also difficult to predict long-term prices, even though they revolve about earnings and tend to establish a "normal" value for securities. For example, the 1969–1970 period was one in which millions of professional and amateur investors suffered huge losses because of a decline in stock prices. Stock prices declined because of a decrease in profits related to inflation, because of high bond yields, and because of monetary and fiscal restraints.

As we have previously discussed, the interest rate risk is related to the variability of bond prices as caused by changes in the level of interest rates. It is related to the fact that yields on bonds vary with the rate and conditions of the money and capital markets. There is an inverse relationship between bond yields and bond prices. As interest rate yields for new issues of bonds increase, yields for existing bonds must also increase. This is accomplished through a decline in the price of an existing bond. Inversely, as yields decrease, bond prices increase.

Bonds have a market risk of their own in addition to a business risk. The business risk results when declining earnings have an unfavorable effect on bond ratings or interest rate payments to investors. If earnings decline substantially, there is the risk that the company will not have sufficient funds available to pay back investors at the maturity on the bond. This is called default risk.

Marketability risk is related to the liquidity of an obligation and the ease with

Table 4.2
Basic Elements of Risk in Fixed-Income Instruments

Element of Risk	Description	Characteristics of Securities
Interest rate risk	Variation in return caused by fluctuations in interest rates.	
Price risk	Variation in return caused by fluctuations in the market value of the securities.	Typically, longer-term bonds with lower coupon rates will vary more in price with a given change in interest rates.
Reinvestment risk	Variation in return caused by reinvesting intermediate interest payments at a rate different from the promised yield.	Usually, bonds with higher coupon rates will have a higher degree of reinvestment risk.
Credit/default risk	Variation in return caused by default on interest payments or repayment of principal	U.S. Treasury securities and GNMA securities are free of credit risk. Corporate and municipal securities are subject to various degrees of credit risk, depending on quality.
Purchasing power risk	Variation in real rate of return caused by inflation.	All fixed-income securities are subject to purchasing power risk.
Marketability risk	Variation in return caused by selling costs or large spreads between bid and asked prices when bonds are sold before maturity.	Depends upon the trading characteristics of the particular issue. U.S. Treasury securities are the most marketable, while municipal bonds are usually the least marketable, although marketability characteristics of these securities vary widely among issuers. For example, issues of the Farm Credit Bank were not as marketable as usual during the farm crises of 1985-86.

which the security can be sold at or near the current market price. Smaller issues and those with thin secondary markets will occasionally experience marketability problems. The larger the assumed marketability risk, the higher the required yield.

Marketability depends on the breadth of ownership of a corporation's securities, on how many securities are outstanding, and on the credit risk of a bond, insofar as issues with low ratings do not attract a wide variety of buyers. The marketability of corporate and municipal issues is reflected in the difference between the bid and offered prices that dealers quote when they make a market in an issue. The dealer spread in a $500,000 to $1,000,000 transaction is about 12.5 basis points or $1.25 per bond, while the spread for less marketable issues ranges up to 400 basis points or $40 per bond. The lowest spreads are for actively traded government securities and are about $\frac{1}{32}$ of a point. It should also be mentioned that relatively new issues of corporate and municipal bonds are usually quoted at narrower spreads than after they have been held in an investor's portfolio for a considerable time since they are traded more actively after the issues are brought to market. Also, the amount of uncertainty about future interest rates will cause spreads to widen.

Fong and Fabozzi (1984) point out that a liquidity reserve may be obtained from the cash flow coupons and maturing fixed income instruments as well as the cash flow from a spaced schedule of maturing obligations. Liquidity can also be achieved by emphasizing portfolio investments that are most readily marketable and liquid. High credit quality and short maturity are the most dominant characteristics of readily marketable bonds. Round lot holdings of corporate bonds (usually $500,000 par value) are more marketable than odd lots. The marketability of round lots is reflected in the narrower dealer spreads between bid and ask prices than occur for odd lots.

Liquidity characteristics are determined by the amount of the issue of bonds outstanding, the amount closely held, the coupon rate, age of issue, quality, callability or sinking fund provisions, and maturity or duration. The greater the amount of bonds outstanding and the less the amount closely held the better the liquidity. Recently issued securities and higher credit quality issues also tend to be more liquid. The closer to current coupon levels in the marketplace the better the liquidity since investors usually have a preference for current coupon securities. Callability and sinking fund provisions tend to reduce liquidity. Bonds with a maturity or duration of less than one year tend to be more liquid than bonds with longer maturities.

The market for long-term corporate and municipal bonds is basically a primary market—a market for new issues. Institutional investors dominate the bond market and often hold the bonds until maturity. Although the secondary market for bonds has become increasingly important, the volume of trading for existing bonds in the secondary market is miniscule when compared to secondary market trading of common stocks. The secondary market for bonds is primarily an over-the-counter market, with commercial bank and brokerage firm dealers making a market in various issues. There are many well-known commercial bank and brokerage firm dealers in governments, agencies, and municipals. Unlike the homogeneous government bond market, the corporate bond market faces growing heterogeneity and declining credit quality. Although a few corporate industrial and utility bonds are actively traded, most other issues are quite inactive. Small positions (under $100,000) in corporate bonds are often relatively illiquid and price concessions on the part of the seller are not unusual.

Just because there are investment risks, this does not mean that there cannot be significant rewards for investors. For example, the price of IBM stock went from 67 in August 1982 to 158 in January 1986, while bond prices showed substantial price increases as long-term rates declined substantially, but not monotonically, during this period. The nature of the investment process suggests that investors be knowledgeable about investment opportunities and the potential risks and rewards. A method for approving, valuing, and managing securities must be established. There also must be a method of analyzing the national economy, particular industries, and individual companies. The knowledgeable investor should also be aware of what the characteristics and technicians on Wall Street are saying. There is a plethora of investment information available from Wall Street brokerage firms and investment advisory services. However, many investors do not have the time nor inclination to manage their own resources and rely on mutual funds, bank trust departments, or insurance companies to manage their portfolios.

Insolvency, Illiquidity, Default, and Interest Rate Risk

The risk of insolvency makes the management of capital or net worth extremely important. Many financial institutions have kept equity capital at minimum levels in order to allow for the maximum use of financial leverage. When profit margins are high, financial leverage is advantageous. However, too much debt can backfire in periods when revenues decline without a commensurate decline in the interest payments on the outstanding debt. Because the cost of debt is usually a fixed obligation, failure to meet required payments can bankrupt a company. Management must be careful that excessive levels of debt do not decrease the liquidity of the company and increase the risk of a corporate bankruptcy. If a financial institution is perceived to be substantially more risky than in the past (for example, Continental Illinois in 1984 and the Texas banks in 1986), it will usually have greater difficulty in attracting funds, will pay higher rates for funds attracted, and could run a chance of illiquidity or insolvency. There is the increased risk of illiquidity or cash-out if a financial institution cannot meet all legitimate demands for cash from customers precisely at the time cash is demanded. Different kinds of assets vary substantially in their liquidity, while the need for liquidity varies significantly among financial institutions.

It must also be remembered that financial institutions face the possibility of default or credit risk whenever they make a loan or an investment. Default risk refers to the possibility of never recovering the full amount originally invested in an asset because of the solvency of the issuer of the claims. For those institutions acquiring fixed rate assets, there exists an interest rate risk that is always associated with the possibility of rising interest rates. This interest rate risk is also called market risk and refers to the risk of flunctuation of market value of the principal invested in a given financial instrument. For example, fixed rate mortgages or bonds held in a portfolio will decline in market value when long-term interest rates rise.

Liquid assets such as government securities and stocks and bonds of the largest corporations can be sold and converted into cash on short notice. However, if a security is not liquid, there is usually a liquidity premium added to the equilibrium interest rate on a security that cannot be converted into cash quickly. Although it is difficult to measure liquidity premiums, there is typically a differential of at least 100 and probably 200 basis points between the least liquid and the most liquid financial assets of similar default risk and maturity.

There is also a maturity risk premium for the risk to which investors are exposed because of a security's maturity. The maturity risk premium is higher the longer the time to maturity.

Credit Ratings and Default Risk

The credit or default risk is the possibility that the principal and/or interest payments on a debt security will not be made in a timely fashion. Obviously, the larger the perceived default risk, the higher is the expected yield to maturity on a security. There is a high correlation between the rating of a bond and its yield, with lower ratings (higher default risk) associated with higher yields. Default risk can be attributed to: (1) the internal risk position of the corporate issuer, (2) the external environment or economic climate within which the corporate issuer operates, and (3) the period to maturity of the security itself. Default risk premiums are not constant and tend to vary contracyclically, widening during recessions and narrowing during prosperous periods. This reflects the fact that most defaults occur during periods of severe economic downturn.[4]

Since the early 1900s, bonds have been assigned quality ratings that reflect their probabilities of going into default. The two major bond rating firms are Moody's and Standard & Poor's (S&P), and their rating classifications are shown in Table 4.3. The ratings are judgmental in nature because no precise formula is used when setting a firm's rating. They are based on qualitative and quantitative factors, some of which are listed below:[5]

1. Financial leverage: The more debt a firm uses, the greater its financial leverage; the magnification of risk and return introduced by the use of fixed cost financing, such as debt and preferred stock.

2. Times-interest-earned ratio compared to the firm's expected cash flows: This ratio measures the firm's ability to pay contractual interest payments. Is the company within its capacity to service the debt? Does the company have assets that could be sold to raise funds?

3. Fixed charge coverage ratio: The amount of the company's fixed contractual payments such as lease, interest, and principal payments. The increased use of debt, with fixed obligations to pay interest and to repay principal, means an increase in the possibility of bankruptcy if earnings decline. Is the company close to its borrowing limit germane to restrictive covenants?

4. The current ratio: A measure of liquidity calculated by dividing the firm's current assets by its current liabilities.

5. The amount of time the company has been profitable.

6. Mortgage provisions: Is the bond secured by a mortgage? If it is, and if the property has a high value in relation to the amount of bonded debt, the bond's rating is enhanced. An FHA mortgage will also enhance the rating.

7. Subordination provisions: Is the bond subordinated to other debt? If so, it will be rated at least one notch below the rating it would have if it were not subordinated. Conversely, a bond with other debt subordinated to it will have a somewhat higher rating.

8. Guarantee provisions: Some bonds are guaranteed by other firms. If a weak company's debt is guaranteed by a strong company (usually the weak company's parent), then the bond will be given the strong company's rating. A third-party guarantee from an insurance company or a letter of credit from a bank will enhance the rating.

9. Sinking fund: Does the bond have a sinking fund to insure systematic repayment? This feature is a plus factor to the rating agencies.

10. Maturity: Other things the same, a bond with a shorter maturity will be judged less risky than a longer term bond, and this will be reflected in the rating. What is the maturity structure of the company's debt? Is it faced with large debt repayments in the near future?

11. Stability or variability of the issuer's sales and earnings: Do high interest rates or a recession have a negative impact on earnings? What is the trend in profitability? Is the improvement due to short-lived supply shortages? opportunistic changes in financial accounting? cyclical factors? improved asset management? Is the profitability sustainable?

12. Regulation: Is the company regulated, and could an adverse regulatory climate cause its economic position to decline? Regulation is especially important for electric and gas utilities and telephone companies.

13. Antitrust: Are there antitrust actions or other lawsuits pending against the firm that could erode its position?

14. Overseas operations: What percentage of the firm's sales, assets, and profits are from overseas operations, and what is the political climate in the host country? How vulnerable are they to exchange rate fluctuations? Are the earnings available to the parent company, or are they blocked in other countries?

15. Environmental factors: Is the firm likely to face heavy expenditures for pollution control equipment? Are the earnings of the firm vulnerable to changes in local taxes?

16. Pension liabilities: Does the firm have unfunded pension liabilities that could pose a future problem?

17. Labor unrest: Are there potential labor problems on the horizon that could weaken the firm's position?

18. Accounting policies: Conservative accounting policies are a plus factor in ratings. For example, are all subsidiaries consolidated? Are there unconsolidated subsidiaries with high debt levels?

19. Resource availability: Is the firm likely to face supply shortages that could force it to curtail operations?

20. Hidden problems: Are there large contingent liabilities or uncompleted contracts?

Bond ratings are periodically reviewed by the rating agencies and are subject to change. A reduction in a bond rating will increase the borrowing costs for a company and could possibly limit its access to both the money and bond markets.

The lower a firm's rating, the smaller the group of available purchases for its new issue. If a firm's bond rating falls below BBB, the lowest investment grate, it could have a difficult time attempting to sell new bonds, since many in the universe of potential buyers will not be permitted to buy them. On the other hand, a higher bond rating usually reduces a company's future borrowing costs and might improve its access to money and capital markets. Standard & Poor's publishes "The Credit Watch," which discusses developing situations that may lead to upgradings or downgradings.

Valuations of the quality and experience of management, the competitive position of a firm within its industry, the prospects for the industry as a whole, financial leverage, the variability of revenues, and the ratio of cash flow to debt are all among the key determinants of credit or default risk. Investors require a higher rate of return to invest in a security with a higher risk.

Bond ratings are important both to companies and investors because the rating has a direct, measurable influence on the bond's interest rate and the firm's cost of debt capital. Most bonds are purchased by institutional investors who are generally restricted to investment grade securities. These quality ratings are closely related to other traditional measures of credit quality, such as relative debt burden, interest or fixed charge expense coverage, and variability in earnings stream. The timely review of credit ratings by the rating agencies is sometimes a problem as a substantial delay may occur between published reviews of ratings. With internal credit analysis it may be possible to anticipate such upgrades or downgrades and profit from the yield and price changes that may follow. The analyst's assessment of credit quality may be more accurate and timely than those of the credit agencies.

The ratings have been good indicators of default risk. Researchers have found a close relationship between bond rating and defaults. The higher the rating given a new issue of corporate bonds, the lower the incidence of subsequent default. Most sophisticated fixed income investors do not rely exclusively on the rating agencies. They also engage in their own credit analysis or assessment of default risk.

Much of the analysis focuses on the character of the industry in which the bond issuer operates. Is the industry growing, steady, stagnant, or cyclical? What are the strengths and weaknesses of the firm within the industry? Rating companies are concerned with the specific nature of the collateral provisions and/or pledges given in the indenture. Recent and probable trends in the issuer's balance sheet and income statement are extremely important with special attention being given to earnings coverage of the outstanding debt burden.

Table 4.3 lists the different categories of ratings available for corporate bonds from Moody's and Standard & Poor's, as well as an explanation of the investment quality of each rating category.

The rating agencies reserve the right to change or withdraw a published rating if there is a change in the financial condition of the company or if a company fails to provide information needed for the periodic review of the company. Rating

Table 4.3
Corporate Bond Rating Systems

Explanation	Moody's	Standard & Poor's	Default risk premium	
Best quality, smallest degree of risk	Aaa	AAA	Lowest	Bonds that are judged to be of the best quality. They carry the smallest degree of investment risk and are generally referred to as "gilt edge." Interest payments are protected by a large or exceptionally stable margin, and principal is secure.
High quality, slightly more long-term risk than top rating	Aa1 Aa2 Aa3	AA+ AA AA–	● ● ●	Bonds that are judged to be of high quality by all standards. Together with the first group, they comprise what are generally known as high-grade bonds. They are rated lower than the best bonds because margins of protection may not be as large.
Upper medium grade, possible impairment in the future	A1 A2 A3	A+ A A–	● ● ●	Bonds that possess many favorable invest-ment attributes and are to be considered as upper medium-grade obligations. Factors giving security to principal and interest are considered adequate.
Medium grade, lack outstanding investment characteristics	Baa1 Baa2 Baa3	BBB+ BB BBB–	● ● ●	Bonds that are considered as medium-grade obligations, i.e., they are neither highly protected nor poorly secured.
Speculative issues, pro-tection may be very moderate	Ba1 Ba2 Ba3	BB+ BB BB–	● ● ●	Bonds that are judged to have speculative elements; their future cannot be con-sidered as well assured. Often the pro-tection of interest and principal payments may be very moderate.
Very specula-tive, may have small assurance of interest and principal pay-ments	B1 B2 B3	B+ B B–	● ● ●	Bonds that generally lack characteristics of the desirable investment. Assurance of interest and principal payments or of maintenance of other terms of the contract over any long period of time may be small.
Issues in poor standing, may be in default	Caa	CCC	●	Bonds that are of poor standing. Such issues may be in default, or there may be elements of danger present with respect to principal or interest.
Speculative in a high degree, with marked short-comings	Ca	CC	●	Bonds that represent obligations which are speculative to a high degree. Such issues are often in default or have other marked shortcomings.
Lowest quality, poor prospects of attaining real investment	C	C		The lowest rated class in Moody's desig-nation. These bonds can be regarded as having extremely poor prospects of attain-ing any real investment standing.
		D	Highest	Rating given to income bonds on which interest is not currently being paid. Issues is default with arrears in interest and/or principal payments.

agencies such as Moody's charge a fee for a rating, which is based on the size of the issue. The fee approximates 0.02 percent of the principal amount of the issue. Fees at Moody's vary from a minimum of $1,000 to a maximum of $20,000. On the other hand, the fee at Standard & Poor's is based on the amount of time and effort involved in rating the security. The minimum fee is $500 and the max-imum fee is $15,000.

The most noteworthy trend with respect to debt ratings of industrial corporations is their general downgrading. During the first half of the 1980s rating downgrades far exceeded upgrades in the industrial sector. For example, there were 187, 98, and 94 downgrades in 1985, 1984, and 1983 by Standard & Poor's compared with 49, 54, and 49 upgrades, respectively, in these years.

From 1981 through mid-1986, industrial ratings changes affected about 15 percent of the universe of industrial ratings. This was far above the historic range of 7 to 10 percent. The rating changes have been attributed to continued recapitalization, increased debt related to merger activities, volatile capital costs, intense worldwide competition, a sometimes inhospitable economic cycle, changes in business fundamentals, sharp currency fluctuations, oil price shocks and other fast moving market conditions.

The increase in major oil company mergers in 1984, which increased debt leverage of the affected firms, resulted in rating reductions for a number of corporations that were originally classified as AAA. Also, numerous AA- and A-rated companies were downgraded, reflecting the numerous mergers, restructurings and writedowns of 1984 and 1985, which led to some deterioration in the key ratio medians. Offsetting this to a degree was the continued economic improvement in 1985.

It is interesting to note that the yield spreads of bonds with different ratings change over time. As can be seen in Table 4.4, spreads between intermediate Treasury securities and BBB corporate bonds have varied between 120 and 355 basis points between 1957 and 1981. These cyclical changes in risk premiums are one reason market interest rates fluctuate. Risk premiums are typically highest at economic troughs when unemployment is high because investors tend to demand larger risk premiums to induce them to buy risky bonds. Also, corporations that issue bonds during recessions often experience reductions in sales and profits. Investors tend to require larger risk premiums since the issuers are subject to a higher probability of bankruptcy during recessions. There are also numerous noncyclical reasons for risk premiums to vary over time.

Table 4.4
Rating Changes

	1986(first half)	1985	1984	1983	1982	1981
Upgrades	66	49	54	49	37	57
Downgrades	74	187	98	94	124	67

Table 4.5
Market Rates and Yield Spreads at Economic Peaks and Troughs

	Rates and Yield Spreads in Percent					
Date	AAA	AA	A	BBB	T	BBB-T
August 1957(P)	4.13	4.27	4.39	5.11	3.84	1.27
April 1958 (T)	3.63	3.82	4.03	4.82	2.58	2.24
April 1960 (P)	4.44	4.56	4.75	5.34	4.13	1.21
February 1961(T)	4.28	4.40	4.66	5.22	3.74	1.48
December 1969(P)	7.65	7.83	8.10	8.67	7.47	1.20
November 1970(T)	7.79	8.31	8.69	9.38	6.52	2.86
November 1973(P)	7.76	7.95	8.17	8.67	6.83	1.84
March 1975 (T)	8.63	8.86	9.08	9.66	6.92	2.74
January 1980(P)	10.98	11.36	11.59	12.12	10.70	1.42
July 1980 (T)	10.63	10.96	11.25	12.10	9.72	2.38
July 1981 (P)	14.11	14.54	14.79	15.74	14.11	1.63

T stands for an average of intermediate-term U.S.Treasury bonds
BBB-T stands for the spread between AAA and intermediate -term

    U.S.Treasury bonds
P stands for business cycle peak
T stands for business cycle trough

Sources: Federal Reserve Bulletins; Moody's; National Bureau of Economic Research.

NOTES

1. J. Loeys, "Low-Grade Bonds: A Growing Source of Corporate Funding," Federal Reserve Bank of Philadelphia, *Business Review* (November/December 1986): 9–10.

2. J. J. O'Leary, "How Life Insurance Companies Shifted Investment Focus," *Bankers Monthly Magazine* (June 15, 1982): 26–28.

3. T. Curry and M. Warshawaky, "Life Insurance Companies in a Changing Environment," *Federal Reserve Bulletin* (June 1986): 449–59.

4. E. F. Brigham, *Financial Management Theory and Practice,* 4th ed. (Chicago: Dryden Press, 1986) pp. 623–24.

5. Ibid.

BIBLIOGRAPHY

Bankers Trust Company. *Credit and Capital Markets.* New York, annually. Board of Governors of the Federal Reserve System. *Flow of Funds Accounts.* Washington, D.C., quarterly.

Cook, Timothy Q. "Some Factors Affecting Long-Term Yield Spreads in Recent Years." Federal Reserve Bank of Richmond, *Monthly Review* (1973): 2–14.

Darst, David M. *The Complete Bond Book.* New York: McGraw-Hill, 1975.

Dougall, Herbert E., and Guamnitz, Jack E. *Capital Markets and Institutions.* Englewood Cliffs, N.J.: Prentice-Hall, 1980.

Fabozzi, Frank J., and Irving M. Pollack. *The Handbook of Fixed Income Securities.* Homewood, Ill.: Dow-Jones-Irwin, 1983.

Fong, H. Gifford. "Portfolio Construction: Fixed Income." In John L. Maginn and Donald L. Tuttle, eds., *Managing Investment Portfolios.* Boston: Warren, Gorham, and Lamont, 1983.

Fong, H. Gifford, and Frank J. Fabozzi. *Fixed Income Portfolio Management.* Homewood, Ill.: Dow-Jones-Irwin, 1984.

Henning, Charles N., et al. *Financial Markets and the Economy.* Englewood Cliffs, N.J.: Prentice-Hall, 1978.

Homer, Sidney, and Martin L. Leibowitz. *Inside the Yield Book.* Englewood Cliffs, N.J.: Prentice-Hall, 1972.

Humphrey, Thomas M. "Can the Central Bank Peg Real Interest Rates? A Survey of Classical and Neoclassical Opinion." Federal Reserve Bank of Richmond, *Economic Review* (September/October 1983): 12–21.

———"The Early History of the Real/Nominal Interest Rate Relationship." Federal Reserve Bank of Richmond, *Economic Review* (May/June 1983): 2–10.

Leibowitz, Martin. "Bond Immunization: A Procedure for Realizing Target Level of Return." Salomon Brothers, October 10, 1979, and November 27, 1979.

Malkiel, Burton, G. *The Term Structure of Interest Rates.* Princeton, N.J.: Princeton University Press, 1966.

Melton, William C. "Recent Behavior of the Risk Structure of Interest Rates." Federal Reserve Bank of New York, *Quarterly Review* (Summer 1977): 21–26.

Robinson, Roland I., and Dwayne Wrightsman. *Financial Markets.* New York: McGraw-Hill, 1980.

Reilly, Frank and Sidhu, Rupinder S. "The Many Uses of Bond Duration." *Financial Analyst Journal* (July/August 1980): 58–72.

Rose, Peter S. *Money and Capital Markets.* Plano, Texas: Business Publications, 1983.

Rosenbloom, Richard H. "A Review of the Municipal Bond Market." Federal Reserve Bank of Richmond, *Economic Review* (March/April 1976): 10–19.

Saloman Brothers. *Prospects for Financial Markets.* New York, annual.

Santoni, G. J., and Courtenay C. Stone. "The Fed and the Real Rate of Interest." Federal Reserve Bank of St. Louis, *Review* (December 1982): 8–18.

Sharpe, William F. *Investments.* 3rd ed. Englewood Cliffs, N.J.: Prentice-Hall, 1985.

Spence, Bruce M., Jacob Y. Graudenz, and John J. Lynch, Jr. *Standard Securities Calculation Methods: Current Formulas for Price and Yield Computations.* New York: Securities Industry Association, 1973.

Trainer, Richard D. C. *The Arithmetic of Interest Rates.* New York: Federal Reserve Bank of New York, 1983.

Twentieth Century Fund Task Force on Municipal Bond Market: Building a Broader Market. New York: McGraw-Hill, 1976.

Van Horne, James C. *Financial Market Rates and Flows.* 2nd ed. Englewood Cliffs, N.J.: Prentice-Hall, 1984.

Zwick, Burton. "The Market for Corporate Bonds." Federal Reserve Bank of New York, *Quarterly Review* (Autumn 1972): 27–36.

5

Bond Portfolio Management

There has been an explosion in the variety of fixed income securities in the last decade. In addition, active bond management has progressed from the status of a novelty to that of the norm within fee-based management organizations.[1] At the same time, bond portfolios began to be subjected to the same type of short-term performance measurement as had been applied to equity portfolios.

Today's portfolio manager has a wide selection of options available daily. The investor can choose from a spectrum of maturities ranging from one day to dates well into the next century, from well-known worldwide names to obscure situations requiring detailed analysis, from coupons ranging from 3 percent to double digit yields, from highest quality U.S. Treasury securities to high yielding "junk" bonds. The investor can also manipulate the timing of commitment of new money flows, try to anticipate overall changes in interest rates, try to take advantage of changing yield curves or of the changing yield spread relationships between market sectors differentiated by quality, by coupon, by type of issuer, and by type of issue.[2] A bond manager can construct swaps and consolidate a large number of fragmented holdings by swapping them for a highly marketable set of issues. These examples are only a sampling of the many possible courses of action available to the bond portfolio manager.

In order to manage bond portfolios, the long-term objectives of the portfolio must be clearly defined. With objectives and horizon well defined, it should be possible to construct a baseline portfolio that corresponds to the long-term objectives. The value added by divergence from the baseline portfolio can be interpreted as the portfolio's risk and return objectives.[3]

BOND STRATEGIES AND MANAGEMENT

Bond investing has become increasingly popular because of record high interest rates in the 1970s and early 1980s. The theoretical framework for bond portfolio

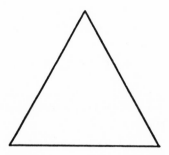

Active Management   Passive Management

1. Rate anticipation   1. Buy and hold

2. Sector valuation   2. Indexing

3. Bond swaps   3. Immunization

4. Use of futures

Figure 5.1
Fixed Income Portfolio Management: Immunization and Cash Flow Matching

management has not been developed to the extent of that for common stocks. Despite the lack of a complete theory of bond management, it is possible to categorize at least two broad strategies: Passive management and active management of bond portfolios (See Figure 5.1).

Passive Management

A passive management strategy suggests that the investor does not actively seek out trading opportunities and searches for mispriced bonds in an effort to outperform the market. Investors still monitor the status of their portfolios in order to match their holdings with risk preferences and objectives, as well as their perception of the outlook for interest rates. Investors seek to earn normal rates of return for a certain risk level and to minimize transactions costs. Management must continually assess default risk, current income requirements, taxes, diversification, callability, and taxes. Strategies for investors following a passive approach to bond management include:

1. Buy and hold
2. Indexing
3. Immunization
4. Contingent immunization

A buy and hold strategy is essentially one that deemphasizes trading activities. It is still important to select bonds carefully and to know the yield advantages of utilities over industrials and agencies over Treasury securities. Some passive investors use timing considerations, switching from long maturities when conditions warrant.

Index funds appeared in the 1980s as a passive management strategy. The strategy does little more than try to keep the fund's investments aligned with the securities that make up the market index the fund is seeking to emulate. Although there is more indexing of stock funds than bond funds, the indexing of both types of portfolios are popular among investors.

Immunization is the strategy of protecting a portfolio against changes in the general level of interest rates. There is both a reinvestment risk and a price risk. The price risk results from the inverse relationship between bond prices and market interest rates. The reinvestment risk results from the certainty about the rate at which future coupon income can be invested. If interest rates fall, reinvestment rates fall and the price of the bond increases. If interest rates rise, reinvestment rates rise and the price of the bond declines. Essentially, the favorable effects on one side can be used to offset the unfavorable results on the other side. Immunization is concerned with protecting the portfolio against interest rate risk by cancelling out its components.

Classical immunization is defined as the process by which a fixed income portfolio is created having an assured return for a specific time horizon regardless of changes in interest rates. An example of a zero reinvestment rate risk portfolio is one consisting of a pure discount instrument maturing at the investment horizon. There is no reinvestment risk because there are no flows to reinvest. Among the important characteristic of classical immunization are a specified time horizon, an assured rate return during the holding period to a fixed horizon date and insulation from the effects of potential adverse interest rate changes on the portfolio value at the horizon date.

Immunization requires offsetting interest rate risk and reinvestment risk. The concept of duration helps accomplish this balancing act. Duration is a measure of the average life of a bond, or the average time necessary to recover the price plus accrued interest of the bond in present value terms where the discount rate is the bond's yield to maturity. A necessary condition for effectively immunizing portfolios is setting the duration of the portfolio equal to the desired portfolio time horizon.

This concept of duration (discussed later) is the basis for current immunization theory. Immunization can be defined as the process of creating a fixed income portfolio having an insured return for a specified time period irrespective of interest rate change. A portfolio is said to be immunized or neutralized against the effects of interest rate risk if the duration of the portfolio is made equal to a preselected portfolio investment horizon. An investment with a 20-year horizon should choose bonds with a duration of 20 years.

Contingent immunization is an approach to integrating a passive immunization strategy with that of a more active strategy. It sets limits on the amount of downside risk associated with an actively managed bond portfolio, while guaranteeing a minimum return. The portfolio manager agrees to a minimum return which will be earned or exceeded over some future period. The portfolio manager is then free to speculate actively until enough of its value has been lost that the only way to guarantee the minimum return is immediate immunization. Essentially, contingent immunization is a risk reduction technique, placing bonds on the risks accepted in an active bond-management program, while guaranteeing a minimum return.

Active Management and Strategies

A basic difference between passive and active management is the use of expectational inputs by active management and the emphasis on risk control by passive management. Immunization and cash flow matching management can be pursued with either emphasis. Dedicated portfolios are often constructed to fund a number or schedule of liabilities over time from portfolio return and asset value, with the value of the portfolio declining to zero after the last liability is paid. Cash flow matching and multiperiod immunization are two approaches for dedicating a portfolio. Cash flow matching allows the portfolio manager to select maturities to match liabilities. The procedure allows the portfolio manager to select a bond with a maturity that matches the last liability. The remaining elements of the liability stream are then reduced by the coupon payments of this bond. Another bond is then purchased for the new, reduced amount of the next to last liability. This process is continued until all liabilities have been matched by the payments on the securities in the portfolio. Sophisticated linear programming techniques can be employed to find a least cost cash flow matching portfolio from a universe of securities. Even with the use of linear programming models, cash flow matching is often technically inferior to multiple liability immunization.

On the other hand, many investors purchase bonds primarily for their appreciation potential. These investors actively manage their portfolios by shifting in and out of various maturities according to their interest rate forcasts or opinions regarding individual bond price. An activist investor should shorten the maturity of a bond portfolio or sell bonds when interest rates are expected to decline. It must be pointed out that the short-term maturities sacrifice capital gain potential and typically (but not always) offer lower coupons. However, short maturities protect the investor when rates are expected to increase. Longer maturities have greater price fluctuations, magnifying the chance for larger gains and losses. With the exception of Treasury issues, longer maturities may be illiquid at times. They are certainly more liquid than Treasury bills.

Activist portfolio managers tend to purchase and sell bonds continually in an attempt to improve the rate of return on the bond portfolio. These bond swaps can be classified as substitution swaps, pure yield swaps, rate anticipation swaps, and intersector spread swaps. These swap strategies are more carefully discussed in another section. Financial futures are used to hedge positions and to gamble on the future course of interest rates.[4]

The most widely implemented and followed active management strategy is the market timing strategy, which emphasizes the cyclical nature of interest rates and the ability to forecast interest rates accurately. Another form of active management is based on determination of value rather than interest rate forecasting. A third active management strategy is a blend of the two aforementioned strategies that captures the advantages of both such that risks offset each other and minimize the risk of the entire portfolio.[5] The active bond portfolio manager makes decisions with respect to interest rate movements, maturity structure, and individual bond selection. Three general maturity structures exist: barbell, laddered, and maturity concentrated portfolios. Maturity concentrated portfolios are utilized when the investment manager has a definite interest rate opinion. If a portfolio manager expects interest rates to decline, the investor would concentrate on long-term maturities because these bonds would have the greatest price appreciation. Laddered portfolios have evenly spaced maturities so that the same amount matures each year. The laddered portfolio structure provides average return over an interest rate cycle and implies no specific interest rate forecast. A barbell structure includes both short- and long-term bonds with no funds investment in intermediate maturities. The barbell structure portfolio has greater liquidity than laddered portfolios because of the larger concentration of short-term bonds. If the yield curve is upward sloping, it should also generate higher returns because more funds are invested in long-maturity issues. The barbell structure does expose the investor to both price and reinvestment risk, which implies an interest rate opinion.

Bond Swaps. A bond swap may be defined as the simultaneous purchase and sale of equal amounts of similar bonds, undertaken in order to increase a bond portfolio's rate of return. Difference among bonds in default risk, coupons, marketability, duration, tax treatment, sinking funds, call provisions, and other factors determine the potential profitability of a bond swap. Bond swapping presupposes that the investor has an ability to identify a short-lived anomaly or mispricing in the markets. The most common bond swaps are substitution, intermarket spread, rate anticipation and pure yield pickup swaps (see Table 5.1). The pure yield spread pickup swap is a transaction based on no expectation of market changes. The swap is accomplished by selling a bond that has a higher yield to maturity.

When the investor anticipates a decline in all interest rates, then long-term bonds should be bought and swapped for holdings of cash or short-term bonds in anticipation of capital gains. On the other hand, when the investor anticipates a rise in interest rates, then long-term bonds should be sold and swapped for cash or short-term instruments in order to avoid capital losses from the expected changing level of interest rates. These last two examples are called rate anticipation swaps. Rate anticipation swaps can lead to the most productive bond port-

Table 5.1
Bond Swaps

Type of Swap	Motivation	Example
RATE ANTICIPATION	To alter the maturity structure of the port- folio to profit from expected movements in interest rates. Can be the most productive action, but it is also the riskiest.	Sell a short-term security and use the proceeds to purchase a long-term security in anticipation of a decrease in interest rates.
SUBSTITUTION	To profit by trading on a market disequilibrium of two similar or sub- stitute securities. When the spread between any two bonds reaches some extreme limit, a swap is executed in the hope of obtaining a profitable reversal as the spread later returns to more normal levels.	Sell a municipal bond of Y maturity at a higher price and purchase a lower-priced but similar risk municipal bond.
INTERMARKET	To profit by trading on a market disequilibrium involving securities that are not perfect sub- stitutes. Also called a sectoral spread swap.	Sell a low-yield Treasury security and purchase a higher-yielding agency security. Trade is motivated by a larger than expected yield of dif- ferential.
YIELD PICKUP	To switch from a lower- yielding security to a higher yielding security. The objective is to increase the total con- tractural return over the bond's life.	Sell an 18-month Treasury note and purchase a 5-year Treasury bond to gain a higher yield.

folio action, but it is also quite risky as interest rate forecasting has become more difficult.

Intermarket spread swaps involve bonds that usually have different coupon rates. Intermarket swaps usually involve buying and selling of bonds in different markets, different quality ratings, or different maturities. For example, buying a Treasury bond and selling a corporate bond or selling an agency security and buying a tax-exempt bond are examples of intermarket swaps. For example, a bond investor may perceive a misalignment between Treasury bonds and corpo- rate bonds. If the yield spread between two sectors is too wide and is expected to narrow, a switch may be made into the security with the higher yield.

The substitution swap involves bonds that are theoretically perfect substitutes for each other in all aspects except in their yield to maturity (or equivalently, their prices). The bonds would have the same quality ratings, similar yields to maturity and coupon interest payments, the same marketability, sinking funds provisions, and call features. The market price differential of these theoretically similar bonds could occur because of a temporary market imperfection. When the spread between any two bonds reaches some extreme limit, presumably as a result of transient market imbalances, a swap is executed in the hope of obtaining a profitable reversal as the spread later returns to more normal levels.[6]

There are also tax swaps. For example, an investor might swap tax-free municipal bonds for taxable corporate bonds of the same risk. This would be done if the swap increased the investor's after-tax return.

All of these bond swaps are undertaken because some bond portfolio managers expect to make a future profit as the price of the bond to be sold is realigned with the price of the bond to be purchased. The workout or realignment time can range from a few days to as long as the time left for the bond to mature. It is of course impossible to know the actual length of the workout time in advance.

Of course, there are risks in bond swapping. These risks include longer than anticipated workout times, an adverse movement of the yield spread, an adverse movement of the level of all interest rates, and an adverse change in quality ratings of the purchased bonds. The swaps should generate a sufficiently large gain in realized yield to pay for the bond brokerage commissions related to the swap, as well as compensation for the risks incurred. Bond swaps require extensive bond market expertise to identify transitory price misalignments. The large number of sophisticated investors and improving technology make bond swapping a challenging and difficult task.

Coupon and Currency Swaps. A currency swap provides a convenient means of altering the quality characteristic of expected cash flows. The key objective is to swap floating rate interest rate payments for fixed rate payments, or vice versa. A coupon swap may be defined as an exchange of a coupon stream with another configuration for the same principal amount.[7]

As in the case of coupon exchange, instruments that enable participants to cover foreign exchange risk of more than one year have been developed. In a currency swap, each party exchanges one currency for another currency with an agreement to reverse the exchange at a specified exchange rate. Currency exchange agreements may consist of a stream of currency in each year, as may be necessary to service the interest payments or receipts on an obligation in foreign currency, or they may provide for a one-time transfer of funds at maturity. The role of the currency cover is to create both a long-term liability in a currency in which an undesired long-term asset position exists and a corresponding asset in an alternative currency in which denominating assets are desirable.[8]

Interest Rate Swaps. Virtually nonexistent as late as 1981, the worldwide interest rate swap market grew to between $350 and $400 billion at the end of 1986. The major cause of the enormous growth has been the increased demand for increased protection against interest rate risk.

Since swaps are agreements between private parties, there is the potential disadvantage that one of the parties may default and be unable to continue the

HOW A SWAP WORKS

The following example is based on an actual transaction that was arranged by an investment bank between a large thrift institution and a large international bank; it is representative of many swaps that have been arranged since 1982. "Thrift" has a large portfolio of fixed-rate mortgages. "Bank" has most of its dollar-denominated assets yielding a floating-rate return based on LIBOR (the London Interbank Offered Rate).

On May 10, 1983, the "Intermediary," a large investment bank, arranged a $100 million, 7-year interest rate swap between Thrift and Bank. In the swap, Thrift agreed to pay Bank a fixed rate of 11 percent per year on $100 million, every 6 months. This payment covered exactly the interest Bank had to pay on a $100 million bond it issued in the Eurodollar market. Thrift also agreed to pay Bank the 2 percent underwriting spread that Bank itself paid to issue this bond. In exchange, Bank agreed to make floating-rate payments to Thrift at 35 basis points (.35 percent) below LIBOR. Intermediary received a broker's fee of $500,000.

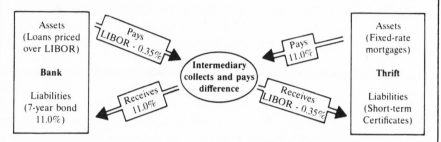

Twice a year, Intermediary (for a fee) calculates Bank's floating-rate payment by taking the average level of LIBOR for that month (Col. 2), deducting 35 basis points, dividing by 2 (because it is for *half* a year), and multiplying by $100 million (Col. 3). If this amount is larger than Thrift's fixed-rate payment (Col. 4), Bank pays Thrift the difference (Col. 5). Otherwise, Thrift pays Bank the difference (Col. 6).

[1] Date	[2] LIBOR	[3] Floating-rate payment 1/2 (LIBOR -0.35%)	[4] Fixed-rate payment 1/2 (11%)	[5] Net Payment from Bank to Thrift	[6] Net Payment from Thrift to Bank
May 1983	8.98%	—	—	—	—
Nov 1983	8.43%	$4,040,000	$5,500,000	0	$1,460,000
May 1984	11.54%	$5,595,000	$5,500,000	$95,000	0
Nov 1984	9.92%	$4,785,000	$5,500,000	0	$ 715,000
May 1985	8.44%	$4,045,000	$5,500,000	0	$1,455,000

The swap allows both Bank and Thrift to reduce their exposure to interest rate risk. Bank can now match its floating-rate assets priced off LIBOR with an interest payment based on LIBOR, while the fixed-rate interest payments on its bond issue are covered by Thrift. At the same time, Thrift can hedge part of its mortgage portfolio, from which it receives fixed interest earnings, with the fixed-rate payment it makes to Bank. However, the floating-rate payment that Thrift receives is linked to LIBOR while its cost of borrowing is more closely linked to the T-bill rate. Since LIBOR and the T-bill rate do not always move in tandem, Thrift is still exposed to fluctuations in the relation between LIBOR and the T-bill rate.

Figure 5.2
How A Swap Works

Source: James A. Wilcox, ed., *Current Readings on Money, Banking, and Financial Markets.* (Boston: Little, Brown & Company, 1987).

agreement. Although there may be no principal at risk between swapping parties, the other party may be stuck with an interest rate exposure. Potential default risk can be reduced by requiring standby letters of credit, third party guarantees or collateral, and by carefully screening participants in swap agreements.

Interest rate swaps usually involve two companies that wish to change their exposure to interest rate fluctuations. For example, a savings and loan has long-term fixed rate mortgages, but it also has liabilities with interest payments that float with market rates of interest. The thrift loses when interest rates rise unexpectedly because the interest cost of its liabilities increase but the revenue from the fixed rate mortgages remain constant. The other company involved in the swap, typically a Eurobank, faces the antithesis: its assets yield a return that fluctuates with market interest rates, but the interest payments on its liabilities are fixed for a longer period of time. Revenues for the nonthrift company rise faster than the costs of borrowing when rates increase. However, a drop in market rates reduces its net earnings (see Figure 5.2).

Increased interest rate volatility has caused bank customers to try new techniques for matching interest rate exposures on assets and liabilities. Technological advances in telecommunications and computer systems have increased international financial mobility. Swaps have provided banks with much needed fee income, while borrowers have sought lower borrowing costs and protection from interest rate risk. Even though banks offer an attractive array of fee-generating and portfolio management techniques they also expose banks to new risks. The leverage capacity of swaps has caused bank regulators to consider these activities for inclusion in a risk-based capital adequacy proposal.

Credit risk is the main concern of regulators and banks because credit risk exists for a bank on all swaps in which the bank is the intermediary between two end users. If one of the end users defaults, the bank loses the hedging value of the offsetting swap and may suffer a capital loss. Banks must make sure that the price of the service they provide adequately reflects the risk they provide in the swap arrangement. The credit risk of swaps can also be eliminated by the enforcement of strict credit standards.

DURATION

Professor Frederick Macaulay derived the basic concept of bond duration in 1938. Although the concept of duration received little attention at the time of publication by the investment community, it has been an extremely popular concept during the 1980s. Although maturity is the traditional measure of a bond's lifetime, it is inadequate because of its focus on only the return of principal at the maturity date. Two 10-year bonds, one with a 10 percent coupon and the other with a 14 percent coupon, do not have identical economic lifetimes because the investor will recover the original purchase price much sooner with the higher coupon bond. Therefore, a measure such as duration is needed that accounts for the size and timing of the cash flows over the life of a bond.

Duration is a weighted average term to maturity where the cash flows are in terms of their present value. Mathematically, duration is measured as follows:

Duration = Number of years needed to recover fully purchase price of given present values of its cash flows
= Weighted average time to recovery of all interest payments plus principal

$$= \sum_{t=1}^{N} t \left[\frac{\dfrac{C_t}{(1 + ytm)^t}}{\displaystyle\sum_{t=1}^{N} \dfrac{C_t}{(1 + ytm)^t}} \right]$$

where

C_t = the cash receipt in period t (interest or principal)
ytm = the yield to maturity on the bond
t = time period when any cash receipt occurs

As with the weighted average term to maturity, the duration of a bond is shorter than its term to maturity because of the interim interest payments. This means that a zero coupon bond yielding no interim payments would have the same duration, weighted average term to maturity, and term to maturity, because all of the total cash flow and 100 percent of total present value would come at maturity. Duration is inversely related to the coupon for the bond, that is, the larger the coupon the greater the proportion of total returns in the interim and the shorter the duration. Duration will always be less than time to maturity for bonds that have paying coupons.

Assume an insurer has a loss reserve liability due in 4.6 years. The amount due of $6 million has a present value of $3.56 million at a 12 percent discount rate [$6,000,000/ $(1.12)^{4.6} = \$3,562,446$] and $3.56 million is the amount of cash the company has on hand to meet this liability. The manager's goal is to invest the cash so as to realize a 12 percent return and thereby have sufficient funds to pay off the liability.

Four bonds are candidates for this investment and their features are summarized in Table 5.2. Bond A is a zero coupon bond which matures in 4.6 years. Bonds B, C, and D all have the same coupon rate and are selling to yield 12 percent. The only difference between them is the time to maturity.

If interest rates do not change during the next 4.6 years, it makes no difference which bond is purchased since all will produce an actual return of 12 percent. If rates change anytime during the next 4.6 years then the insurer may or may not realize a 12 percent return depending upon which strategy is followed. If Bond A is chosen, a 12 percent return will be realized regardless of what happens to interest rates. This occurs because no interest is paid and the insurer need not worry about reinvesting the interest payments. Bonds B and C have interest rate risk; Bond B is exposed to price risk and Bond C is

Table 5.2
Duration Calculations

Bond	Coupon	Maturity (Years)	Yield to Maturity	Market Price	Duration
A	0%	4.6	12%	$ 593.74	4.60
B	12%	20	12%	1,000	8.36
C	12%	3	12%	1,000	2.39
D	12%	6	12%	1,000	4.60

Comparison of Funds Available with Funds Required

Bond	Interest Rate	Funds Available at Horizon Date	Funds Required	Excess (Deficit)
B	10	$6,463,132	$6,000,000	$463,132
B	14	5,646,762	6,000,000	(353,238)
C	10	5,797,453	6,000,000	(202,547)
C	14	6,206,921	6,000,000	206,921[1]
D	10	6,003,826	6,000,000	3,286[1]
D	14	6,002,722	6,000,000	2,722[1]

[1]This figure would be $0 were it not for rounding errors.

Calculation of Bond Duration

Year (1)	Cash Flow (2)	Present Value (3)	Proportion of Total (4)=(3)÷1000	Year (5)	Product (6)=(4)x(5)
1	$120	$107.14	.107	1	.107
2	120	95.66	.096	2	.191
3	120	85.41	.085	3	.256
4	120	76.26	.076	4	.305
5	120	68.09	.068	5	.340
6	1120	567.43	.567	6	3.405
					4.604

exposed to reinvestment risk. Bond D guarantees a 12 percent return regardless of interest rate changes.

The above strategies will be examined in more detail by assuming that interest rates change immediately after the bond is purchased. Only two possibilities will be considered; rates go up to 14 percent or down to 10 percent. Table 5.3 shows the horizon date wealth position per $1,000 investment of the insurer as well as the realized return.

At the end of the year 1 Bond B pays $120 interest which is reinvested to the horizon

Table 5.3
Horizon Date Wealth Positions When Interest Rates Change

			Interest	Value of Interest or Bond at Horizon Date	
1.	Bond B	End of Year	Received	10%	14%
		1	$120	$ 169.12	$ 192.33
		2	120	153.75	168.71
		3	120	139.77	147.99
		4	120	127.06	129.81
		4.6		1,224.54[1]	946.24[1]
				$1,814.24	$1,585.08
	Realized Return			13.83%	10.53%

[1]Value of a 12 percent bond with 15.4 years remaining until maturity.

			Interest	Value of Interest or Bond at Horizon Date	
2.	Bond C	End of Year	Received	10%	14%
		1	$120	$ 169.12	$ 192.33
		2	120	153.75	168.71
		3	120[2]	139.77	147.99
		4	100[2]	105.89	151.45
		4.6		1,058.85	1,081.79
				$1,627.38	$1,742.32
	Realized Return			11.17%	12.83%

[2]Assume a 2 year, 10% bond was purchased with the proceeds from Bond C.
Assume a 2 year, 14% bond was purchased with the proceeds from Bond C.

			Interest	Value of Interest or Bond at Horizon Date	
3.	Bond D	End of Year	Received	10%	14%
		1	$120	$ 169.12	$ 192.33
		2	120	153.75	168.71
		3	120	139.77	147.99
		4	120	127.06	129.81
		4.6		1,685.61	1,046.16
				$1,685.31	$1,685.00
	Realized Return				

date (3.6 years) at a compound annual rate of 10 percent which means the year 1 interest payment will be worth $169.12 in 3.6 years [$169.12 = $120(1.10)$^{3.6}$]. Similarly, year 2 interest is reinvested for 2.6 years at a compound annual rate of 10 percent and years 3 and 4 values are calculated in a similar fashion. The figure of $1,224.54 is the market price of the bond 4.6 years from now. The horizon date wealth position is therefore the sum of each year's interest compounded at interest plus the market value of the bond at year 4.6. If interest rates fall to 10 percent the horizon date wealth is $1,814.24 per $1,000 invested for a realized return of 13.83 percent [.1383 = ($1,814.24/1,000)$^{1/4.6}$ − 1.0]. Realized returns for Bond C are calculated in a similar fashion.

Recall that a 12 percent return on the cash was required in order to have enough money to pay the future liability. If Bond B or C is purchased, the insurer will exceed or fall short of the cash target depending upon interest rate changes. Since interest rate changes cannot be accurately predicted it cannot be immediately known whether sufficient funds will be available to pay off the liabilities. Table 5.2 shows the excess or deficit funds.

The purchase of Bond B or C can produce significant deficits or surplus funds depending upon the magnitude and frequency of interest rate movements. This occurred because the portfolio was *immunized,* which is the term used to indicate that the duration of the bond matched the duration of the insurer's liability.

The duration of a zero coupon bond will always be equal to the time to maturity while the duration of an interest bearing bond will always be less than its time to maturity. In Table 5.2 the last column displayed the duration of each bond. A sample calculation for Bond D appears in Table 5.2.

Bonds A and D have the same duration while Bonds B and C have a longer and shorter duration respectively. An insurer could assure itself of enough cash from its investments to match its liability if Bond A or D was purchased. The purchase of Bond B or C would not provide this assurance.

Immunization works because it balances two offsetting effects if interest rates change. When interest rates decline, cash flows are reinvested at a lower than expected rate but the bond price appreciates. Thus, the reinvestment rate drags down return but the price effect acts in the opposite direction. When duration exceeds the horizon (for example, Bond B), the price effect is larger then the reinvestment effect. If duration is less than horizon date, the price effect is less than the reinvestment effect, but if duration exactly equals the horizon date the effects are offsetting. Simply matching maturities will not immunize the portfolio unless the bonds are zero coupon.

Theoretically, the portfolio should be rebalanced to match durations (the time remaining to horizon) every time interest rates change. However, because rebalancing involves transaction costs, management must weigh the risk of a nonimmunized portfolio against the transaction costs to immunize.[9]

The standard duration measure has limitations in that the yield curve must remain constant or move upward or downward by a constant amount for the portfolio to remain immunized. If the interest change is of any other type, the financial institution will not be immunized against that particular rate change. Another limitation of duration analysis stems from the fact that duration is only an approximation. If the assets and liabilities do not have the same convexity, duration cannot match the market value changes on both sides of the balance sheet. For example, if the asset is a fixed rate mortgage it is likely to be repaid if rates decline, while a bank liability does not have this feature.

Because market yield affects the numerator more than it affects the denominator of the duration computation, there is an inverse relation between a change in the market yield and a bond's duration. This means that an increase in the market yield will cause a decline in duration, other things being equal. As market yields increase, the duration of a bond decreases.

Duration tells us the difference in the effective lives of alternative bonds. For example, with an 8 percent yield to maturity and an 8 percent coupon, a 10-year bond has an effective life (duration) of 7.25 years, whereas a 20-year bond has an effective life of 10.60 years—quite a different perspective, given that the second has a term to maturity of twice the first. Furthermore, under these conditions, a 50-year bond has an effective life of only 13.21 years.[10]

A bond's duration equals its term to maturity only if it is a zero coupon bond or a one-period, coupon-bearing bond, while a coupon-bearing bond with a finite maturity of more than one period has a duration that is less than its term to maturity. In general, duration increases with maturity. Although duration may not be a complete measure of bond risk, it does reflect some of the impact of changes in interest rates.

Duration and Bond Price Volatility

Michael Hopewell and George Kaufman set forth the specific form of the relationship between the duration of a bond and its price volatility in a September 1973 American Economic Review article titled "Bond Price Volatility and Term to Maturity: A Generalized Respecification."[11]

$$\% \triangle \text{ Bond Price} = -D^*(\triangle r)$$

where

$\% \triangle \text{ Price}$ = the percentage change in price for the bond,
$\quad\quad D^*$ = the adjusted duration of the bond in years, which is equal to $D/(1 + r)$, and
$\quad\quad \triangle r$ = the change in the market yield in basis points divided by 100 (for example, a 60 basis point decline would be -0.6).

Consider a bond that has a duration of 10 years and an adjusted duration of 9.259 years (10/1.08). If interest rates go from 6 to 7 percent, then:

$$
\begin{aligned}
\% \triangle \text{ Bond Price} &= -9.259 \, (100/100) \\
&= -9.259 \, (1) \\
&= -9.259\%.
\end{aligned}
$$

The price of the bond should decline by about 9.26 percent for every 1 percent (100 basis point) increase in market rates.

IMPLICATIONS FOR PORTFOLIO MANAGEMENT

The direct relation between duration and interest rate sensitivity is important to an active bond portfolio manager who attempts to derive superior returns by adjusting the composition of the portfolio to benefit from swings in market rates of interest. According to this philosophy, the portfolio manager should attempt to minimize the portfolio's interest rate sensitivity prior to an expected increase in rates and to maximize it when interest rates are expected to decline. Duration is considered rather than term to maturity because duration offers a better meaure of the interest sensitivity of the portfolio.

Duration and Immunization

The concept of duration is important to the bond portfolio manager with a specified investment horizon who wants to reduce the interest rate risk from his long-term bond portfolio. The portfolio manager does not want to predict future market rates, but simply to achieve a specified result regardless of future interest rates. Because the yield curve is usually not flat and because interest rates are constantly changing, the bond portfolio manager faces what is referred to as "interest rate risk" between the time of investment and the future target date. Interest rate risk can be defined as the uncertainty regarding the ending wealth position due to changes in market interest rates between the purchase date and the target date. If interest rates decrease, the realized price for the bond in the secondary market will be above expectations, while if interest rates increase, the realized price will be below expectations. There is also a reinvestment risk because interest rates at which coupon payments can be reinvested are unknown. Price risk and reinvestment risk have opposite effects on the investor's ending wealth position.

A bond portfolio manager with a specific investment horizon will want to eliminate these two risks and "immunize" the portfolio. A portfolio of bonds is immunized from interest rate risk if the duration of the portfolio equals the desired investment horizon. Duration is the investment horizon for which the price risk and the coupon reinvestment of a bond portfolio have equal magnitudes but opposite directions.

Two security characteristics—yield and duration—play a salient role in appraising fixed income securities. Yield gives some indication of the average rate of return on capital, while duration indicates the time span over which that rate of return has relevance, that is, it reflects the "futurity" of a bond's cash flow. A bond portfolio is said to immunize a liability if the duration of the portfolio matches the time remaining before the liability becomes due. For example, a portfolio with a three year duration is said to immunize a liability payable in three years. Unfortunately, merely matching the duration of a bond portfolio to an investor's liability horizon does not eliminate risk; the investor is not left indifferent about future changes in interest rates. Although such matching will eliminate the risk associated with parallel shifts in the yield curve, it will not eliminate other risks associated with changes in the shape of the yield curve, such as a flattening or steepening. Complete immunization or protection is available only from construction of a dedicated bond portfolio.[12]

Suppose we have a schedule of liabilities related to future pension benefit disbursement. A dedicated bond portfolio is one that should generate sufficient cash from the bonds' interest and principal payments alone to cover each and every liability with certainty. Dedication is an extreme form of risk management that guarantees funding of future disbursements regardless of changes in interest rates and securities prices. The success of a dedication program depends only on the timely payment of interest and principal as promised by the issuers of bonds in the portfolio and is independent of any reinvestment of cash receipts or on the sale of a security prior to the final maturity.[13]

Corporate and municipal cash managers have practiced dedication or funding to a specific date for decades as can be seen in the demand for short-term instruments timed to mature on or immediately prior to a dividend payment, interest payment, or other liability date. There is a difference between the dedication techniques used by cash managers and those used by bond portfolio managers. Because most money market instruments, such as Treasury bills, bank CDs, and commercial paper make a single payment at maturity, a cash manager can fund each of these liabilities individually. On the other hand, bonds pay interest prior to maturity and while various payments from a bond can serve to satisfy many different liabilities in part or in whole, the manager of a dedicated portfolio cannot fund particular long-dated liabilities with particular bonds. The manager has to fund every piece of the liability schedule concurrently and must analyze the schedule systematically and in its entirety.[14]

NOTES

1. R. Akhoury, "Bond Management Issues," in *Financial Handbook,* 5th ed., E. Altman, ed. (New York: John Wiley & Sons, 1981), p. 17–19.

2. Ibid.

3. Ibid.

4. C. Seix, "Bond Swaps," *The Handbook of Fixed Income Securities,* F. J. Fabozzi and I. M. Pollack, eds. (Homewood, Ill.: Dow-Jones-Irwin, 1983), pp. 737–42.

5. H. G. Fong and F. J. Fabozzi, *Fixed Income Portfolio Management,* (Homewood, Ill.: Dow-Jones-Irwin, 1985), pp. 3–4.

6. Seix, "Bond Swaps," p. 740.

7. C. R. Beidelman, *Financial Swaps* (Homewood, Ill.: Dow-Jones-Irwin, 1985), p. 4.

8. Ibid., p. 3.

9. A. Gart and D. Nye, *Insurance Company Finance* (Malvern, Pa.: Insurance Institute of America, 1986), pp. 276–80.

10. Ibid.

11. M. Hopewell and G. Kaufman, "Bond Price Volatility and Term to Maturity: A Generalized Respecification," *American Economic Review* (September 1973): 749–753.

12. K. D. Garbade, "Rate of Return and Futurity of Cash Flow from a Bond: Are Yield and Duration Good Measures?" Money Market Center of Bankers Trust (December 1984): 1.

13. K. D. Garbade, "Dedicated Bond Portfolios: Construction, Rebalancing, and Swapping," Money Market Center of Bankers Trust (October 1985): 1.

14. K. D. Garbade, "Managing Yield Curve Risk: A Generalized Approach to Bond Immunization," Money Market Center of Bankers Trust (August 1985): 1.

6

Interest Rate Determination for Bonds

THE BOND MARKET

A bond is a written promise by the issuer to repay a fixed amount of borrowed money on a specified date and to pay a set annual rate of interest in the meantime, generally at semiannual intervals. Corporate bond holders are creditors, not owners. They do not share in profits and losses, but are paid before common stockholders (owners get dividends). Maturities typically range from 5 to 40 years. They are conventionally denominated in units with a principal value of $1,000 and a stated coupon rate.

Almost all bonds have their terms spelled out in a detailed contract called an indenture. This agreement describes the rights of lenders and the obligations of the debtors. The enforcement of this indenture is usually left to a trustee (frequently a commercial bank trust department) who acts for the bond holders collectively. To ensure that bond liabilities do not exceed the value of assets financed by these liabilities, some bonds are often issued with sinking fund provisions. The funds set aside in the sinking fund by the issuer in a reserve account are used to retire a portion of the outstanding bonds.

Failure to pay either interest or principal on a bond constitutes a default for that obligation. Default usually leads to bankruptcy unless quickly remedied by payment or a voluntary agreement with the creditor. A filing of bankruptcy by a corporation initiates litigation and involvement by a court, which works with creditors, other claimants, and the company. The firm could be liquidated with proceeds divided among creditors and other claimants according to bankruptcy procedures. Another option is to seek a reorganization of the firm if its assets appear valuable enough in a going concern. This type of plan requires substantial concurrence by the affected creditors, who receive new claims on the reorganized company. A third alternative for a failing company is to voluntarily seek an "arrangement" under Chapter XI of the Federal Bankruptcy Act. The company is protected by the court from its creditors while it attempts to work out a plan that creditors will accept for paying its debt.

In a bankruptcy claim, secured debt (debt that has specified assets as collateral) has priority over the funds received in the liquidation of that asset. To the extent that the funds received are insufficient to cover the entire allowed claim, the balance is owned by the debtor and is considered part of the remaining unsecured claims: Senior debt has priority over all debt that is specified as subordinated to that debt but has equal priority with all other unsecured debt.

The institutional market for corporate bonds consists primarily of tax-exempt pension funds, life insurance companies, bank trust departments, and mutual bond funds. Individuals are also buyers of these bonds, especially when their yields are relatively high compared to other alternative investments. Bonds provide investors with two kinds of income: (1) they provide current income from the periodic receipt of interest payments and (2) they can generate capital gains whenever market interest rates decline. In addition to investing directly in various bonds, investors can also invest indirectly into these securities via investment company shares (such as mutual funds) and financial futures.

PRICE QUOTES AND YIELDS

The prices of taxable bonds are usually quoted as percentages of par or face value. In order to convert the price quote into a dollar figure, you multiply the price by the par value. For example, a bond with a par value of $1,000 and a price of "$92\frac{1}{2}$" has a market value or price of $920.50. Table 6.1 will illustrate the matter.

The current yield is the ratio of the coupon to the current price. For example, a bond with a price of 92.5 and a coupon of 10 percent has a current yield of 10.81 percent. The yield to maturity is an application of the internal rate of return, that is, the discount rate that makes the present value of the cash flow payments just equal to the price of the asset that generates the flows. For example, suppose a bond is selling at $961.60 and has a coupon of $80 per year for the next 20 years. The holder of such a bond would expect to receive $40 every six months for 20 years and $1,000 at the end of 20 years. The rate of interest on an investment of

Table 6.1
Prices of Taxable Bonds

Par Value	Price Quote	Price as a Percentage of Par	Price in Dollars
$1,000	92 1/2	92.5%	$920.50
$5,000	103	103.0%	$5,150.00
$10,000	80 1/4	89.25%	$8,925.00
$100,000	101 7/8	101.875%	$101,875.00

$961.66 that would be able to produce those cash flows and leave nothing after the payment of $1,000 at maturity is a yearly compounded rate of 8.4 percent, which happens to be the yield to maturity of this bond.

The typical bond expires (matures) on a specified date and is technically known as a term bond. In contrast, a serial bond has a series of maturity dates. One issue of serial bonds may mature in specified amounts year after year, and each specified amount could carry a different coupon.

Bonds track on an accrued interest basis. This means that the bond buyer must pay the bond holders the interest that has been earned (accrued) on the bond since the last semiannual interest payment. An investor can sell a bond anytime without losing the interest that has accrued.

INTEREST RATES AND BOND PRICES

The interest rate is the price of renting money, a rate paid by the borrower to the lender. According to John Maynard Keynes, "The rate of interest is the reward for parting with liquidity for a specified period." A bond is an IOU issued by the borrower who promises to repay the face value of the loan at maturity and to make periodic coupon interest payments (usually semiannually), while the debt is outstanding. The market value of the bond is the present value of all promised future interest payments discounted by the appropriate market rate of interest plus the discounted maturity value of the bond. Therefore, bond prices vary inversely with interest rates. When interest rates go down, bond prices rise. When interest rates go up, bond prices fall.

The coupon rate, maturity, call and put provisions, tax status, marketability, credit rating of a bond, general economic conditions, and current market interest rates help determine the price of a bond. The structure of prices for bonds differing in these dimensions can be examined and used to estimate the prices of other bonds. The overall pattern is called the yield structure, while the set of yields of different maturities is called the term structure, and the set of yields of bonds of different risk is called the risk structure. Risk differentials are added to the interest rates for default-free bonds to obtain the relevant yields for lower quality bonds. Differentials between yields of related bonds, bills, or notes are usually termed yield spreads and are measured in basis points. One basis point equals 0.01 percent. If the yield to maturity for one bond is 10.90 and that of another is 9.80, the spread is 110 basis points.

BOND PRICING

The quoted price of a bond is equal to the present value of the future cash flows to be received, minus the accrued interest. Corporate bonds assume a 180-day coupon period, whereas government bonds use the exact number of days within the coupon period. Bonds are also priced as of the delivery date. If a bond is purchased for delivery at a coupon date, then accrued interest will be zero. If the bond pays interest on a semiannual basis, then all future cash flows to be received will be discounted over full periods at one half of the quoted yield to maturity.

Example: A 9 percent coupon bond has a quoted yield of 10 percent. What is the current price of this bond if interest is paid semiannually and the bond has 20 years to maturity?

In this case, accrued interest is zero and the bond will make 40 semiannual payments of $45, beginning in six months, plus a final maturity payment of $1,000. The appropriate discount rate is one half of the quoted yield, while the current price is equal to the present value of the 40 interest payments plus the present value of the maturity value of the bond. All cash flows to be received are discounted at the six month rate of 5.0 percent.

The bond value is the sum of the present value of the interest payment annuity that the bond holder receives and the present value of the return of bond principal at maturity compounded at the market discount rate of 10 percent paid semiannually. The value of this bond that pays $45 semiannually, given a market discount rate of 10 percent, is $914.16.

Present Value of Bond
= (Present Value of Interest Payments) +
   (Present Value of the Return of Principal)

$$= \$45 \sum_{t=1}^{40} \frac{1}{(1 + .05)^t} + \$1,000 \left[\frac{1}{(1 + .05)^{40}} \right]$$

$$= \$45 \, (17.15) + \$1,000(.142)$$
$$= \$772.16 + \$142$$
$$= \$914.16$$

Yield to Maturity

The yield to maturity for a bond paying interest semiannually can be calculated by solving for r in the present value bond formula given below:

$$PV = \frac{M}{\left(1 + \dfrac{r}{2}\right)^{2n}} + \sum_{t=1}^{2n} \frac{\dfrac{I}{2}}{\left(1 + \dfrac{r}{2}\right)^t} \tag{1}$$

PV = price of bond
m = number of years to maturity
I = annual dollar coupon interest
r = yield to maturity
M = redemption value of bond at maturity

and then adjusting the discount rate by using the following formula: $((1 +$ discount rate$)^2 - 1)$. (2)

This formula implicitly assumes that the periodic payments of interest are reinvested at a rate equal to the yield to maturity. For example, let us consider a bond with a current market price of $814.10, a redemption value at maturity of $1,000, a coupon rate of 8 percent with semiannual interest payments, and seven years to maturity. While the current yield would be 9.8 percent ($80/$814.00), the yield to maturity would be 12.36 percent. When a 6 percent rate is used the present value of the promised cash flow is $814.10, in formula 1. The 6 percent yield is annualized by using the aforementioned formula (2). This would generate $(1 + .06)^2 - 1 = 1.1236 - 1 = .1236$.

Yield to Call

Since some bonds can be called by the issuer before maturity, an investor should compute the yield on a bond (1) assuming the bond is held to maturity and (2) assuming the bond is called by the issuer (yield to call).

The yield to call is defined as the discount rate that equates the present value of the promised cash flow if the bond is called to the market price. For example, suppose a bond is selling for $1,089.37 and is callable in three years at 104.2 or $1,042. A 3 percent discount rate will equate the present value of the cash flow of the bond if it is called to the market price of $1,089.37. Doubling the discount rate to 6 percent gives the yield to call.

A trial-and-error approach is used with the correct solution given below:

$PV =$ (Semiannual coupon rate)(PV Annuity at 3 percent for six periods)
  $+$ (Call price)(PV at 3 percent for six periods)
($40)(5.4172) + (1,042)(.8375) = $1,089.37

The yield to call assumes that the coupon rate will be invested at a rate equal to the yield to call. This is the same drawback suffered by the yield to maturity calculation. Also, the yield to call does not recognize what will happen to the proceeds after the bond is called.

In order to calculate the yield to first call, the yield to maturity formula (equation 1) is used. The number of periods until the first call date is substituted for the number of periods until maturity and the call price is substituted for the face value or redemption value of the bond in equation 1.

INTEREST RATES AND YIELD CURVES

There are many different interest rates in the financial markets. Even though these interest rates often move in the same direction at the same time, the amount of their movements may differ substantially.

The relationship between a security's interest rate and its term to maturity for a given default risk class at a particular point in time is usually called the term structure of interest rates. The yield curve illustrates the relationship between the interest rate and the maturities of securities that are identical in all ways except maturity. The horizontal axis represents the time to maturity, and the vertical axis represents yield to maturity (see Figure 6.1). Yield curves have different

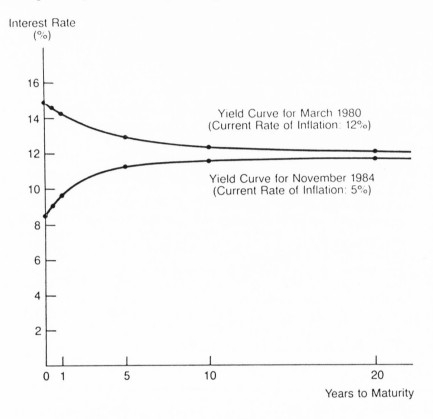

Term to Maturity	Interest Rate	
	March 1980	November 1984
6 months	15.03%	8.81%
1 year	14.03	9.80
5 years	13.47	11.33
10 years	12.75	11.57
20 years	12.49	11.66

Figure 6.1
Yield Curves

Source: Federal Reserve Bulletin.

shapes depending on expected inflation rates and supply and demand. The shape and level of yield curves do not remain constant over time. Yield curves will generally shift up and down and have different slopes as the general level of interest rates increase or decrease.

Figure 6.1 shows some possible yield curves, each of which indicates that interest rates vary with time to maturity. The November 1984 yield is upward sloping, which is considered most typical. It shows that interest rates rise with maturity. The "normal" yield curve is upward sloping, which usually signifies that investors expect inflation to remain steady or increase in the future. The March 1980 yield curve is a downward sloping curve and often occurs when interest rates have reached their peak. The downward sloping yield curve demonstrates investor expectations of a decline in inflation and interest rates. They are also "humped" yield curves, and flat yield curves. For example, when the general level of interest rates is low and yields are expected to increase, many investors shun long-term securities because of the potential for capital losses. This drives down the price of long-term bonds (raising the yield), producing higher long-term rates than short-term rates and an upward sloping yield curve. On the other hand, when all rates are relatively high, investors typically prefer to hold long-term securities over short-term securities because of the limited capital gain potential on shorter-term securities. However, when the overall level of rates is high, long-term yields are often less than short-term yields, resulting in a yield curve that is downward or negatively sloped.

The shape of the term structure of interest rates provides investors with considerable information regarding present market conditions and consensus expectations of future interest rate changes. Market expectations are formed on the basis of available information and frequently change. This implies uncertainty associated with the forecasts implied by a term structure. The fact that rates are expected to increase, for example, does not necessarily mean that rates are at a nadir. Rates may decrease further before increasing. Hence, term structure estimates should be used in a most likely context. The term structure of interest rates represents a useful tool for assessing present market conditions and a consensus forecast. Also, yield curves can be used to find inefficiencies in the market, that is, to find overpriced and underpriced securities.

RIDING THE YIELD CURVE

Obviously, the price of a bond will depend upon the dollar maturity value of the bond, the size and frequency of coupon payments, the term to the final or maturity payment, the frequency and magnitude by which the coupon can change prior to maturity, the risk of default on interest payments and/or repayment of principal, the time value of money, and any options or conditions that affect the timing or size of any of the payments.

In the past, the phrase "riding the yield curve" referred to a policy of buying securities with maturities beyond the investment horizon and selling them prior to maturity at the horizon. The strategy was based on the upward sloping yield curve, where yields on longer-term maturities were higher than those on short-term maturities. For example, suppose that a 60-day T-bill yielded 7 percent and 90-day T-bills yielded 8 percent and that these rates were expected to remain the same over the next month. The investor could earn the higher yield on the 90-day instrument over the 60-day horizon, and sell the instrument at the horizon for a capital gain, because it would then be trading as a 30-day instrument. The current concept of riding the yield curve includes a policy of speculating on shifts in the yield curve relationship. For example, if the yield curve were upward sloping at present and the investor expected the yield curve to flatten out as interest rates declined, the financial manager might extend the average maturity of the portfolio. The danger inherent in this buy and hold strategy is that the level of interest rates may increase or that the short-term end of the yield curve may swing upward. Either of these developments would cause the bond investor to suffer a capital loss.

INTEREST RATE THEORIES

One interest rate theory suggests that the nominal or stated interest rate is composed of a pure rate of interest ($K\sim$) plus an inflation premium (IP), a default risk premium (DP), a liquidity premium (LP), and a maturity risk premium (MP). The pure rate of interest is defined as the equilibruim interest rate on a riskless security if there were no rate of inflation such as the interest rate on a default-free U.S. Treasury security minus the anticipated inflation rate. The inflation premium is added to the pure rate of return because of expected inflation. We then add a default risk premium that reflects the credit risk inherent in the security. In addition, we add a liquidity premium to the equilibrium rate on a security that cannot be converted to cash on short notice. Then we add a maturity premium due to the length of a security's maturity and the risk to which investors are exposed because of changing interest rates.

$$K = K\sim + IP + DP + LP + MP$$

$$
\begin{aligned}
K\sim &= \text{pure, or real, rate of interest} \\
IP &= \text{inflation premium} \\
DP &= \text{default risk premium} \\
LP &= \text{liquidity premium} \\
MP &= \text{maturity risk premium}
\end{aligned}
$$

The actual, or nominal, rate of interest is the real rate of interest plus premiums to compensate investors for inflation and risk. The inflation premium, which is the average inflation premium anticipated over the life of the security, compensates the investor for the possible loss of purchasing power. The default premium compensates investors for the risk that a borrower will default, or not pay principal and interest on a loan. A security that can be sold and quickly converted into cash at a fair price is said to be liquid. A liquidity premium is added to the real rate for securities that are not liquid. Because long-term securities are more price sensitive to interest changes than are short-term securities, a maturity risk premium is added to longer-term securities to compensate investors for interest rate risk. For example, you have determined the following data:

$$\text{Pure rate } (K\sim) = 3\%$$
$$\text{Inflation premium} = 8\%$$
$$\text{Default risk premium} = 2\%$$
$$\text{Liquidity premium} = 1\%$$
$$\text{Maturity risk premium} = 1\%$$

The rate of inflation is expected to be constant and a liquid market exists only for a very short-term Treasury securities. What is the interest rate on a Treasury bill and what is the interest rate on a long-term Treasury bond according to the aforementioned interest rate theory?

The interest rate on the Treasury bill would be 11 percent. It would be calculated by adding the inflation premium to the pure rate of interest. The interest rate on the long-term Treasury bond would be 13 percent. The liquidity premium and the maturity risk premium would be added to the inflation premium plus the pure risk premium. There is no need for a default risk premium in either case since both securities are issues of the U.S. government. If a third question had been added such as what is the interest rate on a long-term corporate bond, the answer would have been 15 percent. We would add the default risk premium to the long-term rate on the Treasury bond. It should be mentioned that the default risk would vary for different types of securities and would be a function of the perceived credit risk as assigned by the credit rating agencies.

Other Determinants of Interest Rates

We have already established that interest rates on debt instruments vary with risk and that different classifications of debt instruments are exposed to different kinds of risk, with the result that interest rates between the classifications are apt to be different. Within each classification, there are additional interest rate differentials owing to differences in the degree of risk exposure. For example, the maturity of a bond and the creditworthiness of its issuer are two fundamental characteristics that determine risk. Interest rates also reflect the presence or absence of bond provisions such as callability and convertibility, market imperfections, tax effects, and other considerations.

Since callability is a disadvantage to the investor, callable bonds command higher yields than noncallable bonds. On the other hand, a sweetener such as convertibility into common stock suggests that investors will often accept a lower interest rate for this feature. However, interest rates on convertibles are not always lower than on nonconvertibles since some companies would have difficulty in finding a market for their bonds without this convertibility feature. This compensates to some extent for default risk.

Interest rates are also classified according to their tax status: The biggest difference appears between the yields on municipal debt issues that are exempt from federal income taxes and those bond yields fully taxable at the federal level. There are also potential differences in interest rates for conventional mortgage loans and for short-term consumer loans in different regions of the United States. Historically, rates in the eastern states tend to be lower than rates in western or southwestern states.

Liquidity preference is an important explanation of short-run changes in interest rates, particularly in response to changes in the money supply. Financial markets respond quickly to weekly Federal Reserve announcements of changes in the money supply. This is particularly true when growth rates in the money supply either exceed or are below Federal Reserve Board target guidelines for money supply growth or when changes in the growth rate of the money supply are enormously different from those expected by Wall Street money market analysts.

Prior to the mid-1970s, if money supply increased substantially, interest rates declined as expected by the liquidity preference rationale. In the 1980s, when money supply has risen substantially, interest rates usually increased rather than decreased, and vice versa. The reason for this change in the direction of interest rates to the response in money supply announcements is rooted in a shift in Federal Reserve operating policy and the fact that inflation has played a more important force in interest rate determination since the oil price shocks of the 1970s. Since the mid-1970s, the Federal Reserve has set target ranges for future money supply growth and has conducted monetary policy so that actual money supply growth fits within these ranges. Therefore, an announcement of a large increase in money supply growth is frequently interpreted by the market as requiring the central bank to subsequently tighten money supply growth in order to remain within the targeted money supply ranges.

TREASURER'S DILEMMA

There is a basic practical question that must be answered by corporate treasurers: How should the treasurer respond to changing term structures and fluctuating interest rates? When interest rates are high the treasurer usually tries to borrow in the money markets or to borrow short term from a bank if funds are available. If the corporation has excess funds that will not be needed in the near term there would be a tendency for the treasurer to invest long term in order to generate a good yield as well as a substantial capital gain when rates decline. As rates reach their nadir, the treasurer will try to lock in these lower rates with long-term borrowing. Some of these funds will be used to reduce short-term debt and the rest will be available for future expansion and working capital if necessary.

When rates are low and the yield curve has a positive slope, corporate treasurers have a bit of a dilemma when they have excess funds to invest. If they invest long term they run the risk of a capital loss. If they invest short term they give up a considerable yield. Their investment decision is often based on their interest rate outlook, their liquidity needs and their willingness to accept risk. Many investment managers diversify their maturity holdings in their portfolio by purchasing short-, intermediate-, and long-term securities.

For the corporate treasurer borrowing short term, there is a choice of a bank loan at a prime related rate or at a spread over the London Interbank Offered Rate (LIBOR). The most creditworthy borrowers are now paying less than prime for their short-term bank loans. For the largest 1,500 corporations there is an option of borrowing in the commercial paper market for those firms that qualify. Although commercial paper borrowers are usually required by dealers to have backup lines at commercial banks, borrowing in the commercial paper market is typically cheaper than borrowing from a commercial bank.

BOND PRICE VOLATILITY

Burton G. Malkiel, in a classic paper titled "Expectations, Bond Prices, and the Term Structure of Interest Rates," published in the Quarterly Journal of Economics, May 1962, has shown that bond price volatility is a function of the time to maturity, coupon, the par value of the bond, and the prevailing interest rate. Coupon and maturity are the most important variables in assessing the change in the price of a bond, given a change in interest rates. Maximum price volatility is achieved with low coupon, long-maturity bonds. A decline (rise) in interest rates will cause a rise (decline) in bond prices, with the most volatility in bond prices occuring in longer maturity bonds and bonds with low coupons. Therefore, a bond buyer, in order to achieve the maximum impact of an expected increase in interest rates, should purchase large coupon bonds with short maturities.

BOND YIELD SPREADS

A yield spread is the difference between the promised yields that exist at a given point in time between a particular bond or segment of the bond market and another alternative issue. Yield spreads come about as a result of different segments (for example, government versus corporate), different sectors of the same market segment (for example, Aa utilities versus Baa utilities), different coupons within a given market sector or segment (for example, current coupon governments versus deep discount governments, or new Aaa corporates versus seasoned A corporates), and differences in maturities within a given market segment or sector (for example, 30-year general obligation prime municipals versus 5-year general obligation prime municipals).

Yield spreads are rather common and vary over time. The size of the yield spread is subject to changing levels of interest rates, variations in investor perception of risk, and supply-demand factors. Yield spreads exist because there are different market rates associated with different types of bonds.

Of course, bond prices change inversely with interest rates and variables such as the coupon rate, the bond's term to maturity, the level of beginning market rates, and the direction and size of the change in rates.

RELATIVE YIELD TABLE

Table 6.2 shows selected market yields on money and capital market instruments for 1975, 1978, 1981, 1983 (February), 1985 (August), and 1986 (October). The three money market rates on Treasury bills, jumbo CDs, and commercial paper tend to cluster together, reflecting substitutability of these instruments in investment portfolios.

Rate Differences—Yield Spreads

Yield spreads are the relationships between bond yields and the particular features on various bonds such as quality, callability, and taxes, holding maturity constant. They are a result of the following factors:

1. Differences in marketability or liquidity. Some bonds can be sold either quicker or with less of a price concession, or both. The more marketable a bond, the lower the yield to maturity.

Table 6.2
Interest Rates on Selected Money and Capital Market Instruments (percent)

	1975	1978	1981	1985	1986 (Oct.)
3-Month Treasury Bills	5.80	7.19	13.14	7.05	5.18
Jumbo CDs	6.43	8.20	15.14	7.80	5.69
90-119 Day Commercial Paper	6.26	10.37	14.60	7.74	5.68
20-Year U.S. Government Bonds	8.19	8.90	15.27	10.54	7.61
AAA Municipal Bonds	6.42	5.52	12.60	9.56	6.44
Federal Funds	8.20	13.36	16.38	7.90	5.85
3-Month Eurodollar Deposits	N.A.	N.A.	16.79	8.10	5.88

Source: Federal Reserve Bulletin.

2. Differences in call features. Bonds that are callable have higher yields to maturity than otherwise identical noncallable bonds.

3. Differences in default risk or quality. A bond with a lower credit rating will offer a higher yield than a similar bond with a higher rating because of the difference in default risk. The actions of both borrowers and investors affect yield spreads. For example, heavy Treasury financing may cause a narrowing of the yield spreads between government bonds and corporate bonds as the big increase in the supply of Treasury securities pushes up the yield on Treasuries.

The size of the yield spread changes over time. Whenever the difference in yield increases, the yield spread is said to ''widen''; as the difference in yield become smaller, it ''narrows.'' Although there is some historic support to the theory that yield spreads widen during recessions since investors demand more of a premium because of greater default risk, the evidence is mixed. The structure of yield spreads and their changes over time are complex. However, some general yield spreads exist:

1. Different types of bonds, for example, corporates versus municipals (see Figure 6.2).

2. Different qualities within the same type of bond, for example, AAA corporates versus AA corporates.

3. Different coupons within the same type or quality, for example, a high coupon U.S. Treasury versus a low coupon U.S. Treasury security.

4. The spread between low rated credits and higher quality credits usually increases with the level of interest rates because of a ''flight to quality'' when interest rates are relatively high.

5. The spread between Treasury and tax-free municipal securities tend to increase as interest rate levels rise (see Figure 6.2).

Often, the holder of a financial instrument may want to liquidate the securities prior to maturity. In that case, the ability to eliminate the security from the portfolio quickly and with little impact on market price is important. Among fixed income securities, U.S. Treasury securities, followed by agency issues, have the best secondary market, while corporate bond issues and municipal securities have a much more limited secondary market. Stocks and bonds listed on exchanges are generally easier to liquidate, although sometimes the market price may be unsatisfactory.

Callability, the ability of a borrower to retire a capital market instrument prior to maturity, is another factor that often influences market yields. With a call-ability feature, the borrower may ''call'' the security at a previously specified price, thereby forcing holders of the security to exchange it for cash. Many corporate bonds are callable, but few U.S. government securities and many municipals are not callable. Since the call feature is desirable to the issuer but undesirable to the investor, many securities that are immediately callable carry higher yields than securities that are not callable or for which the call feature has

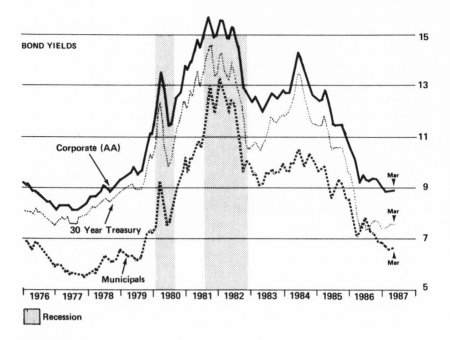

Figure 6.2
Bond Yields

Source: Brown Brothers Hariman and Co.

been postponed or deferred for some period. The investor would demand a call premium only if there was a strong possibility that the issue will be called. Such a call would most likely be exercised when interest rates have declined from the higher levels when the security was initially issued. Many corporations exercised the call options on their bonds in the declining interest rate environment of 1986.

The antithesis of callability is "putability." It offers the investor the option of selling the security back to the issuing company at an agreed upon price at a given point in time. Sometimes, these securities have a lower interest rate than nonputable bonds because the interest rate risk is limited in time. Recently, putable bonds have had a fixed yield for a set number of years and offer a put at the expiration of this time period when a new rate is set for the remaining maturity of the bond.

Both the Treasury bill rate and commercial paper rate are shown at a discount, so that their actual yields are modestly higher. However, the yield on Treasury bills is lower than the yield in other money market instruments. This reflects the lack of credit or default risk of Treasury issues and their superior marketability. In the capital markets, yields on municipal bonds are below yields on either U.S. government or corporate bonds because of their tax-exempt feature. Yields on

U.S. government bonds are also below yields on corporate bonds because of the reduced default risk and their superior marketability.

Taxability refers to the tax status of the return from the security. For example, the interest income from U.S. government issues is exempt from state and local taxes, while it is well known that the interest return on most municipal securities are exempt from federal income tax. Also, the returns of these issues are typically exempt from local and state taxes in the state and locality which issued the security. As a result of this tax exemption, municipal securities generally have substantially lower yields than corporate debt issues with the same maturity and credit rating.

Corporate bond yields are always higher than government bond yields because there is always some risk of default on corporate bonds. Even though this risk may be negligible in the case of the highest quality corporate bonds (AAA), the yield on these corporates is still higher than the yield on government securities of similar maturity. Corporate bond yields are especially important because they represent the marginal cost of long-term funds for corporations. It is interesting to note that utility bonds of similar quality rating and maturity tend to have higher yields than do bonds of industrial corporations.

In comparing the yields on U.S. government bonds, corporate bonds, state and local government (municipal) bonds, and conventional mortgages of similar maturities in July 1986, the yields were 7.27, 8.88, 7.24, and 9.74 percent, respectively, for the four fixed-rate instruments (see Table 6.3). Because government bonds have no default risk, we use them as a basis for comparing the rates of the other bonds. The yield differential for state and local bonds of minus 0.03 is caused primarily by the tax-exempt federal income tax structure. The positive differential of 1.61 on the AAA-rated corporate bonds is caused by the increased credit or default risk, higher transaction costs and the smaller market for indi-

Table 6.3
Yield Differentials for Instruments of Similar Maturities

Instrument	Yield	Differential
U.S. Government bonds	7.27	—
State and Local government bonds(Aaa)	7.24	−0.03
Aaa seasoned corporate bonds	8.88	+1.61
Conventional mortgages	9.74	+2.44

Source: Federal Reserve Bulletin, October 1986, Data for July 1986.

vidual corporate bonds than for the billions of dollars of U.S. government bonds. The conventional mortgage differential of plus 2.44 is because a mortgage has all the disadvantages of the corporate bonds plus increased default risk of an individual homeowner compared to a AAA-rated corporation, reduced marketability of an individual mortgage versus a publicly traded security and a servicing cost of approximately 0.5 percent related to collecting monthly mortgage payments and maintaining the corresponding bookkeeping. Although yield differentials vary over time as institutional characteristics, markets, and supply and demand change, the overall structure tends to remain the same and explains much of the difference in yields among various securities.

Compared with corporate bonds, mortgages have usually had a higher yield because they are liabilities of people with unfamiliar credit ratings. However, many of these individual mortgages find their way into mortgage pools, whose timely payment of interest and principal is guaranteed by GNMA or by the VA or FHA. Even with conventional mortgages that are not insured by any federal agency, the assessed value of the property far exceeds the size of the loan made by the lending institution.

In the 1960s, mortgages yielded much more than corporate bonds because mortgages had limited marketability. The improved marketability and default insurance from private companies have brought mortgage yields closer to the yields on government bonds. Uncertainty over cash flows is probably the key reason for mortgage yields to be higher than bonds of comparable risk and marketability. Prepayment on mortgages is uncertain and are often a function of the level of interest rates, as well as marriages, births, deaths, and the number of corporate transfers of employees. This makes it difficult to know the precise maturity or yield to maturity of a mortgage. For example, there will be a tendency for people to pay off their mortgages early if the holder of a 13 percent mortgage can refinance at 9 percent. This maturity uncertainty makes mortgages undesirable to some institutional investors that require fixed cash inflows to match the profile of their liabilities. Therefore mortgages tend to yield more to compensate investors for the volatile cash flow. The CMO (see Chapter 8) was invented to minimize this problem.

The distinction between the bond market and the mortgage market has faded with mortgage instruments competing in the same capital markets as bonds. The mortgage has been transformed into a security and mortgage instruments have become more uniform and standardized. Securitized mortgages are alternatives to bonds and are used in portfolios as substitutes.

There is a wide variety of corporate bonds with maturities ranging from a few years to 40 years. There are even zero coupon bonds and bonds backed by corporations in foreign currencies such as the German mark. Yields for corporate utility bonds tend to be higher than those of industrial bonds for issues of comparable maturity and credit rating. The quality of corporate bonds is subject to change. Therefore, it is important for investors to monitor credit ratings carefully and to pay close attention to whether a corporation's fortunes might be improving, deteriorating, or remaining the same.

Mortgage backed security bonds pay higher yields than Treasury issues of comparable maturity but usually offer yields that are lower than the yields available on corporate bonds of similar maturity and credit quality. Collateralized mortgage obligations provide investors with yields that are 50 to 300 basis points higher than U.S. Treasury securities (see Figure 6.3). Most CMOs are AAA rated and usually yield more than A-rated corporate bonds. CMOs are generally paid off prior to maturity by prepayments from the underlying mortgage collateral. Average redemption dates from 2 to 20 years are usually available so that investors can select the CMO class that meets their investment needs. While the duration of CMO securities is close to their stated maturity, the duration of most of the collateralized mortgage bonds is considerably less than the stated maturity and is uncertain. The duration is usually a function of mortgage interest rates. Lower interest rates typically induce faster prepayments of mortgages and hence a shorter duration of the mortgage backed securities.

During 1986 corporate yield spreads to Treasuries widened sharply. This movement was unusual because bond rallies are usually associated with a narrowing of yield spreads. In addition to the heavy volume of new issues in 1986, two of the more uncommon factors that contributed to the spread widening were the increased values of the embedded call refund options of corporate securities and a widespread deterioration in the credit quality of industrial corporations, fueled largely by corporate restructuring. It is interesting to note that close to 25 percent of all Standard & Poor's industrial downgradings during 1986 resulted

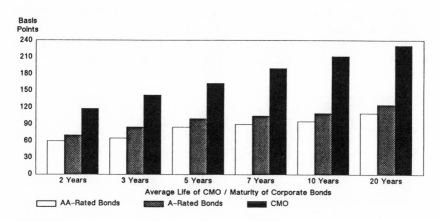

Figure 6.3
CMO Yields vs. Corporate Bond Yields (Spreads over U.S. Treasury Securities, August 1986)

Source: An Investor's Guide To Evaluating CMOs. Smith Barney, October 1986.

from corporate restructurings. Another consequence of the increased merger activity and restructuring for industrial corporations has been reflected in the narrowing and inversion of the spread between long-term utility bonds and industrials.

BOND PRICE REACTION TO BOND RATING CHANGES

Professors that have analyzed the monthly market price changes of different bonds that were associated with rating changes found that bond prices:

1. Do not react after their ratings have been changed
2. Have a tiny abnormal reaction in the rating change month
3. Experience most of their price change reactions about one year in advance of having their ratings changed

The research findings suggest estimators of bonds' true economic values. Bond prices seem to fully reflect all publicly disseminated information because both the price and value of bonds change together in advance of any changes in published bond ratings. The results suggest that the buying and selling done by astute bond analysts anticipated the publicly announced rating changes. Other findings on the equity side of the market suggest that by the time the rating agencies have publicly announced changes in a bond's quality rating, the investing public has already revised the issuer's stock price so that the announcement of the rating change is not going to capture speculative profits.

The studies by Weinstein and Griffin, and Sanvicente have raised serious questions about whether the bond ratings determined the market yields or whether the antithesis was true. The quality ratings for already issued bonds lag the changes in both bond and stock prices by so many months that it seems as if the market prices may be coercing the rating agencies to change quality ratings.

BIBLIOGRAPHY

Backer, M., and M. L. Gosman. "The Use of Financial Ratios in Credit Downgrade Decisions." *Financial Management* (Spring 1980): 53–56.

Belkaoui, Ahmed. *Industrial Bonds and the Rating Process*. Westport, Conn.: Quorum Books, 1983.

Brigham, E. F. *Fundamentals of Financial Management*. 4th ed. New York: Dryden Press, 1986.

Clark, J. L., with B. W. Harries. "Some Recent Trends in Municipal and Corporate Securities Markets: An Interview with B. W. Harries, President of Standard & Poor's Corporation." *Financial Management* (Spring 1976): 9–17.

Fabozzi, F. J., and I. M. Pollack, eds. *The Handbook of Fixed Income Securities*. Homewood, Ill.: Dow Jones Irwin, 1983.

Fabozzi, F. J., and Sauvain. "Corporate Bonds," *The Handbook of Fixed Income Securities*. Homewood, Ill.: Dow Jones Irwin, 1983, pp. 297–332.

Fabozzi, F. J., and F. G. Zarb, eds. *Selected Topics in Investment Management.* Homewood, Ill.: Dow Jones Irwin, 1983.

Ferri, G. "An Empirical Examination of the Determinants of Bond Yield Spreads." *Financial Management* (Autumn 1978): 40–46.

Gordon, A. J., R. D. Stover, and D. B. Kuhnau. "Market Timing Strategies in Convertible Debt Financing." *Journal of Finance* (March 1979): 143–55.

Griffin, P. A., and A. Z. Sanvicente. "Common Stock Returns and Rating Changes: A Methodological Comparison," *Journal of Finance,* (March 1982): 103–119.

Howe, J. T. "Credit Analysis for Corporate Bonds." *The Handbook of Fixed Income Securities.* Homewood, Ill.: Dow Jones Irwin, 1983, pp. 344–371.

Kalotay, A. J. "Innovations in Corporate Finance: Deep Discount Private Placements." *Financial Management* (Spring 1982): 55–57.

————. "On the Management of Sinking Funds." *Financial Management* (Summer 1981): 34–39.

Loeys, J. G. "Interest Rate Swaps: A New Tool for Managing Interest Rate Risk." Federal Reserve Bank of Philadelphia, *Business Review* (May/June 1985): 17–25.

McEnally, R. W. "Duration as a Practical Tool for Bond Management." *The Journal of Portfolio Management* (Summer 1977): 53–57.

Ritchie, John C. "Convertible Bonds and Warrants." *The Handbook of Fixed Income Securities.* Homewood, Ill.: Dow Jones Irwin, 1983, pp. 580–594.

Silber, W. L. "The Process of Financial Innovation." *American Economic Review* (May 1983): 89–94.

Tuttle, D. L., ed. *The Revolution in Techniques for Managing Bond Portfolios.* Charlottesville, Va.: Institute of Chartered Financial Analysts, 1983.

Weinstein, M. I. "The Effect of a Rating Change Announcement on Bond Price." *Journal of Financial Economics* 5, no. 3 (December 1977): 329–50.

Wilcox, J. A. "Inflation Proof Long-Term Bonds." Federal Reserve Bank of San Francisco, *Weekly Letter* (November 30, 1984): 1–2.

Zwick, B. "Yields on Privately Placed Corporate Bonds." *Journal of Finance* (March 1980): 23–29.

7

U.S. Treasury and Agency Securities

TREASURY NOTES AND BONDS

The U.S. Treasury sells financial securities to investors for the purpose of financing the deficits or cash flow problems that arise between tax receipts and government expenditures. The U.S. government enjoys the highest credit rating because of its no-default repayment record. This has resulted from its ability to tax its citizens, as well as the resultant wide acceptance of government securities in the past by institutional investors in this country and abroad. This does not mean that holding government bonds is without risk. Government securities, as well as every fixed rate security, still have an interest rate risk.

Treasury notes have a maturity of not less than 2 or more than 10 years, while bonds generally have a maturity of more than 10 years. Both securities are offered on a definitive or book entry basis in $1,000, $5,000, $10,000, $100,000, and $1 million denominations. Investors pay the face value at purchase and receive interest payments semiannually during the life of the note or bond; face value is returned at maturity. Both notes and bonds are offered quarterly in February, May, August, and November. Two-year notes are offered every month, while 5-, 7-, and 20-year bonds are offered every March, June, September, and December. Federal income tax must be paid on interest earned, but interest earned on bills, notes, and bonds is exempt from state and local taxes.

Although U.S. Treasury bonds are listed on the New York Stock Exchange, most trading in U.S. government securities takes place in the over-the-counter market (OTC). The OTC market consists of a group of large banks and security dealer firms that deal directly with insurance companies, banks, brokerage corporations, and other investors interested in government securities.

Prices of government securities other than Treasury bills are usually quoted in terms of 32nds. A price of 95.8 means that the security is selling for 95 8/32 or 95.25 percent of face value. Dealers usually buy and sell government securities at net prices, that is, no commission is added. A dealer quote such as 95.5 bid and 95.7 asked, indicates that on full lots (usually $100,000 face value or more) the dealer will pay the bid price and will sell at the asked price. For bond transactions under 100 bonds there is usually a service charge or price adjustment. The difference between the bid and asked price is called the spread. The volume of market activity in the issue is a dominant factor in determining the width of the spread. The spread in the quotation on Treasury bills may be only $50 per million, while the spread on the other short-term issues may be 1/32 to 4/32 of a point ($312.50 to $1,250 per million). On the other hand, the spread on longer-term bonds may be somewhat greater.

Treasury issues generally yield less than other market instruments with the exception of the yield on municipal bonds. Treasury obligations are also the most liquid instruments traded. Most issues are exceptionally large and there are a wide array of issues available. A few issues sell at yields to maturity that are substantially different from those issues with reasonably similar maturity. This might be because some issues have fewer securities outstanding. This tends to result in less active trading, poorer marketability and higher yields for these issues. Some issues are known as flower bonds and have a favorable tax treatment, selling at discount, but offering redemption at face value to pay estate taxes.

The Treasury issues three types of coupon-bearing securities, certificates of indebtedness, notes, and bonds. Bonds typically mature in 20 to 30 years from date of issue, while notes have an original maturity from 1 to 10 years. Certificates of indebtedness, which had original maturities of one year or less, have been replaced by one-year Treasury bills.

There are three methods of selling new issues of notes and bonds: subscription offerings (a nonauction technique), price auctions, and yield auctions. The Treasury specifies the coupon rate, maturity, and price in a subscription offering. In a price auction, the coupon rate and maturity of the issue are specified in advance. Investors submit tenders for desired quantities of the issue and specify the bid price they are willing to pay. Competitive tenders are accepted in order of decreasing bid price until the desired quantity of securities has been sold. Noncompetitive tenders are accepted for guaranteed delivery at the average accepted competitive bid price.

Dutch auctions, another form of price auction, have both noncompetitive and accepted bidders, paying the lowest accepted competitive bid price, the stop-out price. Essentially, the Treasury charges everyone the bid price of the marginal or last accepted bidder.

In a yield auction, only the maturity date of a new issue is specified prior to the auction. Investors submit competitive tenders stating the yield to maturity they are willing to accept on the quantity of bonds they wish. The competitive auctions are similar to the T-bill auctions (discussed in Chapter 2) except that bidders submit desired yields to maturity, as opposed to discounts, for bills. The average winning bid is then used to determine the issue's coupon (stated in eighths of a dollar) so that securities can be sold at close to total face value. The Treasury accepts competitive bids in order of increasing yield until it has exhausted the offering.

The market for U.S. government securities helps the Treasury to finance the government debt, and provides the Federal Reserve with an effective means of implementing monetary policy. The impact of Federal Reserve open market operations on the price and corresponding effective yield on government securities is rapidly transmitted to other securities markets. Brokers, dealers, and their customers seek to earn profits by intermarket arbitrage. The huge size of the government securities market and its close linkage to other markets for short-term debt instruments gives U.S. government securities dealers and brokers a key role in the operation of the money market.

Treasury EE and HH Bonds

The Treasury also issues nonmarketable bonds that individuals can purchase. The most popular issues are Series EE savings bonds and Series HH current-income bonds (see Table 7.1). Series EE savings bonds are accrual-type bonds with a maturity of 11 years. The difference between the redemption value and the amount of the purchase price is the interest earned by the bond holder. EE bonds are sold at 50 percent of face value and in denominations of $50 to $10,000. The investor holding these bonds may elect to recognize the increase in the redemption value in the tax year it accrues or accrue the interest until the savings bond is redeemed. However, Series HH savings bonds pay current interest and have a 10-year maturity. HH bonds are sold at face value, pay semiannual interest and are sold in denominations of $500 to $10,000. Holders of Series HH bonds must report the current interest paid in their federal income tax return in the year that the interest is received; they do not have the option of deferring the recognition of interest that Series EE bond holders possess. As in the case of Series EE bonds, the yield from the date of purchase to date of redemption increases with the holding period.

Flower Bonds

Certain U.S. Treasury bonds sell at a slight discount and yield only 3 or 4 percent. About 15 of these issues have a special wrinkle. Although you buy them at a discount, they can be redeemed at par—prior to maturity—to pay federal estate taxes. Even though the open market does not value these bonds at par, the government will pay the face value for them, up to an amount equaling your federal estate taxes. Someone once said that this extra value can pay for the flowers at a funeral and that they "bloom" or can be redeemed at par when federal estate taxes are due. Therefore, these securities are called flower bonds. A spouse or child with power of attorney can buy them for an estate when death appears imminent and use the proceeds to pay estate taxes. The government

Table 7.1

Comparison of Terms and Conditions of Series EE and HH Savings Bonds

	Series EE	Series HH
Denominations	$50, $75, $100, $200, $500, $1,000, $5,000, $10,000.	$500, $1,000, $5,000, $10,000.
Issue Price	50% of face amount.	Face amount.
Maturity	10 years.	Same.
Yield Curve	A fixed graduated rate increasing from 4.16% after six months to 7.5% after five years. Thereafter, the market-based variable investment yield will be used for determining the redemption value of a bond, unless the minimum investment yield of 7.5% produces a higher value.	7.5% for new issues; however, bonds which were sold for cash will have an interest penalty applied against redemption value, if held for less than 5 years.
Retention period	Redeemable any time after 6 months from issue date.	Same.
Annual limitation	$15,000 issue price.	No limit.
Tax status	Accruals subject to federal income and to estate, inheritance and gift taxes—federal and state—but exempt from state and local income taxes. Federal income tax may be reported (1) as it accrues, or (2) in year bond matures, is redeemed or otherwise disposed.	Interest is subject to federal income tax reporting in year it is paid. Bonds subject to estate, inheritance and gift taxes—federal and state—but exempt from state and local income taxes.
Registration	In name of individuals—in single, coownership of beneficiary form; in names of fiduciaries or organization—in single ownership only.	Same.
Transferability	Not eligible for transfer or pledge as collateral.	Same.
Rights of owners	Coownership: either owner may redeem; both must join reissue request. Beneficiary: only owner may redeem during lifetime; consent of beneficiary to reissue not required.	Same.
Exchange privilege	Eligible, alone or with Series E bonds or savings notes, for exchange for Series HH bonds in multiples of $500, with tax deferral privilege.	Issued only in exchange for Series E, EE, and savings notes in multiples of $500, with continued tax deferral privilege.

Source: Handbook of Securities of the United States Government and Federal Agencies. New York: First Boston Corporation, 1986.

essentially subsidizes the payment of estate taxes through the use of flower bonds. These bonds are also taxed to the estate at their market rather than their par value.

For example, the 3 percent coupon issue due on February 1995 had an asked price of 91.16 or 91.5 percent of its par value in January 1987. Even though the bonds had a market value of $91,500 they could be used to satisfy a $100,000 federal estate liability. The only reason for holding flower bonds is for federal estate planning purposes as the yield on the bonds reflects this feature and are consequently lower than the yields on similar maturity treasury bonds.

COMMENTS ON YIELD CURVES

As can be seen in Figure 7.1, long-term bonds offered higher yields than either notes or bills. During 1984–1986, the yield differentials between intermediate-term notes and Treasury bills and long-term bonds and Treasury bills ranged from 25 basis points to 400 basis points. The differential varies over the business cycle and market conditions, expectations of interest rates, and the yield curve. The differential is not always positive as is the case when the yield curve is negative (see Figure 7.1 and Figure 6.1).

In general, when inflation and interest rates are low, the yield curve has a positive slope, that is, interest rates increase with maturity. However, when inflation and interest rates are high, the yield curve often has a negative slope, that is, interest rates decrease with maturity. Short-term interest rates are more volatile than long-term rates. Consequently, the spread between short-term rates and long-term rates varies a great deal over the interest rate cycle. As interest rates increase, the spread becomes more negative.

Arbitrage is buying and selling a security to earn a profit from the difference in prices. A benefit from drawing and studying yield curves is the ability to detect temporary anomolies such as identifying securities that carry a higher or lower than usual yield. Bond house traders monitor market prices closely and try to make short-run profits through arbitrage trading.

Whereas arbitrage transactions embody little risk because purchases and sales cover each other, speculation in the bond market can be quite risky. The investor either takes a buy and hold position (a long position) or the investor sells borrowed securities.

In the latter case, the borrowed securities are repurchased and returned to the original owner (a short position). For example, a trader can sell "short" $5 million of Treasury securities by borrowing them through a broker and selling them; the trader will later repay the loan by repurchasing an equal number of bonds at the prevailing market price. The trader will make a profit if bond prices fall and will suffer a loss if bond prices increase. Successful speculation occurs when the investor forecasts future interest rates more accurately than the market in general.

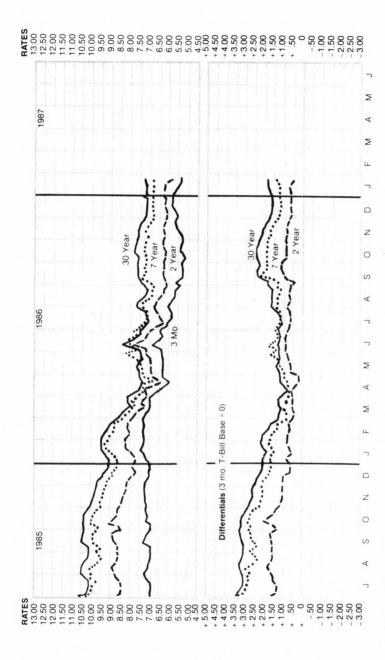

Figure 7.1

Selected Treasury Issues: Yields & Yield Curve

Source: Griggs and Santow Report.

OWNERSHIP

The largest holders of U.S. government and agency securities are classified as private domestic nonfinancial interests, private nonbank institutions, commercial banks, foreign interests, and the Federal Reserve. Households, which are categorized as private domestic nonfinancial, are the largest holders of U.S. Treasury debt. Foreign investors and commercial banks represent the next largest interests. In the private nonbank category, private noninsured pension funds, state and local retirement funds, thrift institutions, and life insurance companies are the biggest owners of Treasury debt. State and local governments are also large holders of U.S. Treasury debt (see Table 7.2). It is interesting to note that at year-end 1986, there was $1.6 trillion of U.S. marketable securities outstanding and $600 billion of nonmarket securities. Of this debt, there is approximately $430 billion in Treasury bills, $927 billion in notes, and $250 billion in bonds among the marketable securities.

Table 7.2
U.S. Treasury Debt (Annual Net Increases in Amounts Outstanding, Dollars in Billions)

	1981	1982	1983	1984	1985	1986E	1987P	Amt. Out. 31 Dec 86E
Outstanding								
Marketables								
Bills	$28.9	$66.8	$32.0	$30.6	$25.5	$29.8	$7.0	$429.7
Notes	53.7	89.7	108.3	131.7	107.4	114.4	115.7	926.9
Bonds	14.5	4.7	29.1	34.2	43.1	38.6	38.7	249.7
Nonmarketables								
Government Account Series	11.6	8.8	26.5	54.3	46.0	51.7	60.0	383.9
State and Local Series	-0.9	2.7	11.1	7.7	43.1	20.2	13.0	107.7
Foreign Gov't. Series (US$)	-2.7	-2.0	-2.5	-1.3	-1.6	-3.9	-4.0	3.6
Foreign Public Series (Non-US$)	-2.4	-2.3	-1.7	0.0	0.1	0.0	0.0	0.0
Savings Bonds	-4.4	-0.1	2.7	2.6	4.5	13.2	12.0	91.2
Guaranteed and Noninterest-Bearing	0.1	0.0	8.1	-8.2	0.9	0.1	0.0	2.8
Total Public and Guaranteed Debt	98.5	168.2	213.5	251.5	269.0	264.1	242.5	2,195.6
Less Trust Fund Holdings	10.8	6.1	26.9	53.3	59.3	52.0	60.0	400.9
Less Agency Holdings	0.2	1.5	-0.8	0.4	1.2	-0.1	0.0	4.0
Less Federal Reserve Holdings	9.6	8.4	12.6	8.9	20.5	18.0	19.0	199.3
Privately Held Treasury Debt	**$77.8**	**$152.3**	**$174.8**	**$188.9**	**$188.1**	**$194.2**	**$163.5**	**$1,591.3**
Ownership								
Thrifts	$-3.7	$8.5	$20.9	$10.7	$-9.2	$7.4	$9.0	$50.7
Insurance and Pensions	17.8	20.2	28.0	50.5	41.8	51.0	37.0	281.5
Investment Companies	19.0	23.4	-19.2	8.9	52.1	52.4	33.0	141.9
Other Nonbank Finance	-0.6	0.4	-12.4	1.0	3.6	3.6	5.0	0.6
Total Nonbank Finance	32.6	52.5	17.3	71.1	88.3	114.4	84.0	474.7
Commercial Banks	1.8	19.4	47.8	1.9	12.1	16.3	25.0	214.5
Nonfinancial Corporations	-1.0	5.2	8.0	7.3	-3.0	8.3	7.4	41.8
State and Local Governments	-0.9	5.7	16.1	13.2	50.2	23.9	12.8	125.2
Foreign Investors	6.7	12.6	16.4	25.4	20.2	60.4	62.0	266.2
Residual: Households Direct	38.6	56.9	69.2	70.1	20.4	-29.1	-27.8	469.0
Total Ownership	**$77.8**	**$152.3**	**$174.8**	**$188.9**	**$188.1**	**$194.2**	**$163.5**	**$1,591.3**

Source: Prospects for Financial Markets in 1987. Salomon Brothers, Inc., December 1986.

DEALERS AND RISK

U.S. government securities dealers and brokers (see Chapter 2) play an extremely important role in purchases and sales of U.S. Treasury securities. Although the largest volume of transactions is in Treasury bills, notes and long-term bonds are also actively traded. There is a broad and highly liquid secondary market for U.S. Treasury securities.

The government securities dealers work closely with the Federal Reserve System and the Treasury. The Federal Reserve Bank of New York conducts its open market operations and its repurchase and reverse repurchase transactions through auctions with the primary dealers. The Fed also obtains financial information about the condition of the market from these dealers.

While U.S. government securities are generally regarded as riskless assets, market prices of these securities can change daily. Moreover, the dealers that trade government securities undertake two kinds of operating risk: trading risk and credit risk. Trading risk arises largely from price changes in the market that are related to interest rate fluctuations and Federal Reserve policy. Credit risk involves the ability of market participants doing business with dealers to meet their financial obligations.

Losses that result from trading and credit risk reduce the capital of the firm. After capital is exhausted, further losses may fall on the dealer's customers, if they have exposure to the dealer in their transactions. The Federal Reserve has recommended standards of capital adequacy in the form of guidelines for a ratio of liquid capital to measured risk. A dealer firm that maintains the minimum standard would not place its customers at risk under normal market conditions. The standard can only be enforced by other dealers, clearing banks, and customers. The most important safeguard in the market is the discipline imposed by market participants who should carefully choose the dealers with whom they do business.

THE AGENCY MARKET

Agency obligations are usually not direct obligations of the U.S. Treasury. Therefore, there is a greater element of credit and business risk. Because of their credit differential from Treasury issues, they sell at higher yields than do Treasury issues of comparable maturity. With the exception of GNMA, FHA, and Eximbank debentures, agency securities are not guaranteed against default by the federal government.

On the other hand, the yields on agency securities are normally considerably lower than those on corporate debt issues of similar maturities. For example, during the 1980s, the yield on agency securities was typically 3 to 25 basis points above the yield on Treasury securities of similar maturities. However, because of the high default rate on farm loans during 1985 and 1986, Farm Credit securities traded as much as 60 basis points above Treasuries. Each federally sponsored agency that issues large amounts of securities typically has one fiscal agent.

The federally sponsored credit agencies usually sell their new debt through a fiscal agent in New York City. When there is an offering to be made, the fiscal agent assembles the selling group of security dealers, dealer banks, and brokerage houses. Unlike the syndicate format to sell stocks and municipal and corporate bonds, members of the agent's selling group do not bid against each other because each agency offering is made through only one selling group. In establishing the price range of the new issue, the fiscal agent consults with the Treasury, the trading desk of the New York Federal Reserve Bank, the issuing agency, and the members of the selling group germane to maturity, coupon amount, and price. On the sale date, the price is telegraphed by the agent to the members of the group, who make subscriptions through the agent. The agent determines the allotments, which are usually a fraction of total subscription.[1]

Bonds sold by fiscal agents require advance notice of their sale. Discount notes do not require advance notice and can be offered on a continuous basis by an agency in a manner similar to the way in which commercial banks sell negotiable certificates of deposit.

The Federal Financing Bank (FFB) was created in 1973 to assist, consolidate, and coordinate the financing activities of agencies that issue small amounts of debt or infrequently enter the money and capital markets. The FFB purchases the securities of participating agencies and issues its own obligations. The primary goal of the FFB is to lower the borrowing costs of participating agencies.[2]

Table 7.3 shows the debt outstanding of federal and federally sponsored agencies, while Table 7.4 shows the salient characteristics of federally sponsored agencies.

Short-term obligations of the Farm Credit Banks, the Federal Home Loan Banks, and Fannie Mae have established secondary markets. The primary selling group of dealers usually maintains a secondary market and sufficient amounts of these securities in inventory. The spread between bid and asked prices is quite narrow on short-term issues.

Most of the federally sponsored credit agencies finance their loan programs and secondary market purchases by issuing debt in the capital and money markets. These securities are not guaranteed by the federal government, but, because of the close ties of the sponsored agencies to the government, these agencies are afforded certain privileges not available to most other issues:

- Exemption from SEC registration requirements
- Exemption of interest income from state and local taxes (except for FNMA and FHCMC issues)
- Eligibility as collateral when depository institutions borrow from the Federal Reserve or from the Federal Home Loan Bank
- Eligibility for purchase by the Federal Reserve in open market operations
- Eligibility as collateral for public deposits, including Treasury tax and loan accounts
- Favorable status in the portfolios of depository institutions; for example, national banks may invest and deal in these securities without limit, while the shorter-term securities

Table 7.3

Federal and Federally Sponsored Credit Agencies (Debt Outstanding, Millions of dollars, end of period)

Agency	1983	1984	1985	1986 July	Aug.	Sept.	Oct.	Nov.	Dec.
1 Federal and federally sponsored agencies	**240,068**	**271,220**	**293,905**	**298,361**	**299,211**	**302,411**	**305,011**	**n.a.**	n.a.
2 Federal agencies	33,940	35,145	36,390	35,768	36,132	36,473	36,716	36,952	
3 Defense Department[1]	243	142	71	45	40	37	36	35	
4 Export-Import Bank[2,3]	14,853	15,882	15,678	14,953	14,953	14,274	14,274	14,274	n.a.
5 Federal Housing Administration[4]	194	133	115	115	115	117	123	124	
6 Government National Mortgage Association participation certificates[5]	2,165	2,165	2,165	2,165	2,165	2,165	2,165	2,165	
7 Postal Service[6]	1,404	1,337	1,940	1,854	1,854	3,104	3,104	3,104	
8 Tennessee Valley Authority	14,970	15,435	16,347	16,562	16,931	16,702	16,940	17,176	
9 United States Railway Association[6]	111	51	74	74	74	74	74	74	
10 Federally sponsored agencies[7]	206,128	236,075	257,515	262,593	263,079	265,938	268,295	n.a.	n.a.
11 Federal Home Loan Banks	48,930	65,085	74,447	83,081	85,997	87,133	87,146	86,891	88,752
12 Federal Home Loan Mortgage Corporation	6,793	10,270	11,926	12,818	12,801	13,548	14,007	n.a.	n.a.
13 Federal National Mortgage Association	74,594	83,720	93,896	93,417	92,286	91,629	93,272	93,477	93,563
14 Farm Credit Banks	72,816	71,193	68,851	62,857	61,575	63,073	63,079	62,693	62,328
15 Student Loan Marketing Association[8]	3,402	5,745	8,395	10,420	10,420	10,555	10,791	11,102	11,795
MEMO									
16 Federal Financing Bank debt[9]	**135,791**	**145,217**	**153,373**	**155,526**	**156,132**	**156,873**	**157,371**	**157,452**	
Lending to federal and federally sponsored agencies									
17 Export-Import Bank[3]	14,789	15,852	15,670	14,947	14,947	14,268	14,268	14,268	
18 Postal Service[6]	1,154	1,087	1,690	1,604	1,604	2,854	2,854	2,854	
19 Student Loan Marketing Association	5,000	5,000	5,000	5,000	5,000	4,970	4,970	4,970	n.a.
20 Tennessee Valley Authority	13,245	13,710	14,622	14,937	15,306	15,077	15,515	15,751	
21 United States Railway Association[6]	111	51	74	74	74	74	74	74	
Other Lending[10]									
22 Farmers Home Administration	55,266	58,971	64,234	65,174	65,274	65,374	65,374	65,374	
23 Rural Electrification Administration	19,766	20,693	20,654	21,321	21,398	21,460	21,506	21,531	
24 Other	26,460	29,853	31,429	32,469	32,529	32,796	32,810	32,630	

1. Consists of mortgages assumed by the Defense Department between 1957 and 1963 under family housing and homeowners assistance programs.
2. Includes participation certificates reclassified as debt beginning Oct. 1, 1976.
3. Off-budget Aug. 17, 1974, through Sept. 30, 1976; on-budget thereafter.
4. Consists of debentures issued in payment of Federal Housing Administration insurance claims. Once issued, these securities may be sold privately on the securities market.
5. Certificates of participation issued before fiscal 1969 by the Government National Mortgage Association acting as trustee for the Farmers Home Administration; Department of Health, Education, and Welfare; Department of Housing and Urban Development; Small Business Administration; and the Veterans Administration.
6. Off-budget.

7. Includes outstanding noncontingent liabilities: Notes, bonds, and debentures. Some data are estimated.
8. Before late 1981, the Association obtained financing through the Federal Financing Bank.
9. The FFB, which began operations in 1974, is authorized to purchase or sell obligations issued, sold, or guaranteed by other federal agencies. Since FFB incurs debt solely for the purpose of lending to other agencies, its debt is not included in the main portion of the table in order to avoid double counting.
10. Includes FFB purchases of agency assets and guaranteed loans; the latter contain loans guaranteed by numerous agencies with the guarantees of any particular agency being generally small. The Farmers Home Administration item consists exclusively of agency assets, while the Rural Electrification Administration entry contains both agency assets and guaranteed loans.

Source: Federal Reserve Bulletin, April 1987.

Table 7.4
Characteristics of Federally Sponsored Credit Agencies

Agency	Stockholders	Influence of the administration	Line of credit with Treasury	Federal tax on income of sponsored agency[1]	State and local tax on interest income of investors
Federal Home Loan Banks	Owned by member thrift institutions but operated by the Federal Home Loan Bank Board	President selects all 3 members of the FHLBs	$4.0 billion	No	No
Federal National Mortgage Association	Owned entirely by private stockholders	President selects 5 of 18 board members; subject to general supervision by HUD	$2.25 billion	Yes	Yes
Federal Home Loan Mortgage Corporation	Nonvoting common stock owned by FHLBs; participating preferred stock issued to member thrift institutions	Same as FHLBs	Indirect line of credit through the FHLBs	Yes[2]	Yes
Farm Credit Banks	Owned by farm cooperatives and credit associations	President selects 12 Board members; Secretary of Agriculture	$112 million for Federal Intermediate Credit Banks; $149 million for Banks for Cooperatives; secretary may deposit $6 million in Federal Land Banks	No	No
Student Loan Marketing Association	Lenders under the Guaranteed Student Loan program may hold voting common stock; individual investors may hold nonvoting common and preferred stock	President selects 7 of 21 Board members including chairman	$1.0 billion[3]	Yes	Yes

1. Interest on all debt of the sponsored agencies is subject to federal taxation.
2. Effective January 1, 1985.
3. Sallie Mae also has the authority to sell to the Federal Financing Bank securities backed by student loans.

may be used to meet thrift institution liquidity requirements at the Federal Home Loan Bank.[3]

Historically, most federal agencies were involved in directing capital flows into agriculture or housing as can be seen in the proliferation of agencies such as the Farm Credit agencies, FNMA, GNMA, and Freddie Mac. However, federal credit agency programs have expanded into other areas. For example, the Environmental Financing Authority (EFA) was created in 1972 to ensure that state and local governments could borrow funds at reasonable rates to finance waste treatment facilities, while the Tennessee Valley Authority (TVA) was established in the mid-1930s to assist in the development of power projects and other economic undertakings in the Tennessee River basin.

The Farm Credit System

The Farm Credit System is the oldest of the federally sponsored agencies, dating back to 1917, and is divided geographically into 12 districts; each district has a Federal Land Bank, a Federal Intermediate Credit Bank, and a Bank for Cooperatives. Also, a Central Bank for Cooperatives participates in large loans, or loans that span more than one district. These 37 banks, along with a number of cooperative associations that own the banks, form the heart of the Farm Credit System. In addition, the Farm Credit Administration, an independent agency of the federal government, provides supervision at the national level.

Federal Land Banks. The agricultural sector was the first recipient of agency funding and the Federal Land Bank (FLB) is the oldest of the debt issuing agencies. There are currently 12 FLBs throughout the country that permit farmers to borrow in order to purchase and develop land, farm equipment, and livestock. FLB bonds are not guaranteed by the U.S. government and usually have maturities between 18 months and 15 years. The proceeds from bond sales are loaned to qualifying ranchers and farmers. The funds must be used for agricultural purposes.

The Federal Intermediate Credit Bank. The 12 regional FICBs borrow to finance the activities of production credit associations. These associations are local mutual associations of farmers that lend money to their members to finance seasonal crops and investment in farm capital equipment. The 12 Banks for Cooperatives and the Central Bank for Cooperatives borrow to finance the activities of agricultural cooperatives, whose activities include marketing farm products, inventorying farm supplies, and providing business service to farmers.

The individual Bank Coops lend within their regions while the Central Bank makes loans to large cooperatives. The 12 FLBs borrow to finance the loan program of local Land Bank Associations (LBAs), which are mutual associations of farmers that service FLB loans to members for construction of farm residences and outbuildings, purchase of farm equipment, and farm land. Neither the individual Farm Credit Banks nor the networks of Farm Credit Banks sell their own debt. Debt of the agricultural intermediaries is sold as the "joint and several" obligation of the 37 Farm Credit Banks. The underlying purpose of all these banks is to provide an adequate flow of credit to the agricultural sector.

The Farm Credit Banks use the subscription method of selling after consulting with commercial bank and broker-dealer underwriters. The banks place a coupon rate on the issue and offer it to the members of the syndicate at a price equal to its principal value less a selling commission. Then syndicate members re-offer the issue to public investors at a price equal to principal value.

Farm Credit Banks discount notes are continuously offered to investors on a tap basis, that is, they agree to satisfy all demands for the notes at rates announced in advance. The rates are raised when the Bank wishes to sell more notes and are lowered when the Bank desires to sell less. The notes are always on "tap," but at a rate that reflects the desire of the Farm Credit Banks in raising money.

The Federal Farm Credit System implemented a discount note program as a source of short-term financing. Notes have a minimum $50,000 size and are sold thereafter in $50,000 increments. Salomon Brothers and Merrill Lynch sell these securities on a discounted basis with maturities ranging from 5 to 270 days. Interest is calculated on actual days, on a 360-day basis. Notes are issued in definitive form for New York delivery and settlement in federal funds in one business day. Round lots trade at a $1 million minimum with odd lots trading at some concession to the round lot rate.

The Federal Farm Credit System sells consolidated system-wide and two-months bonds once a month in increments of $5,000 in book entry form. The rate is set by the Federal Farm Credit System with bonds bearing interest on a 30-day month, 360-day year basis.

The depressed farm economy has created extremely serious problems for both some private banks and Farm Credit Banks because many farmers have gone bankrupt and defaulted on their loans. This had a serious impact on the financial viability of the Farm Credit Banks that required a cash infusion of several billion dollars that was approved by Congress in 1986.

Export-Import Bank

The Export-Import Bank, founded in 1934, is a government agency whose mission is to help finance America's exports. The bank aids in financing exports by extending loans, guarantees, and exports credit insurance. The Export-Import Bank finances its operations through income generated from loans and fees from the sale of participation certificates. The range of bank programs appears in Table 7.5. In this table, FCIA stands for the Foreign Credit Insurance Association, a group of close to 50 of the nation's private insurance companies that cooperate with Eximbank to cover commercial risks on certain export transactions. Commercial banks that participate with the Eximbank and the FCIA are guaranteed by Eximbank against all political risks and some of the commercial

Table 7.5
Export-Import Bank Programs

Product Examples	Appropriate Eximbank FCIA Program
Short Term (Up to 180 days)	
Consumables Small manufactured items Spare parts Raw materials	FCIA policies only
Medium Term (181 days–5 years)	

Capital goods such as:
  Mining and refining equipment
  Construction equipment
  Agricultural equipment
  General aviation aircraft
  Manufacturing equipment
  Communications equipment
  Planning and feasibility studies
	FCIA policies
	Commercial bank guarantees
	Cooperative Financing Facility
	Discount loans
	Bank–to–bank guaranteed lines

Long Term (5 years and longer)	
Commercial jet aircraft or locomotives Other very expensive heavy capital goods	

Projects such as:
  Cement plants
  Chemical plants
  Power plants -- hydro, thermal,
  nuclear
  LNG and gas processing
  Other major projects
	Participation Financing:
	  Commercial bank loan combined with
	  direct Eximbank loan
	Financial guarantee to bank by
	  Eximbank where needed

Source: Export-Import Bank of the United States.

risks on funds provided in export transactions. Eximbank also makes loans to foreign financial institutions to enable them to help finance purchases of exported U.S. goods and services. The discount loan program is used to overcome difficulties that U.S. exporters have in obtaining medium-term financing at fixed rates from commercial banks. The debt of the Export-Import Bank is guaranteed by the full faith and credit of the U.S. government and so is free of default risk.

Federal Home Loan Bank

Federally sponsored home mortgage intermediaries can be categorized into those that lend on ordinary debt contracts against mortgage collateral (Federal Home Loan Banks (FHLB)), and those who actually receive mortgage payments from homeowners (Federal National Mortgage Association). Two other intermediaries, the Federal Home Loan Mortgage Corporation and the Government

National Mortgage Association, issue unique types of securities known as pass-throughs.

Congress established the Federal Home Loan Bank System in 1932 to supervise federally chartered savings and loans and to provide a credit facility for thrift institutions. The system originally was composed only of the Federal Home Loan Bank Board, which is primarily a regulatory agency and 12 regional Federal Home Loan Banks, which carry out Board policies and provide the credit facilities and other services for member institutions. The Federal Savings and Loan Insurance Corporation (FSLIC) and the Federal Home Loan Mortgage Corporation were added to the system in 1934 and 1970, respectively.

Federal Home Loan Bank discount notes are issued by the Federal Home Loan Bank System in maturities from 30 to 270 days in denominations of $100,000 and $200,000 and in increments of $50,000 above $200,000. The notes are sold at a discount to mature at par with interest calculations made on actual days on a 360-day basis. The notes are issued in definitive form on a tap basis with New York delivery and regular settlement on the next business day in federal funds. The FHLBs also sell bonds of short and intermediate maturities on an irregular basis. FHLB debt instruments typically have maturities of up to 20 years and are not guaranteed by the U.S. government. Proceeds from bond sales are used to lend money to FHLB members. Distribution is performed by a national syndicate of dealers, including Discount Corporation, First Boston Corporation, Goldman Sachs, Aubrey G. Lanston, William E. Pollack, and the Bank of America. Members of the underwriting group, as well as other securities dealers, make up an active secondary market. Although a round lot transaction is $1 million, smaller amounts trade at a discount to the round lot rate.

The 12 FHLBs borrow funds by issuing debt securities. They relend the proceeds to the 3,200 savings and loans that are members of the Federal Home Loan Bank System. These thrifts borrow from the FHLBs to finance depositor withdrawals and liquidity problems, not to extend new mortgage loans.

The Federal Home Loan Mortgage Corporation (Freddie Mac). Freddie Mac, a subsidiary of the Federal Home Loan Bank Board, pioneered the conventional mortgage-backed security called pass-through certificates. Freddie Mac buys mortgages, usually from savings institutions and mortgage bankers. It usually sells them as Freddie Mac–guaranteed certificates. The maximum size of the mortgages that it buys was limited to $153,100 in 1987. Freddie Mac is authorized to purchase conventional mortgages from private lenders. Before its creation in 1970, only FHA- or VA-guaranteed mortgages were eligible for purchase by FNMA and GNMA. Freddie Mac was formed, in part, to fill this void. There are some minor operational differences between FNMA, GNMA, and FHLM. Freddie Mac is financed primarily by public borrowings and has created an interesting debt instrument—the mortgage participation certificate—a pass-through security in the sense that Freddie Mac collects the payments on the mortgage and passes them through to the certificate holders. Freddie Mac guarantees payments on the certificates regardless of the fate of the mortgages in its pool. At the end of 1985 Freddie Mac held $15 billion in mortgages for its own account and about $200 billion for mortgage pools.

The Government National Mortgage Association

The Government National Mortgage Association (GNMA) is a federally chartered corporation wholly owned by the federal government within HUD. GNMA was an offshoot of FNMA and was organized to provide special assistance and financing to the mortgage market. It sponsors a program of pass-through securities affectionally referred to as Ginnie Maes. Ginnie Mae securities are backed by the full faith and credit of the United States with respect to principal and interest on certificates that it issues. Ginnie Mae issues mortgage-backed certificates from mortgage pools that it buys from depository institutions and mortgage bankers. At the end of 1985 GNMA held only a few billion dollars in mortgages for its own account and $200 billion for mortgage pools. GNMA securities are treated in more detail in Chapter 10.

Two types of securities are sold by Ginnie Mae. They are participation certificates and pass-through securities. Pass-throughs differ from participation certificates in that pass-throughs provide both interest and principal repayment as the underlying mortgages being used as collateral are repaid. The principal and interest payments on the underlying mortgages are passed through to the bondholder.

Federal National Mortgage Association

The Federal National Mortgage Association (FNMA) is affectionately called Fannie Mae. FNMA is the fifth largest company in the United States in terms of assets. After the U.S. government, it is the second largest domestic borrower of money. Fannie Mae owns one in every twenty mortgages with a mission to provide support to the secondary market for federally guaranteed or insured mortgages. It accomplishes this mission by raising money in the capital markets in order to buy new mortgages from local mortgage lenders. That helps to replenish the lenders' cash, allowing these mortgage lending institutions to offer more mortgages in the primary market.

The Federal government created Fannie Mae in 1938 to provide a secondary market for mortgages on low and moderately priced homes. Additionally, FNMA began to guarantee conventional mortgage-backed securities in 1982. Congress turned Fannie Mae into an investor-owned company in 1968. Although Fannie Mae pays taxes and is owned by stockholders, the president of the United States appoints 5 of its 15 directors. Also, HUD must approve all new programs and limits the maximum size of the mortgages FNMA buys, to a 1987 level of $153,100.

FNMA lost money in 1981 and 1982 because it operated like a conventional savings and loan, buying fixed-rate, long-term mortgages with short-term debt. That strategy only works when interest rates are low and stable and there is an upward (positive) sloping yield curve. FNMA has attempted to reduce its vulnerability to interest rate swings by buying more adjustable-rate mortgages, high yielding conventional mortgages, and mortgages on mobile homes. It has also increased its commitment fees to buy mortgages. FNMA has asked Congress to limit HUD's supervisory authority, to let FNMA buy commercial mortgages and to lift the $153,100 limit on mortgages.

In 1960, FNMA implemented a program of selling discount notes in minimum denominations of $50,000 as a source of short-term financing. The notes are sold through a national syndicate of securities dealers which include Salomon Brothers, Goldman Sachs, Merrill Lynch, Shearson Lehman, Citibank, Bank of America, and Continental Illinois Bank. A secondary market is maintained by the above dealers along with several others not in the syndicate. One million dollars represents a round lot trade. The rates are set by FNMA, quoted on a discount basis and calculated on a 360-day basis. FNMA continues to issue interest-bearing notes at the interest-bearing equivalent of the discount rate. Notes are issued in book entry form for New York delivery in federal funds with settlement typically on the next business day. A variety of different FNMA issues exist, ranging from short-term discount notes to 25-year debentures. Proceeds from bonds' sales are used to purchase mortgages.

FNMA participates in conventional as well as the government-insured sector of the mortgage market. At the end of 1985 FNMA held approximately $100 billion in mortgages for its own account and $50 billion for mortgage pools. FNMA finances its mortgage purchases by issuing various forms of debt or stock. The debt is attractive to buyers who especially like the fact that the U.S. Treasury has guaranteed FNMA a large line of standby credit. However, Fannie Mae issues are sold without guarantee by the U.S. government.

Student Loan Marketing Association

The Student Loan Marketing Association was established by an act of Congress to provide liquidity to lenders (primarily banks and educational institutions) participating in U.S. government–insured student loan programs. Created in 1972, Sallie Mae went public in September 1983 by selling 11.5 million shares. Sallie Mae provides liquidity to the student credit market primarily through the purchase of government-insured student loans in the repayment phase (generally five years after the loan was originated or after the student graduates and is responsible for payment), and through warehousing seasoned student loans for new loan advances.

Sallie Mae's unique operation allows it several advantages over other finance companies. By operating with a ''matched book,'' the company has no significant interest rate sensitivity. It is sheltered from interest rate flunctuations since its assets are all variable rate, with both purchased and warehoused loans tied to the 91-day T-bill. In addition, it obtains funds to finance its loan program primarily through the sale of debt securities that also float with short-term T-bill rates. In addition, Sallie Mae encourages the flow of credit to higher education by providing loans to institutions, often called warehousing advances, so that these institutions can offer additional student loans. The loans purchased by Sallie Mae are usually originated by depository or educational institutions, are guaranteed either directly or indirectly by the federal government and are granted under the Guaranteed Student Loan Program. The return on the loans to the holders is ordinarily set at 3.5 percentage points above the interest rate on three-month Treasury bills (bond-equivalent basis) and is adjusted quarterly. The government makes the entire interest payment while the students are in school, while the students begin repaying the loans based on a fixed interest rate stated at the onset after graduation. In addition, Sallie Mae offers forward purchase commitments, developing special credit plans for medical and law students, and issues letters of credit to back student loan revenue bonds issued by state or local government agencies. Also, Sallie Mae acquired a North Carolina savings and loan in 1984 to assist in providing its education-related financial services.[4]

During 1987 the Student Loan Marketing Association, an innovative borrower in the capital markets, added another variety of debt security called "perls" for principal exchange rate linked securities. Interest and principal on the issue are paid in American dollars, with the size of the principal payment depending on the value of the Australian dollar. Investors in the issue will benefit if the value of the Australian dollar rises against the American dollar but will suffer if the Australian dollar weakens. Sallie Mae arranged swap transactions to eliminate its currency risk and reduce its borrowing cost to less than it would pay in a standard domestic financing.

Ownership of Agency Securities

While the Federal Home Loan Bank, the Federal National Mortgage Association, and the Farm Credit Banks have the largest amount of debt outstanding among the federally sponsored agencies, GNMA, FHLMC, and FNMA have large amounts of mortgage pool securities outstanding. The largest holders of agency debt issues are thrift institutions, households, commercial banks, insurance companies, private noninsured pension funds, state and local retirement funds, and state and local governments (see Table 7.6). Thrifts hold primarily mortgage-related agency securities in their investment portfolios along with a smaller amount of U.S. Treasury instruments. Whereby foreign investors hold considerable positions in U.S. Treasury securities, they hold less than 3 percent of outstanding debt.

Table 7.7 shows the key investment characteristics of agency securities, while Table 7.8 shows the denominations of both U.S. government and agency securities available for purchase.

Table 7.6

Federal Agency Debt (Annual Net Increases in Amounts Outstanding, Dollars in Billions)

	1981	1982	1983	1984	1985	1986E	1987P	Amt. Out. 31 Dec 86E
Outstanding								
Budgeted and Federally Sponsored Agencies								
Federal Home Loan Banks	$17.8	$0.6	$-7.0	$18.4	$4.9	$13.1	$10.0	$89.1
FNMA and Other Housing Credit	4.3	10.3	3.9	7.4	5.7	1.8	2.5	90.5
Total Farm Credit	8.4	0.5	0.5	-1.2	-2.9	-7.8	-8.0	60.5
Other Agencies	-0.2	0.9	1.3	0.6	0.2	8.7	5.0	13.5
Total Budgeted and Sponsored	30.4	12.4	-1.3	25.2	7.9	15.8	9.5	253.7
Mortgage Pool Securities Guaranteed by								
GNMA	11.9	13.2	40.9	20.1	32.2	53.0	60.0	258.3
FHLMC	2.7	22.9	14.8	12.8	29.4	57.0	65.5	165.2
FNMA	0.7	13.7	10.7	11.1	18.8	30.0	35.0	85.0
Farmers Home Administration[a]	-0.3	-0.2	0.0	0.5	-0.5	3.4	-3.1	3.7
Collateralized Mortgage Obligations	0.2	0.2	1.7	2.6	3.1	1.8	2.5	10.6
Total Mortgage Pools	15.2	49.8	68.1	47.1	82.9	145.2	159.9	522.9
Total Agency Debt	45.6	62.1	66.8	72.3	90.9	161.0	169.4	776.6
Less Trust Fund Holdings	0.0	0.0	0.0	0.0	0.0	0.0	0.0	0.0
Less Agency Holdings	0.2	-0.1	-0.4	0.2	0.1	-0.4	0.0	0.4
Less Federal Reserve Holdings	0.1	0.1	-0.7	-0.1	1.1	-1.8	0.0	8.1
Privately Held Fed. Agency Debt	**$45.3**	**$62.1**	**$67.9**	**$72.1**	**$89.6**	**$163.2**	**$169.4**	**$768.0**
Ownership								
Thrifts	$8.3	$31.4	$35.7	$17.6	$1.2	$31.0	$35.0	$186.5
Insurance and Pensions	21.0	20.5	26.7	12.6	22.5	31.0	42.0	190.9
Investment Companies	5.6	1.6	1.4	9.6	10.0	15.0	23.0	47.9
Other Nonbank Finance	0.0	0.0	0.0	2.9	3.2	4.0	4.0	10.1
Total Nonbank Finance	34.9	53.5	63.8	42.7	36.8	81.0	104.0	435.4
Commercial Banks	9.8	7.3	0.7	-1.3	-2.4	9.0	14.0	84.4
Nonfinancial Corporations	0.0	0.1	-0.0	-0.1	-0.1	1.2	3.1	2.8
State and Local Governments	-5.4	1.7	10.2	10.1	8.1	15.0	11.0	75.9
Foreign Investors	0.3	0.2	0.5	1.2	4.6	8.0	10.0	15.2
Residual: Households Direct	5.7	-0.7	-7.2	19.5	42.7	48.9	27.3	154.3
Total Ownership	**$45.3**	**$62.1**	**$67.9**	**$72.1**	**$89.6**	**$163.2**	**$169.4**	**$768.0**
Summary of Privately Held Federal Debt								
Privately Held Treasury Debt	$77.8	$152.3	$174.8	$188.9	$188.1	$194.2	$163.5	$1,591.3
Privately Held Fed. Agency Debt	45.3	62.1	67.9	72.1	89.6	163.2	169.4	768.0
Privately Held Federal Debt	**$123.2**	**$214.3**	**$242.7**	**$261.1**	**$277.7**	**$357.4**	**$332.8**	**$2,359.3**

[a] Excludes holdings of Federal Financing Bank.

Source: Prospects for Financial Markets in 1987. Salomon Brothers, Inc., December 1986.

Agency Summary

FMHA, FHLMC, and GNMA encourage private lenders to originate mortgage loans and to form them into pools, issue securities against these pools, service and guarantee the pool securities. This gives the pools characteristics of both guaranteed loans and direct agency credit.

Regardless of the maturity class, agency securities normally yield a bit more than Treasury securities, because agencies are

Table 7.7
Government Agency Security Investment Characteristics

	1	2	3	4	5	6	7	8	9
Eximbank	x	x	x	x	x	x	x	x	
TVA		x	x	x	x	x	x		x
GNMA	x	x	x	x	x	x	x	x	
FNMA		x	x	x	x	x	x		
Home Loan Banks		x	x	x	x	x	x	x	x
Co-op Banks			x		x	x	x	x	x
FICBs			x		x	x	x	x	x
Federal Land Banks			x		x	x	x	x	x

1. Backed by the full faith and credit of the U.S.

2. Approved by the U.S. Treasury.

3. Issued under an act of Congress.

4. Supported by authority to borrow from the Treasury.

5. Exempt from registration with the SEC.

6. Issued and payable through the facilities of the Federal Reserve Banks.

7. Legal investments for federally supervised institutions.

8. Eligible to be purchased and held without limit by national banks.

9. Exempt from state and local taxation.

1. Smaller issues and less liquid
2. Less marketable
3. Subject to state income taxes, although there are exceptions
4. Generally not backed by the full faith and credit of the U.S. government, that is, have greater default risk

The bid-ask spread is larger for agency securities than for Treasury securities. The longer-term issues tend to have larger spreads than short-term issues. The bid-ask spread is another measure of the security's marketability. Shorter-term issues are actively traded and have good liquidity; longer-term agency issues are traded less actively than Treasuries and command higher yields to maturity as a result.

A few agency issues are backed by the full faith and credit of the United States. Some are guaranteed or supported by the U.S. Treasury. Even though

Table 7.8
Denominations of U.S. Government and Agency Securities

December 31, 1985

Bearer — B
Registered — R
Book-entry — E

Security	Type	$500	$1,000	$5,000	$10,000	$25,000	$50,000	$100,000	$500,000	$1,000,000	$100,000,000	$500,000,000
Treasury bills[1]	E				•							
Treasury notes[2]	B&R&E		•	•	•				•		•	•
Treasury bonds[3]	B&R&E	•	•	•	•				•	•		
Asian Development Bank bonds[4]	R[5]		•									
Department of Housing and Urban Development:												
Federal Housing Administration deb's[6]	R	•	•	•	•							
Local authority bonds[4]	B&R			•								
Export-Import Bank of the United States deb's	B&R&E			•		•	•		•	•	•	
Farmers Home Administration CBOs	B&R&E					•	•		•	•	•	
Federal Farm Credit Banks Consolidated Systemwide:												
bonds[7]	E		•	•								
discount notes[4]	B							•				
Federal Home Loan Banks:												
consolidated bonds[8]	E			•								
consolidated discount notes[9]	E			•								
Federal Home Loan Mortgage Corporation:												
debentures[10]	E			•								
discount notes[11]	B					•			•	•	•	
guaranteed mortgage certificates	R								•	•	•	
participation certificates[12]	R								•	•	•	
Federal National Mortgage Association: notes[10]	E				•	•	•	•	•	•	•	
deb's[6]	B&R&E				•	•	•	•	•			
General Services Administration participation certificates	R				•	•	•					
Government National Mortgage Association:												
participation certificates	R				•	•	•		•	•	•	
pass-through securities[13]	R				•							
mortgage-backed bonds	R						•		•	•	•	
Inter-American Development Bank[14]	B&R&E	•										
Maritime Administration												
notes	R	•										
bonds	R	•										
Short-term tax exempt notes[15]	B			•						•		
Small Business Administration												
deb's[4]	R			•								
pool certificates	R						•					
Student Loan Marketing Association:												
discount notes[16]	R&E							•				
floating rate notes[10]	B&R		•									
Tennessee Valley Authority bonds[17]	B&R	•	•									
United States Postal Service	B&R					•	•		•	•		
Washington Metropolitan Area Transit Authority bonds[18]	B&R		•	•	•				•	•		
World Bank bonds (US$)[17]	B&R	•		•						•		

most agency issues do not have a direct guarantee of payment, they are considered to be of top investment quality because of an implied government backing.

The existence of federal credit programs is related to a government attempt to alleviate economic recessions, correct market imperfections leading to misallocation of resources, redistribute wealth, and rechannel credit into sectors of the economy that should increase economic activity and output such as housing, agriculture, education, and foreign trade. Evidence seems to indicate that the ability of federal credit programs to direct economic resources to special sectors seems to be less impressive than the size of the program would indicate. The federal government's role in credit markets has expanded to become a key force for some of these markets. At the end of 1985 they had provided approximately $621 billion in direct credit to the private sector. However, these magnitudes do not demonstrate that federal credit programs either add to GNP or even allocate credit to the favored sector. Empirical studies of federal credit in the housing sector, where the largest programs operate, suggest that the effects of the programs are still quite small given the size and subsidization of the programs.

NOTES

1. "The Federally Sponsored Agencies: An Overview," *Federal Reserve Bulletin* (June 1985): 379.

2. D. S. Kidwell and R. L. Peterson, *Financial Institutions, Markets and Money,* 3rd ed. (New York: Dryden Press, 1987), p. 441.

---

[1]Minimum order $10,000, then multiples of $5,000. Cash management bills minimum order $1 million.

[2]Bearer notes no longer issued. $1,000 denomination has not been available on most Treasury note issues with a maturity of less than four years since the latter part of 1974.

[3]Bearer bonds no longer issued. $500 denomination eliminated on bonds issued since mid-1971.

[4]Available in this single denomination or in multiples thereof.

[5]Zero coupon notes issued in registered and bearer forms.

[6]$50 and $100 denominations also available.

[7]For maturities less than 13 months issued in multiples of $5,000; for longer maturities issued in multiples of $1,000.

[8]New issues available in book-entry form only. Minimum $10,000, thereafter in multiples of $5,000.

[9]Minimum $100,000, then multiples of $5,000.

[10]Minimum purchase $10,000, thereafter in multiples of $5,000.

[11]Also available in $5,000,000 denomination.

[12]$200,000 and $5,000,000 denominations also available.

[13]Minimum purchase $25,000, then multiples of $5,000.

[14]New issues available in book-entry form only, in multiples of $1,000.

[15]Most issues also have denominations that fall in between.

[16]Minimum purchase $100,000.

[17]Registered bonds are available in any multiple of $1,000.

[18]Registered bonds available in multiples of $5,000.

Note: Domestic marketable obligations issued by the United States or any agency or instrumentality thereof after December 31, 1982 (September 3, 1982 in the case of certain long-term U.S. obligations) are not allowed to be in bearer form. Book entry obligations are transferable only pursuant to regulations prescribed by the Secretary of the Treasury.

3. D. Howell, "Federally Sponsored Credit Agency Securities," in *Instruments of the Money Market,* 5th ed., T. Q. Cook and J. G. Duffield, eds. (Richmond, Va.: Federal Reserve Bank of Richmond, 1981), p. 379.

4. M. J. Moran, "Federally Sponsored Credit Agencies: An Overview," *Federal Reserve Bulletin* (June 1985): 338.

ADDITIONAL READINGS

Handbook of the Securities of the United States Government and Federal Agencies (New York: First Boston Corporation, 1986), published biennially.

8

Corporate Bonds

A corporate bond is an IOU or loan agreement between a lender and a borrower, in some cases backed by specified collateral and in others by the general credit of the issuing corporation. The contract obligates the borrower to repay the lender by a specific date, the full amount being loaned and to make two semiannual interest payments at an agreed upon rate.

Corporate bonds are usually issued by large corporations and foreign governments or their agencies to finance the acquisition of assets. The overwhelming number of corporate bond issuers can be classified as utility, industrial, transportation, bank, and finance company bonds. Financial institutions, banks, pension funds, corporations, professional money managers, and individuals for their IRA and Keogh accounts have been traditionally the principal buyers of corporate bonds.

A number of factors affect the corporate choice between debt and equity financing, including the levels of corporate and personal income tax rates, the rate of inflation and the amount of uncertainty or expected variability of corporate earnings before interest and taxes, and the interest rate that the company will have to pay on a bond issue. Other factors that have an impact on the mix between debt and equity funds are timing, availability, control, and flexibility.

PUTS AND CALLS

Some companies retain the option of redeeming or ''calling'' their bonds before they mature. A call provision allows the bond issuer to redeem the bonds by purchasing them from the holder at a specified price. There is no firm rule, but bond holders usually have a minimum of 5 to 10 years protection before a new issue can be refunded. These bonds are usually sold with a deferred call provision that bars the issuer from calling the bond for a stipulated period of time. Call prices are initially set above face value and decline, in steps, to face value prior to maturity. The typical initial call premium is normally equal to one year's coupon payment. The initial investors require a higher yield when purchasing securities with a call provision. Issuers seem willing to offer the higher yield necessary to obtain these call provisions because of greater uncertainty about future interest rates and capital costs. From the investor's viewpoint, the call provision establishes an upper limit on the amount of potential capital gain that can be obtained should interest rates fall. This is an especially important feature for investors holding current coupon or premium bonds during periods when interest rates are declining. One way to control against call risk would be to purchase low coupon, deep discount bonds. Even though interest rates may decline, prices of these issues are unlikely to increase to their stated call prices.

Research on callable bonds suggests that callable bonds sell at higher promised yields than noncallable issues, that the yield spread between callable and noncallable bonds widens during periods of high interest rates and increases with the maturity of bonds. In addition, immediately callable bonds sell at higher yields than bonds that have a deferred call. "Put" options allow bond holders to redeem their investment at a price usually equal to the principal value of the issue. Because put options work to the benefit of investors, the yield on debt with a put option should be lower than the yield on comparable debt without a put option. Investors will generally exercise put options if interest rates have increased above the coupon rate.

To make sure that the money is available for repayment, some companies create what is known as a sinking fund. The fund is used to buy back some of the issues each year, thus gradually returning the debt over a period of time instead of all at one time. Sinking funds are annual payments made to a trustee to ensure repayment of the bonds. The funds may be left to accumulate as a deposit with the trustee or used to immediately retire a portion of the debt outstanding through purchase in the open market. The retirement of bonds is often accomplished by selling a random set of bonds. Sinking fund obligations are closely related to serial bonds. Sinking fund issues are popular with industrial, electric utility, and pipeline issues, but remain unpopular with telephone and finance company issues.

SOURCES AND USES OF FUNDS

The corporate bond market is a key source of long-term funds for businesses. Borrowing corporations tend to rely more on debt issues than on equity financing because interest payments on bonds are tax deductible, while dividends on common stock are not. In addition, the issuance of bonds does not dilute the equity position of existing stockholders under normal conditions, while the issuance of new shares of stock does have this effect in the short run.

Corporate bonds are negotiable instruments that are usually in bearer form so that they may be easily transferred. The volume of trading is small in corporate bonds compared with that in stocks. Since most corporate bonds are purchased by institutional investors, the secondary market is rather "thin" since these institutions seldom need liquidity.

Corporations borrow long-term funds by issuing bonds when they do not generate sufficient funds internally to meet their needs (see Table 8.1). When retained earnings exceed corporate needs they often use these internally generated funds to pay back part of their external debt. Because of the cyclical pattern of internally generated funds, changing corporate needs and varying business conditions, there are substantial fluctuations in the volume of corporate bond issues. Just as the supply of bonds fluctuates, the demand for corporate bonds also fluctuates among institutional investors. The changing patterns of supply and demand, as well as general financial market and inflationary conditions, often cause yields to fluctuate widely.

Corporate bonds used to have average maturities of 25 to 30 years. By 1980, the average maturity had fallen to 18 years, and by 1984, to 15 years. This reflects the fact that investors desired shorter maturities because interest rates had become so volatile.

In addition to fixed-rate coupon bonds, there are several types of bonds that can be classified as floating-rate notes. This is a term that applies to the note's coupon rate, which changes at regular intervals as other specific interest rates change. There are also both fixed- and floating-rate notes that have "puts" attached. That is an option that enables the holder of the note to put it back to the issuer at an agreed upon date.

Corporate bonds are among the most important source of corporate long-term debt, followed by commercial mortgages for use in the financing of office buildings and shopping centers. Term loans from banks and insurance companies, leasing arrangements on equipment and tax-exempt corporate obligations used to fund some industrial development projects and pollution control equipment are other important sources of funding. Although nonfinancial corporations are the largest demanders of funds in the bond market, there is substantial demand for long-term debt from financial intermediaries such as depository institutions and insurance and finance companies (see Table 8.2). A substantial number of foreign obligations, especially Canadian corporate and municipalities and their agencies, are issued in the U.S. bond market. Corporate long-term debt financing is highly cyclical. It generally expands in the late stages of each economic cycle, in the subsequent recession, and in the preliminary stages of economic recovery. For example, in 1970–1971, 1975–1976, and 1982–1983, corporations issued long-term debt to finance their current needs and to refund part of the short-term debt they had built up in previous phases of the credit cycle. This is often referred to as reliquification and balance sheet restructuring. Electric, gas, and water utility companies have always been steady and heavy borrowers in the long-term marketplace, reflecting the continual capital expenditures and relatively stable internal funds generated by these utilities, while mining and energy-related companies have been big borrowers since the OPEC price hike in 1974. The supply of funds for the corporate bond market comes from life

Table 8.1

Sources and Uses of Corporate Funds[a] (Annual Income, Expenditures and Net Increases in Amounts Outstanding, Dollars in Billions)

	1981	1982	1983	1984	1985	1986E	1987P	Amt. Out. 31 Dec 86E
Analysis in Brief								
Profits Before Taxes and IVA	$181.4	$129.8	$159.5	$189.6	$170.4	$176.6	$205.3	
Inventory Valuation Adjustment	-24.2	-10.4	-10.9	-5.5	-0.6	11.0	-4.7	
Repatriated Foreign Profits	14.5	12.5	11.8	11.3	12.2	12.0	14.6	
Less Federal Tax Payments	71.1	57.7	52.1	69.0	70.3	74.3	108.2	
Less Dividends	67.6	72.0	78.0	83.9	86.2	90.8	95.7	
Plus Depreciation Allowances	184.9	213.0	244.2	269.3	303.3	313.6	345.0	
Internal Cash Generation	218.0	215.3	274.5	311.8	328.9	348.2	356.4	
Total Physical Investment	290.4	263.9	275.6	368.0	357.6	370.8	367.1	
Plus Net Receivables	-2.3	-18.5	29.5	23.7	13.6	6.6	3.0	
Less Internal Cash Generation	218.0	215.3	274.5	311.8	328.9	348.2	356.4	
Capital Requirement	70.1	30.2	30.6	79.9	42.3	29.2	13.7	
Plus Req. for Financial Assets	53.1	70.7	77.1	80.1	65.3	54.9	72.1	
Less Foreign Equity Investment	22.3	16.2	11.9	22.5	16.8	11.3	16.2	
External Requirements	101.0	84.7	95.8	137.6	90.8	72.7	69.6	
Uses of Funds								
Plant and Equipment, NIA	$270.6	$267.9	$261.1	$309.9	$348.8	$348.5	$351.7	
Land[b]	4.6	4.2	4.4	0.3	0.0	0.0	0.4	
Mineral Rights	4.8	7.8	7.8	7.9	4.4	4.3	3.6	
Direct Foreign Investment	-0.5	3.3	-3.6	-3.5	-5.0	-0.7	-2.0	
Residential Construction	-0.8	1.8	5.4	2.3	2.4	5.4	6.0	
Inventory Adjusted for Valuation	11.7	-21.2	0.6	51.2	6.9	13.2	7.4	
Total Physical Investment	290.4	263.9	275.6	368.0	357.6	370.8	367.1	
Plus Net Receivables[b]	-2.3	-18.5	29.5	23.7	13.6	6.6	3.0	$230.5
Liquid Assets	17.5	34.2	54.5	21.7	15.3	33.8	44.0	373.5
Statistical Discrepancy	36.4	22.6	58.4	50.0	31.3	21.1	28.1	
Total Uses of Funds	**$341.2**	**$316.1**	**$382.2**	**$471.8**	**$436.4**	**$432.3**	**$442.2**	
Source of Funds								
Mortgages	$-1.9	$-1.2	$3.5	$0.3	$0.4	$2.2	$2.0	$83.9
Bank Loans	43.5	39.7	18.0	77.0	35.5	27.1	22.0	540.3
Foreign Bank Loans	8.9	2.5	2.7	13.0	-2.3	8.1	4.0	37.1
Thrift Loans	0.4	0.2	2.4	8.7	5.4	4.7	7.0	21.8
Finance Company Loans	9.2	2.0	8.9	20.8	15.8	13.3	12.9	151.5
U.S. Government Loans	1.2	1.3	-0.5	1.2	-4.4	1.4	1.5	15.6
Net Sales of Open Market Paper	16.9	-6.5	2.6	23.1	13.5	8.1	5.3	94.5
Tax-Exempt Bonds	13.4	15.1	9.4	20.5	22.6	-6.3	0.7	120.8
Taxable Corporate Bonds[b]	24.8	32.4	22.1	48.6	66.8	71.8	67.4	634.8
Eurobonds (for Domestic Uses)[b]	3.3	11.8	2.5	6.7	10.2	18.7	20.0	55.5
Stocks[b]	-18.6	-12.7	24.0	-82.4	-72.7	-76.3	-73.4	2,045.6
Total External Sources	101.0	84.7	95.8	137.6	90.8	72.7	69.6	3,801.3
Internal Cash Generation	218.0	215.3	274.5	311.8	328.9	348.2	356.4	
Foreign Equity Investment	22.3	16.2	11.9	22.5	16.8	11.3	16.2	
Total Sources of Funds	**$341.2**	**$316.1**	**$382.2**	**$471.8**	**$436.4**	**$432.3**	**$442.2**	

[a] Nonfarm, nonfinancial corporations.
[b] Salomon Brothers Inc estimates. All other data from Federal Reserve Board of Governors.
IVA Inventory Valuation Adjustment. NIA National Income Accounts.

Source: Prospects for Financial Markets in 1987. Salomon Brothers, Inc., December 1986.

insurance companies and pension funds who between them hold over two thirds of the outstanding bonds (see Table 8.3). The remaining third is divided among individuals, mutual savings banks, educational, religious and charitable institutions, foreign investors, property-casualty insurance companies, mutual funds, and broker-dealers.

Table 8.2

Corporate Bonds by Type of Issue (Annual Issuance, Retirements and Net Increases in Amounts Outstanding, Dollars in Billions[a])

	1981	1982	1983	1984	1985	1986E	1987P	Amt. Out. 31 Dec 86E
Straight Public Debt								
Utility	$11.7	$9.9	$9.7	$8.3	$14.6	$37.8	$34.0	
Industrial	11.1	13.0	9.8	20.2	36.3	56.2	65.3	
Finance	6.4	16.6	18.0	31.1	38.8	45.6	36.0	
Total Public Straight Issues	29.2	39.5	37.5	59.6	89.8	139.6	135.4	
Merger Exch. Bonds for Stock	1.3	14.1	4.8	9.9	9.5	6.1	5.0	
Maturing Public Straights	6.1	7.6	6.8	6.2	11.1	9.6	13.0	
Calls	0.4	2.7	2.0	1.9	8.9	37.8	35.5	
Sinking Fund Retirements	5.8	4.5	6.8	7.7	9.1	7.4	7.6	
Debt/Equity Swaps	0.7	5.9	2.0	0.9	0.0	0.0	0.0	
Net Increase in Public Straights	17.6	32.9	24.7	52.8	70.2	90.9	84.2	$555.6
Straight Private Debt[b]								
Utility	$3.8	$3.2	$3.0	$3.7	$2.0	$1.9	$2.0	
Industrial	9.3	12.7	15.1	21.0	26.4	13.9	13.5	
Finance	3.0	7.5	14.0	17.6	13.3	11.1	9.5	
Total Private Straight Issues	16.2	23.4	32.2	42.3	41.7	26.9	25.0	
Maturing Private Straights	5.2	5.6	6.9	5.8	5.8	5.9	6.0	
Net Increase in Private Straights	11.0	17.8	25.3	36.5	35.9	20.9	19.0	278.1
Convertible Bonds								
Utility	$0.4	$0.5	$0.8	$0.2	$1.4	$0.1	$0.7	
Industrial	3.6	2.0	5.0	3.3	7.5	10.6	9.8	
Finance	0.4	0.5	0.7	0.5	3.1	2.0	2.2	
Total Convertible Issues	4.4	3.0	6.5	4.0	12.0	12.8	12.7	
Merger Exch. Bonds for Stocks	0.2	1.6	0.6	1.4	0.4	0.3	0.3	
Calls	1.8	0.2	6.1	1.2	2.2	3.3	3.5	
Conversions	1.1	1.3	1.2	1.6	1.4	3.5	3.0	
Net Increase in Convertibles	1.8	3.1	-0.3	2.7	8.6	6.3	6.5	35.9
Net Increase in Corporate Bonds	**$30.3**	**$53.8**	**$49.7**	**$92.0**	**$114.7**	**$118.2**	**$109.7**	**$869.6**
Memo: Sector Analysis								
Nonfinancial Corporations	$24.8	$32.4	$22.1	$48.6	$66.8	$71.8	$67.4	$634.8
Finance Companies	1.9	14.0	14.9	24.8	28.9	24.3	21.5	110.5
Commercial Banks	1.4	3.2	8.3	12.7	11.6	13.4	15.0	74.2
Thrifts	-0.5	0.2	-0.0	1.2	3.6	1.1	1.5	9.6
Other Finance and Real Estate	2.8	3.9	4.4	4.7	3.9	7.5	4.3	40.4
Net Increase in Corporate Bonds	**$30.3**	**$53.8**	**$49.7**	**$92.0**	**$114.7**	**$118.2**	**$109.7**	**$869.6**

[a] Salomon Brothers Inc estimates.
[b] Many private placements have equity features.

Source: Prospects for Financial Markets in 1987. Salomon Brothers, Inc., December 1986.

Table 8.3
Holders of Corporate Bonds (September 1985)

Holder	Amount(Billions)	Percentage of Total
Households	$ 37.8	5.3
Foreign	88.8	12.5
Commercial banks	24.8	3.5
Savings banks	20.0	2.8
Life insurance companies	262.6	37.1
Other insurance companies	25.7	3.6
Private pension funds	96.5	13.6
Public pension funds	121.6	17.1
Mutual funds	21.2	3.0
Brokers and dealers	11.0	1.5
Total	$710.0	100.0

Source: Board of Governors, Federal Reserve System, Flow of Funds Accounts, Assets and Liabilities Outstanding, December 1985.

Corporations prefer not to raise long-term funds when long-term rates are high. However, their need for funds tends to peak near the times when long-term rates are high. Nonfinancial corporations seem to be less sensitive to high nominal rates than the other principal long-term borrowers. Just like other bonds, corporate bond prices tend to rise when interest rates fall and vice versa. During periods such as 1970–1971, 1975–1976, and the early 1980s, increasing inflation led to expanded corporate financial needs, increased inflationary expectations, and higher nominal interest rates. The enlarged corporate demand for long-term funds exceeded the available institutional supply, placing additional pressures upon the bond market. The huge corporate demand for long-term funds drove corporate rates upward relative to other issues, increasing the spread between corporate bonds and other long-term bonds until incremental funds satisfied the increased demand. Of course, during these time frames, supply and demand factors were not the only factors influencing corporate yield spreads. Increases in risk perception may have widened the spreads between corporate and government bonds.

At the end of 1985, total outstanding corporate and foreign bonds amounted to close to $775 billion, just slightly more than that of state and local government securities and about half as much as that of home mortgages. Borrowing and lending decisions—particularly those involving substitution between corporate bonds and other instruments by both issuers and purchasers of bonds—affect not only the size and rate of growth of the corporate bond market but also the effectiveness of selective credit and other public policies designed to alter the price and quantity of particular securities, such as home mortgages or state and local government obligations.

Although some bonds are listed on the New York and American Exchanges, most of the trading in outstanding corporate bonds takes place in the OTC market through a group of dealer firms who sell and buy bonds to and from institutional and individual investors. The liquidity of these bonds varies from one issue to another. Small issues from firms with lower credit ratings are not widely traded and may, in fact, be illiquid. On the other hand, dealer firms make active markets in large issues of prime credit, well-known corporations.

INVESTORS IN CORPORATE BONDS

Life insurance companies and pension funds are the largest holders of corporate bonds. These bonds are attractive to these institutional investors because of the predictability of the cash flows and the long-term nature of their liabilities. Foreign investors, households, other insurance companies, banks, mutual funds, and brokers and dealers are among the other major holders of corporate bonds. In the last two decades households and mutual funds have increased their share of corporate bond ownership. Both federal and state laws require many institutional investors to be prudent in their investment decisions, which implies that they limit bond purchases to the top four investment categories that are classified by Moody's and Standard & Poor's.

New corporate bonds are brought to market by a public offering through an investment banking firm or by a private placement to a limited number of investors. Pension funds and life insurance companies are the major purchasers of private placement sales.

Corporate bonds are typically issued in $1,000 denominations with a fully taxable coupon. Most issues are term bonds, which means that all of the bonds that compose a particular issue mature on a single date. In contrast, most municipal bonds are serial issues, which means that the bond issue contains a variety of maturity dates.

During the 1980s many smaller companies and companies with lower credit ratings have been able to sell their corporate bonds in both private placements and in public offerings to what might be called "high yield" mutual funds. These issues are often referred to as "junk bonds" and have been an extremely popular source of funds in leveraged buyouts (see the section on junk bonds later in this chapter). It is interesting to note the percentage distribution of corporate bonds by rating categories at par value, shown in Table 8.4. This table was made prior to the enormous popularity of junk bonds in the mid-1980s. A 1986–1987 table would probably show a large increase in the percentage of junk bonds and a large decline in the percentage of AAA-rated securities being brought to market.

The degree of substitution between corporate bonds and other instruments differs substantially among the major groups of holders. Households substitute

Table 8.4
Percentage Distribution of Corporate Bonds by Rating Categories

	Total Corporate	Utilities	Industrial	Finance	Transportation
AAA	23%	26%	21%	19%	7%
AA	26	25	26	33	10
A	33	·32	34	34	27
BBB	13	16	10	5	18
BB	2	1	3	1	8
B	1	—	2	1	8
CCC and lower	2	—	4	7	22
	100%	100%	100%	100%	100%

Source: Salomon Brothers.

freely among corporate bonds, equities, and short-term securities. While life insurance companies tend to favor long-term corporate bonds and mortgages or mortgage-related securities with long maturities, their unique time pattern of inflows and outflows inevitably tends to reduce their ability to substitute between corporate bonds and other instruments. Although pension funds have shifted more funds into real estate and mortgage-related instruments during the 1980s, they tend to invest heavily in corporate bonds and income-oriented equity issues. There is some modest shifting in and out of corporate bonds on the part of both life insurance companies and pension funds as interest rate peaks and troughs are anticipated.

Another interesting trend taking place in debt markets is the growth of insured issues. For example, nearly 20 percent of the $222 billion in long-term municipal debt issued in 1985 was insured. Increasingly, municipalities are seeking AAA-rated guarantees from insurers to boost the investment grade of their debt and thereby reduce the interest rate they must pay. Major banks have been backing corporate debt as well as municipal bonds with billions of dollars of letters of credit guaranteeing payment of principal and interest. Corporate bonds guaranteed by a bank's letter of credit are exempt from the registration requirement of the Securities Act of 1933. Foreign banks have been given the same favored treatment allowed domestic banks when it comes to corporate guarantees and SEC registration exemption. Insurance companies have sought equal treatment by the SEC when it comes to insurance company guarantees of corporate debt.

CORPORATE BOND DEALERS

Compared with the Treasury market, the interdealer market in corporate bonds is primitive. Dealers cannot afford to maintain a position in more than a handful of issues, so interdealer trading is not a significant source of liquidity to corporate bond dealers. Liquidity is derived by knowing what may be available from, or what may be sold to, public investors.

The frequency of trading in individual corporate bonds is much lower than the frequency of trading in individual Treasury bonds, because of the relatively smaller size of corporate bond issues. Dealers quote bid-ask spreads on corporate bonds considerably wider than the spreads quoted on Treasury issues. The relatively high cost of trading corporate bonds, related to the huge bid-ask spreads, has led to the use of trading mechanisms other than cash sales and purchases. Many dealer-customer transactions are arranged in pairs, where the customer and dealer swap two issues of comparable value, settling only the difference in cash. This eliminates the customer need to first sell one issue and then, with the proceeds, buy another issue. Swaps are also usually more economical.

With the smallest spreads of $\frac{1}{32}$ point in the bond market for U.S. Treasury securities, spreads on corporate bonds are considerably higher. The dealer spread in a $500,000 to $1 million transaction for a highly marketable corporate bond is usually about $\frac{1}{8}$ point, while spreads for less marketable issues range from about $\frac{1}{4}$ to $\frac{1}{2}$ point. A large portion of the differences in bond yields can be explained by both theory and empirical evidence as due to differentials in default risk and marketability of the bonds.

While government, agency, and municipal bonds can be bought from either a banker or a broker, an individual buying or selling a corporate bond must deal with brokers. Commissions on listed corporate bonds are generally $10 per bond for the first five bonds and $5 per bond thereafter. However, some brokerage houses impose a minimum commission of $25 per trade. It is generally wise for the individual investor to buy only listed bonds because prices on unlisted issues may invite unnecessary liquidity problems or unusually steep bid-ask spreads.

While new issues of municipal bonds are usually sold to underwriters through competitive bidding, most corporate new issues are sold to underwriters through a negotiated sale. The corporate issuer chooses the investment banking firm and agrees upon a selling concession which may range from $\frac{1}{2}$ point for a AAA-rated bond in a strong market to $1\frac{1}{2}$ points for a Baa issue sold in a weak market.

The principal secondary market for corporate bonds is a dealer-made, over-the-counter market that accounts for about 95 percent of all corporate bond trading. The remaining 5 percent of secondary trading in corporate bonds occurs on organized exchanges such as the New York Stock Exchange. Trading on the New York Stock Exchange is in small lots because of a rule requiring dealers who are members of the exchange to execute trades on listed bonds on the exchange whenever the trade is for nine bonds or less.

In addition to the greater default risk of corporate bonds versus either government or agency bonds, the greater yield on corporates also reflects the greater bid-ask spreads and the fact that U.S. government securities are not taxed at the state and local level. The spreads between corporates and governments are highly volatile. They have ranged from 25 basis point spreads between Aa public utilities and 20-year Treasuries on several occasions during the 1950s to spreads

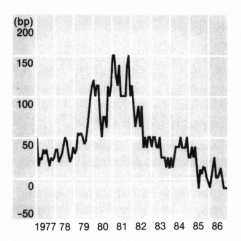

Figure 8.1
Long A Utilities vs. Industrials, 1977–1986
Source: Prospects for Financial Markets in 1987. Salomon Brothers, Inc., December 1986.

of 275 basis points in 1981. The spread between long-term A-rated utilities and industrials ranged from between 25 and 150 basis points during 1977–1984. However, during 1985–1986, the spreads ranged from a negative 15 basis points to a positive 25 basis points (see Figure 8.1). The narrowing and inversion of the spread was related to the heightened risk of restructuring for industrial corporations during 1986. The large positive spreads are unlikely to return until the merger risk for industrials is reduced.

The corporate/government yield spread is usually widest when credit is scarce and interest rates are high. There is an apparent "flight to quality" as investors must feel that corporate bonds are a riskier investment at the peak of the business cycle when rates are highest and a decline in economic activity is expected. The spread between low quality corporates and high quality corporate issues reflects the same pattern as the corporate/government yield spread over the interest rate cycle. Yield spreads on BBB versus Treasury bonds exhibit a more dramatic sensitivity to business cycles than do spreads between corporate AAA and Treasury bonds. Consistent with the fact that AAAs contain small amounts of default risk, the spreads between AAA and Treasury bonds are split.

Types of Bonds

Mortgage Bonds. They are long-term obligations that are secured by specific property. In the event of default, holders of mortgage bonds receive ownership of the mortgage property.

Income Bonds. They pay interest only when the corporation's net income is above a prespecified level. They are sometimes called adjustment bonds because they may be issued to readjust fixed-interest debt by corporations undergoing reorganization.

Guaranteed Bonds. They are instruments guaranteed by the assets of a corporation other than the issuing firm. The guaranteeing firm is often the parent of an issuing subsidiary or a company acquiring another company in a merger.

Participation Bonds. They provide fixed-interest payments and a portion of surplus earnings accruing over the life of the bond if earnings are above the fixed interest.

Pooled Bonds. They are obligations jointly issued by two or more corporations (usually railroads).

Collateral Trust Bonds. They are often used by a parent firm when it pledges the securities of a wholly owned subsidiary as collateral.

Equipment Trust Certificates. They are typically used by trains, airlines, and shipping companies. Equipment trust certificates may be issued by a trustee who holds the specific machinery or equipment, issues obligations, and leases the equipment or machinery to the user corporation, who will usually eventually take title to the equipment. The interest and principal on the equipment trust certificates are paid from cash received from the corporation. They are issued in serial maturities and offer buyers complete protection against call.

Serial Bonds. They are corporate obligations so arranged that specified principal amounts become due on specified dates. The repayment schedule of a serial bond will ordinarily match the decline in the value of the equipment used as collateral, reducing default risk for the investor. Serial bonds have different portions of the issue maturing at different dates. A default on any portion constitutes default on the entire issue.

Voting Bonds. They are generally issued in connection with reorganizations. They give holders the right to vote for directors if interest payments are not made for a certain period of time.

Debenture Bonds. They are unsecured general obligations of the issuing corporation that are protected by their indenture restrictions. These restrictions may include (1) provisions against the issuance of more debt and merger activity and (2) restrictions on dividends payments and on the disposition of the firm's assets. Only corporations of high credit quality can issue unsecured or uncollateralized notes or bonds. It is interesting to note that most defaults on corporate bonds have been on secured issues rather than on unsecured issues. Subordinated debentures represent junior debt. In a bankruptcy claim, subordinated debenture holders' claims are met only after the claims of senior debt holders have been fully satisfied.

Convertible Debentures. They carry a call option, allowing a debenture holder to purchase some underlying asset, typically the common stock of the debenture issuer, where the exercise price of the option is the debenture itself. A convertible bond is a debt instrument of an issuing corporation with a par value, a maturity date, a call price, and an interest rate that, at the holder's option, can be converted into a predetermined number of the corporation's common shares. Convertible bonds offer some of the stability and relative safety associated with straight debt issues, such as regular bonds, but may not appreciate as much as stock might in a rising stock market. On the other hand, it will not lose as much value in a falling stock market because its yield is generally considerably higher than the average dividend available in the stock market. Companies issue convertible bonds with a yield that is below that of otherwise similar nonconvertible issues. The interest on a convertible bond may appeal to investors who desire to have the cash flow and a safety of a bond as well as the prospect for capital gains should the company's stock go up in price. Convertible bonds tend to be subordinated debentures, a form of debt that has a somewhat residual claim on a company's income and assets in the case of bankruptcy. The key to choosing a convertible bond is a thorough knowledge of the company and its common stock—its earnings and dividend expectations and the conversion premium of the bond over the stock value.

Zero-Coupon Bonds. They are essentially deep discount bonds that pay no interest but can be redeemed at par at maturity. One typically buys these securities at a discount of 20 to 90 percent off each $1,000 of face value. These bonds have proved popular for investors in IRA accounts who do not wish to be concerned with reinvesting typical interest payments. Since zero-coupon bonds have no cash flows before maturity, they are free from the problem of coupon reinvestment. Zero coupons also save money for the issuing corporation or municipality. However, they are not particularly good investments for accounts that must pay current income taxes, because yearly taxes must be paid despite the fact that no interest payment is received in that year by the investor.

An investment banker or brokerage house creates a clip and strip by purchasing an outstanding bond issue and formulating an instrument that will mature on a series of dates that correspond to the underlying bond's annual interest dates and maturity date. Depending upon the brokerage house, when the underlying security is a Treasury note or bond, one of the following names is used: CATS, TIGRs, COUGARs, or Treasury bond receipts. The broker will place the purchased Treasury bonds in trust and issue a series of Treasury receipts sold at a discount and maturing either on the same date as the underlying coupon payments or the underlying maturity date. The resulting instrument is similar to a zero-coupon bond and has little reinvestment risk. It is popular for use in IRA, KEOGH, and other tax deferred accounts.

The major Zero Coupon Treasuries issued include

CATS—Certificates of Accrual on Treasury Securities

TIGRs—Treasury Investment Growth Receipts

TRs—Generic Treasury Receipts

STRIPS—Separate Trading of Registered Interest and Principal of Securities

Zero-coupon bonds are attractive to some investors because they eliminate reinvestment risk and permit the investor to lock in the yield to maturity when the bond is purchased. Investors have no danger of a call and are guaranteed a "true" yield irrespective of what happens to future interest rates.

Zero-coupon bonds expose the investor to greater interest rate risk and, in the case of tax-free or corporates, to greater default risk than for non–zero-coupon bonds. Because there is no reinvestment risk, investors are often willing to accept a lower return, depending on their expectation of the future course of interest rates.

Zero-coupon bonds, or original issue discount bonds, were first used in a major way in 1984. IBM, J. C. Penney, Alcoa, GMAC, Martin-Marietta, ITT, Cities Service, and many others have raised billions of dollars by issuing "zeros." The advantages of the zeros to the issuing corporation include the following:

1. No cash outlays are necessary for either principal or interest payments until the bonds mature.
2. The bonds have a lower yield to maturity than if the issue had been a regular coupon bond.
3. The issuing company receives an annual tax deduction equal to the yearly amortization of the discount. The bonds provide a positive cash flow in the form of tax savings over their life.

The disadvantages of zeros to the issuing corporation include the following:

1. The bonds are not callable because the issuing company would have to pay the $1,000 par value at a date earlier than the maturity date. In effect, the corporation cannot refund the issue if interest rates should decline.
2. The issuing corporation will have a large nondeductible cash outlay in the year in which the bond matures.

Commodity-Backed Bonds. They have face values indexed to certain commodity prices that might be expected to outpace inflation. Bonds have been indexed to oil, silver, and gold.

Stock-Indexed Bonds. They link the interest paid on a bond to stock market factors such as trading volume on the NYSE.

Warrants. Bonds are often sold with warrants attached. They allow bond owners to buy, within a stated period, more bonds at the same yield or a certain number of common shares at a specified exercise price anytime before a specified exercise date. These warrants are generally detachable from the bonds and can be sold in the marketplace to speculators. Like a convertible provision, bonds with warrants provide the owner with a fixed income plus the ability to share in future stock price increases. Equity kickers such as conversion options, warrants, and unit packages of debt issues and common stock have appeared as sweeteners to attract investors. With a sweetener package, the bonds may be offered at a reduced cost. The issuing corporation hopes to save through lower required bond yields and automatic future equity sales at the exercise date.

Bearer Bonds. Bearer bonds are presumed to belong to whoever has them. The owner of registered bonds has his or her name registered with the issuing corporation or its agent. Bearer bonds have coupons attached. However, more and more issuing corporations and municipalities have issued registered bonds. Aside from the banishment of new municipal bearer bonds from the marketplace on July 1, 1983, another reason was to protect bond owners from theft or loss of their bonds and to protect corporations from forgeries (see Table 8.5).

Adjustable or Variable Rate Bonds. Interest rates on these securities are indexed to the rates on Treasury securities or other money or capital market instruments. They provide a type of interest rate hedge or protection. Investors usually earn a spread of 50 to 300 basis points above the Treasury rates or a percentage above the Treasury rate (for example, 109 percent) to adjust for different levels of interest rates. These rates are typically adjusted every six months or once a year. Although financial companies have floated these securities frequently, the wave of new adjustable debt has spread to industrial and public utility companies. Corporate issuers are essentially making a choice between a floating rate, which can go up or down, and a high fixed rate, which the corporation could be forced to pay for up to 30 years. Adjustable rate debt is most popular for issuing companies when interest rates are quite high and expected to decline, while they are popular for buyers when rates are expected to increase. During the early 1980s, inflation pushed interest rates to record double-digit levels. This caused large declines (in some cases in excess of 50 percent) in the value of long-term bonds. As a result, many institutions became reluctant to lend or invest money at fixed rates on a long-term basis, but corporations needed long-term money. The problem was solved with the introduction of long-term, floating-rate debt. Floating-rate debt is advantageous to lenders because the yield increases if market interest rates rise. It is also advantageous to corporate borrowers because by using it they can obtain long-term funds without committing themselves to paying high rates of interest for the entire term of the loan. Of course, if rates increase, the borrower would have been better off issuing conventional, fixed-rate debt.

High Yield or Junk Bonds. During the 1980s, a growing part of corporate borrowing took the form of "low grade," high yielding bonds, commonly called "junk bonds." These low grade bonds are below investment grade, carrying S&P credit ratings of BB, B, CCC, or CC. They are regarded as "speculative" with respect to the issuer's capacity to meet the terms of the debt obligation.

Although "junk bonds" received a lot of attention because of their use in corporate takeovers, most junk bond issues are not used for this purpose. Low grade bond issues actually involved in takeovers and leveraged buyouts make up less than half the market. It is estimated that out of the $14 billion in publicly

Table 8.5
Differences between Bearer and Registered Bonds

	Bearer Bonds	Registered Bonds
Ownership	The bonds belong to bearer, or holder, of the certificate... easy to trade, but also vulnerable to loss or theft...the anonymity provided by these bonds is said to encourage tax evasion by providing a haven for unreported income.	The issuer of these bonds must keep records of ownership. Bonds are less negotiable, but easier to replace in case of theft or loss..
Interest Payment and Redemption	Certificates are issued with coupons that must be clipped and presented to a paying agent in order to be paid interest... Investor receives no money until the paying agent has processed the coupon	Since issuer has records of the bondholders, interest payments may be mailed directly to the investor and interest check can be cashed.
Back Office Impact	State and local governments must maintain extensive operations that process the interest coupons...redeeming an issue via a call can be difficult because bondholders can be notified only through newspaper advertisements. Municipalities no longer issue bearer bonds.	Municipal governments have to hire transfer agents to keep records of bondholders and to issue new certificates when a bond changes ownership...Redeeming issues via a call is simpler as investors can be notified by mail.

issued low grade bonds in 1984, approximately 12 percent were issued in acquisition or leveraged buyouts. By 1985, the proportion had risen to 38 percent. Prior to the 1980s, not many companies with speculative credit ratings were able to borrow in the public bond market because of prohibitive underwriting costs associated with their risk, their lack of size, track record, and name recognition. These companies previously borrowed in the form of commercial loans from banks or privately placed bonds.[1]

Low grade bonds have been in existence for over half a century. In fact, during the 1920s and 1930s, about 17 percent of domestic corporate new bonds issues were low grade.[2] Following the Depression, many bonds that were originally issued with high grade credit ratings were downgraded to below investment grade. (During the 1980s Lilco, Bethlehem Steel, and Beatrice Foods would have joined the aforementioned list of "fallen angels" because they were all downgraded to speculative grade securities.) By 1940, low grade bonds made up more than 40 percent of all bonds outstanding. After 1940, the market for new public offerings of low grade bonds shrank considerably. By the mid-1970s, only about 4 percent of all public corporate bonds outstanding in the United States consisted of low grade corporate bonds.[3] However, during the 1980s, low grade bond issuance grew from $42.8 billion or 6 percent of total corporate bonds issued in 1982 to close to $32 billion or about 21 percent of total corporate bonds issued in 1986 (see Figure 8.2 and Table 8.6).

Junk bonds have emerged as an important type of debt in the 1980s. The investment banking firm of Drexel Burnham Lambert is the leading underwriter of these bonds and has actively campaigned to persuade certain institutions to buy junk bonds. The number of high yield corporate bond mutual funds has grown from 10 in the late 1970s to 50 in 1986 as interest rates declined in general and as spreads between investment grade and junk bonds widened.

There were an estimated $125 billion worth of junk bonds held in the United States in 1986. There are no precise figures on the overall distribution of junk bonds, but it is estimated that insurance companies and mutual funds each hold about $40 billion, pension funds hold between $10 and $15 billion, thrift institutions about $10 billion, individuals about $15 billion, foreign investors about $5 billion, and securities dealers about $2 billion. Corporations probably hold the remainder of the securities.

Historically, default rates on low grade bonds have been considerably higher than those on investment grade bonds. Between 1970 and 1984, the average annual default rate for junk bonds was only 2.1 percent, while the default rate for investment grade debt was negligible. The average default rate hides year-to-year variability. For example, the default rate varied from a high of 11.4 percent in 1970, when Penn Central failed, to just .15 percent in 1981, when only two companies defaulted on their bonds (see Figure 8.3). In 1986, the default rate approximated 3 percent, primarily because of the LTV bankruptcy. It should be pointed out that most default statistics fail to take into account "soft defaults"—instances where issues come close to a bankruptcy, but are rescued by an exchange offer. Some analysts expect the percentage of junk bond defaults to rise

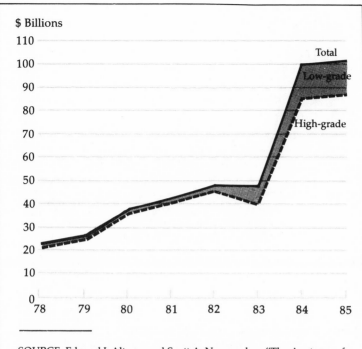

$ Billions

SOURCE: Edward I. Altman and Scott A. Nammacher, "The Anatomy of the High Yield Debt Market: 1985 Update," Morgan Stanley (June 1986) Table 2. Data do not include exchange offers, secondary offerings, tax exempts, convertible bonds, or government bonds.

Figure 8.2
New Domestic Corporate Bond Issues: 1978–1985

Table 8.6
Selected Debt Issues

DEBT ISSUED	1985	1986 (through 12/3)
Junk Bonds (BBB and under)	$22.1	$29.8
Medium Term Notes	19.6	11.4
Foreign Bonds	41.0	38.3
Private Placements	73.9	35.3
Corporate Bonds	72.0	91.9
	(billions of dollars)	

Source: Salomon Brothers, Inc.

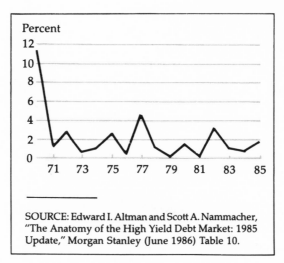

SOURCE: Edward I. Altman and Scott A. Nammacher,
"The Anatomy of the High Yield Debt Market: 1985
Update," Morgan Stanley (June 1986) Table 10.

Figure 8.3
Historical Default Rates on Low-Grade Bonds 1970–1985

substantially. They sight statistics such as the fact that the proportion of new junk bond issues in the lowest rated or unrated categories has jumped from 6.3 percent of new issues in 1980 to more than 40 percent in 1986. In addition, some economists feel that the next recession could lead to massive failures of junk bonds.

The lower a firm's bond rating, the higher the interest rate that it must pay on its bonds. As revealed in Figure 8.4, AAA bonds usually yield only 25 to 125 basis points more than Treasury bonds, while BBB-rated bonds may yield from 150 to 300 basis points more. The risk premium of lower grade bonds over Treasuries has run from 300 to 600 basis points during the first half of the 1980s.

The impact on bond yields of the boom in corporate restructurings has been most evident in the high yield (junk bond) market, where much of the financing for these activities took place. The spread between BB- and A-rated industrials reached a record 300 basis points early in 1986 (see Figure 8.5). Later in 1986, the insider trading investigation hurt the high yield sector. The widening in spreads between different rated corporate bonds in this market reflected increased concern about credit risk and market liquidity.

The impact of corporate balance sheet leverage on credit ratings and bond yields is exemplified by the $6.2 billion Beatrice Companies leveraged buyout, which was partially financed with $2.35 billion of debt securities. The securities were rated BB by Moody's—a large change from the once AAA-rated corporation. Consequently, the 10-year bond was trading at a 375 basis point spread over Treasuries in 1986 in contrast to the 50 basis point spread of a Beatrice issue with 10 years remaining to maturity that prevailed prior to the buyout announcement.

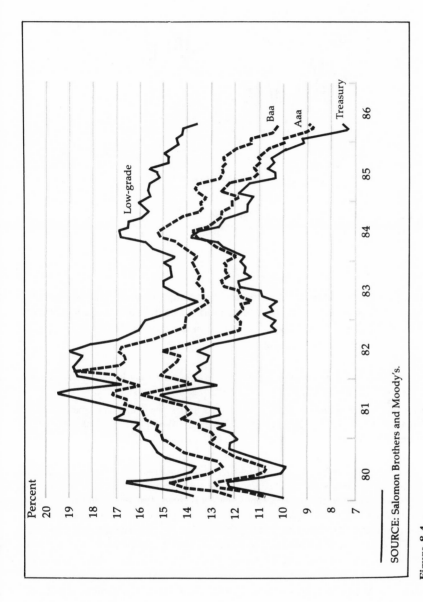

Percent

SOURCE: Salomon Brothers and Moody's.

Figure 8.4
Promised Yields on Treasury and Corporate Bonds

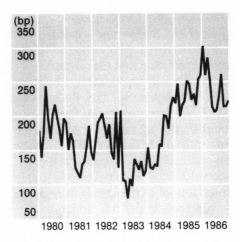

Figure 8.5
Long BB- vs. A-Rated Industrials, 1980–1986
Source: Prospects for Financial Markets in 1987. Salomon Brothers, Inc., December 1986.

The 1986 LTV bankruptcy and the insider trading scandals temporarily hurt the high yield bond sector. Spreads increased substantially between high yield bonds and Treasuries. The reasons for the re-emergence of a market for public original issue, low grade bonds are:[4]

1. A greater demand from investors for marketable assets, particularly from life insurance companies, the dominant factor in the private placement market.

2. Investors appear more receptive to riskier securities, including low grade bonds. Perhaps this is related to the relatively favorable post–World War II default experience on low grade bonds and their relatively high yields.

3. Improvements in computer technology have lowered the information and monitoring costs of investing in securities issued by smaller and lesser known corporations. It has become easier for investors to obtain and maintain information about the condition of these corporate borrowers. Lenders are finding it cost effective to lend directly to these companies, rather than indirectly through financial intermediaries such as commercial banks. The growth in low grade publicly offered bonds is a rechanneling of corporate borrowing away from individually negotiated loans (for example, a shift away from private placements toward publicly issued bonds)[5].

4. Altman and Nanmacher (1986) found that a portfolio of junk bonds would have resulted in an annual compound return spread of 580 basis points over a portfolio of long-term government bonds in the period from December 31, 1977 to December 31, 1983.

5. The large differential between junk bonds and bonds of investment grade quality.

6. The junk bond market is not as volatile as government or high-grade bonds; junk bonds react more to changes in the economy than to shifts in interest rates.

Foreign and Eurobonds. A foreign bond is a debt instrument sold by a foreign borrower but denominated in the currency of the country in which it is sold. For example, a Canadian manufacturer will on occasion raise money in the capital markets of the United States. The bond will be underwritten by a syndicate of U.S. investment bankers, denominated in U.S. dollars, and sold to U.S. investors in accordance with SEC and applicable state regulations. Except for the foreign origin of the borrower, the bond will be indistinguishable from bonds issued by equivalent U.S. corporations.

Another type of international bond is the Eurobond, which is a bond that is sold in a country other than the one in whose currency it is denominated. For example, if Texaco, a U.S. corporation, sold bonds in England that were denominated in Japanese yen, these would be Eurobonds. Most Eurobonds are not rated by Moody's or Standard & Poor's and are underwritten by an international syndicate of banks and securities dealers. These bonds tend to be issued in bearer form. A bond issued in bearer form increases the marketability of the issue because the identity of the owner is not a matter of public record. Eurobonds are marketed with a far lower level of required disclosure than would be the case for bonds issued in the United States markets. In general, governments do not usually apply as strict regulation on securities denominated in foreign currencies as they would on home currency securities because of the nature of the probable purchasers of the bonds. Eurobonds are considered a cost-effective means of raising long-term debt capital because of the lower disclosure and regulation costs. Although transaction costs are usually lower and interest costs are sometimes lower, a corporation does take on a foreign exchange risk when it borrows money in a foreign currency.

Eurobonds are normally issued as unsecured obligations of the borrower. Therefore, only borrowers of good quality are able to market new issues successfully. Eurodollar bonds are described as those securities that are denominated in U.S. dollars, underwritten by an international syndicate and sold when originally issued to non-U.S. investors. A single bank is usually responsible for assembling and coordinating the selling group of banks and dealers. The number of banks and dealers involved in the placement of the issue may range from 1 to as many as 100 institutions. The head of the syndicate is known as the lead managing bank.

Private placements are usually issued on behalf of prime borrowers by a smaller syndicate of banks and placed directly with a single institution or a small group of institutional investors. Private placements are usually not quoted on a stock exchange and are ordinarily not negotiable in the secondary market.

Because Eurodollar bonds are not registered with the SEC, they are less expensive to bring to market abroad than in the U.S. domestic bond market. The size of the Eurodollar market has grown substantially from a nominal amount in the early 1960s to more than $33 billion of new issues in 1984. In addition to fixed-rate securities, there are floating-rate notes, original issue discounts, index-linked securities, and issues convertible into the stock of a foreign-based company or a domestic company. The attraction of Eurodollar bonds to foreigners is often related to judgments on the prospects for the U.S. dollar, the level of U.S. interest rates relative to other foreign markets, and expectations for capital gains. It is interesting to note that most Eurodollar bonds pay interest only annually compared to U.S. domestic issues, which pay interest semiannually.

The Eurobond market was given a strong stimulus during its infancy in the early 1960s when the U.S. government, concerned about the increasing volume of dollars held in foreign hands, placed a 30 percent withholding tax on interest paid to overseas investors holding American bonds. The move drove investors away from Wall Street and into the Euromarket, where they could buy dollar-denominated securities tax free. It is primarily because some foreign companies earn and trade in dollars and that foreign governments hold reserves in dollars that the Euromarket originally developed. The Eurodollar bond market is the largest of all the Eurobond markets in terms of the value of outstanding issues and of secondary market turnover.

The main borrowers in the Eurobond market in 1985 came from the United States, England, Japan, France, and Canada. American concerns that borrow in the Euromarket are generally multinational institutions taking advantage of temporary interest rate or currency advantages available there. For example, a gap of 20 basis points on a $200 million issue amounts to a savings of $400,000 annually for the issuer. New U.S. issues in the Eurobond market reached a level of $36.2 billion in 1985 compared to a level of over $100 billion in the domestic capital markets.

There is a secondary market for Eurobonds in the over-the-counter market. Secondary market spreads range from about 50 to 100 basis points. The buyers of Eurobonds are primarily foreign institutions and corporations. U.S. residents are not permitted to buy new issue Eurodollar bonds unless they are private placements. There is a highly active secondary market that takes place through a bank or a dealer in the over-the-counter markets of Europe and the Far and Middle East. Publicly issued Eurobonds are quoted on one or more stock exchanges such as in London, Luxembourg, or Zurich.

Most Eurobonds are publicly marketed, callable, and have maturities of 10 to 15 years. Some Eurobonds have been denominated in several currencies and have had currency options in which bond holders can ask for payment and principal in one of several currencies. Others have been denominated in the European Unit of Account (EUA). The EUA was defined as a weight of gold in U.S. dollars and was instituted to eliminate the risk of currency devaluation.

In addition to fixed rate Eurobonds, there are also floating-rate issues, convertible issues, and bonds with warrants. The special feature of floating-rate notes (FRNs) is that the coupon is set at some margin over the London Interbank Offered Rate. This margin can be as low as 12.5 basis points or as high as 150 basis points, depending on the quality of the issuer and market conditions. Floating-rate issues keep a market price close to the par value of the bonds. Most FRNs state minimum rates of return such that if LIBOR plus the predetermined margin falls below a certain level the investor receives the stated minimum rate of interest. Some Eurobond issues have "drop lock" clauses, whereby if interest rates according to the predetermined formula fall below a specified minimum rate, that interest rate is fixed at the minimum and "locked in" for the remaining life of the loan.

Convertible Eurobonds are similar to convertible bonds that are issued in the United States. They give the investor the right to convert the fixed-interest bond into common stock of the issuing company. The bonds themselves have fixed rates of interest, which because of the attached conversion right are normally lower than coupons on straight bonds of comparable terms. Convertible bonds have on occasion offered an additional advantage to the investor that is not available with domestic convertible bonds. They may be issued in a currency that differs from the currency in which the shares of the company are denominated.

Bonds with warrants are less frequently issued than convertible bonds. The warrant can be detached from the bond and traded separately. These warrants give the holder the right to buy a specified number of shares of the company at a predetermined price during a specified period of time.

Yankee Bonds. They are U.S. dollar denominated bonds that have been registered with the SEC by foreign-domiciled issuers and issued in the United States. Canadian issues dominate this market in the United States. Some foreign buyers prefer U.S.-pay international bonds over U.S. Treasury or U.S. corporate issues because they are familiar with Yankee bond credits and because the yields on these instruments are usually higher than U.S. government or domestic corporate issues. Also, Yankee and Eurodollar bond maturities are usually shorter than many U.S. domestic issues, while call protection is sometimes longer.

Bonds issued in the U.S. capital markets by nonresidents of the United States, primarily foreign governments, public authorities, or corporations are colloquially known as Yankee bonds. Many foreign institutions publicly issue securities in the United States to tap the large supply of private capital. Although the Yankee bond market is the largest foreign bond market in the world in terms of issues outstanding, the Swiss foreign bond market has greater volume of new issues. Investors have shown a penchant for issuing dollar denominated bonds in the Euromarket rather than in the U.S. domestic market because the Eurodollar market is less restrictive and issuing costs are lower.

Yankee bonds are issued in both bearer form and registered form with maturities ranging from 5 to 30 years. The secondary market is moderately active with most transactions taking place in the over-the-counter market. Many of the foreign government issuers of Yankee bonds carry AAA ratings.

Perpetual Notes. Citicorp issued the first perpetual American bank holding company notes in the fall of 1986. The perpetual notes count as primary capital and may become a harbinger of future capital issues.

Historically, U.S. banks were wary of perpetual issues because the Internal Revenue Service interpreted the absence of maturity as evidence that the securities were not debt, and their interest payments could not be deducted as a business expense. However, the IRS has allowed interest to be deducted on the

Citicorp issue because investors may redeem the notes after 30 years and annually thereafter at face value.

INNOVATIVE FINANCING

The 1980s have been a period of major financial innovations, as evidenced by the promulgation of new products and concepts. Included among these innovations were original issue discount bonds, zero-coupon bonds, stripping of coupons from principal, partly paid bonds, options on almost anything, coupon and currency swaps, dual currency issues, floating rate preferred stocks, adjustable rate preferred stock mutual funds, adjustable rate mortgages, and the securitization of mortgage instruments and consumer installment paper (see Table 8.7).

There have been a number of innovative financing products with optionlike features that are allowing companies to raise capital at lower costs than many traditional forms of financing. Some bonds now include a choice of currencies in which they can be repaid. Floating-rate debt is being sold with "collars," limiting how high or low the interest rate can move. Some deals give the purchaser of a note the right to buy more securities later at higher interest rates. For example, the buyer has the right, but not the obligation in one particular issue, to redeem the security after five years and obtain a return of principal or to receive another five-year note at a much higher rate of interest. Under these terms, the issuer pays a lower interest rate for the first five years than it would have on a note issued without an option feature.

Another innovative development is the detachable option, in which the option portion of the securities deal can be stripped and sold separately. In one particular case, a corporation issued notes that had an interest rate cap giving the issuer the right, but not the obligation, to pay only the interest rate at which the debt is capped if rates should rise. The issuer can also sell the cap to an investment banker for a lump sum. If it does so, the issuer gives up protection provided by the cap, but in return the interest rate it pays on the debt is effectively lowered because of the sum received in the sale. Meanwhile, the investment bank sells the cap to a corporation that already has the same amount of floating-rate debt on its books and wants to protect the debt against increases in interest rates. The corporate customer buys the cap option from the investment bank, presumably at more than the investment bank had paid.

Asset-based securitization reached an estimated record level of $270 billion in 1986. This increase was primarily related to the huge increase in the issuance of residential mortgage-backed securities, which reflected record refinancings by homeowners. Although home financing dominated the market, other securitized assets included automobile loans, credit card loans, and commercial mortgages.

Innovations included "stripped securities," which enable issuers to segment cash flow payments into two or more pass-throughs with different coupon rates. In addition, floating-rate collateralized mortgage obligations (CMOs) tranches and the sale of CMO equity were introduced into the marketplace during 1986.

Table 8.7
Recent Innovation in the Financial Markets

International Markets

Nondollar Floating-Rate Notes	Mark- and yen-dominated F.R.N.s
Nondollar Zero-Coupon Bonds	Mark-, swiss franc-and yen-dominated issues
Shoguns	U.S. dollar bonds issued in Japan
Sushis	Eurobonds issued by Japanese entities that do not count against limits on holdings of foreign securities
Down-Under Bonds	Euro-Australia dollar and Euro-New Zealand dollar bond issues

Domestic Markets

Zero-Coupon Convertible Collateralized Securities	Zero-coupon bond with option to convert to common stock
Multifamily Pass-Through	Securities backed by multifamily mortgages where the principal and interest is passed through to the investor
Lease Backed	Leases on plant and equipment serve as collateral
Automobile Backed	Pools of car loans serve as collateral
Commercial Real Estate Pass-Through Securities	Pass-through securities backed by commercial mortgages
Daily adjustable Tax-Exempt Securities	Long-maturity bonds with coupon rate adjusted daily; investor has right to sell bond back to the issuer
Stepped Tax-Exempt Appreciation on Income Realization Securities	Zero-coupon bonds for an initial period, after which they are converted to interest-bearing securities
Municipal Option Put Securities	Bonds that can be sold back to the issuer at specific dates. The put option is sold separately from the bond itself.

Collateralized Mortgage Obligations

The major growth of the secondary market for mortgage loans is usually attributed to government-chartered entities such as GNMA, FHLMC, and FNMA. These organizations were formed to create and maintain liquidity in the mortgage loan market. FNMA, GNMA, and FHMLC transform pools of mortgage loans into pass-through securities that are standardized, highly liquid, and extensively traded.

These securities represent an undivided interest in a pool of mortgage loans, with the monthly principal and interest payments on the mortgage loans being passed through to the holders of the securities. The governmental agencies enhance the credit of the mortgage pool, as they guarantee the payment of principal and interest to holders of the pass-through securities. Although all three are government-chartered corporations with AAA-rated credit, their structures vary:

- GNMA is a wholly owned corporation within the U.S. Department of Housing and Urban Development. Their securities are backed by the full faith and credit of the U.S. government.
- FHLMC is a private corporation owned by the nation's savings and loans and operated by the Federal Home Loan Bank Board.
- FNMA is a public corporation. Its stock is traded on the New York Stock Exchange.

Although the payment of principal and interest on these securities is guaranteed by institutions of the highest credit quality, the timing of principal payments is uncertain, since prepayments on the mortgage loans are passed through to the holders of the securities. Prepayments usually occur as falling interest rates induce homeowners to refinance their mortgages, but can also occur when a homeowner moves or if the mortgage property is foreclosed. Therefore, pass-through securities are partially or totally "called" because of prepayments during their 30-year life, resulting in an average life, cash flow, and duration that are subject to uncertainty.

Despite high credit quality and high yield relative to other investments, mortgage pass-through securities have two drawbacks: (1) a monthly payment frequency that may include some repayment of principal and (2) a security partially or totally callable at any time.

CMOs were introduced in 1983 to improve the appeal of pass-through securities to investors by giving different call protection features. Unlike pass-through securities callable at any time, CMOs are debt obligations collateralized by pass-through securities and are structured into classes or tranches in a predetermined order. The most common structure contains four classes, usually labeled A, B, C, and Z. While all classes of bonds receive interest payments, principal payments are allocated only to the A bonds until the A bonds are fully repaid. Following the A bond repayment, the B bonds are then fully repaid, and so on until all the classes have been repaid. The Z bonds are usually an accrual bond having characteristics similar to those of zero coupon bonds because they receive no interest payments until all other classes have been repaid (see Figure 8.6 and Table 8.8).

CMOs are bonds issued in several classes and collateralized by mortgage loans or mortgage pass-through securities. Principal payments on the bonds are made sequentially to each class of the CMO, creating short-, medium-, and long-term

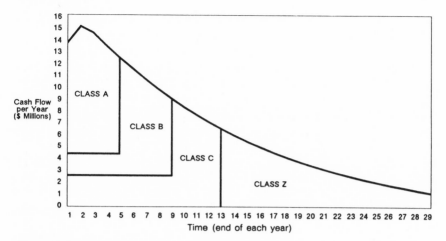

Figure 8.6
Cash Flow of a Typical CMO
Source: An Investor's Guide to Evaluating CMOs. Smith Barney, October 1986.

securities that are generally rated AAA by Standard & Poor's and whose yields exceed those available even on AA- or A-rated single maturity bonds of similar average life. For example, during 1986, a AAA-rated CMO with a three-year average life yielded 60 to 70 basis points more than a three-year, A-rated industrial bond; while for a CMO class with a 10-year life, the average differential ranged from 90 to 100 basis points. In general, the longer the average life of a CMO the higher the yield compared to a "bullet" maturity bond. Figure 8.7 illustrates the historical yield relationship between 10-year, AA-rated corporate bonds, a typical CMO class with an expected average life of 10 years and 10-year Treasuries. Between August 1984 and August 1986, CMOs yielded between 50 and 220 basis points more than Treasuries of the same maturity (see Figure 8.8). In exchange for a higher yield, investors must accept some uncertainty germane to repayment of principal.

Investors who prefer CMOs to Ginnie Maes prefer them because they have more call protection and a more predictable repayment schedule. In a Ginnie Mae issue, the interest and principal payments are passed directly to the investor, which means that the investor cannot be certain as to what interest rate he is getting.

CMOs do not eliminate interest rate risk, but they do minimize it by creating several different maturities. Payments on principal go first to pay off the first class or tranche, then the second tranche, and so forth. Following retirement of the first bond tranche, the next class in the sequence becomes the exclusive recipient of principal payment until this class is retired. This sequential process continues until the last class of bonds is retired.

Table 8.8
Profile of Various Classes of CMOs

	Class A Bonds	Class B Bonds	Class C Bonds	Class Z Bonds
Typical Average Life:	2 to 3 years	5 to 7 years	7 to 10 years	14 to 25 years
Yield:	85 to 115 basis points over 2- or 3-year Treasuries	120 to 185 basis points over 5- or 7-year Treasuries	170 to 220 basis points over comparable Treasuries	200 to 250 basis points over 20-year Treasuries
Appeal:	Class A bonds are an excellent alternative to short-term investments. The yield differential is significant enough to attract commercial banks and thrift institutions. Often they can identify a portion of their short-term portfolio that could remain slightly less liquid.	Class B bonds are very attractive to insurance companies for their investment portfolio as a way to match liabilities in the 5- to 7-year range such as Guaranteed Investment Contracts (GICs) and Single Payment Deferred Annuities (SPDAs).	Class C bonds are particularly attractive to insurance companies who want to match liabilities longer than 7 years. They are also attractive to bank trust departments who want a portion of their portfolio in medium-term investments.	Class Z bonds are generally purchased by pension fund and bank trust departments attracted to high credit quality and high yield and not subject to income taxation. Class Z bonds provide the greatest degree of call protection and eliminate the reinvestment risk associated with coupon payments. Class Z bonds also offer yields that greatly exceed those of zero coupon bonds.

Source: An Investor's Guide to Evaluating CMOs. Smith Barney, October, 1986.

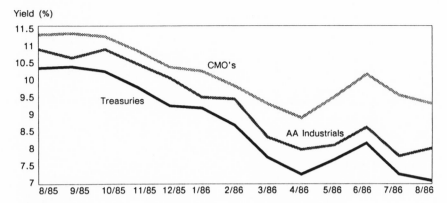

Figure 8.7
Comparison of Ten-Year Securities (August 1985–August 1986)
Source: An Investor's Guide to Evaluating CMOs. Smith Barney, October 1986.

CMOs are multiclass pay-through bonds and are general obligations of the issuer backed by mortgage collateral. The cash flows generated by the collateral are linked to the cash flows of the bonds. At each bond payment date, sufficient cash should be available from the collateral to pay all interest and some principal on the bonds. Each bond class has a stated maturity date and a fixed coupon rate.

Floating-rate collateralized mortgage obligations and stripped mortgage-backed securities were offered initially to the public in the fall of 1986. Other varieties of mortgage securities are likely to be developed in the future.

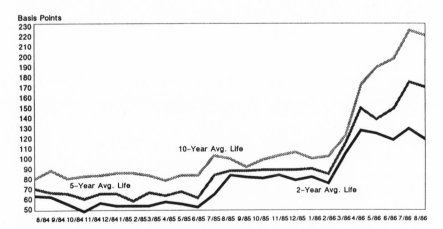

Figure 8.8
Spreads of CMO Classes Over Treasuries (August 1984 to August 1986)
Source: An Investor's Guide to Evaluating CMOs. Smith Barney, October 1986.

Real Estate Mortgage Investment Conduits

Real estate mortgage investment conduits (REMICs), authorized by the Tax Reform Act of 1986, are an improved version of mortgage-backed securities such as Ginnie Maes. GNMA securities pass through to investors the principal and interest payments from single family mortgages. The major flaw in Ginnie Mae securities is that when interest rates fall, homeowners tend to refinance their high rate mortgages. Investors receive a premature return of principal as soon as the total mortgage is paid. The REMICs are a form of bond designed to be rated AAA and to minimize the prepayment problem.

The first REMICs were backed by mortgages guaranteed by Ginnie Mae securities (the reason for the AAA rating). However, future REMICs are expected to be backed by more speculative commercial mortgages. When first issued in January 1987, AAA-rated REMICs yielded approximately 200 basis points more than a Treasury security of comparable maturity. For example, two-year REMICs yielded 7.2 percent, compared to a 6.2 percent yield for a Treasury note. Twenty-year REMICs yielded 9.7 percent compared to a yield of 7.7 percent for 20-year Treasuries.

The first REMICs were put together by a brokerage firm and sold in minimum amounts of $1,000 or more. They consisted of bonds with four separate maturities or tranches: 2, 4, 10, and 20 years. Mortgage prepayments are assigned to the shortage tranche, usually assuring something close to the original yield for the full term that has been chosen.

Other Forms of Securitization

The wide acceptance by investors of mortgage-backed securities has led recently to a similar securities phenomenon—asset securitization. The securitization of assets theoretically transforms an illiquid loan or lease agreement into a liquid security. Pooled corporate receivables, such as computer leases and automobile loans, have already been securitized, while outstanding balances on credit cards or other revolving credit plans, as well as loans for planes, boats, and even time-sharing vacation homes, are being considered for the future. Unlike Ginnie Maes, which are guaranteed against credit loss by the full faith and credit of the government, the other securitized assets do not have a federal guarantee. However, many of these issues contain loans guaranteed by an insurance company and are therefore granted a higher rating by the rating agencies than they would have otherwise received. Some experts believe that virtually every asset with a payment stream and a long-term payment history is a candidate for securitization. This would open the door for the eventual creation of billions of dollars worth of marketable securities to finance the loans traditionally offered by finance companies, banks, thrifts, merchants, and other lenders.

There exists the potential for abuse of securitization because of misconceptions about marketability and the possible transfer into marketable form of poor quality assets. Many institutional lenders do not want to be bound to borrowers so they seek to disengage the link between creditor and borrower through securitization. The credit scrutiny at the inception of a loan or investment should be meticulous. In a nonmarketable relationship the lender is linked to the borrower for the life of the loan. In a securitized arrangement scrutiny of the borrower may not be quite so intensive since the initial pressure to be highly circumspect in the creation of the obligation does not exist. The illusion of marketability is that the holders of the obligations will be able to sell their investment before a deterioration in credit quality is perceived that will negatively affect the price and/or the demand for the security. Some of the collateralized obligations have yet to be tested by adverse business conditions. There exists the risk that if the market detects poor underwriting standards for the basic bonds and/or a deterioration in the underlying financial conditions, the owners of the securitized obligations may not be able to divest from their portfolio credit obligations that are unwanted by the market.

Automobile Receivable–Backed Securities

The market for publicly registered automobile-backed securities began in May 1985 and has developed as a sequel to the collateralized mortgage market. Automobile receivable–backed securities have aided consumer installment lenders in liquifying assets previously held in portfolio. Issuers have included banks, thrifts, and automobile finance companies. As of December 1986, GMAC accounted for 80 percent of the total. Most of this was accomplished when First Boston Corp. sold $4.0 billion of AAA-rated securities backed by General Motors' low interest rate loans in late 1986. This was the biggest corporate underwriting in the domestic capital markets. It is the first offering to apply a structure that revolutionized the mortgage-backed bond market to bonds backed by other types of assets. The bonds are modeled on collateralized mortgage obligations. Rather than simply passing principal and interest payments through to bond holders, as previous asset-backed offerings have done, First Boston's offering splits that cash flow into three separate securities with different maturities. Although all three security holders get interest payments, principal payments are made in sequence, first to the shortest-term securities, then to the intermediate securities, and finally to the long one.

A First Boston subsidiary bought 2.9 and 4.8 percent loans from GMAC at a substantial discount. While GMAC has promised to buy back up to 5 percent of nonperforming loans in the pool—a promise backed up by a letter of credit from Credit Suisse—investors have no recourse to First Boston or to GMAC and must look to the loans for repayment. Unlike mortgage-backed securities, First Boston's offering has a set payment schedule. Since car loans, like mortgages, can be paid at any time, investors could theoretically get their principal back sooner than they expect. First Boston has assumed that consumers are less likely to prepay below-market loans and that they will prepay at a much more consistent level than mortgages.

Automobile receivable–backed securities have expected average lives of about two years when issued and have typical spreads over two-year Treasuries of between 80 and 100 basis points. Unlike mortgages, automobile receivable securities are backed by assets that generally depreciate over time. Of the issues in the market at this time about half have received a AAA rating, while the other half have received AA ratings. In assessing the creditworthiness of these issues, the rating agencies review not only the quality of these assets, but also pay attention to the servicer and its ability to collect the funds due and make advances on behalf of delinquent accounts. Upon receiving the asset and servicer quality, the rating agency sets the level of credit enhancement necessary for the rating desired by the issuer. The credit enhancement is usually provided by a guarantee or repurchase commitment from an entity rated at least equal to the proposed issue. The guarantor then commits to repurchase defaulted receivable contracts at a price equal to their remaining principal balances, up to the maximum amount specified.

SUMMARY

Corporate bonds are fully taxable debt contracts that are usually issued in denominations of $1,000 requiring borrowers to make semiannual payments of interest and repay principal at maturity. Corporate bonds can be registered bonds, where the bond owner is recorded and interest payments and principal payments due are mailed to the owner, or bearer bonds, where coupons are attached and the holder presents them for payment when interest or principal payments come due.

If no assets are pledged, corporate bonds are secured only by the company's potential to generate cash flows and are called debenture bonds. The debentures can be senior debt, giving the owners first priority to the company's assets in the event of default, or subordinated debt, where holders' claims to the firm's assets rank behind senior debt. Also, many bonds have sinking fund provisions and call provisions. With a sinking fund provision, the issuer must retire a portion of the bond as promised in the bond indenture. On the other hand, a call provision is an option of the issuing corporation to retire bonds prior to maturity.

The major investors in corporate bonds are life insurance companies and pension funds. The principal secondary market for corporate bonds is a dealer-made, OTC market that accounts for about 95 percent of all corporate bond trading.

During the 1980s, zero-coupon bonds, high yield (''junk'') bonds, and collateralized mortgage obligations became extremely popular. Real estate mortgage investment conduits were introduced in 1986. They are an improved version of mortgage-backed securities and are designed to minimize the prepayment problems. The wide acceptance by investors of mortgage-backed securities has led recently to other types of asset securitization. Computer leases and automobile loans have already been securitized, while outstanding balances on credit cards or other revolving credit plans, as well as loans for planes and boats, are being considered for future securitization.

CMOs were developed to deal with the uncertainty of the final maturity of GNMA pass-through securities. CMOs are multi-class pay-through bonds that are liabilities to the issuer backed by mortgage collateral. Each bond class, or tranche, in a CMO has a stated maturity date and a fixed coupon rate. The cash flows generated by the mortgage collateral are used to make interest and principal payments on the various tranches of the CMO. Interest payments have priority over principal payments. After all interest payments due have been met, all available cash goes to repay the principal of the first class. Following the retirement of this tranche, all principal payments go to the next tranche in the CMO sequence until that tranche is also retired. The process of sequential payment of principal continues until the last tranche has been paid off. Under these procedures, each class is retired upon the maturity date of that class if there are no prepayments in the collateralized mortgage loans. If principal payments on the collateral occur, some or all of the tranches in the CMO will be retired earlier than the original maturity dates.

The Tax Reform Act of 1986 led to the introduction of mortgage-backed securities vehicles known as a Real Estate Mortgage Investment Conduit, or REMIC. A REMIC is not a new type of mortgage-backed security nor is it a new form of business organization. REMICs are essentially "pass-through" tax entities that can issue mortgage-backed securities, often with multiple maturity classes, under a variety of legal forms. For the most part, REMICs that were issued in 1987 resembled CMOs. The type of collateral used has consisted largely of securities from FNMA, GNMA, and FHLMC.

NOTES

1. J. Loeys, "Low Grade Bonds: A Growing Source of Corporate Funding," Federal Reserve Bank of Philadelphia, *Economic Review* (November/December 1986): 12.

2. Ibid.

3. W. B. Hickman, *Corporate Bond Quality and Investor Experience* (Princeton, N.J.: Princeton University Press, 1958), p. 153.

4. E. I. Altman and S. A. Nammacher, "The Anatomy of the High Yield Debt Market," Morgan Stanley, September 1985 (Table 2).

5. Loeys, "Low Grade Bonds," p. 12.

9

Tax-Exempt Securities

STATE AND LOCAL DEBT

The doctrine of reciprocal tax exemption outlined by Chief Justice Marshall in 1819 in the case of *McCulloch* v. *Maryland* declared that interest income received by investors from the debt securities issued by state and local governments and their agencies is not subject to federal taxation. Not only are holders of municipal bonds not required to pay federal income tax on their interest income, but their interest is also frequently exempt from state and local taxes. For example, residents of New York State are exempt from the payment of state and local taxes on the interest earned on their New York State bonds. The tax-exempt feature permits state and local governments to borrow at interest rates below those available to other types of borrowers, whose interest payments on debt represent taxable income to investors. These tax-exempt securities have a special appeal to high-income individuals, commercial banks, municipal bond funds, and property and casualty insurance companies who account for over 90 percent of the holdings of outstanding municipal securities (see Table 9.1).

Table 9.1 also shows a considerable degree of volatility in the participation rate by banks, households, and property and casualty insurance companies. Bank demand varies as a function of loan demand, tax position, and liquidity levels, while insurance company demand is generally a function of the underwriting cycle and profitability levels, as well as tax position. Households appear to be most sensitive to changes in interest rates and substitute between tax-exempt and taxable bonds on the basis of relative after-tax yields. Households also compare equity yields with tax-exempt rates, although the extent of portfolio switching based on relative yields is much less significant.

VOLUME TRENDS

The dollar volume of new bond and note issues has expanded from $17.3 billion in 1966 to $180 billion in 1985. The issuance of notes or short-term tax-exempt

Table 9.1

State and Local Government Securities (Annual Issuance, Retirements and Net Increases in Amounts Outstanding, Dollars in Billions)

	1981	1982	1983	1984	1985	1986E	1987P	Amt. Out. 31 Dec 86E
Net Increases								
Corporate Purpose	$6.9	$10.1	$7.4	$13.8	$15.6	$1.2	$2.0	
Hospitals, Education, etc.	9.5	16.3	15.6	15.0	45.5	7.2	15.0	
Housing	6.8	15.7	16.8	18.6	34.3	3.6	8.0	
Utility and Public Facilities	8.5	15.1	18.2	27.2	48.4	59.6	32.0	
Other	11.9	20.0	21.0	24.7	40.3	46.0	42.0	
New Bond Issues	43.6	77.2	79.1	99.4	184.1	117.6	99.0	
Less Refundings[a]	2.1	1.3	4.4	8.5	25.3	19.2	11.0	
Less Maturities[b]	18.4	20.7	22.0	23.0	25.1	26.7	28.0	
Less Sinking Fund Purchases[b]	10.0	11.5	13.0	15.0	17.3	19.4	20.0	
Net Increase in Bonds	13.1	43.7	39.7	52.9	116.3	52.4	40.0	$720.5
New Note Issues	34.4	43.4	19.3	22.1	21.8	18.0	22.0	
Less Maturities[b]	33.3	36.7	20.8	25.7	20.5	21.7	16.0	
Net Increase in Notes	1.1	6.7	-1.5	-3.7	1.3	-3.8	6.0	15.1
Bank Loans to State and Local Gov'ts.	4.0	4.0	4.0	17.8	6.8	5.7	8.5	61.0
Total Net Issuance	**$18.2**	**$54.4**	**$42.2**	**$67.0**	**$124.4**	**$54.4**	**$54.5**	**$796.7**
Ownership								
Thrifts	$0.0	$-0.3	$-0.2	$-0.3	$0.6	$1.0	$0.0	$4.4
Insurance and Pensions	4.2	4.2	-0.5	-3.7	3.3	4.4	9.0	102.7
Investment Companies	7.5	29.1	23.1	25.8	49.2	70.7	60.0	232.0
Other Nonbank Finance	0.2	-0.2	0.4	0.6	1.0	0.3	0.5	3.3
Total Nonbank Finance	11.9	32.9	22.7	22.4	54.2	76.4	69.5	342.4
Commercial Banks	5.0	4.5	4.7	10.8	57.2	-5.0	-25.0	226.4
Nonfinancial Corporations	-0.0	0.1	0.7	-0.1	0.8	1.6	4.0	6.5
Residual: Households Direct	1.3	17.0	14.1	34.0	12.1	-18.7	6.0	221.3
Total Ownership	**$18.2**	**$54.4**	**$42.2**	**$67.0**	**$124.4**	**$54.4**	**$54.5**	**$796.7**
Construction Expenditures	46.0	43.7	43.2	47.0	53.5	63.9	66.5	
Housing Finance Issues	7.7	5.2	7.9	10.2	9.8	11.9	3.0	86.1
Corporate Tax-Exempt Bonds	13.4	15.1	9.4	20.5	22.6	-6.3	0.7	120.8
Advance Refundings (Federal)	-0.9	2.7	11.1	7.7	43.1	20.2	13.0	107.7

[a] Omits advance refundings.
[b] Salomon Brothers Inc estimates.

Source: Prospects for Financial Markets in 1987. Salomon Brothers, Inc., December 1986.

securities (final maturity of 13 months or less) generally increases during periods of high or rapidly rising interest rates and declines during periods of low or falling rates. Long-term issues (bonds) have been in a consistent upward trend since 1966 (see Figure 9.1). The record of the past 15 years shows that new issues of tax-exempt bonds have doubled approximately every five years. The average size of new bond issues also increased significantly. However, upon passage of President Reagan's tax reform measures, the volume of municipal bond new issue financing (particularly revenue bonds) (see Figure 9.2) declined dramatically in 1986. On the other hand, talk of federal income tax reform during 1985 threatened to eliminate the tax exclusion for interest on certain types of revenue bonds. This caused a huge flood of financing during 1985 in order to lock in favored tax treatment. The total volume of tax-exempt financing set a record in 1985 compared with previous years.

UNDERWRITING SECURITIES

The new bond issues of well-known cities, states, and state agencies attract bidding syndicates of major underwriters nationwide and are sold nationally. On

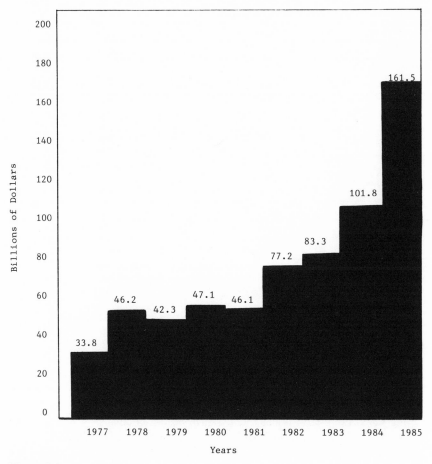

Figure 9.1
Municipal Long-Term Debt Issues

QUARTERLY

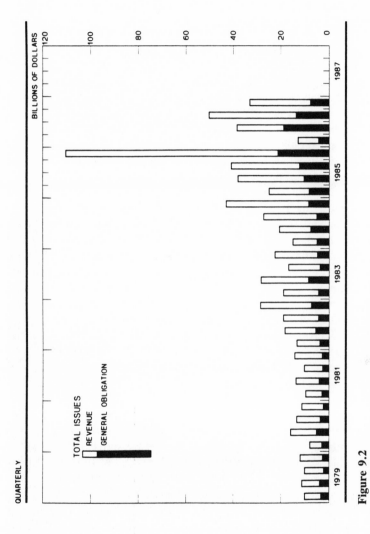

Figure 9.2
Tax-Exempt Bond Issues (Gross Proceeds)

Source: Federal Reserve Chart Book. Washington, D.C.: Federal Reserve Publications Services, February 1987.

the other hand, the primary market usually consists of a large number of relatively small bond issues that are underwritten by small regional dealers in the immediate locale of the issuing municipality. The reason for the existence of local markets is related to the high cost of gathering information about smaller issues and the tax exemption from local as well as federal taxes on interest earned from these bonds.

Most new tax-exempt issues are sold to underwriting syndicates, although some states and municipalities have sold bonds directly to the public. Underwriters may be investment bankers and/or commercial banks, with syndicates ranging from a single firm to 100 firms. The syndicate purchases the entire issue from the issuer and attempts to resell the bonds to investors. The issuer of the bonds can select underwriters by negotiating as is the case with most revenue bonds, or by competitive bidding as is the case with most general obligation bonds. Revenue bonds are limited obligation bonds secured by special user charges and not by general taxing power, while general obligation bonds are secured by the full faith and taxing power of the governmental unit.

In competitive bidding, issuers receive bids from competing underwriting syndicates and award the bonds to the syndicate with the lowest interest cost bid. In negotiation, the underwriting syndicate is selected in advance of the sale date. The terms of the bond issue are negotiated between the syndicate and the issuer.

The compensation received by underwriters is called a spread, which is the difference between the price at which bonds are sold to investors and the price received by the issuer of the bonds. This spread ranges between one half of 1 percent and 2.5 percent of the total value of the issue, or $5 to $25 per $1,000 bond. The spread is subdivided into expenses incurred by underwriters for legal fees, advertising, travel expenses, computer costs, a management fee for organizing and structuring the actual syndicate operations, the concession that is paid to underwriters and dealers and their sales people for the selling of the bonds, and an underwriting profit that is distributed among the syndicate members in proportion to the participation of each firm.

Gross spreads, the income derived by investment firms for underwriting a tax-exempt issue, fell an average of 30 percent in 1986 from 1985 and 38 percent from 1984 according to Securities Data Co. The average spread of a $10 to $50 million tax-exempt issue fell from $25.65 per $1,000 bond in 1984 to $22.46 in 1985 and to $17.66 by the end of 1986. The spreads for larger issues were equally lower. The decline in underwriting spreads demonstrates that the municipal bond market is becoming more efficient and more competitive.

Merrill Lynch, Goldman Sachs, First Boston, Kidder Peabody, E. F. Hutton, Salomon Brothers, Smith Barney, and Paine Webber were the largest underwriters of municipal bonds and notes during 1985. These firms participated in bringing to market between 285 and 610 issues during that year (see Table 9.2).

The issuer takes the responsibility of securing a credit rating from one of the bond rating agencies, and prepares an official statement or prospectus of information necessary for underwriters and investors to gauge the investment merits

Table 9.2
The Municipal Underwriting Leaders

A summary of the top firms according to *Institutional Investor*'s bonus-credit-to-lead-manager ranking method.

1984	1985		$ Volume (millions)	No. of Issues
1	1	Merrill Lynch	$13,554.0	610
6	2	Goldman Sachs	10,234.4	331
9	3	First Boston	8,353.6	229
5	4	Kidder, Peabody	8,237.3	424
2	5	E.F. Hutton	8,156.3	407
3	6	Salomon Brothers	8,155.0	345
7[1]	7	Shearson Lehman Brothers	7,927.3	349
4	8	Smith Barney, Harris Upham	7,476.6	285
8	9	Paine Webber	7,452.8	363
13	10	Morgan Stanley	4,088.9	131
[2]	11	Drexel Burnham Lambert	3,873.7	210
12	12	Bear Stearns	3,531.5	175
10	13	Prudential-Bache Securities	3,320.4	199
16	14	Rauscher Pierce Refsnes	2,315.0	118
—	15	Matthews & Wright	2,176.8	76
14	16	L.F. Rothschild, Unterberg, Towbin	2,036.8	147
11	17	Dean Witter Reynolds	2,022.7	150
21	18	John Nuveen	1,899.9	97
—	19	Donaldson, Lufkin & Jenrette	1,874.0	86
15	20	Dillon Read	1,822.1	85
17	21	Miller & Schroeder	1,709.0	94
19	22	Howard, Weil, Labouisse, Friedrichs	1,554.2	66
—	23	Citicorp	1,546.5	100
22	24	Underwood, Neuhaus	1,373.7	70
—	25	Russell Rea & Zappala	1,341.3	44

[1] *Includes Robinson-Humphrey.*
[2] *Drexel Burnham Lambert, 20; Kirchner Moore, —*

Source: Institutional Investor.

of the bonds. The underwriter specifies the coupons and yields necessary to sell the bonds and the dollar amount to be paid to the issuer for the bond issue.

The risk-bearing services include the uncertainty faced by the underwriting syndicate over the price at which these securities can be sold to markets once the issue has been purchased at a fixed price. The inventory risk is lower for negotiated issues than for competitive issues because in the negotiated sale the underwriter can engage in substantial presale marketing efforts. Presale marketing does take place in competitive bidding, but there is less incentive for underwriters to perform these services because there is uncertainty as to whether they will win the bid. Distribution services are independent of the method of sale, be it competitive or negotiated. They include the costs involved in selling and delivering bonds to investors.

THE SECONDARY MARKET

The secondary market is an over-the-counter market. The Blue List of Current Municipal Offerings, a daily financial publication that carries a listing of bonds offered for sale by about 700 dealers and banks, is the most complete source of information on volume and activity in the municipal bond market.

Although the bonds of some states and cities do have active secondary markets, small local issues are traded infrequently. Local brokerage firms and banks made markets in these securities. The bottom line is that the municipal market is not as liquid as the Treasury market. It can sometimes be difficult to sell issues of large size ($25 million or more) and the spread between bid and asked prices can be large. The large spreads are also the result of the relatively inactive secondary market for lesser known municipal bonds and the difficulty in matching buyers and sellers of these issues. The difference between the dealer's bid and asked price ranges from as low as 25 basis points on large blocks of actively traded bonds to 400 basis points for odd lots of inactive issues. The average spread for retail investors is approximately 200 basis points, while the average spread rarely exceeds 50 basis points for institutional investors. In the municipal market, an odd lot of bonds is $25,000 or less in par value for retail investors. On the other hand, an odd lot is anything below $100,000 for institutional investors.

There do exist municipal bond brokers who serve as intermediaries in the sale of blocks of municipal bonds among dealers and large institutional investors. These brokers are primarily located in New York and include J. J. Kenny, Titus and Donnelly, Chapedelaine & Co., and Drake & Co., among others.

SECURITIES FEATURES

General obligation bonds are backed by the ability of the municipality, city, or state to levy *ad valorem* taxes on all taxable real property. The bonds are repayable from the general revenues provided from such taxes as well as from other available revenues and are backed by a pledge of full faith and credit and taxing power of the issuer.

Revenue bonds are payable entirely from revenue received from the users or beneficiaries of the projects financed. Examples of these might include utility revenue bonds, mortgage-backed revenue bonds, and limited-liability special tax bonds that might be used to finance state highway or construction, bridges, ports, airports, parking garages, state university dormitories, hospitals, and so on. Fees and user charges for services provided furnish the revenues available for meeting both interest and principal payments on the bonds. Under the lease-rental bond approach, public borrowing entities issue tax-exempt bonds and use the proceeds to construct facilities that are then leased to other governmental units, to private enterprises, or to nonprofit groups. Lease-rental payments are pledged to cover the borrower's debt service requirements. Mortgage revenue bonds are typically issued by state finance agencies, by cities and countries, as well as by local housing agencies in order to purchase pools of mortgages. Mortgage loan repayments are used to meet the debt service requirements. Housing authority bonds are issued by local authorities to finance low-rent housing projects. These bonds are secured by the pledge of unconditional, annual contributions by the Housing Assistance Administration, a U.S. government agency.

The recent trend toward larger yield spreads on revenue bonds has occurred in tandem with a marked shift in the type of financing from tax-supported debt to revenue bonds. These new financings can be highly complex and generally have higher yields than those of similarly rated general obligation bonds of the same maturity.

Moral obligation bonds are primarily secured by project revenues and have the moral pledge of a state to make up any deficiency in the capital reserve fund of the issuer in the event that revenues are insufficient to cover debt service. That pledge is not legally binding. Pollution control bonds are tax-free municipals issued by local authorities but supported by corporations using the pollution control facilities financed by the bonds.

Investors can also purchase option tender bonds. These bonds combine a rare degree of liquidity in the tax-exempt market with yields above those of short-term, tax-exempt instruments. Although issued as long-term bonds with maturities between 20 and 30 years, these issues are really short-term notes for a number of reasons. The interest rate is adjusted periodically to reflect changes in the prevailing interest rates. The bond owner has the option of accepting the new rate or tending the bond to the trustee for payment at par value plus accrued interest.

In addition to being able to purchase shares in a mutual fund holding tax-exempt notes or bonds, investors can participate in a unit trust. A unit trust is a diversified portfolio of tax-free bonds in which one unit represents a pro rata ownership of each of the bonds in the trust. The investor can choose from long-term, intermediate-term, short-term, insured, and unit trusts that are free of state and sometimes local taxes.

A super sinker is a maturity for a single-family housing revenue bond issue in which all funds from early mortgage prepayments are used to retire the bonds. A super sinker has a long stated maturity but a shorter uncertain actual life. Investors have the chance to realize a return that is priced as if it had a maturity considerably longer than its anticipated life. This is advantageous to investors when the yield curve has a positive slope.

Long-term municipal issues are usually sold as serial bonds as opposed to term bonds. Serial bonds have a predetermined series of bonds maturing each year until final maturity, while term bonds are repaid in full at one terminal maturity date. In a serial bond issue, when a portion of principal is retired each year, the default risk might be lower because the issuer is forced to have capital available each year for repayment instead of waiting until maturity to repay the entire issue. Serialization is believed to aid the initial marketing of the bonds since many financial institutions like to stagger the maturity distribution of their bond portfolios over a number of years. The issuer can sell part of the issue with a given maturity to an institution that desires more bonds of that particular maturity.

MUNICIPAL BOND YIELDS

The basic factor determining the interest rate on the sale of new municipal bonds is the current market yield on bonds of similar quality, maturity, and liquidity. During the early 1980s state and local governments had to pay high interest rates—rates they may be locked into when interest rates decline, making them unable to pay off previous high cost debt or to sell new bonds at lower interest costs.

In response to this problem, state and local borrowers used to issue refunding bonds to pay off old debt. Proceeds from the sale of refunding bonds are used to pay off old debt at its earliest call date. Such funds were frequently invested in the purchase of special nonmarketable Treasury securities with maturities matching those of the first call date on the debt to be refunded. Interest rate earnings on these special Treasuries were above those paid by borrowers on their new debt, reducing the issuer's borrowing costs and offsetting the cost of the call premium. After the call and redemption of the older debt, the new lower cost debt remained. Both general obligation and revenue bonds may be repaid at the earliest call date by the issuing of refunding bonds. The financial aspect to be covered is the yield on municipal securities. The federal tax exemption of interest earned on municipal securities is an important factor in the evaluation of municipal yields. For the issuer, the tax-exempt status of the interest paid on municipal securities does not increase the yield payable. For the bond's owner who pays federal income taxes, such a bond has a taxable equivalent yield higher than the actual interest stated on the bond. The taxable equivalent yield is the gross yield that, before applicable income taxes, would provide the same interest paid on a taxable bond. For example, an investor who pays taxes at the rate of 28 percent of taxable income would have to earn a 12.5 percent gross yield on a taxable bond to realize a net or after-tax yield equal to the 9 percent yield for a tax-exempt municipal.

The taxable equivalent yield for municipals is found by using the following formula:

$$\text{Taxable Equivalent Yield} = \frac{\text{Nominal Tax-Free Yield}}{1 - \text{Marginal Tax Rate}}$$
(as a decimal)

Assume that a commercial bank pays a marginal tax rate of 34 percent. The taxable equivalent yield of a 9 percent tax-exempt bond would be 13.63 percent. A comparison of the two taxable equivalent yields—12.5 on a 9 percent bond at a 28 percent marginal tax rate and 13.63 on a 9 percent bond at a 34 percent marginal tax rate—shows an important feature of municipals. The higher the marginal tax rate, the greater the advantage of the tax exemption. It is obvious for those in high tax brackets that municipals offer substantial yield benefits.

The spread between yields on municipals and other types of debt is not constant but fluctuates in response to changing factors, including supply and demand. Most major shifts in yield spreads are the result of changes in supply and demand for amount of investable funds held by the principal owners of municipals, changes in the highest personal tax rates, and changes in the perceived risk of individual issues. Even proposals to remove the tax exemption or to change tax rates may cause the yield spread to narrow or widen.

While the yield curve can have a positive, flat, or negative slope for taxable securities, the yield curve for municipal bonds has a positive slope. The positive slope of the municipal yield curve is usually greater than that for U.S. government securities, that is, yield spreads between maturities are usually wider in the tax-free market than in the Treasury market.

The differences in yield between municipal bonds with different credit ratings are not constant over time. The spread between the A-rated and AAA-rated 30-year general obligation bonds has ranged from 30 to 160 basis points between 1973 and 1986, while the spread between AAA and BAA bonds has ranged from 50 to 185 basis points.

The changes in spreads related to ratings can be explained by the outlook for the economy, federal budget financing needs, and municipal market supply and demand factors as well as changes in the tax laws. When interest rates are low investors often increase their holdings of low credit rated bonds in order to obtain higher yields. Also, during periods in which market participants anticipate a poor economic climate, there is a "flight to quality," as investors pursue a more conservative credit risk posture. There are occasional conditions of oversupply in certain market sectors that impact spreads. In a weak market, it is easier for high grade municipals to come to market than for weaker credits. High grade issues flood markets, while at the same time creating a scarcity of low and medium grade issues. These factors tend to decrease the quality spread between high grade and lower grade bonds.

The spreads between corporate and municipal bonds also tend to fluctuate. These spreads are often a function of tax rates, interest rates and supply and demand for these particular securities. For example, yields on long-term AAA general obligation municipal bonds averaged 70 percent of the yields on AAA corporate bonds between 1970 and 1984. However, with a change in tax rates, municipal yields were 82 and 74 percent of corporate bond yields in mid-1985 and year-end 1986, respectively.

The ratio of municipal bond to corporate bond yields exhibits considerable variability, part of which takes the form of explainable short-term cyclical movements. While the supply of municipal bonds typically rises at a steady rate each year, demand is continually changing in composition because of the influence of profitability and tax factors and of other capital markets on municipal bond investors.

OTHER TYPES OF MUNICIPAL BONDS

Lease Secured Bonds

Lease secured bonds are backed by a pledge of fixed dollar amount by a party other than the issuer to make payments to the issuer over the life of the bonds to cover principal and interest requirements on the tax-exempt bonds. Normally, the payment is made pursuant to a lease and trust agreement. Frequently, the lessee's credit background is far superior to that of the issuer.

"Double Barreled" Bonds

Double barreled is a term applied to tax-exempt bonds that are backed by a pledge of two or more sources of payment. For example, some special assessment or special tax bonds are additionally backed by the full faith, credit, and taxing power of the issuer. Similarly, one occasionally finds a bond secured by the joint and several pledges of more than one party, any of which would give adequate protection.

Housing Bonds

Housing bonds are revenue issues secured by mortgage repayments on homes and rental buildings. They are issued by both state and local housing authorities. A first mortgage on the property and reserve funds may provide additional backing. Sometimes federal subsidies for lower income families (sections 8 and 2361, plus FHA insurance, VA guarantees, and private mortgage insurance) add extra protection. New or Public Housing Authority Bonds (PHABS) are no longer issued, but are still available in the secondary market. They are backed by the full faith and credit of the U.S. government.

Project Notes

Project notes are short-term, tax-exempt notes issued to finance urban renewal projects or low income housing projects. Project notes are binding and valid obligations of the local issuing agency that are fully secured by a pledge of the full faith and credit of the United States.

Authority and Agency Bonds

Authorities and agencies are created by states or their subdivisions to perform specific functions, such as the operation of water, sewer, electric systems, bridges, tunnels, or highways, and, in some states, to construct schools or public facilities. In some cases, the authority has the right to levy fees and charges for its services. In others, it receives lease rentals that may be payable from specific revenues or may be general obligations of the lease.

Limited and Special Tax Bonds

Limited and special tax bonds are payable from a pledge of the proceeds derived by the issuer from a specific tax such as an *ad valorem* tax levied at a fixed rate, a gasoline tax, or a special assessment. Sometimes, a bond is secured by the first $250,000 annually of a special tax, thereby giving unusual ability to the bond to withstand a weakened economy.

Territorial Bonds

Territorial bonds are issued by U.S. territorial possessions such as Guam, Puerto Rico, and the Virgin Islands, and are tax exempt throughout most of the United States.

Troubled City Bailout Bonds

Troubled city bailout bonds were created to bail out underlying general obligation bonds issuers from severe budget deficits, for example, the State of Illinois Chicago School Finance Authority Bonds and the New York State Municipal Assistance Corporation for the City of New York Bonds (MAC). Although these bonds appear to be structured as revenue bonds, revenues actually come from general purpose taxes and revenue.

PROFILE OF MUNICIPAL BOND HOLDERS

There has been a progressive change in the profile of municipal securities holders. Although individuals, investment companies, and commercial banks are the dominant holders of municipal bonds, property-casualty companies also have large holdings (see Table 9.1). The share of municipal bonds held by banks has declined from about 51 percent of outstandings in the early 1970s to about 29 percent in 1986. The large decline in the bank share over the years reflects bank expansion into leveraged leasing activities, growing lending subject to foreign tax credits, reduced earnings performance over the last year or so among some of the largest banks, increased loan loss provisions, and the reduction in federal tax deductions on municipal securities purchased by financial institutions since January 1, 1983.

With the exception of 1985, when bank demand for municipal bonds ballooned because of a provision in the House of Representatives' tax reform bill that would eliminate the deductibility of the carrying costs on tax-exempt instruments purchased after December 31, 1985, banks have played a leading role in the tax-exempt market during the early 1980s. In 1981, 1982, 1983, and 1984 commercial banks' net purchases of tax exempts represented only 21.3, 9.8, 6.7, and 19.0 percent, respectively, of the total net issuance of tax-exempt instruments. The Tax Reform Act of 1986 should only accelerate the withdrawal of commercial banks from the tax-exempt market.

Property-casualty insurance companies have traditionally purchased long-term tax-exempt bonds, with a preference toward higher yielding revenue rather than general obligation bonds. However, between 1983 and 1985, property-casualty companies have been only a minor factor in the tax-exempt market because of large underwriting losses that have led to negative taxable income for the industry as a whole. Consequently, the industry actually reduced its holdings of tax-exempt securities in 1983 and 1984 and purchased a modest net $2 billion in 1985. But as the underwriting cycle improved during 1985 and 1986, property-casualty insurance companies began to increase their purchases of municipal bonds. Despite the lackluster purchases of municipal bonds during 1983–1985, the share of total outstanding municipal bonds going to property-casualty companies has risen from 10 percent in 1967 to approximately 13 percent in early 1986. During the best years of the underwriting cycle (1976–1980), the share had risen to net purchases of 37.4 percent.

On the other hand, individuals became more active buyers as relatively high tax-free interest rates made municipal bonds attractive. Many individual purchases were made through investments in tax-exempt mutual funds in 1985 and 1986 instead of by direct purchase. Also, the availability of insured municipal bonds and insured tax-free investment trusts have attracted additional individual investors into the marketplace.

Following a number of municipal bond defaults, the area of bond credit research has come into its own in the past decade and a half. A key reason for this fact is that credit rating assignments have changed between the late 1960s and the early 1980s. For example, Detroit Edison and Boston Edison were AAA-rated credits in 1968 whose credit ratings had slipped to Baa/BBB by 1983. Over the course of the 1968–1983 period, there were upwards of 200 rating changes per year, the majority of which represented downgradings.

THE RATING AGENCIES

There are three credit rating agencies that evaluate municipal bonds: Moody's Investors Service, Standard & Poor's Corporation, and Fitch Publishing Company. These agencies are concerned with the ability of the borrower to repay.

They evaluate (1) the economic base of the issuer, (2) the financial condition of the governmental units, (3) administrative factors such as tax assessment and collection systems, budgeting practices, and the contingent costs of possible litigation, and (4) the debt burden.

Municipal Debt Rating Definitions

Aaa/AAA. Bonds rated Aaa/AAA are judged to be of the best quality. They carry the smallest degree of investment risk and are generally referred to as "gilt edge." Interest payments are protected by a large or by an exceptionally stable margin and principal is secure. While the various protective elements are likely to change, such changes as can be visualized are most unlikely to impair the fundamentally strong position of such issues.

Aa/AA. Bonds rated Aa/AA are judged to be of high quality by all standards. Together with the Aaa group they comprise what are generally known as high grade bonds. They are rated lower than the best bonds because margins of protection may not be as large as in Aaa securities or fluctuation of protective elements may be of greater amplitude or there may be other elements present which make the long-term risks appear somewhat larger than in the Aaa securities.

A/A. Bonds rated A/A possess many favorable investment attributes and are to be considered as upper medium grade obligations. Factors giving security to principal and interest are considered adequate but elements may be present that suggest a susceptibility to impairment sometime in the future.

Baa/BBB. Bonds rated Baa/BBB are considered as medium grade obligations, that is, they are neither highly protected nor poorly secured. Interest payments and principal security appear adequate for the present but certain protective elements may be lacking or may be characteristically unreliable over any great length of time. Such bonds lack outstanding investment characteristics and, in fact, have speculative characteristics as well.

Ba/BB. Bonds rated Ba/BB are judged to have speculative elements, their future cannot be considered as well assured. Often, the protection of interest and principal payments may be very moderate and thereby not well safeguarded during both good and bad times over the future. Uncertainty of position characterizes bonds in this class.

B/B. Bonds rated B/B generally lack characteristics of the desirable investment. Assurance of interest and principal payments or of maintenance of other terms of the contract over any long period of time may be small.

Caa/CCC. Bonds rated Caa/CCC are of poor standing. Such issues may be in default or there may be present elements of danger with respect to principal or interest.

Ca/CC. Bonds rated Ca/CC represent obligations that are highly speculative. Such issues are often in default or have other marked shortcomings.

C/C. Bonds rated C/C are the lowest rated class of bonds and issues. C/C-rated bonds can be regarded as having extremely poor prospects of even attaining any real investment standing.

RETAIL MARKET FOR TAX-EXEMPT BONDS

The municipal bond market is a dual market consisting of institutional investors and retail investors. Commercial banks and property-casualty insurance companies, as well as tax-exempt municipal bond funds, are the largest buyers and sellers in blocks of between 250 and 1,000 bonds. A relatively small number of well-capitalized dealers bid on blocks of bonds that institutional investors wish to sell. The dealers then offer those bonds for sale from their own inventories to their institutional investors. Salomon Brothers, Goldman Sachs, and Merrill Lynch are among the largest institutional municipal bond dealers.

The retail market for tax-exempt bonds is characterized by a large number of brokers seeking to buy and sell for individual investors. Retail market transactions are typically for 5 to 100 bonds. The salient determinants of the structure of the retail market are the existence of a larger number of small municipal debt issues and the fact that the tax-free interest payments are attractive to a large number of individuals in high income tax brackets.

The retail municipal bond market is primarily a brokered rather than a dealer market. Many of the bonds trade infrequently because they are part of relatively small issues. An investor is likely to obtain a more favorable price by selling through a broker to another investor rather than to a dealer because the dealer may not be able to sell them immediately.

When an investor wants to sell a small block of tax-free bonds in the retail market, he will usually instruct the bond firm to act as a broker to locate a compatible trading partner. The broker might call several other brokers, use the Blue List or the Kenny wire.

The Blue List of municipal bonds, published daily by Standard & Poor's, contains lists of bonds brokers want advertised for sale. The offerings are arranged by state, by issuer, by specific bond, maturity, coupon, the yield to maturity at which the bonds are being offered for sale, and the broker making the offering. The potential buyers call the offering broker directly and try to negotiate a transaction price.

The value of the Blue List is impaired by its lack of timeliness because the offering yield on a bond can change between the time the yield is submitted for the Blue List and the time in which an inquiry is made. Also, the Blue List has no facility for completing transactions, it only provides a means for brokers to advertise offerings of bonds, as actual transactions must be negotiated directly between buyer and seller. The Kenny wire, sponsored by New York broker-dealer J. J. Kenny and Co., is an electronic auction of offerings of municipal bonds, identifying the offering and the size of the issue. Kenny places the offering details onto a computer that drives a network of teletype terminals in the offices of close to 700 banks and municipal bond firms throughout the country. A participant in the Kenny wire auction may bid before 4 p.m. on any offering in the system. At 4 p.m., Kenny identifies the highest bid on an offering and calls the original offerer to see if that bid is acceptable. There is a difference between the Kenny wire and the Garban Treasury securities electronic quotation system. Garban shows Treasury securities offered at firm prices. If a participant chooses to buy, the offerer must sell at his offering price. However, with the Kenny wire, firms are invited to bid for the offered bonds. The seller has no obligation to accept a bid.

MUNICIPAL BOND INSURANCE

From virtual insignificance a decade ago, third party guaranteed municipals have become an important factor in the tax-free market, accounting for more than 40 percent of all newly issued tax-exempt debt in 1985. Most of these issues carry AAA ratings from one or both of the major rating agencies. However, investors should understand that bond ratings with the exception of perhaps that of the U.S. government are neither absolute nor permanent. The AAA ratings of insurance companies and financial institutions, like those of cities and states, are subject to both interpretation and change.

The best known and most widely used form of third party guarantee is bond insurance that provides an irrevocable lifetime guarantee of principal and interest. Insured bonds accounted for about 23 percent of the tax-free new issue volume in 1985.

Bank letters of credit (LOCs) are the second major form of municipal bond guarantee, capturing 12 percent of all newly issued tax-exempt debt in 1985. An LOC is a line of credit held by a bond trustee for use in the event of default. While insurers continue to pay interest on the maturity, bank LOC agreements usually require trustees to redeem defaulted issues immediately at par. Also, bank LOCs rarely run longer than 10 years. Issuers of longer-term LOC-backed bonds are required to either renew their LOCs after 10 years or redeem their bonds. Letters of credit backing municipals range in quality from A2 (Bank of America) to Aaa (Morgan Guaranty). Downgradings in the ratings of most U.S. commercial banks have reduced most domestic LOC ratings to Aa, while most Japanese banks maintain their AAA ratings.

As a matter of fact, foreign bank LOCs accounted for over half of all bank guarantees of municipals. While insurance companies insist that they are not in the business of enhancing poor credits but rather in the business of arbitraging the disparity between the cost of insurance and the spread between high grade and medium grade credits, banks take a different approach. Bank LOCs are frequently designed to help them win new business, to protect existing loans, to assist clients (for example, builders and contractors) in obtaining tax-free financing. For this reason, and because of the slightly lower ratings carried by the banks, bank LOC-backed municipals tend to yield more than other third party guaranteed tax frees, as much as 50 basis points more than Aaa insured bonds.

A third category of third party guaranteed bonds are collateralized issues, which are secured by assets whose value exceeds the outstanding face value of a bond issue. The most common examples are housing or mortgage issues backed by bank CDs or insurance company ''guaranteed investment'' contracts (GICs), whose interest and principal payments exactly match debt service requirements on the bonds they secure. Some collateralized issues use marketable securities to provide security. For example, university and hospital bonds are often backed by operating revenues of the issuing institutions and are further secured by endowment portfolios with a value exceeding that of the bond's face value by 110 or 120 percent.

There are various mortgage insurance policies used to facilitate the sale of housing issues. These policies are only as good as the organizations that write them, which range from the FHA (Aaa rating) to Ticor Mortgage Insurance Co. (Ccc rating). These insurers guarantee timely payment of principal and interest of the mortgages that underlie housing bond issues. They do not directly guarantee interest or principal on tax-free mortgage bonds.

The availability of bond insurance from private insurers such as MBIA and AMBAC has proved to be quite attractive to both investors and issuers. It is interesting to note that AMBAC is now 85 percent owned by Citibank. Four of the world's strongest insurance companies guarantee bonds issued by MBIA in predetermined proportions. Members of the Municipal Bond Insurance Association are Fireman's Fund Insurance, Aetna Life and Casualty, Continental Insurance, and Aetna (a subsidiary of CIGNA). In late May 1987, MBIA announced plans for an initial public offering of common stock. Proceeds of the stock offering will be divided among those four companies that are liquidating about 15 percent of their holdings. MBIA will not receive any proceeds from the sale. If a participating insurance company chooses to withdraw from MBIA at some future date, its existing liabilities remain in force. The insurance companies guarantee the payment of interest and principal on insured bonds. Retail investors have been willing to give up yield for insurance protection to help sell issues that might face some marketing difficulty or to broaden their marketability. Issuers have also sought insurance coverage in order to cut their costs of debt service since the cost of insurance is less than the savings to the municipality from lower interest rates on the bonds. Both individual issues and entire portfolios can be insured. The marketplace gives the insurance a lot of weight as evidenced by the fact that yields on insured issues are between 15 and 100 basis points lower (net of insurance premiums that average about 25 basis points) than on noninsured issues with similar financial ratios.

Another form of insurance has been a bank letter of credit standing behind a bond. Moody's has given an AAA rating to insured bonds, while Standard & Poor's rates insured bonds on their underlying credit rating without taking into account the insurance protection. In evaluating such bonds, the rating services consider not only the issuer's debt servicing capacity but also the resources of the insuring organization. It should be noted that as of this writing, MBIA has never faced a default on a bond, while AMBAC has made good on their guarantee on a dozen occasions. MBIA has concentrated on insuring individual municipal bond issues, while AMBAC has concentrated on insuring entire portfolios of municipal bonds, particularly tax-free unit investment trusts. In addition to MBIA, AMBAC, FGIC, and BIG, Guaranty Holdings Corporation and Enhance Reinsurance have entered the market to offer the reinsurance of municipal bonds. Another participant is Capital Guaranty Insurance, whose officers previously operated the financial guarantee business of USF&G. This company assumed the $1.2 billion portfolio of insurance policies previously written by USF&G. They will concentrate on writing primary insurance on tax-exempt and taxable securites. Industrial Insurance Corp., Continental Casualty Corp., and Industrial Development Bond Insurance Co. are other insurers of municipal bonds (see Table 9.3). Although insured municipal bonds are practically all rated AAA by

Table 9.3
Municipal Insurers

Primary Insurer	Current Ownership
Municipal Bond Insurance Association (MBIA)	Aetna Casualty & Surety Co.; Fireman's Fund Insurance Co.; Travelers Idemnity Co.; Aetna Insurance Co.; Continental Insurance Co.
Financial Guaranty Insurance Co. (FGIC)	Merrill Lynch & Co. Inc.; Shearson Lehman/American Express Inc.; General Electric Credit Corp.; General Re Corp.; Lumbermens Mutual Casualty Co.; J.P. Morgan & Co. Inc; Public Stockholders
Bond Investors Guaranty Insurance (BIG)	American International Group Inc.; Bankers Trust New York Corp; (GEICO); Philbro-Salomon Inc,; Xerox Credit Corp.
AMBAC Indemity Corp.	Citibank, N.A.; Xerox Financial Services; Stephens Inc.; AMBAC management
Financial Security Assurance	Group of 26 investors including: Equitable Society of the United States; Ford Motor Credit Co.; John Hancock Mutual Life Insurance Co.; New England Mutual Life Insurance Co.
Capital Guaranty Corp.	Constellation Investments Inc.; Fleet Financial Group Inc.; Norstar Bancorp; Safeco Corp.; Sibag Finance Corp.; U.S. Fidelity & Guaranty Co.
Monoline Reinsurer	**Current Ownership**
Enhance Reinsurance Co.	Group of investors including: Manufacturers Life Insurance Co.; Merrill Lynch & Co.; Commonwealth Bank of Australia; Midlantic Bank

the rating agencies, the bonds sell and trade at yields between AA- and AAA-rated bonds.

The amount of insured municipal debt has increased since its inception. The par amount of insured debt increased substantially to $47 billion in 1985 from $12 billion in 1983. Insured municipal bonds represented close to 23 percent of long-term municipal debt in 1985. The growth of bond insurance in part reflects its appeal to some investors and issuers. An important boost in investor demand came after the well-publicized default of Washington Public Power Supply units 4 and 5, as well as the complexity of bond financings (see Figure 9.3).

For issuers, interest rate savings can be substantial when interest rates are high and the spread between AAA rating and the actual debt rating on the issue is large. However, when rates are low, the value of bond insurance is reduced as the yield differential between lower investment grade and the AAA rating is compressed.

MUNICIPAL BANKRUPTCIES

Washington Public Power Supply System (WPPSS), commonly known as "Whoops," defaulted on $2.25 billion worth of bonds related to uncompleted nuclear power plants 4 and 5. This was the largest municipal default in history. In a surprising court ruling, the Washington State Supreme Court ruled that 88 utilities were not required to help pay off WPPSS bonds sold to finance the aforementioned two nuclear power plants that were canceled in early 1982. The utilities had signed contracts obligating them to pay for the plants if they were never completed. The state court ruled that the utilities lacked the authority to enter into such agreements. The federal government, through the Bonneville Power Administration (BPA) has a major stake. The BPA sells the power output of federally owned dams in the Northwest to utilities. The participating utilities have assigned their share in WPPSS projects numbers 1, 2, and 3 to the BPA, which is responsible for meeting its creditors. The BPA provided the $150 million to finish number 2, while it has refused to help WPPSS obtain the bank credit line it needs for number 3 (74 percent complete). Work on number 1 (63 percent complete) was suspended in 1982.

Municipal bankruptcies are rare and the legal implications of a massive one such as WPPSS are unclear. In the wake of WPPSS, municipalities will be pressured for financial disclosure. Also, more bonds will be insured against default, potentially increasing the cost to the issuer. The rating agencies and Wall Street firms will expand their municipal bond research staffs. There are also negative implications for the cost and availability of municipal financing that could spread throughout the tax-exempt market, especially in the Pacific Northwest. Many other electric power bonds are backed by such "take or pay contracts" that are in effect for WPPSS plants numbers 1, 2, and 3. Brokerage firms and the supply system itself are bracing for a possible avalanche of lawsuits from debt holders. The property-casualty industry, tax-exempt bond funds and trusts,

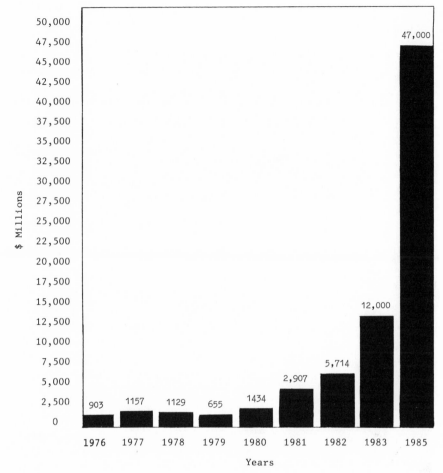

Figure 9.3
New Issue Insurance Par Value Long-Term Municipal Bonds

as well as individuals were among the largest holders. The default has robbed thousands of investors of their savings, shaken confidence in the municipal bond market, angered and humiliated the people in the Northwest, and tarnished the reputations of some of Wall Street's leading institutions. The only beneficiaries may be law firms collecting fees from the anticipated lawsuits that could clog the courts for years.

Defaults on tax-exempt municipal bonds like those issued by WPPSS have been relatively infrequent and have usually involved small sums. Only 685 defaults have occurred since 1940, out of 301,020 municipal bond issues. In terms of money lost, each of the three largest was around one-twentieth the size of the WPPSS loss. The West Virginia Turnpike Commission defaulted on $133 million in bonds in 1958. Chicago's Calumet Skyway defaulted on indebtedness of $101 million in 1963, while the Chesapeake Bay Bridge and Tunnel Commission reneged on $100 million worth of bonds in 1948.

New York City's near miss in 1975 does not count as a default, at least technically, because the city secured moratoriums on short-term interest payments until it could again start paying its creditors. If the Big Apple had defaulted, it would have been slightly ahead of the WPPSS record at $2.4 billion.

Until the WPPSS debacle, the biggest bond defaults had come in the private sector. The Penn Central ran out of cash in June 1970, forcing it into what remains America's biggest bankruptcy: $3 billion in liabilities, including $1 billion worth of bonds.

Crises of municipal credits in the 1970s were associated with short-term debt issues such as the New York State Urban Development Corporation. BANs defaulted in 1975, when the market was unwilling to accept long-term bond issues backed by project revenues of dubious magnitude. A de facto default also took place on notes maturing in the same year by New York City because short-term borrowings had been used to fund years of operating deficits as an alternative to raising taxes or reducing government spending. Also, the city of Cleveland defaulted on notes issued in 1978 when investors' concern about Cleveland's credit quality and financial practices closed the door to further bond financing.

Although municipal bond ratings have been for the most part reliable indicators of credit quality, they are not foolproof, as can be seen in the default of two Washington Power Supply System bonds in 1983 after the bonds had received an investment grade rating. Following this default, investors have shown greater concern over bonds secured by legally untested structures and to sources of cash flow that will be used to pay off interest and principal on the bonds.

INVESTOR RED FLAGS

There have been a number of well-publicized failures of municipal bonds in the 1970s and 1980s. This followed a lengthy period where the measure of safety had been considered second only to that of U.S. Treasury bonds. In analyzing the creditworthiness of either a general obligation or revenue bond, the investor must make inquiries into (1) the legal documents and opinions, (2) the politics, (3) the management, (4) the underwriter, (5) the financial adviser, (6) the local and national economies and general credit indicators, and (7) red flags, or danger signals. Many institutional investors have learned to judge issuers by the company they keep, that is, they are more comfortable with financial information provided by established financial advisers and underwriters and legal work provided by established law firms who have recognized reputations for honesty.

The debt quality of revenue authorities is measured in a manner similar to corporate debt quality, with particular emphasis on the income of the authority relative to its debt service requirements. In the case of tunnel, bridge, or highway revenue bonds those issues that have defaulted have done so because of unexpected competition from toll-free bridges or roads, highly inaccurate traffic projections, or a substantial underestimate of construction costs. For example, investors in toll road, bridge, or tunnel revenue bonds would like answers to the following types of questions:

1. What is the traffic history?
2. How inelastic is the demand?
3. Can the facility be damaged and how well is it maintained?
4. Has the issuer established an adequate maintenance reserve fund?
5. Does the issuer have the ability to increase tolls to meet covenant and debt reserve requirements?
6. What is the debt to equity ratio?
7. When was the facility constructed?
8. Could the bonds be refunded early?
9. What has been the coverage trend of the available revenues over the past decade?
10. From what source do revenues come to pay back bondholders?

Investors in utility authority bonds would like to have answers to the following questions:[1]

1. Does the bond issuer have the authority to raise its electric rates in a timely fashion without going to any regulatory agencies?
2. How diversified is the customer base among residential, commercial, and industrial users?
3. Is the service area growing with respect to population, personal income, and commercial/industrial activity so as to warrant the electric power generated by the existing or new facilities?
4. What are the projected and actual costs of power generated by the existing or new facilities?
5. How diversified is the fuel mix?
6. Why are there frequent or large rate increases?
7. Why are capital plant improvements or maintenance deferred?
8. Is there a shrinking customer base or unexpected competition?
9. Is the coverage of debt service by net revenues increasing or decreasing?
10. Is there excessive management turnover and chronic lateness in supplying investors with annual audited financials?
11. Have there been unanticipated cost overruns and schedule delays on capital construction projects?
12. Has there been growing financial dependence of the issuer on federal and state aid appropriations for meeting operating budget expenses?

The accident at Three Mile Island nuclear plant in Pennsylvania pointed out the potential dangers of nuclear fuel and nuclear installations; it raised legal, political, ethical, and financial questions for investors in municipal power authority bonds. Investors must factor into their evaluation of each public power authority issue the impact of nuclear power and the effects of threats to its issuer's fuel supply over its lifespan. Slowdowns or cutoffs in OPEC oil supplies, uncertainty over supplies of domestic oil, coal, nuclear, and solar power are all legitimate concerns for investors.[2]

The key measures of quality for general obligation bonds are the level and trend of the community's debt outstanding relative to the value of the real estate in the community debt per capita relative to income per capita, and debt service as a percentage of the operating budget of the state or local government. For example, debt per capita of between 10 and 15 percent is about average, while per capita debt in excess of 15 percent of per capita income is viewed as risky. Similarly, a debt service as a percent of operating budget that approaches 20 percent is viewed as potentially risky.

Those investors seeking red flags for general obligation bonds of states, counties, cities, and school districts should be concerned with the following:[3]

1. Declining property values and increasing delinquent taxpayers.
2. An increasing property tax in conjunction with a declining population.
3. An increasing property tax burden relative to other regions.
4. General obligation debt increasing while property values are stagnant; an extremely high ratio of tax-dependent debt as a percentage of the assessed valuation of taxable real estate.
5. Declining economy characterized by increased unemployment and declining personal income.
6. Increasing unfunded pension liabilities.
7. Actual general fund revenues consistently falling below budgeted amounts and/or increasing general fund deficits, that is, a high level of debt service as a percent of operating budget.

Since municipal bonds are not subject to the SEC's registration requirements, it is even more important to read both the summary and the fine print in a municipal bond offering statement or circular. Revenue bonds backed by a specific revenue stream from a prospect like a toll road or bridge usually have a summary statement containing details about the securities. Although the official statement of general obligation bonds may not have such a summary, they do contain an enormous amount of valuable information. The information includes the issue's purpose, its security, the source of the revenue, definitions of terms used, and an opinion from the issuer's bond counsel. It is most important that the bond buyers analyze the listing of the debt service coverage of the bonds to help them determine if it is adequate to pay the principal and interest on a timely basis. The annual revenues required after expenses are paid tend to range from 1.1 to 1.5 times the debt service, with the more speculative issues requiring the higher coverage. It is also important to check the call or redemption features on a bond, as well as the tax status of the bond, especially whether the security is subject to the alternative minimum tax under the new Tax Reform Act rules.

STATE TAXES

Tax treatments of municipal bonds vary by state. Forty-three states plus the District of Columbia levy an individual income tax. Six of these states exempt coupon interest on all municipal bonds, whether the issue is in state or out of state; 32 states exempt coupon interest from in-state issued bonds, while only 5 states levy individual income taxes regardless of whether the issuer is in state or out of state. Of the 20 states that levy a personal property tax, 11 apply this tax to municipal bonds. Bonds in states such as California and New York yield less than identically rated issues with similar investment characteristics that trade in the national market. One of the reasons for this is that there is a high income tax levied by these states, and, consequently, there is a strong demand from residents of these states to own bonds that are exempt from both state and federal taxes. This factor reduces the yield on these bonds below those available in states where local and state taxes are nonexistent or quite low (for example, Florida and Illinois). Other states require acceptable collateral for pledging for public deposits held in banks. For those qualifying in-state municipal issues, pledging tends to increase demand and reduce yields relative to nonqualifying comparable issues.

There are only eight states in which the total effective state tax rates exceed 5 percent for investors in the highest tax brackets. Therefore, it is important for an investor to compare after-tax yields on both in-state and out-of-state bonds before making a purchase.

TAX REFORM AND INDIVIDUAL INVESTORS

The Tax Reform Act of 1986 has established three categories of municipal bonds for individuals:

The first is exempt from federal income taxation and alternative minimum tax.

The second category is exempt from federal taxation but is subject to alternative minimum tax. This category includes qualified redevelopment and mortgage bonds, qualified redevelopment bonds and student loan bonds, and certain private activity bonds such as mass commuting facilities, solid waste disposal, water and sewage facilities, docks, wharves, and airports.

The final category is subject to federal income tax and alternative minimum tax. These federal tax categories apply to municipal bonds issued after August 7, 1986.

Municipal bond offerings carry an opinion of recognized bond counsel in the official statement with a summary at the top of the cover page of the prospectus. This opinion should be studied germane to the tax status of the interest payments the bond holder will be receiving according to federal and local laws.

Private purpose municipal bonds whose income may be subject to the alternate minimum tax offer to many individual investors (those not subject to the alternate minimum tax) a chance to earn an additional 25 to 50 basis points in yield over other similarly rated securities. Investment income generated by such bonds must be limited lest excessive tax preference items subject the investor to the alternate minimum tax.

Other changes in the tax laws have sparked an interest in zero-coupon municipal bonds in the portfolio of investors under the age of 14 since children with incomes above $1,000 will be taxed at the same tax rate as their parents. These bonds are purchased at a deep discount, mature at the par value, and offer the investor a specified compounded annual yield that is the difference between the original issue discount price and par.

TAXABLE MUNICIPAL BONDS

The terms *tax-exempt* and *municipal* bond have been virtually synonymous for years. This has changed with the advent of a growing market in taxable municipal bonds. These bonds are taxed like a corporate bond issue but structured like a tax-exempt municipal bond. While corporate bonds are usually issued as a single, fixed-rate term maturity vehicle, municipal bonds are traditionally issued with a number of serial maturities and one or more term bonds. Taxable municipals are a classic hybrid product incorporating the features of both markets. While income from these issues is fully taxable at the federal level, a number of these issues have been exempt from state and local taxes.

MUNICIPAL BOND FEATURES

Municipal bonds have been issued with put features that allow the investor to resell the bonds to the municipality that issued the bond at a stated price. This option provides a floor for the price of the bond and protects investors from most of the loss arising from interest rate risk.

Some municipal bonds are also issued with an irrevocable guarantee by a private party other than the issuer. (Usually an insurance company or bank.) Essentially the issuer has insured the bonds because the guarantor is a source of collateral. Guaranteed bonds help the issuer by lowering interest rate costs and may help investors by improving the marketability of the issue.

Another relatively new feature of municipal bond issuers is to offer a replacement issue for an outstanding issue of high coupon bonds and to use the proceeds to buy enough Treasury bonds to cover the interest payments on the old issue until they can be called. The federal backing raises the effective rating of the old bond to the highest category, increasing the market value of the bond. The new quality rating and shorter maturity raise the value of the bonds. The owners are then able to trade these bonds for a larger number of the new issue. They now own more bonds at no additional cost.

Private purpose municipal bonds issued to finance not-for-profit hospitals can provide higher tax-free yields to investors without exposing the investor to the alternate minimum tax. The yields on these bonds in January 1987 were about 50 basis points higher than most alternate minimum tax-free municipal bonds, reflecting their greater credit risk. Unlike public purpose bonds, which are usually backed by reliable tax revenues, the interest and principal on hospital bonds come from the often unpredictable revenues generated by the hospital itself.

Prerefunded municipal bonds are high coupon bonds that municipalities have in effect turned into tax-free Treasuries. They do it by floating new bonds at lower rates and investing the proceeds of the second issue into Treasury bonds. Income and principal from the Treasuries pay the interest on the old bonds and will eventually retire the issue. In January 1987 prerefunded municipal bonds yielded as much as 270 basis points more after taxes than taxable Treasuries of comparable maturity.

Even though prerefunded bonds usually carry a AAA rating, these bonds traded at higher yields than many AA- and A-rated securities in the municipal bond market in January 1987. These loftier yields reflected the abundant supply of prerefunded issues and the fact that the bonds will be called within a few years.

Industrial development bonds (IDBs) are a specific type of revenue bond that was first issued to help stimulate local business following the Depression of 1929–1933. When issuing an IDB, the municipality merely gives its approval to the sale of the revenue bonds and assumes no legal liability in the event of default. The recipient of the funds is able to borrow money at a lower cost because of the federal tax exemption accorded revenue bond holders.

Industrial development bonds and pollution control bonds are really corporate bonds disguised to resemble municipal bonds. Although each is officially a type of municipal revenue bond, they differ from all the other types of revenue bonds that have a direct backing of a municipality or public authority. These bonds are backed solely by the corporation and not by any governmental unit. Therefore, industrial development bonds and pollution control bonds are actually corporate credits.[4]

The abuse of IDBs has come from commercial banks that have aided local governments in setting up municipal development agencies. This allowed commercial banks to make tax-free loans to qualified borrowers at lower than normal interest rates. The issuance of mortgage-backed municipal bonds by housing agencies or authorities has also abused the tax-exempt privilege of municipal bonds. The low cost funds are usually used to offer low interest mortgage loans to low and moderate income people. However, this has not always been the case as favoritism and political abuse have played a large role. Federal legislation passed in the mid 1980s has limited the amount of IDBs sold in each state.

Of the $220 billion in tax-exempt bonds issued in 1985, $120 billion were private purpose bonds. Likewise, of the $115 billion in tax-exempt bonds issued in 1984, $71 billion were private purpose bonds. The Tax Reform Act of 1986 severely limited the issuance of industrial development bonds for nonmanufacturing businesses. Although factory owners can still obtain low cost financing through IDBs, such funding has been eliminated for shopping centers, offices, industrial parks, supermarkets, and warehouses. A cap has also been placed on housing agency bonds. In addition, developers of multifamily housing units have to set aside 40 percent of the units for people making less than 60 percent of the median income in order to qualify for tax-exempt financing.

The Tax Reform Act of 1986 also reduced incentives for commercial banks and thrift institutions to purchase municipal bonds for their portfolios. These financial institutions are no longer permitted to deduct as an expense the interest paid for deposits used to buy the tax-exempt bonds.

SUMMARY

There is an implicit understanding between the federal government and state and local governments that each shall respect the other's right of taxation. Both have generally agreed not to tax the interest that investors receive from the other's bonds. States do not tax the interest on Treasury securities and the IRS does not tax the interest from state and local obligations. In addition, as an added incentive to residents of the state, states will usually not tax the interest received on bonds issued in that state.

Because of the tax-exempt nature of municipal bonds, investors are generally those persons and institutions subject to high marginal income tax rates. The key holders of municipal bonds are individuals and individual trusts, mutual funds, commercial banks, and property-casualty insurance companies.

Municipal bonds are issued by about 37,000 out of about 80,000 potential state and local governments and their special government agencies and authorities to finance capital outlays that are too large to finance out of current revenues. There are two special types of municipal bonds: revenue bonds and general obligation bonds. General obligation bonds are "full faith and credit" obligations of the issuing body and are secured by the taxing power of the issuer. Revenue bonds are issued by governmental authorities that have no taxing power and are secured solely by the revenue collected from the issuers of that particular capital project funded by the debt issue. In the case of revenue bonds, the credit quality of such bonds is related to the ability of the issuer to collect revenues from the project involved.

The ratio of municipal bond to corporate bond yields shows considerable variability, some of which takes the form of explainable short-term cyclical movements. An analysis of the municipal bond market indicates that while supply usually rises yearly, demand is continually changing in competition. These changing demand patterns are primarily due to the influences of other capital markets and changes in the tax laws. Commercial bank demand for tax-exempt bonds is a function of loan demand, tax position, and alternative yields on other investment opportunities. The profitability or lack of profitability of insurance company underwriting and other tax and alternative yield factors influence the demand for tax-exempt securities by property-casualty insurance companies. The changing demand of individuals for municipal bonds is a function of the outlook for the stock market, the after-tax yield on corporate bonds and the outlook for interest rates.

The market for municipal bonds is segmented into a national market in which large well-known municipalities sell their bonds and into various local markets in which smaller municipalities sell their bonds. Many municipal bonds now carry third party guarantees such as bond insurance, bank letters of credit, or collateralization. Although the terms *tax-exempt* and *municipal* have been virtually synonymous for decades, this has changed with the advent of a growing market in taxable municipal bonds. Municipal bonds have also been issued with put features that enable the investor to resell the bonds to the issuing municipality at a stated price.

Risk, marketability, and maturity of municipal bonds vary considerably. General obligation issues are typically less risky than revenue bonds, but risks may vary widely among different issuers. For example, the Ohio Turnpike Authority revenue bonds are presently less risky than the general obligation bonds of several large eastern cities. Maturities of municipals range from short-term tax anticipation notes to 40-year bonds. Most long-term issues are sold as serial bonds, maturing each year until final maturity.

NOTES

1. Sylvan G. Feldstein, "Guidelines in the Credit Analysis of General Obligation and Revenue Municipal Bonds," *The Handbook of Fixed Income Securities* (Homewood, Ill.: Dow Jones Irwin, 1983), pp. 411–37.

2. Robert Lamb and Stephen P. Rappaport, *Municipal Bonds: The Comprehensive Review of Tax-Exempt Securities and Public Finance* (New York: McGraw-Hill, 1980), p. 319.

3. Feldstein, "Guidelines," p. 437.

4. Lamb and Rappaport, *Municipal Bonds*, p. 221.

SELECTED BIBLIOGRAPHY

Andrews, Suzanna. "The Creative Surge in Tax-Exempt Finance." *Public Finance* (December 1984): 211–12.

Fabozzi, Frank J., and Irving Pollack, eds. *The Municipal Bond Handbook*. Vols. 1 and 2. Homewood, Ill.: Dow Jones Irwin, 1985.

Feldstein, Sylvan G. "Guidelines in the Credit Analysis of General Obligation Bonds." In *The Handbook of Fixed Income Securities,* F. J. Fabozzi and I. M. Pollack, eds. Homewood, Ill.: Dow Jones Irwin, 1983.

Hawthorne, Fran. "The Boom for Financial Guarantees," *Institutional Investor* (February 1985): 124.

Peek, Joe, and James A. Wilcox. "Tax Rates and Interest Rates on Tax-Exempt Securities." Federal Reserve Bank of Boston, *New England Economic Review* (January–February 1986): 29–41.

Pozdena, Randall J. "Municipal Bond Behavior." Federal Reserve Bank of San Francisco, *Weekly Letter* (February 22, 1983): 1–2.

Rosenbloom, Richard H. "A Review of the Municipal Bond Market." Federal Reserve Bank of Richmond, *Economic Review* (April 1986): 10–19.

Rubins, Laura S. "Recent Developments in the State and Local Government Sector." *Federal Reserve Bulletin* (November 1984): 792–801.

Skelton, Jeffrey L. "Relative Risk on Municipal and Corporate Debt." *Journal of Finance* (May 1983): 625–34.

Twentieth Century Fund Task Force on Municipal Bond Market. *Building a Broader Bond Market*. New York: McGraw-Hill, 1976.

White, Wilson. *The Municipal Bond Market*. New York: Financial Publishers Press, 1985.

10

The Mortgage Market

Jerry Belloit and Alan Gart

In the United States the dollar value of mortgage debt (loans collateralized by land and buildings) is the largest type of debt outstanding. At the end of 1985 there was slightly over $2.2 trillion in mortgage debt outstanding (see Figure 10.1) compared to approximately $775 billion in outstanding corporate and foreign bonds and $1.1 trillion in privately held Treasury bills, notes, and bonds.

Mortgages differ from other capital market instruments because:

1. Real estate is pledged as collateral.
2. The amount borrowed is not standardized.
3. The issuers are usually small, unknown financial units.
4. The secondary markets are limited.

The bulk of mortgage financing is for single-family homes. In addition, there are markets for multifamily structures, commercial and industrial structures, and farms. Savings and loans hold more mortgage debt than any other financial intermediaries, with commercial banks in second place. Savings and loans are the dominant factor in one to four family mortgages, while commercial banks and life insurance companies are the dominant providers of funds in the commercial mortgage market (see Table 10.1).

Mortgages are extremely important in the United States, not only because of their enormous volume, but because they finance the biggest single expenditure most household units make during their lifetimes. The United States is considered a nation of homeowners with two thirds of all households owning at least one home. As a matter of fact, the income tax laws of the United States provide a subsidy for home ownership for many families. Mortgage interest rate payments and local real estate taxes are deductible from gross income for up to two houses for taxpayers who itemize deductions on their federal income tax.

Figure 10.1
Long-Term Borrowing (Private Domestic Nonfinancial Sectors)

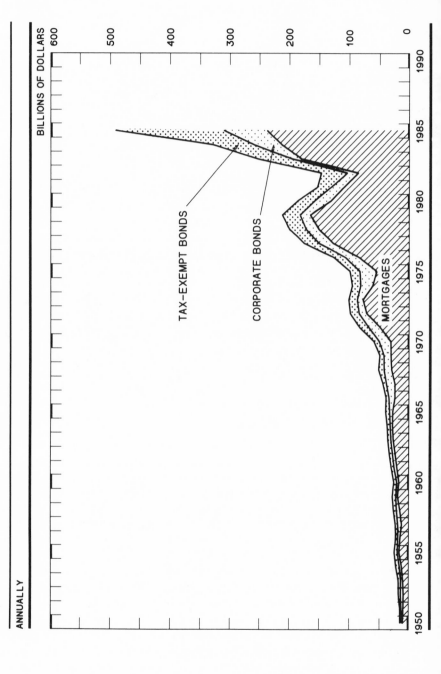

Table 10.1
Mortgage Debt Outstanding (Millions of dollars, end of period)

Type of holder, and type of property	1984	1985	1986
1 All holders	2,036,158	2,268,423ʳ	2,556,620
2 1- to 4-family	1,320,444	1,468,273ʳ	1,668,285
3 Multifamily	185,414	213,816ʳ	244,122
4 Commercial	418,300	480,719ʳ	545,185
5 Farm	112,000	105,615	99,028
6 Selected financial institutions	1,272,206	1,391,894ʳ	1,504,721
7 Commercial banks[1]	379,498	429,196ʳ	500,163
8 1- to 4-family	196,163	213,434ʳ	240,378
9 Multifamily	20,264	23,373ʳ	30,010
10 Commercial	152,894	181,032ʳ	216,771
11 Farm	10,177	11,357	13,004
12 Savings banks	154,441	177,263	224,901
13 1- to 4-family	107,302	121,879	155,229
14 Multifamily	19,817	23,329	30,291
15 Commercial	27,291	31,973	39,277
16 Farm	31	82	104
17 Savings and loan associations	555,277	583,236	553,552
18 1- to 4-family	421,489	432,422	404,034
19 Multifamily	55,750	66,410	67,282
20 Commercial	77,605	83,798	81,734
21 Farm	433	606	502
22 Life insurance companies	156,699	171,797	190,869
23 1- to 4-family	14,120	12,381	13,027
24 Multifamily	18,938	19,894	20,709
25 Commercial	111,175	127,670	145,863
26 Farm	12,466	11,852	11,270
27 Finance companies[2]	26,291	30,402	35,236
28 Federal and related agencies	158,993	166,928	157,049
29 Government National Mortgage Association	2,301	1,473	897
30 1- to 4-family	585	539	47
31 Multifamily	1,716	934	850
32 Farmers Home Administration	1,276	733	480
33 1- to 4-family	213	183	140
34 Multifamily	119	113	50
35 Commercial	497	159	120
36 Farm	447	278	170
37 Federal Housing and Veterans Administration	4,816	4,920	4,899
38 1- to 4-family	2,048	2,254	2,303
39 Multifamily	2,768	2,666	2,596
40 Federal National Mortgage Association	87,940	98,282	97,895
41 1- to 4-family	82,175	91,966	90,718
42 Multifamily	5,765	6,316	7,177
43 Federal Land Banks	52,261	47,498	40,719
44 1- to 4-family	3,074	2,798	2,396
45 Farm	49,187	44,700	38,323
46 Federal Home Loan Mortgage Corporation	10,399	14,022	12,159
47 1- to 4-family	9,654	11,881	10,927
48 Multifamily	745	2,141	1,232
49 Mortgage pools or trusts[3]	332,057	415,042	575,301
50 Government National Mortgage Association	179,981	212,145	259,373
51 1- to 4-family	175,589	207,198	253,388
52 Multifamily	4,392	4,947	5,985
53 Federal Home Loan Mortgage Corporation	70,822	100,387	170,393
54 1- to 4-family	70,253	99,515	165,856
55 Multifamily	569	872	4,537
56 Federal National Mortgage Association	36,215	54,987	97,174
57 1- to 4-family	35,965	54,036	95,791
58 Multifamily	250	951	1,383
59 Farmers Home Administration	45,039	47,523	48,361
60 1- to 4-family	21,813	22,186	21,682
61 Multifamily	5,841	6,675	7,453
62 Commercial	7,559	8,190	8,459
63 Farm	9,826	10,472	10,767
64 Individuals and others[4]	272,902	294,559	319,549
65 1- to 4-family	153,710	165,199	177,133
66 Multifamily	48,480	55,195	64,567
67 Commercial	41,279	47,897	52,961
68 Farm	29,433	26,268	24,888

1. Includes loans held by nondeposit trust companies but not bank trust departments.
2. Assumed to be entirely 1- to 4-family loans.
3. Outstanding principal balances of mortgage pools backing securities insured or guaranteed by the agency indicated.
4. Other holders include mortgage companies, real estate investment trusts, state and local credit agencies, state and local retirement funds, noninsured pension funds, credit unions, and other U.S. agencies.
NOTE. Based on data from various institutional and governmental sources, with some quarte s estimated in part by the Federal Reserve. Multifamily debt refers to loans on structures of five or more units.

Source: Federal Reserve Bulletin.

213

WHAT IS A MORTGAGE?

A mortgage is a loan secured by a lien on real property. A lien gives the lender the right to have the property sold at a public auction in the event that the borrower defaults on the terms and conditions of the mortgage contract. Mortgage lending is often referred to as secured lending because the mortgage is "secured" not only by the borrower's promise to pay, but also by the value of the collateral in the form of real estate. A mortgage can take any form that is satisfactory to the lender and the borrower so long as it does not involve an illegal transaction.

THE HISTORY OF THE MORTGAGE MARKET

Prior to the 1930s, mortgage maturities were typically no more than a few years, interest was payable periodically, and principal was due at the end of the mortgage period. There was no amortization (payment of principal). The idea of amortized mortgages was actually popularized by the Federal Farmers Home Administration in the 1930s. Since the end of World War II, the typical residential mortgage has been for relatively long periods and has included both principal and interest in the monthly payment. With the escalation in home prices and the resulting increase in mortgage amounts, amortization periods have been lengthened from 10 to 20 to 30 years and, more recently, occasionally as long as 40 years.

There was basically little change in the typical mortgage of the period 1945 to the early 1970s. Interest rates rose slowly and the amortization period stretched, but there was no alteration in the basic form. With the rapid escalation in the price of housing and the interest rates that followed the oil crisis in the early 1970s, real estate financing was forced to respond. So-called creative financing, including mortgages held by the seller, became commonplace. A variety of innovative mortgage instruments were developed that have become more and more popular today.

These mortgage instruments were developed to meet the needs of both the buyers and the lenders in the marketplace. The needs of the buyer included offsets to high interest rates and loan values. For the institutional lender, the problem was a rapid increase in the cost of lendable funds that sometimes produced negative spreads on fixed rate mortgage portfolios that were already on the books of the lending institution.

TYPES OF MORTGAGES

High inflation in the 1970s generated serious problems for thrift institutions that held primarily fixed-rate mortgages in the early 1980s. As a result, a variety of new mortgages were developed that included variable rate (VRM), renegotiable rate, adjustable rate (ARM), reverse annuity mortgages (RAM), graduated payment, and shared equity or equity participation mortgages. Many of the new mortgage instruments shortened the effective length of time for which the mortgage holder is "locked in" to a specific interest rate. Consequently, mortgage holders bear less interest rate risk and mortgage borrowers bear more interest rate risk when these new instruments are utilized.

To best understand the types of mortgage that we have today, it is useful to discuss how today's mortgage forms have evolved. The earliest mortgage loans were given by the sellers of property. The loans were very short term, often a year or two. They contained no provisions for interest. If the borrower failed to repay the loan within the specified period, the borrower was forced to vacate and forfeited the down payment. (A current analogy to this early type of mortgage loan occurs when the seller gives an option to purchase and allows the option holder possession of the premises until the option expiration date.)

With the development of savings institutions, it became possible for a borrower to turn to another source to obtain the funds necessary to purchase the property. Early mortgages often paid interest only. These interest-only mortgages (often called bullet loans today) were mortgages with relatively short terms, typically three to five years. No principal repayment was made during the term of the loan. There are still two primary sources of this type of loan available to a home buyer, the ordinary lending institution, and the property seller. Short-term interest-only mortgages benefit the buyer in that the monthly payments are lower than would be the case if principal were amortized. The buyer often expects to refinance at more favorable rates at some future time and views the short-term mortgage as bridge financing. The home seller often views the short-term mortgage as a necessary evil. In a tight mortgage market, it is not unusual for a prospective buyer to be unable to find affordable financing or meet the credit standards required by institutional lenders. In order to induce or enable the potential home buyer to purchase a home, the seller often must either provide the financing or pass up the sale. Institutional lenders, providing short-term interest-only mortgages, may view it as providing liquidity and protection against volatile interest rates. If rates rise in a period covered by the loan, the institution has the option of requiring a higher rate at the termination of the relatively short period, or calling the loan.

Historically, the problem of potentially having to renew the loan led to the evolution of the conventional amortized loan. After the Great Depression many lenders found themselves in the position of either having to foreclose on mortgages or to continually extend them. Thus the need for a new type of mortgage loan was created. The level payment, amortized loan that was developed is one in which the payments remain constant over the entire life of the loan and every payment contains a principal portion along with an interest portion. The nature of the loan is such that the amount of the loan is simply the present value of mortgage payments to be made discounted at the mortgage interest rate.

While the amortized loan is still the most common loan available today, there have been a few refinements upon the basic form. To ensure that the borrower pays his property taxes and keeps the property adequately insured (thus protecting the lender's collateral security), the lender collects the proportional amount of taxes and insurance along with the monthly payment of principal and interest; this became known as a budget mortgage or PITI mortgage (principal, interest, taxes, and insurance). Since this additional payment is usually kept by the lender in a low yielding or non–interest-bearing account, these escrow accounts, as they are sometimes called, can be a significant source of profitability to the mortgage lender.

Another refinement on a conventional amortized loan was to allow the inclusion of certain items of personal property in the mortgage such as the range, refrigerator, washer, dryer, and so on. This type of mortgage, known as a package mortgage, was developed to reduce the level of installment debt that a borrower might have to incur. As interest rate volatility increased, the lenders found themselves in positions where the spread between the interest paid on the mortgages and the cost of funds to the lender narrowed and became negative. This was the case when fixed-rate mortgages issued in the 1970s at 6 to 9 percent had to be financed with funds costing double digit levels in the early 1980s. Lenders felt compelled to devise ways to restructure lending instruments to better match up their maturities with liability maturities, thereby stabilizing yield spreads.

One simple way to shorten the term of the mortgage without making the payments unreasonably high was simply to call the loan due and payable after a certain number of years, even though the loan might be amortized for a much longer period of time. At the time the loan is due and payable a final, large payment would be due. This partially amortized mortgage became known as a balloon mortgage. Often the loan was reduced in term to a period of three to five years. Every three to five years the interest rate would be renegotiated and the appropriate amortization calculated such that the loan would pay off at the end of perhaps 30 years. This became known as a renegotiable rate mortgage (RRM) or rollover mortgage.

Lenders also developed another type of mortgage with an even shorter term of six months to three years. At the end of every adjustment period, the interest rate on the mortgage would adjust to some prevailing market index. Unlike provisions in the renegotiable rate mortgages or rollover mortgages, this shorter mortgage, called a variable or adjustable interest rate mortgage, typically had a full term of about 30 years. The interest rate on the mortgage would vary at the appropriate intervals. In all of these loans where the lender is attempting to shorten the period between changes in interest rates, it becomes difficult for the consumer to anticipate the level of monthly future mortgage payments. This has led to some consumer reluctance to enter into this type of contract unless a "teaser" or incentive rate is offered for the initial period of the mortgage.

In an effort to compromise with the consumer's reluctance to have the payment constantly changing over the term of the loan, two other variations of adjustable-rate mortgages have developed. The first of these involves a variable interest rate mortgage with a constant payment over the term of the loan. As interest rates fluctuate, the term of the loan is either extended or reduced. A second program developed to compensate for changing mortgage payments is the cap adjustable mortgage loan. The chief difference between an adjustable rate mortgage and a traditional mortgage is that the ARM has no fixed interest rate. In this program there is an interest rate cap on the maximum interest rate that can be charged. In addition, the interest rate decreases or increases at the end of the adjustment period (which is usually one, two, or three years) based on the index chosen (most often a fixed spread over a Treasury rate).

For example, the maximum increase at the end of any adjustment period is typically two percentage points (200 basis points) with 5 percentage points (500 basis points) lifetime maximum increase. Since the ARM reduces interest rate risk for the lender and better matches the maturity of assets with liabilities, the borrower is initially often offered an interest rate that is 100 to 200 basis points under the rate for conventional fixed rate mortgages. It is often referred to as a "teaser" rate. ARMs are especially attractive to lending institutions during periods of increasing interest rates because the mortgage rate can be increased at the adjustment date. During periods of rapidly increasing interest rates, many lending institutions offer only ARMs to potential borrowers. ARMs are also attractive to borrowers who will be in the home only a few years and can take advantage of the teaser rate without having to worry about substantial increases in monthly mortgage costs that might occur in the fourth or fifth year if rates rise.

Another way lenders devised to help offset the problems of increased interest rate volatility was to provide additional lender incentives in the form of what were called equity kickers or bonus interest. The first program to include a kicker was the shared appreciation mortgage (SAM). In the shared appreciation mortgage, the lender would receive a percentage of the capital gain in the property made during the term of the loan. The mortgage lender would provide funds at a substantially reduced rate of interest. In return for the discount on the mortgage interest rate, the borrower would agree to share part of the increase in the property value with the lender when the property was sold, when the loan matured, or at some other agreed upon time. A second program that provided more immediate bonus income to the lender was the income participation mortgage, or sales kicker. In this type of mortgage the lender actually received some percentage of gross sales as a bonus. During periods of rapidly increasing prices, interest rates typically rose with inflationary increases. As long as the lender is receiving a bonus that should be increasing with inflation, the lender is not as badly damaged by the increasing rates that might have been the case with a conventional fixed-rate mortgage. This type of mortgage has not proved to be popular with homeowners.

Other forms of mortgages that were developed came in response to the rapidly increasing housing prices of the 1970s. With rising inflation it became increasingly difficult for a prospective buyer to qualify for a mortgage, and several programs were developed to assist with this problem. These programs provided for reduced payments in the early years of the loan, allowing the homebuyer to carry a larger mortgage than he or she could have qualified for if it were a straight amortized loan.

These loans were the deferred interest mortgage (DIM) and the graduated payment loan. In the DIM, loan payments are structured for a few years so that the payments only cover part of the interest due on the loan, and there is no payment toward the principal. The difference between the interest due and the interest paid is then added to the balance of the loan, creating negative amortization. (The outstanding balance on the loan actually increases.) After the initial period, the payment increases, and the mortgage becomes positively amortized.

The graduated payment loan was another attempt to lower monthly payments. The monthly payments in the early years of the loan are actually less than the interest due on the loan. The difference between the interest charged and the actual amount of the payments is added to the balance of the loan. Payments rise gradually each year until they reach a level that will be required to amortize the balance due over the remaining life of the loan. The annual increase in payments is generally about 7.5 percent per year. Typically, by the sixth or seventh year, the payment is sufficiently high to amortize the loan over the remaining life. Normally, this type of loan is a fixed interest rate loan, although it is possible to include a feature that makes the interest rate adjustable.

Loans that reduce the payment in the early years of the loan are particularly important to young families and first-time homebuyers as they fit the repayment pattern to the probable income stream pattern of the family. Most young families can look forward to rapidly increasing incomes in the early years through promotions and seniority increases. A graduated payment loan allows them to fit their house payments to their income and purchase their "dream" house earlier in life than would otherwise be possible.

There was an uneasiness on the part of lenders in having their balance of the mortgage increasing and the loan to value ratio diminishing. To counter this problem, lenders have allowed the interest to be "bought down" by payment of a sufficiently large fee to offset the deferred interest. This fee was usually paid by the seller, and that type of mortgage was often referred to as a "buydown." The Glossary of Mortgage Terms provides a summary and explanation of the various mortgage forms.

Glossary of Mortgage Terms

Adjustable Mortgage Loan. An AML is the broadest of the new loan categories. The fourth generation of loans with variable interest rates, it is the designation used by federal savings and loan associations.

Adjustable Rate Mortgage. An ARM is the third generation of mortgages with variable rates. It is the designation used by national banks. The rate on an ARM issued by a national bank may not increase by more than 1 percent each six-month period. The common feature of ARMs is that the interest rate is not fixed but varies according to some preselected index or reference rate. The adjustments are made at the end of a predetermined period, which may be as short as three months or as long as five years.

Balloon Mortgage. A balloon mortgage is any mortgage that is due and payable before all the principal is repaid.

Base Index Rate. The base index rate is the reference point from which all index rate changes are measured on a mortgage with a variable rate. The base index rate is known at the time of origination, and it is the most recently available value of the index series at, or within six months prior to, the date of the closing of the loan. In general, the maximum rate change from the origination of a mortgage with a variable rate may not exceed the difference between the current value of the index and the base index value.

Debit Rate. The debit rate is the rate at which the borrower is charged interest. In some mortgage plans, the debit rate and payment rate are different.

Graduated Payment Mortgage. The GPM has a fixed interest rate. The initial payment is lower than that on a standard fixed-rate mortgage, and the payments gradually increase for the first 5 or 10 years. The graduated payment adjustable mortgage loan is any mortgage that has a variable interest rate and the initial payment is insufficient to pay all the interest due. GPAMLs involve future increased payments.

Growing Equity Mortgage. The GEM carries a fixed interest rate and a scheduled annual increase in monthly payments. Since the increase in monthly payments is applied to retirement of principal, the final maturity is shortened considerably.

Index. The subsequent movement of the rate on a mortgage when a variable interest rate is governed by an index rate. Rate movements on the mortgage must correspond to movements in the index. The index rate must be an interest rate series that is readily verifiable by the borrower and not under control of the lender.

Negative Amortization. Any increase in the loan balance arising from a mortgage payment being too small to pay all the interest due that month is called negative amortization. The lender effectively makes the borrower an additional loan at the mortgage rate for the amount of unpaid interest. This loan must be repaid over the remaining term of the mortgage. On some new mortgage plans, the payment rate (the size of the monthly payment) is less than the debit rate, and negative amortization thus occurs.

Pledged Account Mortgage. The PAM is a special type of GPM in which the interest due in excess of the monthly payment is deducted from a savings account pledged by the borrower.

Price Level Adjusted Mortgage. The PLAM has a fixed interest rate and an indexed principal. Because repayments are in inflation-adjusted dollars, the PLAM has a real interest rate, which is in the range of 3 percent. Although the interest rate is fixed, the outstanding balance and monthly payments vary according to changes in some price index.

Shared Appreciation Mortgage. In return for a low initial (below market) interest rate, the borrower agrees to pay the lender an amount of "contingent interest" that depends upon the appreciation of the property. In other words, the borrower agrees to share with the lender the appreciation in the underlying property. The outstanding indebtedness and contingent interest are normally refinanced at the end of 5 or 10 years.

Renegotiable Rate Mortgage. The RRM is the second generation of mortgages with variable interest rates. The rate on an RRM can change by no more than 1.5 percent every three years and by no more than 5 percent overall.

Reverse Annuity Mortgage. The RAM is a stream of monthly payments that is provided to homeowners through an annuity purchased by a loan against the owner's accumulated equity in the home.

Variable Rate Mortgage. The VRM is the first generation of mortgages with variable interest rates. The rate on a VRM can change by no more than .5 percent annually and by no more than 2.5 percent overall.

Wraparound Mortgage. A wraparound mortgage is one method of providing the incremental financing a borrower may need when a loan is assumed. The borrower makes a single payment to the wraparound lender who, in turn, makes the payment on the underlying final trust.

SOURCES OF MORTGAGE FUNDS

The major suppliers of funds to the mortgage markets have been thrift institutions, commercial banks, and life insurance companies (see Table 10.2). Although mortgage banking companies have a large share of the original market for home mortgages, they tend to quickly sell mortgages in the secondary market. A relatively new source of mortgage funds comes from pension funds. With the

Table 10.2
Mortgage Loans Outstanding, by Type of Property and Lender, Year-End 1985*
(Billions of Dollars)

	Residential Properties			Commercial Properties	Farm Properties	Total Mortgage Loans
Lender	One- to Four- family	Multi- family	Total			
Savings Associations.....	$ 430.9	$ 66.5	$ 497.3	$ 88.4	†	$ 585.7
Savings Banks...........	122.1	23.2	145.4	31.7	†	177.2
Savings Institutions.....	$ 553.0	$ 89.7	$ 642.7	$120.2	†	$ 762.9
Commercial Banks........	214.3	22.9	237.2	174.3	$ 11.4	423.0
Life Insurance Companies.	13.5	19.5	33.0	122.9	12.0	167.9
All Others..............	686.4	70.8	757.2	53.9	83.7	894.7
Total..................	$1,467.2	$202.9	$1,670.1	$471.3	$107.1	$2,248.5

Note: Components may not add to totals due to rounding.
*Preliminary.
†Less than $50 million.
Sources: Federal Home Loan Bank Board; Federal Reserve Board.

development of the secondary market and insurance that reduces the credit risk involved, pension funds have become increasingly active in the mortgage markets. It seems likely that pension funds will continue to be active both as lenders and equity investors in real estate in the years to come because mortgage securities have tended to outperform high grade corporate bonds and both long Treasuries and 10-year Treasuries. It is interesting to note that while real estate investment is a relatively recent innovation for pension funds in the United States, it has been common in Europe for many years.

THE ECONOMIC BASIS OF THE MARKET

Like any market, there must be an economic basis for the mortgage market. It reflects the transfer of savings from surplus units (savers) to deficit units (borrowers). The function of the financial intermediary is the aggregation of the savings of a large number of relatively small savers for transfer to the home buyers. Relatively few savers would be willing or able to invest directly in mortgages in residential real estate and even fewer in mortgages on commercial and industrial property. The relatively long periods of time involved in the mortgage financing, the large unit size of mortgages, and their relative illiquidity would make them unattractive to all but a select investment market. In exchange for providing mortgage funding, savings institutions are compensated by a spread between the amount paid for savings deposits and the amount earned as interest on mortgages, as well as origination fees at settlement time.

The federal government has been extremely active structuring and helping to create liquidity for the real estate market. Through a variety of federal agencies that are discussed in more detail later in this chapter, a secondary market in mortgages has been established. The secondary mortgage market provides a source of liquidity for mortgage lenders. The secondary market also facilitates the transfer of savings capital between geographic areas of the country. The development of secondary markets has fostered the development of the mortgage banking industry and has encouraged the participation of a wide variety of institutions other than savings and loans in the mortgage market. The secondary market has made it possible for intermediaries such as insurance companies to participate in the market without originating mortgages themselves. A mortgage originator deals directly with the individual borrower and handles all the numerous details involved in the closing of the real estate transaction. The originator creates the actual mortgage, lends the funds to the borrower, and then services the mortgage. Servicing refers to the detail work involved in collecting the monthly payments and making sure the taxes and insurance are kept current on the property.

The secondary market permits the separation of these specialized functions from the actual long-term investment in the mortgage. Normal practice is for the originator of the mortgage to provide these functions for a fee paid by the holder of the mortgage. The borrower makes payments required to the originator who sets up escrow accounts for taxes and insurance and remits principal and interest payments to the holder as they are received by the servicing agency. A fee is charged that is generally between one quarter and one half of a percentage point (25 to 50 basis points) for providing these functions on single-family loans. The servicing of the mortgage can also be sold for a one-time fee of close to 200 basis points for conventional fixed-rate mortgages.

LENDING POINTS

Lending points, often referred to as origination fees, are usually added to the initial cost of a residential mortgage loan. Each point is equal to 1 percent of the amount of the loan. These points are typically paid at the time the loan is made and are not returned to the borrower even if the loan is paid off prior to the original maturity date. Prepayment is quite common in residential mortgage lending because homeowners frequently repay their loans when moving to a new location. It is also quite common for a homeowner to pay off a mortgage with a high interest rate and to refinance at a lower interest rate if market conditions are favorable.

For example, suppose that a lending institution charges 12 percent plus 2 points for a 20-year mortgage requiring a $100,000 loan. The 2 point loan fee on the mortgage would involve the payment of $2,000 at settlement. This 12 percent, 20-year mortgage with 2 points yields 13.12 percent to maturity and even more if the loan is repaid prior to maturity.

PROBLEMS IN ESTABLISHING A SECONDARY MARKET

Most securities are essentially homogeneous. One share of stock in General Motors is exactly equivalent to another. In the bond market, there is a clear similarity between bonds of well-known companies, and there are a number of credit rating services that provide ratings to make comparisons easy between bonds of various issuers. In the mortgage market, there is no homogeneity between mortgages. Each property is distinct: there is only one property at 123 Main Street, Any Town, USA. While the originator of the mortgage may have some idea of the value of 123 Main Street, the lender at some remote location does not even know where it is. Furthermore, terms on most securities are relatively standard. A mortgage is simply a contract to pay and can be in any form that is satisfactory to both the lender and the borrower. Finally, the originator can make a credit decision on the borrower, but it is more difficult and involves incremental costs for the purchaser in the secondary market to establish the creditworthiness of the borrower.

It was necessary for some institutions to resolve these problems before a really effective secondary market could become operational. Mortgage terms had to be standardized, collectibility of principal and interest had to be established, and the form of exchange to provide liquidity had to be established. Since the standardization of commercial mortgage loans has never really taken place, we do not have a well-developed secondary market for commercial mortgages. Whereas most residential mortgages are readily salable in the secondary market, most commercial mortgages are illiquid.

FEDERAL GOVERNMENT PARTICIPATION IN DEVELOPING A SECONDARY MARKET

The first step was the Federal Housing Act of 1934, which provided that the Federal Housing Authority Insurance (FHA) reduce the problem of credit-worthiness of the individual by transferring most of the risk to the government. The insurance provided that in the event the borrower defaulted, and the value of the property was not sufficient to cover the balance due on the mortgage, the federal government would make up the difference. In practice, when there is a default on an FHA-insured property the government pays the lender the balance due and takes possession of the property. It then undertakes to dispose of the property and recover its funds. In any event, there is no risk of principal loss on the part of the lender.

At the same time, the problems of differences in terms of details were eliminated. In order to qualify for FHA insurance the form of the mortgage and documentation was specified. The purchaser of a FHA mortgage therefore had a completely homogeneous investment with minimum terms exactly like those in any other FHA mortgage, and credit risk was significantly reduced by the FHA insurance. It was thought ironically that these features would be sufficient to permit a spontaneous development of a secondary market. In time such a market might have developed, but the country was still recovering from a Great Depression. Government planners felt that the secondary market was needed to further government policy on housing.

The U.S. government has played a key role in the development of the secondary mortgage markets. Federal mortgage insurance, federal agency purchases of mortgages issued by private individuals, and federal agency development of pass-through securities and mortgage-backed bonds have all initiated corresponding developments in the private sector and enhanced the ability of the mortgage markets to attract funds from the conventional capital markets. Mortgage rates are more closely linked to rates on capital market securities than they were previously because of the development of the secondary markets and the new mortgage-backed securities. In addition to the insurance and secondary market functions, some state and local government housing authorities have made direct mortgage loans at reduced rates.

THE FEDERAL NATIONAL MORTGAGE ASSOCIATION

Today, Fannie Mae is a quasi-public company with aspects of both a government agency and a private corporation. It is chartered by the federal government with a broad franchise to foster the development of a secondary market and support that market. Fannie Mae used to hold periodic public auctions at which it purchased mortgages from private holders. Now, FNMA has an administered rate in the form of a daily price quote for mortgages that is available on a tape recorded message. You can call during the day and buy a commitment for delivery at various times, that is, 10, 30, 60, or 90 days in the future at specific yields and fee levels. The purchases are funded by offerings through the bond market. This allows Fannie Mae to tap into the long-term market for debt, which in turn allows a better matching of assets with liabilities (the bonds). The willingness and ability of Fannie Mae to purchase or sell virtually any amount of mortgages provides a high level of liquidity in the mortgage market. It should be noted that there is sometimes a fee associated with the sale of a mortgage in the secondary market.

Fannie Mae issues its own security, called a mortgage-backed security (MBS) in $25,000 denominations, guaranteeing both timely payment of principal and interest. An important difference between Freddie Mac PCS and the Fannie Mae MBS is the time it takes you to get your first payment. You get your first payment earlier with a Fannie Mae security.

OTHER GOVERNMENT AGENCIES

In addition to Fannie Mae there are two other government agencies that are active in the mortgage markets—the Government National Mortgage Association (GNMA) and the Federal Home Loan Mortgage Corporation (FHLMC), known as Ginnie Mae and Freddie Mac, respectively. The Government National Mortgage Association was created in 1968 as an agency within the Department of Housing and Urban Affairs. It was created in order to assume some of the subsidy functions that were previously the responsibility of Fannie Mae. Unlike Fannie Mae, Ginnie Mae does not hold mortgages in its permanent portfolio. Most of its purchases are resold within one year. Its primary function is the guarantee of securities either through mortgage-backed bonds or pass-through securities. Mortgage-backed bonds are simply bonds secured by a pool of mortgages. Pass-through securities also involve pools of mortgages but the investor purchases a direct interest in the underlying mortgages and the interest and principal payments are passed directly through to the investor either on a monthly basis as they are collected (the so-called standard form) or quarterly or semiannually (the so-called modified form). The Department of Justice has rendered the opinion that the guarantee of Ginnie Mae constitutes the full faith and credit of the United States. This makes the risk of timely payment of principal and interest equal to the risk of U.S. government bonds, or default-free (from credit risk) for all practical purposes. However, payments received from Ginnie Mae securities are subject to state and local income taxes, while Treasury securities are tax-exempt at the state and local level.

Ginnie Mae yields compare favorably with other government agency securities or even with returns on high grade corporate bonds. Ginnie Maes have typically yielded as much as 100 to 150 basis points more than comparable term treasury securities. The yield differential involves the taxability of Ginnie Mae securities at the state and local level and the uncertainty of the final maturity of the pass-through securities because of early prepayments of principal by some mortgage holders. In contrast to the usual twice a year interest payment schedule of most debt instruments, interest and principal on Ginnie Mae securities is paid monthly. Because of the reinvestment value of the monthly cash flow, these securities can offer a higher effective yield than a comparable security with the same coupon and price.

Individual Ginnie Mae certificates are normally traded in blocks of $1,000,000. They are generally available to investors in minimum denominations of $25,000. However, many mutual funds have been established that specialize in Ginnie Mae securities. The small investor can have access to these mutual funds with an initial investment of only $1,000.

Government National Mortgage Association guaranteed mortgage-backed securities have been issued exclusively in book entry form since 1987. The system replaces paper certificates with electronic entries held in a computer. Records of ownership and trades are maintained electronically, which should reduce expenses and problems normally related to the trading of paper.

Freddie Mac, the Federal Home Loan Mortgage Corporation, was organized to provide a secondary market for the mortgages held by savings and loans, credit unions, and life insurance companies. It also issues securities of its own, backed by pools of mortgages. While there are also some technical differences in the operations of Freddie Mac and Fannie Mae, there are also some important differences in risk. FNMA is exposed to significant interest rate risk since it borrows in the short-term markets and lends in the long-term markets. On the other hand, FHLMC buys, packages, and resells mortgages, limiting its exposure to interest rate risk.

The FHLMC was a wholly owned subsidiary of the 12 Federal Home Loan Banks. Recognizing that ultimately the thrift institutions that are members of the Federal Home Loan Bank Systems that have a claim on its income, Freddie Mac issued $600 million of participating preferred stock to these institutions in 1985. Congress created the FHLMC to improve the liquidity of residential mortgage investments. The corporation attempts to accomplish this by maintaining a secondary market in conventional mortgages that are neither insured by the FHA nor guaranteed by the Veterans Administration. Freddie Mac purchases mortgages typically from institutions originating the loans, thereby replenishing the lender's cash positions so that they can make new loans. Although Freddie Mac sometimes purchases mortgage loans for its own portfolio, it is more common for Freddie Mac to place them in pools and issue pass-through certificates backed by their mortgage loans.

Freddie Mac essentially serves as a conduit that links mortgage spending and capital markets. The corporation purchases mortgages from mortgage lenders and sells securities backed by those mortgages to investors. In its purchase programs, Freddie Mac encourages standardization of mortgage documents and assures mortgage quality by following precise underwriting guidelines. The result is a high volume of mortgages that have common characteristics and that can be grouped into pools to underlie high quality pass-through securities. Freddie Mac sells the securities to mortgage originators and in capital markets. The Freddie Mac Mortgage Participation Securities can be held, bought, traded, sold, hedged, or borrowed against. Principal and interest payments made by the homeowner are passed through to the investor in proportion to that investor's participation in the underlying mortgage pool. Freddie Mac guarantees timely payment of interest and ultimate collection of mortgages supporting the securities.

Freddie Mac issues its own mortgage-related security called a participation certificate (PC). Participation certificates represent conventional loans that are not insured by the government. However, the Federal Home Loan Bank System itself insures the timely payment of principal to investors. Freddie Mac PCs do not offer the backing of the full faith and credit of the United States (as is the case with Ginnie Mae securities) so that the yields on Freddie Mac PCs average about 10 basis points higher than Ginnie Maes with a comparable maturity. Freddie Mac PCs sell in $25,000 minimum denominations but are available in $1,000 units in mutual funds.

Freddie Mac has also issued collateralized mortgage obligations. They offer the safety and high yield of mortgage-backed securities with the semiannual interest payments of bonds. Instead of buying mortgage securities directly, you buy a bond that is backed by mortgage securities or by mortgages themselves.

OTHER PARTICIPANTS IN THE SECONDARY MORTGAGE MARKET AND JUMBO MORTGAGES

From the foregoing discussion it might appear that the principal buyers in the secondary market are government entities. The importance of the agencies created by the federal government in the secondary market cannot be overemphasized, but there are a large number of other participants, and the market is by no means a creature of the government entirely. The Automated Mortgage Market System (AMMINENT) was created by the FHLMC in 1974 to provide information on purchasing sale opportunities to other participants in the market. Insurance companies, banks, savings institutions, and pension funds are all substantial participants in the secondary markets, both as purchasers and sellers of mortgages.

Besides the very important role of providing liquidity to these other participants, the secondary market also serves to provide opportunities for short-term risk hedging. Risk hedging in Fannie Mae, Ginnie Mae, and Freddie Mac is accomplished through vehicles called forward commitments. The financial institutions such as savings and loans may hedge by obtaining a forward commitment to either purchase or sell mortgages in the marketplace. For example, a savings and loan that may be undertaking a joint venture with a local developer in the construction of a condominium unit may obtain forward commitments to provide mortgage money at reasonable rates during the marketing phase of the project, thereby improving the likelihood of success in the venture. Many smaller financial intermediaries such as mortgage brokers would be almost unable to participate in the marketplace without being able to obtain these forward commitments.

As of January 1, 1987, the secondary market for mortgages for Fannie Mae and Freddie Mac accepts only mortgages up to $153,100 for single-family homes. Mortgages that need to be sold in the secondary markets above the $153,100 currently are serviced by other institutions such as PRIME and are known in the trade as "jumbo mortgages."

One of the functions of the secondary market was originally to move funds from capital surplus areas to capital deficit areas, usually from the eastern seaboard with its capital excess to California, which was a capital deficit area. But the secondary market has more recently started to take on the more important function of attracting investors from outside the traditional mortgage investment community, providing the mortgage market as a whole with a supply of funds from capital markets, thus increasing the net supply of mortgage credit. For such a market to be effective and worthy of acceptance, private or governmental funds must be available at all times to permit the purchase of mortgage loans meeting prescribed standards. The investor in mortgages can deal with greater confidence if he can be assured of a secondary market where he can liquidate his holdings on a reasonable basis under the current conditions.

One of the new buyers in the secondary market, providing an added conduit for Wall Street financing of mortgage loans, is the Residential Funding Corporation (RFC), a subsidiary of Bancorporation's Banco Mortgage Co. This entrant into the market in November of 1982 was formed for the purpose of specializing in purchasing and pooling nonconforming loans such as mortgage-backed securities through Salomon Brothers. (Fannie Mae and Freddie Mac are limited by law to buying loans up to $153,100 for single family homes.) RFC, however, will offer a 30-year fixed-rate mortgage up to $250,000. After RFC buys the loans, Banco packages them for sale as mortgage pass-through securities by Salomon Brothers, insured by the Mortgage Guaranty Insurance Corp. (MGIC).

Banco, the third largest mortgage banking firm in the country, has set up the conduit program on the premise that the secondary market will become the primary source of mortgage funding. Although Fannie Mae and Freddie Mac buy about 42 percent of the conventional mortgages sold in the secondary market, several private conduits sponsored by mortgage insurers and securities firms are also active. Most existing private conduits are regional rather than national.

Another private participant is General Electric Credit Corporation. Through its subsidiaries, GE Mortgage Securities Company and GE Mortgage Insurance Corporation, it is purchasing, underwriting, and insuring mortgages and issuing mortgage-backed securities with AAA ratings to capital market investors. First Boston Corporation, which was already packaging mortgages from mortgage bankers, set up a new subsidiary in 1983, First Boston Capital Group. The new subsidiary was set up for Shelternet, a new computerized banking system that links home buyers directly to the mortgage capital market, bypassing thrifts or mortgage bankers. Real estate brokers who sign up for the system will originate the mortgages and sell them directly to First Boston who will package them to investors. Fixed rate, growing equity, FHA, VA, and second mortgages are all part of the program. First Boston will make money from servicing the mortgages and from a charge to the brokers. Brokers will have the advantage of direct access to mortgage funds and keeping the points up front which would normally have accrued to the financial institutions.

Coldwell Banker, the Sears subsidiary that is one of the country's biggest mortgage banking companies, has installed computers that will let its realty agents obtain mortgage interest quotes and financing for clients more rapidly. The technology should enable Coldwell Banker to update its rates quickly, allow buyers to apply for a loan using the terminals and should shorten the application processing time. This network, called "Mortgage One," is a private label version of Shelternet. Other companies, such as Better Homes and Gardens Real Estate Service and Realty World Corp., use Shelternet technology in similar networks that they operate.

The development of Shelternet and other competitive systems, the appeal of adjustable rate mortgages to commercial banks, as well as the entry of some life insurance companies in home mortgage origination could lead to some fundamental changes in the financial marketplace. It could eventually lead to the removal of thrift institutions as the primary originator of home mortgages.

The techniques of mortgage-backed securities developed years ago is now catching on among investment bankers. Merrill Lynch, which has acquired numerous residential real estate brokerage firms, has been active in the market, introducing serial mortgage certificates in 1981, with maturities from 1 to 15 years. Merrill Lynch has the essential resources to create a competitive advantage in the secondary market, becoming more and more a full service financial services supermarket.

Home Investors Fund, promoted by the National Association of Realtors and the National Association of Home Builders, is a mutual fund that is administered by the Vanguard Group. The fund invests in Securities of Ginnie Mae, Fannie Mae, Freddie Mac, and the private mortgage pools. The thrust behind the fund is to prove the viability of mortgages and mortgage-backed securities as investments. The Home Builders Association felt that by tapping the capital market through mutual funds, the sources of funds for local lenders will not dry up during high interest rates and might also prevent mortgage rates from escalating as they have in the last several years. It is just another effort to ease the housing industry's dependence on lenders working with depositors' money.

Essentially, individual mortgage contracts have been made more marketable by standardizing the contract, separating the servicing from the financing, and pooling them into packages that can be used to secure new mortgage pass-through securities, mortgage bonds, or collateralized mortgage obligations.

The cash flow to an investor from a pass-through security consists of coupon income, principal amortization, and prepayments. Coupon interest and principal amortization are predictable quantities. However, prepayments are inherently unpredictable, since they depend on the actions of individual property owners. As a matter of fact, the analysis of pass-through securities would be quite routine if it were not for the existence and unpredictability of prepayments. The key factors for prepayment of the principal balance are the sale of the property, refinancing of the original mortgage at a lower interest rate, and payment with insurance proceeds resulting from some disaster.

PRIVATE MORTGAGE INSURANCE

There is also private mortgage insurance (PMI) available on conventional and nongovernment insured mortgages. Insurance companies such as Mortgage Guaranty Insurance, Verex Insurance, Ticor Mortgage Insurance, and PMI Mortgage Insurance, recognizing the low default rate on home mortgages, have become heavily involved in insuring individual mortgages and packages of mortgages. Private mortgage insurance is a guarantee by private insurance companies on payment of principal and interest to the lender in the event of default. Often, this applies only to a portion of the loan. For instance, a lender might require any portion of the loan exceeding 80 percent of value to be covered by private mortgage insurance. The private mortgage insurance did not become an important element in the marketplace until the mid-1970s (see Table 10.3).

Table 10.3
Private and Government Mortgage Insurance (Dollar Amounts in Billions)

Year-end	Private Mortgage Insurance	One- to Four-family FHA/VA Insurance	Insurance as a % of Home Mortgage Debt	Year-end	Private Mortgage Insurance	One- to Four-family FHA/VA Insurance	Insurance as a % of Home Mortgage Debt
1960	$ 0.3	$ 56.4	40.0%	1977	$ 62.8	$141.6	31.8%
1965	3.3	73.1	34.6	1978	80.5	153.4	31.0
1970	7.3	97.3	35.2	1979	95.2	172.9	30.8
1971	9.6	105.2	35.2	1980	105.2	195.2	31.2
1972	17.5	113.0	35.6	1981	114.3	207.6	31.0
1973	27.4	116.2	35.2	1982	124.2	217.9	31.8
1974	33.6	121.3	35.1	1983	148.0	248.8	33.3
1975	40.0	127.7	34.8	1984	192.0	265.9	34.4
1976	49.3	133.5	33.5	1985*	223.7	n.a.	n.a.

n.a. = not available.
*Preliminary.
Sources: Department of Housing and Urban Development; Federal Housing Administration; Federal Reserve Board; Mortgage Insurance Companies of America; Veterans Administration.

Case A		Case B	
Uninsured Conventional Mortgage		*Privately Insured Conventional Mortgage*	
House Value		House Value	
$120,000 Equity	$24,000 Down payment	$120,000 Equity	$12,000 Down payment
		Insured Risk	
		$12,000 mortgage insurance	
Uninsured $96,000 mortgage at 10% APR		Uninsured $108,000 mortgage at 10% plus insurance premium = 10.25 to 10.5 APR on $108,000 balance	

In case A the lender extends a $96,000 mortgage at 10 percent and is in risk in case of default only if the house value falls by more than $24,000. In case B the lender extends a $108,000 mortgage at 10 percent and is still at risk only if the house falls by more than $24,000. The private mortgage insurer in case B bears the risk if the value of the house falls by $12,000 to $24,000 and the borrower defaults. The insurer receives an insurance premium equal to between one-fourth and one-half percent additional interest on the $108,000 debt.

Private mortgage insurance companies have helped fill the need for low down payment conventional mortgages by insuring the riskiest 10 to 20 percent of the total mortgage debt in return for a relatively high premium. This availability of insurance can allow a borrower to purchase a home with as little as 5 percent down. Unfortunately, when prices on homes stagnated in the early 1980s, many borrowers defaulted on low down payment loans, causing many private insurers to suffer huge losses. The financial problems of these mortgage insurers almost led to the collapse of private mortgage insurance.

SUMMARY OF MORTGAGE-TYPE SECURITIES

Since their introduction, mortgage-backed securities have often been called the real estate financing innovation of the 1970s. They have gained rapid acceptance by financial markets and have emerged as serious competition for corporate and municipal bonds.

At the most basic level, there are three types of securities that are classified according to the manner in which payments are made to the investor (see Figure 10.2):

1. Pass through
2. Pay through (cash flow)
3. Straight bond

A pass-through security represents an ownership interest in the underlying mortgages, providing monthly collections on the mortgage pool, less a service fee that is paid, interest and principal payments are "passed through" to the investor. The pass through is further broken down into three variations:

1. Straight pass through
2. Partially modified pass through
3. Modified pass through

A straight pass through pays principal and interest as and when collected from the pool to the investor. This is rarely used in public offerings, but is used in private placements. The often used participation mortgage loan by two or more lending institutions typically involves a type of straight pass through, since none of the lenders guarantees to the other receipt of principal or interest.

```
            Financial institutions make mortgage loans

            Mortgages are bundled and sold as securities

            These securities fall into three major types


        Pass-Throughs          Mortgage -Backed         Pay-Throughs
    ─────────────────      ─────────────────       ─────────────────

  * Ownership of mortgages   * Ownership remains     * Ownership remains
    goes to investor           with issuer             with issuer

  * Repayment goes to        * Repayment not dedi-    *Repayment Dedicated
    investor                   cated to investor       to investor

  * Debt does not appear     * MBBs show as liabil-   *Appears as debt on
    on bank's books            ity : mortgages         banks
                               appear as assets

  * Banks collects
    service fee
```

Figure 10.2
Securitization in the Mortgage Market
Source: Federal Reserve Bank of Chicago, Economic Perspectives (July–August 1986).

A partially modified pass through provides that monthly principal and interest payments will be made to the investor even if not collected from the mortgage pool. The best example of this type is the Bank of America mortgage-backed certificates, which guarantee payment of principal and interest to the investor up to 5 percent of the principal amount of the certificate.

A modified pass through guarantees and pays to the investor the scheduled monthly principal and interest payment, regardless of what amounts are collected from the pool mortgages. Just about all GNMA pass throughs are fully modified, while FNMA mortgage pass through securities are usually modified pass throughs.

The pay through or cash flow bond is an obligation secured by a mortgage pool, not a certificate evidencing ownership of an interest in a pool, whose payment features closely resemble those of a modified pass through security. In the simplest sense, a pay through bond is a fully amortizing instrument with scheduled principal and interest payments that closely track the scheduled collections on the collateral mortgage pool. The bonds are designed so that the required amortization from the collateral pool will at all times at least equal the payments of interest at the bond coupon rate and principal on the pay through bonds. Additional payments of principal are made to bond holders upon prepayments on the mortgage collateral pool, which implies that the life of the bonds is determined by the life of the pool.

The straight bond is also an obligation secured by a mortgage pool. It is similar to a corporate bond, with scheduled interest payments on a monthly, quarterly, or annual basis. Principal repayment is usually at the end of the bond term; however, scheduled interim principal reductions are not uncommon. These types of instruments often have call provisions and require that the issuer at all times maintain a specified amount of mortgages in the collateral pool. If a mortgage in the collateral pool is prepaid or is foreclosed, the issuer must substitute similar mortgages into the pool.

The market has seen a number of different instruments that are combinations of the pay through and straight bond in that principal reductions may be more erratic than the monthly pay down or call of the requisite number of bonds through the use of sinking funds and reserve accounts. This tends to make the bonds appear more as straight bonds than as mortgage instruments.

MORTGAGE BANKERS

No discussion of the mortgage market would be complete without the mention of mortgage banking. There are just over 800 mortgage banking firms. A mortgage bank is not a conventional bank in the sense that they do not accept deposits. However, a number of commercial banks have developed mortgage banking subsidiaries under the umbrella of a holding company. The salient function of the mortgage bank is to make or originate mortgage loans. The loans are funded primarily with short-term bank credit and a small amount of equity. As mortgages are accumulated, they are "packaged" or combined into substantial blocks of mortgages that vary in size from a few hundred thousand to several million dollars, and are sold to investors or Fannie Mae.

The mortgage banker has four potential sources of income. He can generate a profit or loss on the sale of mortgage packages. If he can lend at a rate that is higher than the rate demanded by investors for his packages, there is a profit. When rates are falling, it is not unusual for a mortgage banker to generate gains on the sale of a mortgage package. Naturally, it is also possible to generate losses when rates are rising.

There is also a potential for a "positive carry" on the mortgages the banker is holding while accumulating sufficient mortgages to make up a package while waiting for the sale to be consummated. A positive carry is generated if the short-term bank rates a mortgage banker pays for his funds are lower than the yield of the mortgages in the inventory. A "negative carry" occurs when short-term rates (the cost of the funds) are higher than the yield from the mortgages.

They earn origination and servicing fees, profits on resale of loans, and a profit or loss from the spread between mortgage yields and the cost of their borrowings during the short time that a given mortgage is "warehoused" before sale. In order to protect against negative spread (the mortgage yield is less than the cost of borrowed funds to make the mortgage) and to assure the presence of a subsequent buyer for mortgages originated, mortgage bankers typically secure commitments from institutions such as thrift institutions and life insurance companies to purchase on delivery by the seller a specified amount of mortgages within a certain time frame.

Part of the cost to the borrower is the so-called origination fee that is part of almost every mortgage loan. These costs are paid to the lending institution in the form of "points." For example, mortgage rates are ordinarily quoted as "11 percent, 30 years, with $3\frac{1}{2}$ points." This means that the lender gets a fee equal to 3.5 percent of the amount of the mortgage or $35 per $1,000 of face value. There are legal and clerical costs in generating a mortgage loan, but a large part of this front-end fee accrues to the lender as income.

In addition, there is "service income" in the form of fees paid by the final investor for collecting the payments as they come due and collecting and disbursing escrow funds for property taxes and hazard insurance. The mortgage servicer must remind borrowers when payments are overdue, record prepayments, keep records of mortgage balances, administer escrow accounts for payment of property taxes or insurance, send on year-end tax information and initiate foreclosure proceedings. The mortgage originator, the original lender, may service the loan or the mortgage servicing might be sold to another party. In addition to servicing fees, there are occasionally other fees that the servicer may keep. Some servicers are entitled to keep late payment fees paid by the borrower and foreclosure penalties.

The mortgage banker can also obtain fees associated with change of title, commissions from writing insurance on property, and, in some cases, property management fees. Service income is ongoing, risk-free revenue as opposed to one-time revenue generated by a loan origination payment. The service phase of mortgage banking can be an attractive business. Again, there are clerical costs involved but in sufficient volume, loan service may be highly profitable and provide an income stream similar to an annuity (see Table 10.4).

Institutional investors have sought the yields available on mortgages but have often not been willing to accept the risks of conventional mortgages on single-family homes. Also, these investors were often located at a great distance from where property expansion was occurring and did not wish to set up their own facilities for investigation of a large number of small loans. The mortgage banker can offer these investors insured mortgages and the servicing of these mortgages. Mortgage bankers fill an important niche in the mortgage market, and they depend on the existence of the secondary market for their continued operation. At the same time, they provide an important service to the secondary market by both originating mortgages to supply that market and by providing facilities to service mortgages that form the secondary market.

Mortgage bankers tend to originate between 10 and 30 percent of one- to four-family residential mortgages but tend to hold less than 1 percent of these mortgages at any point in time in their portfolios. Mortgage bankers came into being following the development of government insurance programs after the Great Depression.

MORTGAGE BROKERS

Mortgage bankers and mortgage brokers are rather different. A mortgage broker does not really make any loans or usually provide any significant amount of loan servicing. Instead, the mortgage broker simply serves as an intermediary between the borrower and the lender. The importance of this function should not be overlooked. Since the mortgage broker has a clear fiduciary responsibility to the borrower, there is freedom to search out the lowest rate, thereby encouraging competition among lenders.

SECOND MORTGAGES

It is possible to use the same piece of real estate to secure more than one loan. If the lender feels that the value of the property is in excess of the amount owed under the first mortgage, he may be willing to make a loan secured by the remaining equity in the property. The easiest way to explain the situation is with a simple illustration. The owner of a home with a market value of $100,000 owes $40,000 on the first mortgage. He wishes to borrow an additional $25,000 to invest in some other asset. He has two choices: either take out a new mortgage for $65,000 and use $40,000 to pay the existing mortgage, or take out a second mortgage. If the terms of the first mortgage are advantageous, the latter course may be more attractive. This is more common in situations where the home has

Table 10.4
Five of the Largest Mortgage Servicing Companies (June 30, 1986)

	Volume of Mortgages Serviced	Number of Mortgages Serviced
GMAC Mortgage Co.	$21,761,283,000	355,225
Lomas & Nettleton	21,299,782,000	684,736
Citicorp Homeowners Services	15,023,550,577	235,183
Fireman's Fund Mortgage Corp.	14,792,230,000	365,857
Metmor Financial Inc.	11,655,158,000	246,686

Source: Various Annual Reports and the *American Banker.*

been owned for several years and the interest rate on the first mortgage might be quite low. A market value has risen over those years to provide a large equity, thus providing sufficient collateral to the lender.

The second mortgage holder has the same rights as the first mortgage holder, and the only real difference occurs in the event of default. The entire balance of the first mortgage must be repaid before any funds are available to the second mortgage holder. In the event that the buyer defaults, it is therefore usually necessary for the second mortgage holder to repay the holder of the first mortgage entirely in order to foreclose on the property. There is obviously a significantly greater risk exposure in second mortgages. Holders of second mortgages should be prepared to repay the first mortgage holder in the event that they must take title to the property. Common clauses in second mortgages, however, frequently provide that the second mortgage holder may make the payment on the first mortgage loan, thus keeping it out of default and add those payments to the amount owed under the second mortgage. In this way, when the second mortgage holder forecloses on the property the first mortgage lien is kept intact and potential buyers at the foreclosure may be able to take advantage of the existing first mortgage.

Second mortgages were common in Rome in 400 B.C., so they are hardly a recent financial innovation. They have become increasingly common in recent years. Historically, the second mortgage lender was an individual or specialized institution such as a loan company. Most conventional mortgage institutions such as banks or savings and loans associations try to avoid second mortgages because of the risk factors and problems involved in the event of foreclosure. With the movement of the secondary market to include second mortgages, more and more of the traditional lenders have entered into this marketplace. Typically, interest rates on second mortgages are higher than rates for first mortgages and repayment terms are considerably shorter. In some markets, where prices have rapidly escalated even more than the national levels such as in California and Florida, third and fourth mortgages are not uncommon.

REAL ESTATE INVESTMENT TRUSTS (REITs)

REITs were set up to increase the flow of funds into the mortgage market. Many of the REITs are affiliated with bank holding companies, life insurance companies or mortgage banking firms. It was hoped that REITs would expand the availability of funds for the construction of housing when Congress set up the special tax benefit for REITs investors in the early 1960s. The Real Estate Investment Trust Act of 1960 exempted REITs from federal corporate income taxes, provided they met certain requirements such as the distribution of at least 90 percent of the ordinary income to its shareholders and the requirement that the REIT be owned by at least 100 shareholders with not more than half of the trust being owned or controlled by five or fewer stockholders.

REITs are analogous to closed-end investment companies for those who wish to invest in real estate. The principal difference between the two is that real estate investment trusts make extensive use of borrowed funds, while investment companies are not permitted to borrow funds. In both cases there is a fixed number of shares, and the trust or fund does not stand ready to sell additional shares or to buy back shares outstanding.

The main assets of REITs are mortgages and owned properties, while the main liabilities are outstanding credit market loans such as commercial paper or loans from commercial banks. Although REITs raise their initial capital through equity shares, most of their funds are raised through the selling of debt instruments.

The REITs industry grew rapidly from its initiation until 1974, when REITs held assets of approximately $17.5 billion. Throughout much of the post World War II period, short-term interest rates were lower than long-term interest rates. Many REITs assumed that this condition would continue and borrowed large amounts of short-term funds, which they used to make long-term mortgages. During 1973–1974, short-term rates exceeded long-term rates and this reduced the profitability of or caused actual losses for REITs. Because of the highly leveraged financial structures of REITs, the earnings of many REITs fluctuate considerably. These volatile fluctuations in earnings have led several REITs to bankruptcy and have caused financial difficulty for many others. In addition, too many bad loans were made in support of commercial and apartment construction projects. The problems were magnified by substantial overbuilding. Hence, the market value of industry assets declined rather rapidly to about $9 billion by 1984. However, during 1985, 36 new REITs filed with the SEC and industry assets appear to be beginning to expand once again on what some analysts have called the REIT rollercoaster ride.

SUMMARY

The dollar value of mortgage debt is the largest type of debt outstanding in the United States. The bulk of financing is for single-family homes. However, there are large markets for multifamily structures, commercial and industrial structures, and farms. Savings and loan associations are the dominant providers of one- to four-family homes, while commercial banks and life insurance companies are the major providers of funds in the commercial mortgage market.

In addition to conventional fixed-rate mortgages, lending institutions have developed a plethora of newer mortgage instruments. Adjustable rate mortgages, the most popular of the new mortgage instruments, have captured a large share of the market for home mortgages. The ARM has helped shift most of the interest rate risk from the lending institution to the mortgage borrower.

A secondary mortgage market has developed for home mortgages that is dominated by several government agencies, including GNMA, FHLMC, and FNMA. The secondary market provides a liquidity option for mortgage lending institutions. Another result of the development of secondary mortgage markets is that residential mortgage rates have become more uniform nationwide. In addition, mortgage markets have become more clearly linked to conventional capital markets.

Mortgage securities issues by quasi-government agencies with anthropomorphic nicknames such as Fannie Mae, Ginnie Mae, and Freddie Mac have become quite popular among institutional as well as individual investors. These securities, which entitle the investor to a portion of homeowners' monthly mortgage payments, have yielded as much as 150 basis points more than a Treasury bond. Each of the aforementioned agencies offers a different type of mortgage-related security with varying structures, yields, and guarantees.

It is possible to use the same piece of real estate to secure more than one loan. Second mortgages have become quite popular in California, where the value of most properties exceeded the amount owed under the first mortgage. Second mortgages have provided homeowners with liquidity. Many economists expect second mortgages to become popular throughout the country under the tax bill passed in 1986 because interest payments on conventional installment loans will no longer be tax deductible.

SELECTED BIBLIOGRAPHY

Alton, G. R., and A. S. Holland. "Has Deregulation of Deposit Interest Rates Raised Mortgage Rates?" Federal Reserve Bank of St. Louis, *Review* (May 1984): 5–15.

Beckman, N. G. "Mortgage Finance and the Housing Cycle." Federal Reserve Bank of Boston, *New England Economic Review* (September–October 1979): 54–76.

Federal Trade Commission. *The Mortgage Maze*. Washington, D.C., 1983.

Jones, Marcos T. "Mortgage Designs, Inflation, and the Real Interest Rates." Federal Reserve Bank of New York, *Quarterly Review* (Spring 1982): 20–27.

Lea, Michael J. "Adjustable Rate Mortgage." *Financial Markets Instruments and Concepts* 2nd ed. J. H. Brick et al., eds. Reston, Va.: Reston Publishing Co., 1986, pp. 207–18.

Marcis, Richard G. "The Shakeout in Alternative Mortgage Instruments." *Real Estate Review*, Vol. 13 (Spring 1983): 29–33.

McConnell, John J. "Survey of the Impact of Regulation on the Residential Mortgage Market." In D. S. Kidwell et al., eds., *The Impact of Regulation on the Provision of Consumer Financial Services by Depository Institutions: Research Background and Needs*. Monograph no. 10. West Lafayette, Ind.: Purdue University Credit Research Center, 1978.

McKenzie, Joseph A. "A Borrower's Guide to Alternative Mortgage Instruments." *Federal Home Loan Bank Board Journal* (January 1982): 16–22.

Melton, William C., and Diane L. Heidt. "Variable Rate Mortgages." Federal Reserve Bank of New York, *Quarterly Review* (Summer 1979): 22–31.

Peterson, Richard L. "Creative Financing: Its Nature and Risks." *The Bankers Magazine* (September–October 1982): 87–92.

Polish, C. J., and R. S. Stoddard. "ARMs: Their Financing Rate and Impact on Housing." Federal Reserve Bank of New York, *Quarterly Review* (Autumn 1985): 39–49.

Sivesand, Charles M. ''Mortgage Backed Securities: The Revolution in Real Estate Finance.'' Federal Reserve Bank of New York, *Quarterly Review* (Autumn 1979): 1–10.

Stern, R. L., and M. Clifford. ''Trouble at Home.'' *Forbes* (August 12, 1985): 31–34.

11

Stock Markets and Exchanges

WHAT IS A STOCK EXCHANGE?

A stock exchange is a securities market that provides a way in which investors may trade securities, easily, quickly, and efficiently. The stock exchange permits its members to trade stocks between themselves. In order to use the facilities of the exchange, it is necessary to become a member and to meet the requirements of the exchange in terms of capital, knowledge of trading techniques, and to maintain an acceptable standard of ethical conduct. Exchanges have only a limited number of members. If an individual or corporation wishes to become a member, it is necessary to purchase a membership, usually referred to as a seat, from an existing member. There are 1,366 seats on the New York Stock Exchange (NYSE), a number that has been fixed for decades. In 1968, seats on the NYSE sold for $515,000, but in 1977 they sold for as little as $35,000. However, NYSE seats sold for a record $1,100,000 in April 1987. This price was approximately 3 times the average price of a seat on the American Stock Exchange and 14 times the price on the Pacific Exchange.

Membership may be divided into classes based upon the members' activity. These classes are the commission broker, odd-lot broker, floor broker, floor trader, and bond broker. The bond broker handles a part of the close to 3,000 bond issues traded on the New York Exchange. A commission broker deals primarily with the public, buying and selling stocks for customers. The commission broker acts as an agent to the customer and receives a commission. The business is obtained through registered representatives or account executives who work for member firms and who are engaged in buying and selling securities on behalf of their employers. Every member firm must have at least one partner or stockholder who is a member of the New York Stock Exchange.

The odd-lot broker executes buy and sell orders for stocks in amounts from 1 to 99 shares. The customers of the odd-lot brokers are the odd-lot firms or other commission brokers that are member organizations and channel their odd-lot business to the odd-lot houses. There is typically a 12.5 or 25 cent service charge added to the price of each share. The approximately 200 floor brokers buy and sell shares for other brokers on the floor of the exchange, while the floor trader buys and sells for his own account; they do not do business with the public or another broker.

A specialist is a member of the exchange that is charged with the responsibility of maintaining a "continuous and orderly market" in a specific stock. Specialists can buy and sell for their own account or for the account of others. Each stock listed on the exchange is assigned a specialist and a trading post. The posts are large circular counters staffed with specialists and clerks. A specialist may have a responsibility for a number of different stocks, the number of which will depend on his capabilities in terms of capital and expertise. He must always be ready to either buy or sell shares of any stock for which he is responsible if there are no other sellers or buyers at the moment. He is also responsible for seeing that the variations in price between successive trades are not unusually large. He does this by continuously offering to buy or sell at prices that are close to the previous trade. While members trade between themselves, the rules of the exchange assure that the specialist can participate in any trade that takes place in his stocks. In addition to his functions as a buyer or seller, referred to as a market maker, he also maintains a "specialist's book," in which offers to buy or sell given amounts at specified prices are recorded.

Suppose, for example, that a broker has an order to sell 100 shares of XYZ Corporation at $60 per share. The last trade executed was at $55 per share. If the most recent price is $55, clearly there will be no one willing to buy at the moment at $60. The specialist would not be doing his job of maintaining a continuous and orderly market if he permitted the price to jump directly from $55 to $60 with no intervening trade. The selling broker will inform the specialist that he has an order for $60 and the specialist will record this in his "book." If and when additional buy orders are received, and the prices of the stock rise to $60, he will execute the orders he has recorded in the order they were received. In this way, he is acting in effect as a broker's broker, or acting for the broker that has originally received the order from the public. It is the specialist's functions that are the heart of the exchange system. As soon as a dealer and a specialist, or two dealers, agree on a transaction, the price, volume, time, and date are recorded on a machine-readable card that is fed into a computer system that flashes the quotation on the ticker service and records the order for the exchange's back office clearing operation.

In most cases, an order to buy or sell a stock on the New York or American Stock Exchange is telephoned from brokerage office to a floor broker, who hand carries it to the specialist in that stock. The specialist keeps a ledger that enables him to pair off buy and sell orders. Trading on NASDAQ needs no auction floor and does not utilize specialists. By pushing a few buttons on a terminal a buyer or seller summons up the latest bid and asking price offered by each of the market makers in any NASDAQ stock. After reviewing the prices on the screen, a broker or institutional trader can consummate a deal by telephoning or teletyping the market maker who offers the best price.

ORGANIZED EXCHANGE MARKETPLACE

The New York Stock Exchange, the largest stock exchange in the United States, moved to its present headquarters at Broad and Wall in 1903. It has a structure that closely parallels a private holding company, with a limited total voting membership of 1,366. Close to 550 brokerage firms are represented on the Exchange which had 2,332 stocks traded in 1985. The trading amounted to 35.68 billion shares in 1986 with a market value of $1.37 trillion compared with 27.71 billion shares with a market value of $970.5 billion traded in 1985. The daily volume averaged 141 million shares in 1986 compared with 109.2 million in 1985 and 28.6 million in 1978 (see Figure 11.1).

The American Stock Exchange (AMEX), also located in New York City, is the fifth largest exchange in the country in terms of trading volume. The total volume of shares traded on the AMEX reached 3 billion shares with a daily volume of 11.8 million shares during 1986. That accounted for under 4 percent of share volume in U.S. stocks. Other large regional exchanges are the Boston, Midwest, Pacific, PBW (Philadelphia, Baltimore, Washington), and Chicago Board Options Exchange. In addition, there are about a dozen active commodity exchanges in the United States, with options and financial futures among the fastest growing lines of business.

The largest public corporations are generally listed for trading on the NYSE, but there are thousands of traded securities that remain unlisted, as well as thousands of individuals and firms that are not exchange members. Regulation of these smaller brokerage firms and over-the-counter securities is provided by the National Association of Securities Dealers (NASD).

The NASD has helped provide a structure for the training and registering of individuals and firms that are not exchange members and to oversee the trading and clearance of OTC traded securities. NASD and private computer firms have been developing a computerized communications network (NASDAQ) that displays price information and does computer-linked trading for the more active OTC stocks and some exchange-listed securities. Dealers are linked in a nationwide computer system with video display units that enable them to make a market in a particular security by entering bid-ask quotes for a minimum of 100 shares. Another dealer may place the stock of interest on the screen and call the dealer, offering a market if the price seems attractive to arrange a transaction at the desired volume. Of the 50.3 billion in shares traded on the NYSE, AMEX, and NASDAQ in 1985, NASDAQ accounted for 41.1 percent, the NYSE 54.7 percent, and the AMEX 4.2 percent. NASDAQ's share volume accounted for 37% of equities trading in domestic securities markets during 1985. This was equivalent to more than three quarters the share volume of the NYSE and 10 times the share volume of the AMEX (see Figure 11.1). Share volume in NASDAQ issues was more than three times the combined share volume of the AMEX, Boston, Cincinnati, Midwest, Pacific, and Philadelphia-Baltimore-Washington Stock Exchange. In terms of companies, the NASDAQ market had

	NASDAQ			NYSE			Amex		
Year	Companies	Issues	Share Volume (Millions)	Companies	Issues	Share Volume (Millions)	Companies	Issues	Share Volume (Millions)
1985	4,136	4,784	20,699	1,540	2,298	27,511	783	940	2,101
1984	4,097	4,723	15,159	1,543	2,319	23,071	792	930	1,545
1983	3,901	4,467	15,909	1,550	2,325	21,590	822	948	2,081
1982	3,264	3,664	8,432	1,526	2,225	16,458	834	944	1,338
1981	3,353	3,687	7,823	1,565	2,220	11,854	867	919	1,343

Figure 11.1
Five-Year Comparisons of NASDAQ, NYSE, and AMEX

Source: National Association of Securities Dealers.

4,136 and the number of securities reached 4,784. NASDAQ has grown rapidly because it is an electronic stock market with 5,200 NASD member firms linked through a computer complex in Trumbull, Connecticut.

There are three service-related corporations that partly are controlled by the NYSE. The National Securities Clearing Corp (NSCC) is essentially a channel through which the books of brokerage firms, exchanges, and other clearing corporations are brought into balance. The Depository Trust Co. is a central certificate depository organized to immobilize the physical transfer of securities. It holds in its vaults $1.4 billion of stocks and $800 million of bonds. The Securities Industry Automation Corp. (SIAC) provides much of the communications and computer facilities and systems necessary to run the New York and American Stock Exchanges.

EXCHANGES AND MARKETS

Security markets exist to aid the allocation of capital among households, corporations, and governmental units, with financial institutions acting as intermediaries. Markets also provide liquidity in two ways. They enable corporations to raise funds by selling new issues of securities and they allow the investor who purchases securities to sell them with relative ease and speed. Without markets, governmental units and corporations would not be able to raise the large amounts of capital necessary for economic growth. The New York Stock Exchange is the place where the stocks and bonds of the largest U.S. corporations are traded.

The U.S. stock exchanges could undergo a radical transformation as computers become widely used in trading markets. Before 1990, regional stock exchanges could become part of an electronically linked National Market System. Such a system should enable all investors, regardless of their location, to buy and sell securities at the best prices available anywhere in the country. This electronic hook-up would permit interaction among customers' orders without necessitating intervention by a dealer. Investors would be provided not only with a wider choice of prices on a larger choice of stocks, but with a faster action on orders. Although the National Market System was mandated by Congress in 1975, full-scale implementation lies in the future. Brokers, who would sometimes be by-passed in electronic trading, have resisted such computerization. This has slowed the establishment of a national exchange.

The national securities market is under study by the SEC and the National Market Association, an industry group representing seven major stock markets. The latest proposal would be a communications system linking the New York, American, PBW, Midwest, Boston, and Pacific Coast Stock Exchanges and the over-the-counter trading in listed stocks. The communication system would be supervised by the National Association of Securities Dealers. At present, these markets are tied together with the consolidated tape. The result would be not a national securities market, but several different markets competing for business. In late 1985 the SEC brought a national market system closer when it allowed the stock exchanges to begin trading in a limited number of over-the-counter stocks on an experimental basis.

Other changes in the stock exchanges are forthcoming. The current auction market system with stocks traded on an exchange floor may evolve into a system resembling the dealer market that now exists in bond trading and in OTC stocks, where securities are traded off the trading floor. The new system could develop into a hybrid of the dealer and auction market, where only trades are handled off the board. Some stock specialists will survive, but they could become a rare specimen. The stock certificate could become extinct as a growing number of transactions are recorded in computer memory and a book entry system is used.

Technological development in the securities industry has been instrumental in facilitating the processing of transactions, helping to reduce costs, improving marketing efforts, creating new products and services, and stimulating unprecedented competition. Considering that 100 to 200 million shares a day were traded on the NYSE in 1986–1987, it is difficult to believe that the NYSE had to close the trading floor early because brokers could not keep up with 10 to 12 million share days in 1967.[1]

Automation has helped to reduce costs and to speed up the flow of orders to the markets. Regional stock exchanges such as the PBW and the Pacific Exchange were quick to grasp the competitive advantage of automated execution systems in their efforts to gain market share away from the NYSE. Another salient event has been the inauguration of the Intermarket Trading System, an electronic network that links seven regional stock markets and the OTC market. The system allows for a given stock order to be executed immediately in whichever market has the best price quotation.[2]

The NYSE has developed Super Dot, an order-routing system through which members can transmit their order directly to the post on the floor of the exchange where the securities are traded and quickly receive a return execution report. Electronic books are currently available for filing limit orders to buy and sell at specified prices, replacing the handwritten order books that used to be maintained by specialists. Specialists can also utilize a touch-sensitive TV screen to perform reporting, trade, and quote dissemination tasks for orders.[3]

NYSE LISTING REQUIREMENTS

The securities traded on the floor of the New York Stock Exchange are those that have been listed. The NYSE has more stringent listing requirements than any other securities exchange in the United States.[4] In order to have its common stock listed on the NYSE, a U.S. company must:

1. Have at least 2,000 holders of 100 shares or more.
2. Have at least 1 million publicly held common shares.
3. Have a total of at least $16 million for the current market value of its publicly held common stock.

4. Have net tangible assets of $16 million.

5. Have before-tax income of $2.5 million in the year prior to listing and $2 million in before-tax income for each of the preceding two years.

Following listing, the NYSE can choose to delist or suspend a security. Causes for delisting include, in addition to a failure to maintain listing requirements, mergers, consolidations, and name changes.

MARKET STRUCTURE

There are two basic types of markets for stocks and bonds. The primary market is the market for new issues of stock. If the proceeds of the sale of a share of common stock benefit the issuing corporation, it is a primary market sale. If the proceeds of a stock sale are remitted to any other entity, it is a secondary market sale.

The primary market is a source of equity funds to corporations. The secondary market provides the liquidity that makes investment in stocks attractive to investors. Trading in the secondary market is continuous, and while there are considerable variations in the total number of shares traded day to day, the volume is always substantial.

In the primary market, there are greater variations in the volume of new issues depending on market conditions. Generally, there will be substantial activity in the new issues market when stock prices are rising. Corporate issuers naturally wish to sell stocks at the highest possible prices.

While it is theoretically possible for a corporation to sell stock directly to the public, stock issues virtually always involve an investment banker. The exceptions generally involve shelf registrations, which are permitted under SEC rule 415. An investment banker or investment bank is a highly specialized financial organization that provides or arranges financing for businesses. The investment banker has the ability to distribute securities to institutional investors and the investing public. The distribution is accomplished through his own sales force and through his ability to enlist the aid of other investment bankers through syndicates. It is this reselling network that allows broad public participation in the issue. The investment banker usually purchases the stock from the issuing company and resells it to the public, earning a modest underwriting spread. This initial issuance of stock is considered the primary market. The actual check received from the corporation is from the investment banker, who is actually a conduit for the funds of the public to the corporation.

The structure of the secondary market is considerably more complex than that of the primary market. It involves exchanges such as the New York and American Stock Exchanges and the over-the-counter market. Only a relatively small percentage of corporations have publicly traded stock, and only a fraction of these have shares that are listed on an exchange. The balance of the shares of public corporations are traded over-the-counter.

Security markets are often classified into four divisions: exchanges, over-the-counter, third, and fourth markets. The third market developed in response to the absence of volume commission rate discounts on the NYSE. The main participants in the third market are institutions such as bank trust accounts, pension funds, insurance companies, mutual funds, and a few select private individuals. These customers reduce their brokerage costs and obtain better prices on exchange listed securities that they buy and sell at negotiated commissions in the third market (part of the over-the-counter market). Since the third market makers deal almost exclusively with broker-dealers and institutions, the services offered are minimal. Trading in the third market reached its peak in 1972, when it accounted for 8.5 percent of the volume traded on the NYSE. Since then, third-market volume as a percentage of NYSE volume has steadily declined, presumably because the era of negotiated commissions has decreased the need for the third market.

The fourth market refers to those institutions and wealthy individuals who buy and sell securities directly among one another, completely bypassing the broker. The market is essentially a communications network among block traders. The fourth market organizer may collect a small commission or a flat annual retainer for helping to arrange these large annual transactions. The fourth market represents a competitive force in the marketplace and encourages the exchanges and the OTC to handle blocks efficiently at a lower cost. Several privately owned fourth market organizers facilitate this type of transaction.

COMMISSIONS CHARGED FOR COMMON STOCK PURCHASE

Prior to 1975, the New York Stock Exchange, with the approval of the SEC, specified the minimum fees that a member of the NYSE could charge. These fixed commissions applied not only to the small investor but to institutional investors. Since these large investors did not receive lower per share fees to reflect the economies of scale for large volume transactions, they were largely responsible for bringing about the third and fourth markets. As part of the Securities Act Amendments of 1975, all fixed commissions were eliminated in May 1975 and fees were supposed to be negotiated, with each firm acting independently (see Table 11.1). One salient result of the "May Day" change insofar as brokerage commissions were concerned, was the birth and growth of the discount brokers. One result of the change in 1975 was the unbundling of brokerage services so that customers pay only for the services they really want. For example, discount brokers concentrate on executing orders and charge only for that service, while full service brokerage houses offer advice, research, recommendations, and order execution. For example, for a small institutionalized order of 1,000 shares of a $45 stock, the 1975 basic cost might have been 35 cents a share (100 shares would have sold at 65 cents a share), the rate today would be between 5 cents and 15 cents a share for a 1,000 share purchase. For individuals, "discount brokers" are offering 30 to 90 percent discounts from the 1975 rates for no-frills brokerage service.

Initially the deregulation of commission rates reduced the profits earned in

Table 11.1
Fixed-Commission Rates for Stock Trades Prior to May 1975

				Stock Price				
Shares Traded	$5	$10	$15	$20	$25	$50	$75	$100
100	18	28	35	42	49	71	81	81
200	36	55	68	77	87	143	161	161
300	54	74	89	117	134	215	242	242
500	82	107	148	176	204	325	400	404
1000	140	214	270	325	363	499	623	748
2000	263	375	450	499	549	797	1046	1294

Source: NYSE Board of Governors. *The New York Stock Exchange Fact Book* (New York: New York Stock Exchange, 1976), p. 59.

commission business by most brokerage firms. Many smaller and troubled firms elected to go out of business or to sell out to larger firms. Other firms began diversifying into new activities, placing more emphasis on noncommission businesses. The biggest firms have become even larger and more dominant in the securities brokerage industry.

The small investor might not enjoy the same access to inside markets available to institutions. Consequently, he may seek ways to invest through mutual funds or other types of institutional vehicles that are large enough to have access to the inside market. Mutual funds will represent a popular way for the small investor to tap the equity market. The small investor in the year 2000 is likely to be older, better educated, wealthier in terms of assets and income, and better informed. At the same time, he will have the luxury of expanded communication channels, with more investor affairs conducted over the telephone. He may even have at his fingertips a cathode ray tube where he can observe transaction data, as well as a printer for presenting hard copy for tax records. The investing consumer could routinely pay bills from the home via terminals or phone as EFT, home computers, and videotex systems become more accessible and acceptable to consumers.

THE OVER-THE-COUNTER MARKET

Compared to the approximately 2,300 companies that have listed their shares on the New York Stock Exchange, there are more than 30,000 stocks that are traded over-the-counter. Most of these are relatively small companies with only a limited number of followers and/or shareholders. When a stock is traded over-the-counter, a trade is usually still arranged by a broker, but the trade is executed without the intervention of an exchange.

The key element in the over-the-counter market is the "market maker." A market maker in the over-the-counter market is a brokerage institution that buys and sells shares in one or more OTC stocks for his own account. In most transactions, the broker is acting as an agent, but in the OTC market, the market maker is acting as a principal on one side of the transaction.

The trade may take place in a variety of ways. The simplest is a case where a single broker or market maker purchases the stock offered for his own account or sells from his own inventory. A somewhat more complex transaction would involve a trade arranged by the broker between two individuals. Still more complex is the simultaneous purchase and sale of a security by the market maker. Finally, there are trades involving brokers that are not market makers in a specific security. Here, a purchaser calls his broker to buy a stock. The broker with the purchase order calls one of the market makers in the stock to effect the trade. It is theoretically possible to have as many as four people involved in a single transaction: a buying broker, a buying market maker, a selling market maker, and a selling broker.

The over-the-counter market maker is not under any obligation from an organization like the exchange to maintain the market, and can enter the market or leave it at his discretion. Any broker can become a market maker in any stock he chooses at any time. While there is only one specialist designated for each stock on the organized exchanges, there can be any number of market makers in a stock traded over-the-counter. Because there is no authority to control trading in the over-the-counter market, there is no assurance that there will be a bid for a stock at any given time, or conversely, there is no assurance that an investor can purchase a specific stock at any time. If the stocks are traded on an exchange, the investor is assured that he can buy or sell any stock listed on the exchange at any time during trading hours.

There is no law or rule that specifies that stocks can only be traded by brokers or on exchanges if they are listed stocks. There is nothing that would prevent two individuals from executing a trade between themselves even in a listed stock. All it would take is the desire on the part of the owner to sell and another individual to buy. If they could agree on price and terms, they could execute the trade without the assistance of any third party. This is, in fact, fairly common among professional investors. The advantage of third market trades to the professional investor is lower transaction costs and some measure of privacy. Any trade executed on the exchange is immediately recorded and reported to all the members via ticker tape. In an over-the-counter or third market transaction, there is no public reporting of the transaction at any time. There is still a broker involved to whom the buyer and seller both pay a commission or transaction cost.

There are a finite number of major institutional investors. Depending on the definitions involved, the number may run from a few hundred to a few thousand. It is not difficult for major institutions to identify their opposite numbers in the marketplace and contact them directly. In this way, they can avoid transaction costs almost entirely, and preserve almost total anonymity. The technique is simplicity itself: The traders simply call their colleagues at other institutions and offer to buy or sell stock directly. A variety of computerized systems have been developed to assist in the process of trading large blocks of stock between institutions.

EXCEPTIONS AND SPECIAL CASES IN SECURITY TRADING

Almost 70 percent of corporate stock is held by major institutional investors, bank trust departments, insurance companies, mutual funds, pension funds, and other similar organizations. When these investors buy or sell, the problems are far different from those involved when individuals trade a few hundred shares at a time.

Major institutions may trade in "blocks" valued in millions of dollars. Clearly, trades of this magnitude can influence the market price of the shares involved. The market has developed a number of devices to facilitate trades of this type. Every major broker has a "block desk" that does nothing but attempt to put together trades of large blocks. A "block" is usually defined as 10,000 shares or more of a single stock in a single transaction. The block desk, upon receiving an order, will immediately contact every other large institution in the world to try and find "the other side," the buyer or the seller. If the block desk is successful in finding the other side of the transaction, the buy and sell orders are simultaneously transmitted to the floor, and the stock is "crossed" by the floor broker. This involves no risk on the part of the broker. In the event that the broker is not successful in finding the required buyer for the full amount of shares involved in the trade, he may "block position" or take some of the shares into his own inventory to complete the trade for the client. The broker now has a substantial risk in the transaction so he may try to execute the transaction on the floor. He will handle it like any other transaction and go to the specialist involved.

The specialist's position is now rather uncomfortable. He has his duty to provide a market for the stock but he knows that every potential major buyer in the world has already been contacted. If he buys the stock offered, it goes into his inventory, and his capital is at risk. The market will be aware of his inventory position and the fact that he will have to be a seller on balance until his inventory is back to something approaching normal levels. This will tend to put pressure on the stock and prevent normal buying from taking place at anything but deteriorating levels. In fact, the specialist may not have available sufficient capital to purchase large blocks of stock from institutions.

Rather than permit discontinuities in the trading pattern of the stock, the specialist has the right to request suspension of trading in his stocks until he has time to arrange a trade at close to the preceding price. In reality, the specialist can decline to participate in a major way in a trade. In addition trading can be suspended for "order imbalance" on significant news. This makes the specialist's job easier. He can appeal for assistance to another group of traders on the floor known as floor traders. These are individuals that own exchange seats but trade only for their own accounts and do not act as brokers or agents for others. They provide depth and liquidity to the market and are governed by still another set of exchange rules. They may act individually or in groups to assist the specialist with large quantities of stock when it is either demanded or offered. Usually, a specialist can arrange resumption of trading in a period of a few hours when large blocks are offered to him. There is no similar arrangement in the over-the-counter market to facilitate large block transactions.

In 1965 only 3.1 percent of NYSE reported volume was in the form of large blocks, while by 1985 block shares accounted for more than half the NYSE volume. Since institutional trades account for more than 50 percent of the value of NYSE transactions, special methods have been devised to handle large block trades of 10,000 shares or more away from the auction market at the specialist's post. At any given point in time, orders arriving at the trading post for a particular stock may not be in balance. The specialist must decide how much to adjust the quote on a stock to bring the market closer to balance. The quote is in terms of a bid price and an ask price where the standard spread is between $\frac{1}{8}$ and $\frac{1}{4}$ of a point. For small imbalances, the specialist may buy and sell from his own inventory, with the expectation of rebalancing the position by a transaction on the other side of the market.

In the past decade, a practice known as "dual listing" has developed. A corporation may list its shares on more than one exchange. It should be noted that a corporation that lists its shares on an exchange must meet the requirements of that exchange in terms of number of shares outstanding, number of shareholders, and history of profitability. They must also pay for the privilege of being listed. In the case of dual listed stocks, there is the possibility that there may be price variations on the same stock at the same time. It is the responsibility of the broker to secure for his client the most advantageous price, the lowest available price for buyers, and the highest available price for sellers. It is also the right of the investing public to know all the activity in given stock if the activity takes place on an exchange. These problems have led to the development of the so-called composite tape, a system that will provide information simultaneously on all trading that takes place on any exchange in any stock listed. The primary problem is in stocks listed on the NYSE or AMEX that are also listed on one or more of the regional exchanges. The composite tape must still be considered experimental, and the final form of this truly national information system has yet to be determined.

TYPES OF SECURITY ORDERS

Market orders are orders to buy and sell at the market price prevailing when the order reaches the specialist's post on the floor of the exchange. Limit orders are orders by the customer to place limits on the price at which the order can be executed. Day orders are canceled at the end of the day that the order is received if it is not executed. Good till canceled orders remain on the books until executed or canceled by the customer. Stop-loss orders are orders that can be used to help limit losses on existing positions. They can only be executed for listed stocks. Short selling consists of selling securities that are not owned by the seller. Customers expect to be able to buy the stock later at a lower price, therefore making a profit. The Federal Reserve Board requires short selling customers to deposit 50 percent of the net proceeds of such sales with the brokerage firm effecting the transactions. Also, a short sale can take place only on either an "up tick" in the stock price or a "zero tick" (no price change) that follows an "up tick." This regulation militates against successively lower prices instigated by a series of short sales.

When an order is placed with a stockbroker and is executed on the exchange floor, the transaction must be settled within five working days. The investor who placed the order must deliver cash for a purchase or security certificate for a sale to the broker.

The purchase of securities may be for cash or on margin, where a customer initially pays only a fraction of the price of the security. Margin is simply the equity that a customer has in a transaction. The balance is loaned to the customer by the brokerage firm for an interest charge. Basic margin requirements are set by Regulation T of the Federal Reserve Board with additional conditions imposed by the customer's brokerage firm or by the stock exchanges. Currently, Regulation T permits brokers to lend up to 50 percent of the value of stocks or convertible bonds acquired or sold short by customers, 70 percent for corporate bonds, and about 90 percent for U.S. government securities (see Table 11.2). When the margin in an account becomes inadequate, a "margin call" is sent to the customer requesting payment of the deficiency. If the payment is not immediately made, the broker may sell the margined stock at market and close out the transaction.

Most common stocks and bonds listed on exchanges can be purchased on margin. The securities being purchased are used as collateral for the loan and are registered in the "street name" of the brokerage firm or other financial institution as custodian for the purchasing investor. When a customer borrows on margin, the brokerage firm is permitted to use the securities as collateral at the bank from which the brokerage firm borrowed the money to finance the customer loan. The bank charges the broker the broker loan rate, and the broker in turn charges the customer this rate plus an additional 100 to 150 basis points.

In addition to Federal Reserve regulation of credit, the NYSE has certain credit requirements. For example, no person may open a margin account without depositing at least $2,000 or its equivalent in securities. The NYSE imposes special margin requirements on special issues, which show a combination of volume, price variation, and turnover of unusual dimensions. The special margin requirements were not imposed on any issues in 1985. Margin debt rose to a

Table 11.2
Initial Margin Requirements

Effective	Rate
10/15/34	45%
2/ 1/36	55
11/ 1/37	40
2/ 5/45	50
7/ 5/45	75
1/21/46	100
2/ 1/47	75
3/30/49	50
1/17/51	75
2/20/53	50
1/ 4/55	60
4/23/55	70
1/16/58	50
8/ 5/58	70
10/16/58	90
7/28/60	70
7/10/62	90
11/ 6/63	70
6/ 8/68	80
5/ 6/70	65
12/ 6/71	55
11/24/72	65
1/ 3/74	50

Source: NYSE Board of Governors, *The New York Stock Exchange Fact Book* (New York: New York Stock Exchange, 1986).

record $28.4 billion in 1985, while the number of accounts in debit status exceeded one million for the first time.[5]

STOCK MARKET INDICATORS

Stock market indicators such as the Dow Jones Industrial Average (DJIA) and the New York Stock Exchange Composite Index perform a variety of functions that range from serving as benchmarks for sophisticated performance analyses to answering the question, ''How did the market do today?'' Each market indicator measures a different facet of the market.

There are three factors that differentiate stock market indicators:

1. The universe of stocks represented by the indicators
2. The relative weights given to the stocks
3. The method of averaging used

In general, the indicators rise and decline together; however, there are differences in the magnitude of these moves.

An index or average can be designed from all publicly traded stocks or simply from a sample of publicly traded stocks. The NYSE Composite Index reflects the market value of all issues traded on the NYSE, while the S&P 500 consists of stocks chosen from the major exchanges and the OTC market. The Value Line Average Composite (VLA) consists of about 1,700 widely traded stocks; while the DJI monitors 30 of the largest blue chip companies traded on the NYSE. These companies have changed over time due to bankruptcies, mergers, or a low level of trading activity. The NASDAQ Composite Index reflects changes in the market value of the OTC stocks traded by the NASD.

Each stock in an index or average is assigned some relative weight. The three ways that weights are assigned are:

1. Weighting by market value of the company (S&P 500)
2. Weighting by the price of the company's stock (DJIA)
3. Weighting each company equally, regardless of its price or value (VLA)

With the exception of the VLA, which is based on a geometric average, market indicators are based on arithmetic averages (see Table 11.3).

In addition to the DJIA, which was first computed on May 26, 1896, Dow Jones and Company computes and publishes three other stock price averages: the Public Utility Average, consisting of 15 electric and natural gas utilities; the Transportation Average, consisting of 20 stocks drawn from the railroad, airline, and trucking industries; and a 65-stock Composite Average, which combines all stocks into one average.

Table 11.3
Market Indicators

	S&P 500	NYSE Composite	VLA	DJIA	NASDAQ Composite
Relative Weighting scheme	MVA	MVA	EW	PW	MVA
Method of Averaging	A	A	G	A	A
Base Year	1941–43	1965	1961	N/A	1971
Value of Indicator in base year	10	500	100	N/A	100
Number of Stocks in Indicator	500	1520 a	1700 a	30	3500 a
Markets Where Stocks Are Traded	NYSE AMEX OTC	NYSE	NYSE AMEX OTC CANADIAN	NYSE	OTC

N/A = not available

MVA = market value weighted

PW = price weighted

EW = equally weighted

A = arithmetic

G = geometric

a = approximately

Among the shortcomings of a stock price average, such as any of the Dow Jones averages, is that components with the highest share prices have the biggest influence on the level of the composite average. The DJIA, which accounts for about 20 percent of the market's total equity, is a price weighted average of the 30 component stocks. Critics of the DJIA do not regard it as a particularly good indicator of the general price movement over the long term because it is not typical of the overall stock market and doesn't have the same level of risk as the market. It is also dominated by a few companies and is price weighted. The DJIA is likely to underperform the market over the long term, since riskier stocks tend to outperform less risky stocks. The Dow can also be a weak indicator of short-term movements as can be seen by examining the DJIA increase of 4.81 on September 24, 1985. On that day General Foods rose by $16\frac{5}{8}$ points. The DJIA would have fallen 9 points without the General Foods increase. On the same day, the S&P Index fell 1.78 and the NYSE Index fell 0.91.

COMPOSITE TICKER TAPE

The stock ticker tape is a familiar feature of brokerage firm boardrooms. Each trading day, a live report of round-lot (100 shares) transactions in listed stocks, which have taken place on the NYSE and AMEX, is transmitted electronically to brokerage houses in the form of a continuous, one-half inch wide paper strip, or electronic representation of it presented in the board room for all to see. The top line contains stock symbols, which may consist of one, two, or three letters. The numerals on the bottom line indicate volume and price for each transaction reported. For example, an average day might look something like this:

EK	T		IBM
$72\frac{1}{2}$	$2S\ 23\frac{1}{8}$	$4S\ \frac{1}{8}$	$1000S\ 150$

The following is a translation of the above ticker tape:

Name of stock price	Number of shares traded
Eastman Kodak (EK) $72\frac{1}{2}$	100
AT&T (T) $23\frac{1}{8}$	200
AT&T (T) $23\frac{1}{8}$	400
International Business Machines (IBM) 150	1000

The price of shares of common stock reflect supply and demand. By custom, trading on U.S. stock exchanges takes place in most securities at one-eighth dollar intervals. Thus, trading may take place at $35\frac{1}{8}$, or $35\frac{3}{8}$, but not at $35\frac{1}{3}$. A few stocks trade at one sixteenth point intervals and options and "penny" stocks (priced under one dollar) on some regional exchanges may trade at even narrower intervals.

STOCK MARKET INFORMATION AND AVAILABILITY

Investors can obtain information on the performance of individual stocks and various market averages such as the Dow Jones Industrial average or the Standard & Poor's 500 from national publications such as the *Wall Street Journal*, the *New York Times, Barron's, MIG Financial Weekly, Commercial and Financial Chronicle,* and most local newspapers. Standard & Poor's *Stock Guide* (a monthly publication) provides a rating system for common stock so as to identify the investment characteristics about specific securities, while Standard & Poor's *Stock Reports* or *Fact Sheets* provide on both sides of one page, a concise and factual interpretation of data about most companies whose stock is actively traded.

In addition, *The Stock Survey* (a weekly publication of Moody's), *The Outlook* (a weekly publication of Standard & Poor's), and the reference manuals issued by Moody's and Standard & Poor's, as well as the weekly *Value Line Investment Survey* provide information to investors that permits them to make a proper assessment and analysis of a company for investment purposes. These services also review market conditions and make specific recommendations about common stocks. Lots of information is available from members of the brokerage community that provide an abundance of factual information and opinion about common stocks. A company's annual report and 10K report gives a statement on the financial affairs of the company and the products and services offered. The *Wall Street Transcript* reproduces select brokerage house reports and interviews with securities analysts on specific companies and industries.

Economic forecasts and various industry forecasts are available from most brokerage firms, money center banks, large regional banks, the Federal Reserve Banks, *Business Week, Fortune* magazine, the Conference Board, Wharton Econometrics, Data Resources, and Chase Econometrics. The *New York Times, Washington Post, Dun's Magazine, Money Magazine, Forbes,* and the *Nation's Business* frequently provide excellent reports on economic, business, and investment conditions. There is also a popular television show, "Wall Street Week," which provides a review of the past week's investment and economic news and interviews with Wall Street money managers and analysts who offer their opinions on particular investments and the stock market outlook.

Additional journals and periodicals on investments include *Financial World, Institutional Investor, Financial Analysts Journal, OTC Review,* and *Journal of*

Portfolio Management. Industry data is available from *Statistical Abstract of the United States, Business Statistics,* Standard & Poor's Statistical Service, *Basebook, Predicasts, U.S. Industrial Outlook, F&S Index to Corporations and Industries, Dun and Bradstreet Key Business Ratios, Robert Morris Associates Annual Studies, Value Line Investment Surveys, Moody's Manuals,* and Standard & Poor's Investment Advisory Service, Industry Surveys, and *Outlook.* U.S. government publications include: *Census of Mineral Industries, Census of Selected Services, Census of Construction Industry, Census of Transportation, Census of Retail Trade, Census of Wholesale Trade,* and its *Annual Survey of Manufacturers.* There are also various trade journals covering different industries such as *Chemical Week, Modern Plastics, Pulp, Paper Board Packaging, Electrical World, Petroleum Times, Ward's Auto World, Automotive News,* and *Textile World.* Studies of various industries are available from Arthur D. Little, Inc., SRI, Predicasts, Business Trend Analysts, and Data Resources Inc.

Information on money market instruments and bonds is readily available in *Money Manager, Weekly Bond Buyer, Banker's Trust Credit and Capital Markets, Moody's Bond Survey, Value Line Options and Convertible, Moody's Bond Record, Moody's Municipal and Government Manual, Moody's International Bond Review, Standard & Poor's Bond Guide,* and *Standard & Poor's Convertible Bond Reports.* Mutual fund information is available in *Vicker's Guide to Investment Company Portfolios, Weisenburger Investment Companies, Investment Dealers' Digest Mutual Fund Directory, Investment Company Institute's Mutual Fund Fact Book,* and various publications by Donaghue on money market funds. *Business Week, Forbes,* and *Money Magazine* have special annual issues featuring mutual funds.

SUMMARY

New issues of equity securities may be sold directly to investors by the issuing corporation or they may be underwritten and distributed through an investment banker. The secondary market for corporate stock is the largest in dollar volume and number of trades of any security. Trading takes place on either organized exchanges, such as the NYSE or the AMEX, or in the over-the-counter market. The largest public corporations are usually listed for trading on the NYSE. During 1987 a seat on the NYSE sold for a record breaking $1.1 million.

Prior to 1975 the NYSE specified minimum fees that a member of the NYSE could charge for both small investors and institutional investors. However, fixed commissions were eliminated in May 1975, with fees to be negotiated with each firm independently. Many discount brokerage firms were established that concentrate on executing orders and charge only for that service. On the other hand, full-service brokerage houses offer advice, research, recommendations, and order execution.

Accounts at brokerage firms can be either cash accounts or margin accounts. With a margin account, the customer can pay part of the total due and borrow the rest from the broker. The Board of Governors of the Federal Reserve System has the authority to specify the initial margin or equity that a customer has in a transaction.

Although the DJIA is the best known of the stock market indicators, it is not considered a particularly representative index of overall market activity. This is because it is price weighted, contains only 30 stocks, and does not truly reflect overall market risk.

The National Association of Security Dealers introduced an automatic computer-based quotation system in 1971 that provides continuous bid and ask prices for more than 3,000 actively traded OTC stocks. Market makers enter any change in bid and ask prices into the computer. When a dealer wishes to obtain a buy or sell quote for a particular stock for a customer, the memory is accessed and all current bid and ask prices are printed out with the name of the dealer to contact.

The U.S. stock exchange could undergo a radical transformation as computers become widely used in trading markets. Regional stock exchanges could become part of an electronically linked National Market System. The national securities market, which was mandated by Congress, is under study by the SEC and an industry group representing seven major stock markets. The latest proposal would be a communications system supervised by the NASD, linking the New York, American, PBW, Midwest, Boston, and Pacific Coast stock exchanges and the over-the-counter trading in listed stocks. At present these markets are tied together with the consolidated tape. The result would be not a national securities market but several different markets competing for business. It is also likely that the stock certificate could become extinct as a growing number of transactions are recorded in computer memory and a book entry system is developed.

NOTES

1. W. C. Freund, "The Securities Industry in the Financial Services Marketplace: A Review of Dynamic Trends," *Business Economics* (April 1987): 49.

2. *Ibid.*

3. *Ibid.*

4. The two largest exchanges, the NYSE and the American Stock Exchange, are usually referred to as "national" exchanges, whereas the Pacific, Boston, Cincinnati, Midwest, Detroit, Philadelphia-Baltimore-Washington, Intermountain, and Spokane Stock Exchanges, as well as the Chicago Board Options Exchange, are called "regional" exchanges. Although the Midwest and Pacific Coast Stock Exchanges are the largest of the regional exchanges, they also trade issues of large national companies. The other exchanges are more regional in the sense that most of the companies listed on them are headquartered in or do their principal business in the region in which the exchange is located.

5. New York Stock Exchange, *Fact Book, 1986.* Published annually.

12

Stock Valuation and Performance

The most interesting aspect of the stock market is what determines the value of a stock. Why do stock prices fluctuate from day to day, indeed from hour to hour? If you follow the stock pages of the local paper for a period of a few days, you are certain to see a headline about a stock that rose or fell in value by several points or dollars in a single day. Although it is not unusual to see the value of a particular stock behave in a volatile fashion by doubling or declining by half in a period of a few weeks or months, it is not a typical occurrence. We have seen the value of the Dow Jones Industrial Stock Average rise from a low of 777 in August 1982 to just above 2,700 in August 1987. What has caused this enormous increase in stock prices?

There are a variety of explanations and they do not all agree. In financial theory, we learn that any investment has a value that is the equivalent of the discounted present value of the future cash flow that it will generate. In the specific case of stocks, this would be the present value of the dividend stream plus the value of the stock at the end of a holding period. The professional securities trader would say that the price at any given moment and the fluctuations from moment to moment are caused by the supply and demand position of the stock in the marketplace. These in turn are reflections of investors' sentiment and belief that are influenced by a variety of factors. Still another theory states that the value of a stock is a representation of the actual market value of the firm, and this market value varies with the purchase of the entire firm. A strong argument can be made relating the last theory with the first, the present value of future cash flows.

THE SECURITY ANALYST AND THE FUNDAMENTAL APPROACH

A large amount of time, money, and effort are expended on "fundamental" research in the investment community. The fundamental analyst will attempt to estimate future earnings and dividends for any company he is researching for at least a year and generally for several years. He will further try to determine the relative position of the firm within its industry and the position of the industry in the economy. The analyst will then examine the financial position of the company and the technology involved in the product or service produced, attempt to relate them all with the cost of capital, and determine if the cost reflected by the valuation of the company is in line with that of other companies of similar quality. Most of these relative valuations are based on the "multiple," or the relationship between the projected earnings per share and the price of the shares. The earnings multiple is nothing but a proxy for the firm's cost of capital.

Most fundamental analysts rely heavily on financial statements in an effort to predict earnings, dividends, and price-to-earnings ratios. A company's quick, current, and inventory turnover ratios (working capital ratios) are used to determine the firm's liquidity and to measure the efficiency of its current assets. On the other hand, a firm's debt-to-equity ratio (capitalization ratio) measures the proportions of borrowed funds and equity used to finance a company. A firm that is heavily in debt will have suboptimal capital ratios, a high break-even point, and usually volatile profit rates. The rate of return on assets or equity (income ratios) measures the productivity of money invested in the enterprise.

Financial ratios are of greater value when they can be measured against the company's historical ratios, competitors' ratios, and published industry average ratios, which can be found in *Moody's Industrial Manuals, Value Line Investment Survey, Standard & Poor's Corporation Records,* Robert Morris Associates, as well as other sources. The ability to compare ratios may enable the analyst to detect deviations from the normal way of doing business and may reveal the source of the deviation.

FUNDAMENTALS OF STOCK VALUATION

Common stock represents a share in the ownership of a company. It has the last claim on earnings and assets of all other securities issued by the firm. However, it also has unlimited potential for dividend increases and capital gain through price increases of the common stock. If the company should fail and be forced to liquidate, common stockholders receive what is left after everyone else has been repaid. Therefore, risk is highest with common stock and so must be its expected return.

In a previous chapter it was pointed out that the value of a bond at a given time was the present value of a stream of coupon payments plus the present value of the principal payment to be received at maturity, both discounted at the prevailing rate of interest for that maturity. In an analogous manner, the value of common stock can be defined as the present value of the future dividend stream in perpetuity. In terms of a formula, we have:

$$V = \frac{D}{r}$$

where

V = value
D = dividends per share
r = percentage discount rate

If the dividends were assumed to grow at a constant rate, the formula becomes

$$V = \frac{D}{r - g}$$

g = annual percentage growth in dividends per share

The fundamental approach to valuation of stocks states that stock values depend on:

1. The expected earnings over whatever time horizon is foreseen by investors
2. The expected price at the end of the time horizon
3. The appropriate rate of discount, based on other yield opportunities available in other capital markets, with adjustments for risk and differentials

The market for common stocks is a market for claims on future earnings of dividends. Since future earnings and dividend payments are uncertain, there is not really any simple formula that can explain common stock prices. The movement in stock prices can often be volatile and respond to many factors. However, if we assume that we know future earnings and dividends and the expected price at the time of sale of the stock, we can use the following formula to estimate the present value of the stock:

$$PV = \frac{D_1 +}{(1 + i)} \frac{D_2 +}{(1 + i)^2} \cdots + \frac{F_e}{(1 + i)^n}$$

where

D_i is the expected dividend at the end of the ith period
F_e is the final expected price of the stock at the time of sale
i is the appropriate discount rate

Determining whether stock is correctly valued requires the investor to estimate the value of the stock and compare the estimated value to the current market price. The key variables in valuation models are a required return, an expected growth rate, and expected generation of earnings or dividends. There are numerous factors behind each of these estimates. For example, growth estimates of earnings and dividends require analysis of sales, margins, debt, and dividend policies, while an estimate of required return requires an analysis of the risk of the individual common stock.

The Dividend Valuation Model[1]

The dividend valuation model reflects the present value of all expected future cash dividends. Simply stated, the model says that capitalizing the expected dividend by the difference between the required rate of return and the expected growth rate gives an estimate of common stock value.

today

$$(1)\ P_0 = \frac{d_1}{R-g} \quad \text{or} \quad (2)\ R = \frac{d_1}{P_0} + g$$

P_0 = value of common stock
d_1 = next expected annual cash dividend
g = expected growth in dividends
R = required return
$R > g$

It is clear in model 1 that, as dividends and growth increase or as the required rate of return declines, the stock would take on a higher value. In the restated form, model 2, the return of a common stock is defined as the dividend yield plus the expected growth in dividends, which happens to work out mathematically to be the expected capital gains.

In the models the investor must eliminate the required rate of return (R), the return an investor should expect based on the level of risk undertaken. It requires the investor to make a forecast of future returns and risk. This boils down to the expected return on a risk-free asset (a Treasury bill), plus a premium that compensates for risk multiplied by the beta value. This is the capital asset pricing model and is treated in more detail later in this chapter.

$$R = R_f + B\ (R_m - R_f)$$

where

R_f = expected return on a riskless asset such as a Treasury bill
R_m = expected return on the market
B = relative risk measure of how a stock reacts relative to the market. The beta of the market is always 1.0. A beta of 1.5 means that the total return of a stock is 50% more volatile than the total return of the market. Beta values for individual

stocks are available from Value Line and from most major brokerage firms.

$R_m - R_f$ = equity risk premium

R = required rate of return for an asset

Based upon historical figures for the last 50 years, the equity risk premium, the amount by which the return on equities have exceeded the return on Treasury bills has averaged 6.2%. The Treasury bill rate in 1985 was 7.3%, while the beta of the Dow is always 1.0. Thus, the required return is

$$R = 7.3\% + 1.0\,(6.2\%)$$
$$= 13.5\%$$

The growth rate (g) can be calculated by rearranging the dividend model and solving for g using the current dividend divided by the stock price today—or 4.86%, the current Dow Jones average, rather than expected yield:

$$g = R - \frac{d_0}{P_0} = 13.5\% - 4.86\% = 8.46\%$$

The remaining variable is the next expected annual cash dividend. This is simply the current dividend times one plus the growth rate. Now that all the variables have been estimated, they can be substituted into the dividend valuation model to estimate the value for the Dow.

$$P_0 = \frac{d_1}{R - g} = \frac{\$61.56\,(1.0864)}{0.135 - 0.0864} = \$1{,}376.11$$

With the Dow around 1,320 in September 1985, this valuation concluded that the Dow was undervalued. To value an individual stock, the same procedure would be followed using the estimated values for that stock; the final value would then be compared with the current market price.

The Earnings Valuation Approach

The dividend valuation is not useful for stocks that do not pay dividends or are considered primarily for their growth characteristics. Therefore, the earnings evaluation approach may be more appropriate.

The most common earnings approach is the price-earnings (P/e) ratio approach. Based upon 1985 figures, the

$$\frac{P}{e} = \frac{1{,}266.78}{107.87} = 11.7$$

On the other hand, using historical averages for dividend yield, the P/e ratio for the Dow would be lower.

$$\frac{P}{e_0} = \frac{0.57}{0.056} = 10.17$$

The idea behind the price-earnings ratio approach is to arrive at the expected price-earnings ratio, use this as a multiplier for the expected earnings, and to arrive at a valuation. Mathematically, the equation is

$$P_0 = P/e_1 \times e_1$$

$$P/e_1 = \text{the expected price-earnings ratio}$$

$$e_1 = \text{earnings.}$$

An estimate of earnings for 1985 was produced by using historical growth rate figures, adding one and multiplying this by the current earnings. The 1978 to 1984 annual growth rate in earnings for the Dow was 2.75 percent. Substituting this into the equation, along with the price-earnings estimate based on historical ratios, tended to undervalue the Dow.

$$P_0 = P/e \times e_0 (1 + g)$$
$$= 10.17 \times 107.87 (1.0275) = \$1,127$$

If you used a 10 percent growth rate assumption and the historical price-earnings ratio, the Dow would be

$$P_0 = 10.17 \times \$107.87 (1.10) = \$1,207$$

On the other hand, if we returned to the original price-earnings ratio equation and used a 5 percent dividend yield along with a 10 percent growth rate, the Dow valuation would be

$$\frac{P}{e_1} = \frac{0.57}{0.05} = 11.4$$

$$P_0 = 11.4 \times 1.10 \times \$107.87 = \$1,353$$

These valuation techniques can be adopted to the valuation of individual stocks and provide investors with a tool to judge current prices of specific stocks.

MODERN PORTFOLIO THEORY

Modern portfolio theory tells us we can estimate the future dividends, the terminal value of the shares, the risks of achieving these values, and model the valuation of the stock based on these variables. This "black box" approach to portfolio management has gained considerable acceptance among institutional investors in recent years. Some early empirical studies, including various measures of performance or the value of portfolios relative to similar portfolios managed, have used valuation models. As the quantitative approach becomes more widely used, it is possible that the results of all portfolios will become increasingly similar. Most of the models are similar in construction: hence, with similar inputs they tend to yield similar results. The element that will differentiate performance will become the quality of the inputs, and this will move back full circle to the very elements that fundamental analysts have been using for many years.

It should be clear that modern portfolio theory and fundamental analysis are in reality only two sides of the same coin and complement each other. Neither can replace the other. Each can only enhance the results that can be produced by application of the other.

Modern portfolio theory (MPT) broadly speaking, is an investment decision process that quantifies the relationship between risk and return. What has evolved from once theoretic constructs is a practical decision-oriented process that allows an investor to classify, estimate, and then control both the type and amount of expected risk and return. MPT is composed of four distinct steps: security valuation, asset location, portfolio optimization, and performance measurement. Security valuation is the description of a universe of stocks in terms of expected return and expected risk. The description information from the security valuation step is used for the asset allocation decision. Information on the expected risk and expected return for stocks, bonds, and so on is arrayed so that the decision maker is able to compare the relative attractiveness of investments. This aids the investment strategist in determining the proportion of assets to be allocated to each category. Portfolio optimization in the case of stocks involves determining which portfolio of stocks offers the lowest expected risk for a given level of expected return or, conversely, the highest expected return for a given level of expected risk. Portfolio optimization decisions use information on relative expected returns and risks for each stock in order to select the best portfolio of stocks within a valuation universe.

An efficient market is said to exist if all known information about a security is fully reflected in its price. The efficient market theory (EMT) suggests that fundamental analysts are so good at their jobs that all mispriced securities have been identified and therefore no longer exist. The market price of a security will equal its calculated fundamental intrinsic value. If the notion of an efficient market is correct, portfolio selection involves defining the level of risk that is acceptable for a given portfolio and creating a combination of broadly diversified holdings of bonds and stocks that provide that risk level. Since prices are always fair, you buy or sell only when you have excess cash, need cash, or desire tax advantages. Extensive research has shown that while EMT is an overstatement of reality, the security markets are considerably more price efficient than many people think.

CAPITAL ASSET PRICING MODEL

The components of risk have been categorized traditionally into business risk, interest rate risk, market risk, inflation risk, liquidity risk, and financial risk (see Chapter 6). However, the modern components of risk are systematic risk that is attributable to exogenous or market forces and unsystematic risk that is attributable to unique or nonmarket forces.

Variability in a security's total return that is directly related to overall movements in the general economy is called market or systematic risk. Just about all securities, whether stocks or bonds, have some systematic risk because systematic risk includes inflation risk, interest rate risk, and market risk. Systematic risk is nondiversifiable.

Unsystematic or nonmarket risk is the variability in a security's total return that is not related to overall market variability. Unsystematic risk is the risk that is unique to a particular security and is related to such factors as financial and business risk. Unsystematic risk is diversifiable, that is, an investor can construct a diversified portfolio and eliminate most nonmarket or unsystematic risk. The sum of systematic risk and unsystematic risk is total risk.

$$\text{Total Risk} = \text{Systematic Risk} + \text{Unsystematic Risk}$$

Investment risk can be measured by calculating the standard deviation and the beta coefficient. Beta is the measure of risk relating the movements in the return of a given security to the movements in the market's return. While the beta of the market is 1.0, a higher beta indicates more volatility and more risk and a lower beta indicates less volatility and less risk than the market as a whole. Betas are estimated from historical data, regressing the holding period yields for the individual security against the holding period return for the market index.

The capital asset pricing model (CAPM), the graph of which is referred to as the security market line (SML), relates the required rate of return for any security j with the relevant risk measure for that security, its beta. The CAPM says that the required rate of return on an asset is a function of the two components of the required rate of return: the risk-free rate and the risk premium. The risk premium is the product of the beta for a particular security j and the market risk premium, $R_m - R_f$. The relationship is expressed in equation form as

$$R_j = R_f + B_j (R_m - R_f)$$

A diagram of the relationship between the required rate of return and beta is given in Figure 12.1. Until recently, the CAPM had been the predominant theory of risk and return in equilibrium and has been the subject of hundreds of empirical tests. The CAPM has been extremely popular because of its intuitive appeal and because it explains the relationship between risk and opportunity costs in the form of a simple equation. The CAPM theory does not hold up well in empirical testing. The intercept term is generally larger than the risk-free rate

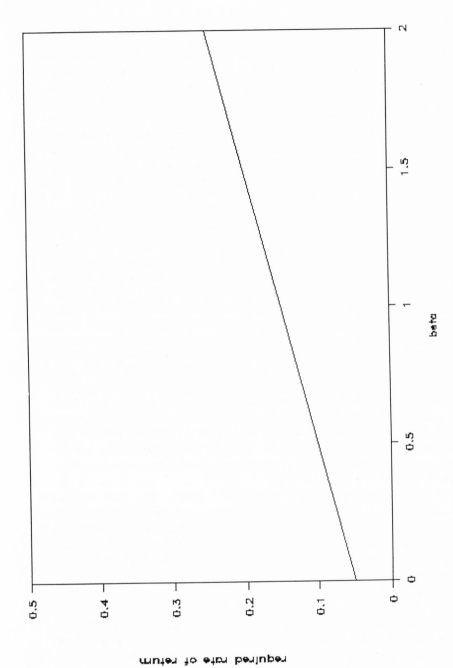

Figure 12.1
Security Market Line

and the relationship implied in the CAPM doesn't hold up well for short intervals below five years or so. However, the relationship between beta and average returns appears to be linear. The CAPM is similar to the concept of perfect competition in economics.

The slope of the preceding risk-return trade-off diagram is the market risk premium, $R_m - R_f$, which is the excess return for the market as a whole, that is, the return above the risk-free rate for assuming the risk of the market as a whole. This market risk premium reflects the additional return that investors typically expect for buying risky securities rather than the riskless asset. Investors expect larger returns to be associated with larger risks. An investor cannot reasonably expect to earn greater returns without assuming greater risks.

THE RANDOM WALK HYPOTHESIS

The financial theorists contend that past price action is no indication of future price action and that no amount of study of past price performance can give any hint of future price performance. There is no denying the mathematical validity of their work or the "random walk theory." A random walk describes a statistical process where successive changes in price are independent, that is, using the previous changes in the price for a security to predict the next change in price is no more helpful than using the previous flips of a coin to predict the outcome of the next flip of a coin. The random walk theory only says that prices move in a random fashion. Obviously, new information about earnings, dividends, growth, stock splits, and market psychology may influence prices. New information is considered information that is unforeseen or unpredictable. Therefore, new information, whether good or bad, that does influence prices arrives at random times. The random walk theory suggests that prices react quickly to new information and move in a random fashion, determined by the information's random time of arrival. This implies that investors will use new information immediately and the price will react immediately.[2]

In summary, empirical research studies have indicated that security prices and the market follow a random walk, that is, price changes are substantially independent. The quest for an explanation led to the efficient market hypothesis in three forms: weak, semistrong, and strong. The weak form extends the random walk theory, which implies that technical trading strategies, based on the history of prices, are not of value in investment decision making. The semistrong form implies that all public information is fully reflected in stock prices, that stock prices incorporate new information in a prompt and unbiased manner, and that for most investors fundamental analysis is of limited value. Finally, the strong form suggests that even nonpublic or inside information cannot be used consistently to capture above normal trading profits. However, some corporate insiders have been able to capture above normal trading profits in some circumstances with special information. On the other hand, studies of professional portfolio managers, who presumably have more access to nonpublic information than most investors, support the strong form of the hypothesis. In addition, secondary distributions by "knowledgeable sellers" have preceded large price declines. Also, for certain periods of time, following the advice of the Value Line Investment Survey has produced above average returns for investors. The same has been true of investment strategies concentrating on the selection of stocks with low P/e ratios or with an emphasis on stocks of small rather than large companies. In summary, there is considerable evidence that supports the efficient markets hypothesis in the weak and semistrong form. This implies that most investors in most circumstances cannot expect consistently to outperform the market.[3] However, corporate insiders and some security analysts have been able to outperform a buy-hold strategy.

THE TECHNICAL APPROACH

Despite the findings of the random walk and efficient market theorists, many people have believed and continue to believe that stock price movements exhibit trends, cycles, and other recognizable patterns. Technical security analysts spend much of their time looking for patterns in stock price movements that will indicate the future direction and strength of price movements. The technical analyst studies trading patterns for stocks in an attempt to understand the force of supply and demand as they are reflected in past history. The technical analyst looks at considerably more elements than simply price movements. Volume plays an important part in most technical analyses as do a variety of other indicators. The technical analyst generally tries to relate individual price performance to overall market performance. They use terms like *buying pressure, selling pressure, resistance level, support level,* and *breakout* to add pizzazz to their analyses. Chartists usually disregard the fact that there must be a sale for every purchase and a purchase for every sale.

Technical analysis is a method of predicting the appropriate time to buy or sell a stock by making and interpreting stock charts. These chartists study past movements of stock prices and the volume of trading for a clue to the direction of future stock prices. Chartists tend to believe that (1) all information about earnings, dividends, and the future performance of a company is automatically reflected in the past market prices of a company and (2) prices tend to move in trends, that is, a stock that is increasing in price tends to keep on rising.

Scientific scrutiny of chart reading has not consistently outperformed the placebo of a buy and hold strategy. Why then are there so many chartists? These technicians play an important role in enriching the coffers of brokerage firms by generating commission income through their buy and sell recommendations.

In spite of a lack of theoretical support in the academic community, and some logical lapses in many of their presentations, technical analysts continue to flourish. Some have developed reasonably good historical records of predicting the direction of the stock market. Burton G. Malkiel's *A Random Walk Down Wall Street* tells a story about Joseph Granville, a famous Wall Street technician of the early 1980s.[4] Granville's record had been good in the late 1970s and in his heyday, he had the power to move markets. For example, his buy recommendation in April 1980 helped send the Dow up 30 points in one day, and his sell recommendation in January 1981 helped to send the market down 24 points the next day. However, his accuracy left much to be desired in future forecasts after a few successful market predictions. When Granville was asked how his "foolproof" system had led him to make egregious errors, he calmly responded that he had been on drugs and had not paid proper attention to his charts. Granville predicted not only stock tremors, but the destruction of Los Angeles in May 1981 by an earthquake.

THE TOTAL VALUE APPROACH

In the late seventies and early eighties, a number of companies were acquired either by other even larger companies, or by foreign investors. This is an example of the "total value" approach at work. There is a school of thought that says that a stock is only a fractional ownership share of the company and the total market value of the outstanding shares represents the market value of the company. There can be no argument with a theoretical basis of this approach, and the acquisition of a number of large companies in a period of depressed stock prices is a reflection of this approach. Investors felt that the depressed prices of the shares in the period of the late seventies and early eighties represented an opportunity to acquire control of various companies at bargain prices.

THE CAUSES OF FLUCTUATION IN PRICE

So far, we have raised the question of why stocks fluctuate in price, and outlined a variety of analytical approaches, but the question remains, "Why do we have the fluctuations from day to day?" It should already be obvious that there is no simple or direct answer to the question. Each of the elements we have discussed can contribute to the fluctuations.

Various empirical studies indicate that there are three elements in the price of any individual stock. The level of the overall market contributes about 60 percent of the price level at any given time, the action of the group of stocks to which it belongs about 30 percent, and the performance of the individual company about 10 percent of the price action. The group's performance refers to the tendency of stocks in the same industry to move together. For example, Alcoa and Alcan will tend to move in the same basic direction as the same economic influences affect both companies in a similar manner. It is possible that Alcoa could have a record year in sales and profits while Alcan is doing poorly, but it is not likely. If demand for steel is strong for U.S. Steel, it is not likely that either Bethlehem Steel or Inland Steel will be doing poorly. It is also unlikely that the demand for autos will be poor when the economy is strong and consumer credit is plentiful, or that either group will do well in a recession. The performance of the basic economy and the performance of the industry within the economy is therefore a major component in the movement of stock prices.

In another empirical study, B. J. King suggested that of 63 firms listed on the NYSE, on average, 31 percent of the variation in a stock's price could be attributed to changes in the level of the whole stock market; 20 percent to changes peculiar to each company that were assumed to come from within the firm; 12 percent to changes in the industry; and 37 percent to changes in industry subgroups.[5] These percentages varied from industry to industry and indicated the necessity for the fundamental analyst to look beyond the company itself in forecasting future earnings, dividends, and price-to-earnings multipliers. It is also prudent for the fundamental analyst to consider the quality, depth, and experience of management, as well as their ability to react effectively to changes. In some industries, such as chemicals, drugs, aerospace, computers, and other technological areas, the research and development program should also be analyzed for new discoveries or advanced technology that might give a company a future competitive advantage.

Investor perception of the economic situation and the probable course of the economy is therefore a key element in stock price movement. It is also possible that investors may believe that a given group will not be influenced by the economy. Stocks of food companies are generally perceived to be less affected by economic fluctuations than many other industries. Much the same could be said of stocks in the drug industry. Most investors feel that consumers will continue to purchase drugs and food even in periods of economic slowdown, and therefore the performance of companies involved in these markets will be less volatile than the economy is in an expansionary phase. While this may appear to be little more than common sense, considerable resources are devoted to determining the economic outlook for the economy and individual groups.

The performance of an individual company is also important, and there are numerous instances of a specific company moving in a direction contrary to either the market or its group. It may have developed a new process or product that its investors perceive as giving it at least a temporary advantage. A new management may give investors the hope that a previously marginal company will gain market share and become desirable, or the departure of a management that is highly regarded may cause investor disenchantment with a stock that was previously a market favorite. There is little question that the stock market anticipates future developments or at least attempts to do so. Stocks will react to investors' anticipation of future results, and the failure to achieve those expectations. It is common to see a stock price react sharply to earnings that are either above or below those anticipated. The announcement of some event that will have an effect on future performance of a company will also cause changes in stock prices. A lawsuit against a company can cause the price to decline.

There is also a connection between the cost of capital and the level of stock prices. There have been numerous studies that have attempted to relate capital costs and stock prices, but no one so far has definitely related the two. If we hold all else constant, expected earnings, dividends, and so forth, and assume that the cost of capital doubles, the price of stock should fall by half. In practice, when capital costs rise or interest rates increase, the attraction of alternative investments such as bonds increases and money appears to flow from stocks into fixed income investments. In short, while we cannot directly relate costs of capital to price fluctuation the interrelationship is obvious, and stock prices will vary as capital costs, or put another way, interest rates, fluctuate.

Stock prices are affected by the outlook for the economy, the level and outlook for interest rates, the outlook for the dollar vis-à-vis other currencies, the industry relative to the economy, the performance of the company relative to the industry, the dividend and growth in earnings potential, and the quality of management.

Technical factors such as the position of institutional investors, interest rates available in alternative investments in the money and bond markets, corporate takeover fever, the effects of trends in stock market prices in influencing stock price expectations, and the short-run impacts of orders to buy and sell at certain prices, as well as the computerized programs that compare option prices and futures prices to current stock market prices all have an impact on stock prices to some extent.

It seems clear that fundamental considerations such as expected growth, dividend payouts, risk, and the rate of interest do have a profound influence on market prices. Higher anticipations of earnings and higher dividend payouts tend to increase stock price-earnings multiples, while higher risk and higher interest rates tend to reduce price-earnings ratios. Another key determinant of stock prices is the state of market psychology. Stocks are often purchased on expectations rather than facts.

Successful investing demands both intellectual and psychological acuteness. Stocks that produce "good vibes" in the minds of investors can sell at premium multiples for long periods even if the growth rate is only average. There is also no scientific evidence to indicate that the investment performance of professionally managed portfolios as a group has been any better than that of randomly selected portfolios.

The key determinants of a *P/e* ratio for an ordinary stock would be determined by the extent to which the following variables exceed or fall below S&P averages: expected growth rate of earnings, sales stability, dividend payout ratio, financial leverage, and institutional stock ownership. A rational investor should be willing to pay a higher price for a share, the longer the growth rate is expected to last, the larger the rate of dividends, the less risky a company's stock, the lower are interest rates and financial leverage.

The price of any stock reflects the overall level of stock prices, the fundamental nature of the company's business and investor expectations about the future. Expectations change as events unfold and the ability to correctly anticipate changes in expectations impacts investment results. The most important macro or market factors affecting stock prices include:

- The level of inflation and interest rates. This affects the choice between real (tangible) assets and financial assets and between stocks and fixed income securities.
- Fiscal and monetary policies. These determine the outlook for the capital markets. For example, many commentators feel that the 1982–1987 bull market was fueled primarily by declining interest rates during much of the period.
- Level and trend of economic activity. This affects the ability of companies to increase earnings per share.
- Internationalization. This reflects the fact that business is exposed to greater foreign competition and the impact of foreign exchange rates on the demand for specific products.

The key company or micro factors affecting stock prices include:

- Profits. Stock prices of companies that consistently attain high growth are rewarded with a premium value or high price-to-earnings ratio.
- Dividends. Profit growth is often translated into increased dividends over time.
- Excess cash flow. This is the ability to generate large amounts of excess cash (after providing for capital spending and dividends). Companies with good earnings growth and low debt ratios are often rewarded with a higher valuation.
- Changing fundamentals for industries or companies. An example of this occurred in the rise of energy stocks during the late 1970s and their subsequent collapse in the 1980s.
- Changing investment attitudes. This reflects the fact that at various times investor interest switches from stocks to bonds, from asset plays to growth stocks, from growth stocks to cyclical stocks, from cyclical stocks to stocks offering high yields and from high yielding stocks to those offering steady growth in earnings such as consumer stocks.

STOCK MARKET OWNERSHIP AND PERFORMANCE

Attitudes about common stock ownership change as market conditions change. For example, following the precipitous drop in equity prices in the period from 1969 to 1970, there was great reluctance on the part of the public to invest in equities with any substantial force. Instead, funds were placed into real estate, commodities, and savings institutions. However, during the biggest stock market rally in history that extended from the summer of 1982 to the summer of 1987, common stock once again captured the imagination of financial investors and speculators. The number of Americans owning common stock rose to an all-time high and the assets of equity oriented mutual funds more than tripled over this period.

There are certain advantages involved in common stock ownership, including:

1. The right to receive dividends
2. The right to vote shares
3. The right to maintain the proportional share of ownership in the company (preemptive right)

Stock ownership allows the investor to participate in dividends that might be in cash or stock in an amount determined by the directors of the company. Dividend policies vary from company to company and from industry to industry. Electric utilities tend to pay out in excess of two thirds of their earnings in dividends, while high technology companies tend to make minimal dividend payments to stockholders. Stock dividends are paid by just about 3 percent of the companies listed on the New York Stock Exchange, while some companies pay a dividend in some combination of cash and stock.

The salient advantage of common stock ownership is the potential for profit in the form of capital gains. There is also the potential for dividend growth as the company grows. The major disadvantages of common stock ownership are the lack of stability of earnings, the uncertainty of the price of common stock, which can fluctuate up and down, and the lack of a guarantee that dividends will increase or even be paid.

The total market value of equity securities has grown from year-end 1981 when the value of holdings was at $1.5 trillion to a value just under $3 trillion at year-end 1986. Households own about 62 percent of the market value of equities, while institutions and foreign investors own 38 percent (see Table 12.1). While households dominate the holdings of equity securities, pension funds are the next largest holder of equities, followed by insurance companies, mutual funds, and foreign investors. The trust departments of commercial banks own a few hundred billion dollars in common stock in a fiduciary capacity for their trust and pension accounts that are managed for individuals, partnerships, and companies. It is interesting to note that the number of individual owners of corporate stock and mutual funds has grown from under 6.5 million in 1952 (4 percent of the U.S. population) to about 50 million in 1987 (20 percent of the U.S. population).

When values of common stocks are low it can be difficult for companies to raise new capital in the equity market. Some firms are tempted to buy up shares of their own stock instead of investing in additional real assets. This tends to increase earnings per share by removing shares from the marketplace. When common stocks are increasing, it is much easier to raise new capital in the equity markets. In addition, the increasing value of real capital assets, which are reflected in the values of common stock prices, tend to induce companies to increase investment.

BUSINESS CYCLES AND INVESTMENT STRATEGIES

A major investment banking firm studied relative stock market performance during the first six months of bull market cycles and the last four months of bear market cycles for market segments of 1966–1967, 1970, and 1974–1975. Some of the findings of the study were:

1. Industries that outperform the market in the early phase of a bull market are those that are characterized by superior growth qualities or that are especially sensitive to the expected turning of the business cycle. Credit-sensitive stocks, excluding utilities, that

Table 12.1
Corporate Stock Issues—Common and Preferred (Annual Issuance, Retirements, Net Issuance and Net Purchases, Dollars in Billions[a])

	1981	1982	1983	1984	1985	1986E	1987P	Amt. Out. 31 Dec 86E[b]
Gross New Cash Offerings								
Utility	$7.6	$9.8	$7.9	$2.9	$3.3	$2.8	$3.0	
Industrial	9.2	8.0	30.5	8.8	17.1	26.6	33.0	
Finance	1.1	2.8	8.9	4.6	15.1	26.9	26.0	
Div. Reinvest., Stock Options and Foreign Sales	7.5	9.8	9.8	9.1	10.8	9.0	8.0	
Total Cash Offerings	25.5	30.4	57.1	25.4	46.3	65.3	70.0	
Conversions of Bonds	1.1	1.3	1.2	1.6	1.4	3.5	3.0	
Equity Swaps for Bonds	0.7	5.9	2.0	0.9	0.0	0.0	0.0	
Merger Exchanges for Debt	1.6	15.7	5.4	11.3	9.8	6.4	4.4	
Merger Exchanges for Cash	49.2	42.2	29.2	98.3	99.4	125.0	138.0	
Net Issuance of Corporate Stock	**$-23.5**	**$-20.3**	**$25.8**	**$-81.7**	**$-61.4**	**$-62.6**	**$-69.4**	**$2,990.0**
Ownership								
Thrifts	$-0.6	$-0.5	$0.3	$-0.2	$-0.1	$0.4	$0.0	$6.8
Insurance and Pensions	18.4	25.5	27.4	-0.7	20.8	9.3	16.0	795.0
Investment Companies	-0.6	3.5	13.7	5.9	10.3	21.7	17.0	163.0
Other Nonbank Finance	2.7	-0.9	5.3	3.3	0.0	-0.2	1.0	7.2
Total Nonbank Finance	19.9	27.6	46.8	8.3	31.1	31.2	34.0	972.0
Commercial Banks	-0.1	0.0	0.0	-0.1	0.1	0.2	1.5	0.3
Foreign	5.8	3.9	5.4	-3.0	5.0	20.0	30.0	171.0
Residual: Households Direct	-49.2	-51.8	-26.4	-86.9	-97.6	-114.0	-134.9	1,846.7
Total Ownership	**$-23.5**	**$-20.3**	**$25.8**	**$-81.7**	**$-61.4**	**$-62.6**	**$-69.4**	**$2,990.0**

Table 12.1 cont.

Memo: Sector Analysis

Nonfinancial	$-18.6	$-12.7	$24.0	$-82.4	$-72.7	$-76.3	$-73.4	$2,045.6
Financial	-4.9	-7.6	1.7	0.7	11.3	13.7	4.0	944.4
Net Issuance of Corporate Stock	**$-23.5**	**$-20.3**	**$25.8**	**$-81.7**	**$-61.4**	**$-62.6**	**$-69.4**	**$2,990.0**
Volume of Secondary Mkt. Transactions on Registered Exchanges	490.7	603.8	984.8	950.4	1,196.9	1,730.6	1,850.0	

Changes in Market Value of Holdings

Institutions and Foreigners

Market Value, Start of Period	$469.3	$449.1	$545.3	$697.4	$693.1	$916.7	$1,143.3
Plus Net Purchases	25.6	31.5	52.2	5.3	36.1	51.4	65.5
Plus Appreciation	-45.9	64.6	99.9	-9.6	187.5	175.2	194.2
Market Value, End of Period	449.1	545.3	697.4	693.1	916.7	1,143.3	1,403.0

Households

Market Value, Start of Period	1,102.9	1,055.8	1,175.9	1,324.9	1,329.1	1,668.4	1,846.7
Plus Net Purchases	-49.2	-51.8	-26.4	-86.9	-97.6	-114.0	-134.9
Plus Appreciation	2.1	171.8	175.4	91.1	437.0	292.3	335.2
Market Value, End of period	1,055.8	1,175.9	1,324.9	1,329.1	1,668.4	1,846.7	2,047.0

All Holders

Market Value, Start of Period	1,572.3	1,505.0	1,721.1	2,022.3	2,022.1	2,585.1	2,990.0
Plus Net Purchases	-23.5	-20.3	25.8	-81.7	-61.4	-62.6	-69.4
Plus Appreciation	-43.8	236.4	275.3	81.6	624.4	467.5	529.4
Market Value, End of Period	1,505.0	1,721.1	2,022.3	2,022.1	2,585.1	2,990.0	3,450.0

a Salomon Brothers Inc estimates.
b At market.

Source: Prospects for Financial Markets in 1987. Salomon Brothers, Inc., December 1986.

277

are sensitive to the business cycle should be beneficiaries of the anticipated decline in interest rates. Utility stocks were not found to be particularly strong bull market performers. While utilities tend to perform well immediately following turns in interest rates, they lose relative momentum fairly quickly.

2. Basic industries do not perform well in the early bull markets.

3. Stocks in industries with high betas tend to outperform other groups in the early phase of the bull market, while industries that outperform the market in the late phase of a bear market usually have low betas.

4. Intermediate goods and services industries should be underweighted in the early phase of a bull market, but tend to thrive in the economic environment of high capacity utilization that generally occurs in the late middle stages of a recovery (see Table 12.2).[6]

Although economists have only mediocre records for forecasting recessions and recoveries, some of the key strategies followed by investment professionals depend upon accurate business cycle forecasts. They include:

1. If investors are convinced that a recession is imminent, even though the stock market is still strong, they might continue to buy stocks but confine purchases to companies whose sales are likely to be least vulnerable to recession and to stocks whose price-to-earnings ratios seem relatively attractive. These investors should also place funds into liquid money market instruments because of a flat or downward sloping shape of the yield curve.

2. Once the recession is under way and the stock market begins to decline, interest rates are likely to be at a peak. Liquid funds should be shifted into long-term bonds in order to take advantage of price appreciation that would follow from the cyclical decline in interest rates.

3. Income-oriented investors may wish to shift funds from high quality bonds to lower quality bonds in the midst of a recession when yield spreads begin to widen. However, one must carefully monitor the credit quality of all investments and potential investments.

4. A renewed stock buying program is in order when investors feel the end of a recession is near. It is appropriate to buy stocks of cyclical and glamour growth companies whose prices appear to be depressed.[7]

The relative price changes over short periods of time reflect factors such as relative changes in company sales, earnings, dividends, and the degree to which different stocks had been over- or underpriced prior to the turning point of the general market. Some industry groupings usually achieve gains in years when overall profits decline. Financial (interest rate related) and retail-oriented securities such as department stores, food chains, and the general merchandise categories tend to outperform the market during periods of overall corporate profit declines. Industries with below average earnings sensitivity to the business cycle such as soft drink, food, tobacco, and soap companies tend to outperform the market in the six-month period after a peak of the last six economic cycles.

Table 12.2
Group Performance in the Business Cycle

Master Group	Dominant Investment Characteristics	Best Relative Performance	Worst Relative Performance
Cyclical Stocks			
Credit Cyclicals	Sensitive to interest rates-performance best when interest rates low.Most groups building related.	Early and middle bull markets.	Early and middle bear market Exception- forest products
Consumer Cyclicals	Consumer durables and non-durables.Profits vary with the economic cycle.	Early and middle bull markets.	Early and middle bear market exception- hotel/motel.
Capital Goods	Many groups depend on capacity utilization.	Middle and late bull markets.	Late bear markets.
Basic Industries	Profits depend on capacity utilization.Prices may benefit from supply shortages near economic peaks.	Early and middle bear markets.Economic peaks	Early or middle bull market, depending on source of demand for products.
Financial	Banks,insurance and gold mining.	Late bull and late bear markets.	Early bull markets.
Transportation	Surface transportatio.	Early bull markets.	Early bull markets.
Defensive Stocks			
Consumer Staples	Nonvolatile consumer goods.	Late bear markets.	Early bull markets.
Utilities	Operating stability.	Late bear markets.	Early bull markets.
Growth Stocks			
Consumer Growth	Combination of growth and defensive characteristics.	Late bear markets: cosmetics,soft drinks and drugs.	Cosmetics,soft drinks and drugs do not vary in any regular cyclical pattern.
Capital Goods-technology	Linked to capital spending cycle;lags economic cycle.	Early and middle bull markets.	Late bear markets.

Even though the aforementioned industries outperformed the market during these periods of earnings declines, only aerospace, food chains, food companies, soap, and tobacco firms actually advanced in price during this interval.[8]

Investors often ask what kind of return they can expect to receive by investing in common stocks. Although it is impossible to answer this question in a precise way, it is possible to offer some guidance to investors based upon historical annual rates of return.

Prior to the 1970s extensive studies for over 40 years had shown that total return on stocks had been approximately 4 percent higher than yields on bonds. Also, investments in the stock market were considered as a hedge against inflation. However, during the 1970s the total return to the stockholders was much lower than the return on bonds and some other financial assets.

The period 1968–1981 was a period of a general rising trend in inflation, culminating in double digit inflation at the beginning of the 1980s. The stock market averages had almost no net increase during this period, rising in some years and falling in others. The value of stocks adjusted for inflation had fallen by close to one half by 1981. What was the explanation for the poor performance of the stock market in the 1970s? Academic researchers have concluded that taxes were not a major factor and that the relative attractiveness of assets such as land, homes, oil, art work, and gold were key factors at certain times. When investors become nervous about values of assets that are expressed in monetary terms (because they see inflation eroding the value of money), they tend to turn to physical assets. It appears as if the relatively low stock market prices of the later 1970s were the result of the fact that reported profits were overstated and, therefore, that when profits were adjusted for this overstatement they were lower enough possibly to justify the relatively low level of stock prices. When inflation occurs, accuracy of profit measures is diminished by accounting problems that arise when companies value assets at historical costs rather than replacement costs. Essentially illusory inventory profits occur and depreciation charges are less than they should be. Analysts did not recognize that there is a need to adjust for the fact that stockholders are residual claimants to the values of business firms. When profits increase the share of creditors' claims, the value of companies must decline and the share of stockholders' claims must increase.

Recognition of the increasing relative share of stockholders as claimants to the value of companies, and of the correctness of discounting current earnings by an interest rate containing an inflation premium probably contributed to the decline in stock prices. Stock prices were also hurt because a decline in productivity of capital reduced possible future earnings and because investors may have ignored the gain by debtors obtained during periods of inflation.

Table 12.3 shows the correlation coefficients between investment returns from different markets in the United States. For example, the table shows that the stock markets are all highly positively correlated, but that stock market returns are slightly negatively correlated with the returns from real estate investments and several types of bonds.

It appears as if the prices of all common stocks are systematically and simultaneously affected by the basic economic forces so that they tend to move through alternating price appreciation trends (bull market) and price depreciating trends (bear market) together. Therefore, an inferior average like the DJIA is highly positively correlated with a more scientifically constructed index. On the other hand, different markets, such as the real estate and bond markets, tend to "march to a different drummer." There was an exception during the 1982–1986 bull market when the stock market and bond markets rallied together for much of this period as interest rates declined substantially, but not monotonically during the record increase in the stock averages.

PREFERRED STOCK

While common stocks have no maturity value or date and do not promise fixed payments, common stockholders do have a residual claim on the earnings and assets of the issuer after all prior claims, including those of bond holders, have been satisfied. Since stocks have no maturity value, they are secured only by a company's earnings. Since future earnings are uncertain, investors often disagree more about the prices of individual stocks than about those of bonds.

Preferred stock has a preferred position in terms of income payments and liquidation payments in case of bankruptcy. Most preferred stock is similar to a bond in that there is a fixed dividend payment each year. The major difference between the bond and preferred stock is that the payment stipulated on the preferred stock is not legally binding. The dividend must be voted on and approved by the board of directors as is the case with common stock. Given the possibility that the board of directors could vote to pass the preferred dividend, it is important to determine if the preferred stock is cumulative or noncumulative. In the case of cumulative preferred stock, if the dividend is not paid, the unpaid dividend is accumulated and is considered in arrears. All of these arrears on the preferred stock must be paid before any dividends can be paid to the common stockholders. In contrast, if the dividend is not paid on noncumulative preferred stock, it does not accumulate and it is not necessary to pay these passed dividends prior to paying dividends on the common stock. However, there is a requirement that during a specific year, the firm must pay the preferred dividend before it can pay a common dividend.

During 1984, corporations began to issue adjustable or variable rate preferred dividends. The dividend rate generally floats quarterly at a fixed spread below the highest of the 3-month Treasury bill, the 10-year Treasury bond, or a 20-year Treasury bond.

Convertible preferred stock is similar to convertible bonds. A bond or preferred stock may offer a conversion privilege that gives the holder the right to exchange the security for the common stock of the issuing corporation under specific conversion conditions. Convertible preferred stocks are equity securities with a priority to dividend payments over common stockholders that offer the

Table 12.3
Correlation Matrix for HPRs from Various Market Indexes

	NYSE	AMEX	OTC	Total common stock	Preferred stock	LT corp. bond	Int. corp. bond	Commercial paper
NYSE	1.000							
AMEX	0.884	1.000						
OTC	0.876	0.897	1.000					
Total common stock	0.998	0.911	0.902	1.000				
Preferred stock	0.371	0.439	0.178	0.356	1.000			
LT corp. bond	0.282	0.313	0.124	0.266	0.863	1.000		
Int. corp. bond	0.422	0.322	0.254	0.405	0.827	0.897	1.000	
Commercial paper	-0.454	-0.576	-0.343	-0.450	-0.067	0.029	0.027	1.000
Total corp. fixed	0.279	0.309	0.120	0.263	0.894	0.986	0.925	0.089
Total corporations	0.982	0.906	0.910	0.987	0.424	0.354	0.473	-0.395
Farms	-0.101	-0.281	-0.144	-0.109	-0.144	0.055	0.146	0.327
Housing	-0.271	-0.206	0.241	-0.270	-0.068	-0.004	0.121	0.635
Total real estate	-0.227	-0.312	-0.232	-0.231	-0.122	0.017	0.153	0.576
U.S. Treasury bills	-0.459	-0.574	-0.317	-0.450	-0.084	0.019	-0.010	0.980
U.S. Treasury notes	-0.174	-0.037	-0.264	-0.187	0.574	0.669	0.606	0.517
U.S. Treasury bonds	-0.041	-0.005	-0.176	-0.059	0.737	0.754	0.695	0.184
U.S. govt. agencies	-0.073	-0.025	-0.171	-0.088	0.657	0.739	0.682	0.412
Total govt. bonds	-0.229	-0.194	-0.314	-0.244	0.648	0.688	0.611	0.470
Short munic.	-0.439	-0.573	-0.314	-0.435	-0.057	0.048	0.049	0.981
LT munic.	0.201	0.268	0.089	0.191	0.782	0.877	0.789	-0.043
Total munic.	0.192	0.261	0.080	0.182	0.783	0.878	0.789	-0.031

Table 12.3 cont.

	Total corp. fixed	Total corporations	Farms	Housing	Total real estate	U.S. Treasury bills	U.S. Treasury notes	U.S. Treasury bonds
Total corp. fixed	1.000							
Total corporations	0.352	1.000						
Farms	0.063	-0.126	1.000					
Housing	0.056	-0.258	0.427	1.000				
Total real estate	0.062	-0.233	0.767	0.906	1.000			
U.S. Treasury bills	0.072	-0.393	0.380	0.641	0.604	1.000		
U.S. Treasury notes	0.678	-0.106	0.059	0.254	0.194	0.439	1.000	
U.S. Treasury bonds	0.770	0.004	-0.053	0.029	-0.013	0.131	0.832	1.000
U.S. govt. agencies	0.757	-0.009	0.018	0.157	0.108	0.328	0.962	0.855
Total govt. bonds	0.724	-0.170	0.032	0.203	0.141	0.417	0.911	0.934
Short munic.	0.104	0.376	0.298	0.600	0.537	0.956	0.524	0.180
LT munic.	0.847	0.257	0.048	-0.107	-0.056	-0.048	0.688	0.762
Total munic.	0.850	0.248	0.053	-0.100	-0.049	-0.036	0.695	0.767

	U.S. govt. agencies	Total govt. bonds	Short munic.	LT munic.	Total munic.
U.S. govt. agencies	1.000				
Total govt. bonds	0.910	1.000			
Short munic.	0.431	0.467	1.000		
LT munic.	0.748	0.688	-0.032	1.000	
Total munic.	0.755	0.698	-0.020	1.000	1.000

Source: R. C. Ibbotson and C. L. Fall, "The United States Market Wealth Portfolio," *Journal of Portfolio Management* (Fall 1979), Table 6.

opportunity to share in potential corporate growth. The investor pays for the conversion privilege by accepting a lower yield than could be obtained by purchasing nonconvertible preferred stock. The option to convert is solely at the discretion of the holder of the security and should only be exercised when and if the holder finds an exchange desirable. Conversion should be considered when the annual total dividends from the common shares obtained through conversion exceeds the annual dividend payments offered by the convertible security. The convertible security should also be sold when the price of that security exceeds the estimated value of the underlying stock into which it is convertible and/or prospects for price appreciation in the common stock become unfavorable.[9]

The advantage of convertible preferred stock is that the price should increase just like the common stock when it gets above the parity price. Also, if the common stock declines substantially, the convertible preferred will probably not decline as much since it has a stabilizer because of its stated dividend. Therefore, convertible preferred stock enjoys the upside potential of common stock and the downside protection of preferred stock.[10]

Preferred dividends are not tax deductible expenses for the issuing corporation like the interest of bonds. However, the law allows corporations to exclude 80 percent of dividends received from other firms from their taxable income. Therefore, the yield on high grade preferred stock has been below the yield of high grade corporate bonds.

Preferred stock, which averaged 6 percent of long-term corporate financing for the period 1970 to 1985, is the least used of all corporate securities. Given a choice between issuing bonds or preferred stock most corporate treasurers would choose bonds because they have a lower after-tax cost of capital. Since the dividends cannot be counted on as an expense by the issuing company, preferred stock has not been a popular source of capital for corporations (except utilities) compared to bonds and common stocks.

VALUATION OF PREFERRED STOCK

The price of a nonparticipating preferred stock is equal to the present value of its infinite stream of promised dividend payments. For example,

$$P_0 = \frac{D}{R}$$

where

P_0 = price of the nonparticipating preferred
R = appropriate discount rate
D = stated annual dividend rate

If we assume that a preferred stock pays an annual dividend of $10 per share, then the value of a share to an investor requiring a 10 percent rate of return would be

$$P_0 = \frac{\$10}{0.10} = \$100$$

When investors purchase a corporation's preferred stock, they expose themselves to more risk than they would assume by owning the firm's bonds, but less risk than if they had purchased the common stock. Therefore, the yield on preferred stock might be expected to be higher than the yield on bonds of comparable quality and maturity. However, yields on preferred stocks are almost always below yields on bonds. Prior to the passage of the Tax Reform Act of 1986 only 15 percent of the dividends earned by corporate holders of preferred stock were subject to federal income taxation. The tax rate is now 20 percent.

PERFORMANCE: STOCKS VERSUS BONDS

Although equities have historically been considered as superior investment vehicles relative to fixed-income securities, the comparative advantage has shifted in the decade through 1980. For example, Fisher and Lorie (1968) revealed that over the period from 1926 to 1965, the average return from common stocks was 9.3 percent compared to a meager performance of about 3.5 percent for bonds. A National Bureau of Economic Research study by Hickman (1958) showed a return on bonds of 5.6 percent for the period 1900–1943. However, in the period from 1969 through 1980, fixed income returns were higher than equity returns about half of the time. As a matter of fact, aggressively managed bond funds far outperformed the Standard & Poor's 500 Stock Average in the first half of the 1970s according to a study by Daniel Ahearn (1975). Currently, fixed income investments are viewed as highly competitive in return to the equity side of the market.

Ibbotson Associates of Chicago in their annual statistical analysis showed that the total returns for common stock were far greater than the total return on bonds or U.S. Treasury bills in the period 1925–1985 (see Table 12.4). As a matter of fact, small stocks showed higher returns than the common stock averages. The Ibbotson analysis also gives yearly returns for stocks, bonds, and Treasury bills. It shows that yearly performance is quite volatile and that only Treasury bills had a positive return in almost every year (59 out of 60 years) (see Table 12.5). Stocks that had the greatest return over this 60-year period had 19 years in which their return was negative. The average annual return (using both the arithmetic and the geometric mean) for common stocks was 9.8 and 12.0 percent, for small stocks 12.6 and 18.3 percent, for long-term government bonds 4.8 and 5.1 percent, for Treasury bills 3.4 and 3.5 percent, compared to an average inflation rate of close to 3.1 percent during the period 1926–1985 (see Table 12.6). The

Table 12.4
Basic Series: Invoices of Year-End Cumulative Wealth, 1925–1985

Year	Common Stocks Total Returns	Common Stocks Capital Appreciation	Small Stocks Total Returns	Long-Term Corp. Bonds Total Returns	Long-Term Government Bonds Total Returns	Long-Term Government Bonds Capital Appreciation	U.S. Treasury Bills Total Returns	Consumer Price Index
1925	1.000	1.000	1.000	1.000	1.000	1.000	1.000	1.000
1926	1.116	1.057	1.003	1.074	1.078	1.039	1.033	0.985
1927	1.535	1.384	1.224	1.154	1.174	1.095	1.065	0.965
1928	2.204	1.908	1.710	1.186	1.175	1.061	1.099	0.955
1929	2.018	1.681	0.832	1.225	1.215	1.059	1.152	0.957
1930	1.516	1.202	0.515	1.323	1.272	1.072	1.179	0.899
1931	0.859	0.636	0.259	1.299	1.204	0.981	1.192	0.814
1932	0.789	0.540	0.245	1.439	1.407	1.108	1.204	0.730
1933	1.214	0.792	0.594	1.588	1.406	1.073	1.207	0.734
1934	1.197	0.745	0.738	1.808	1.547	1.146	1.209	0.749
1935	1.767	1.053	1.035	1.982	1.624	1.170	1.211	0.771
1936	2.367	1.346	1.705	2.116	1.746	1.225	1.213	0.780
1937	1.538	0.827	0.716	2.174	1.750	1.194	1.217	0.804
1938	2.016	1.035	0.951	2.307	1.847	1.228	1.217	0.782
1939	2.008	0.979	0.954	2.399	1.957	1.271	1.217	0.778
1940	1.812	0.829	0.905	2.480	2.076	1.319	1.217	0.786
1941	1.602	0.681	0.823	2.548	2.095	1.305	1.218	0.862
1942	1.927	0.766	1.190	2.614	2.162	1.315	1.221	0.942
1943	2.427	0.915	2.242	2.688	2.207	1.310	1.225	0.972
1944	2.906	1.041	3.446	2.815	2.270	1.314	1.229	0.993
1945	3.965	1.361	5.983	2.930	2.513	1.423	1.233	1.015
1946	3.645	1.199	5.287	2.980	2.511	1.392	1.238	1.199
1947	3.853	1.199	5.335	2.911	2.445	1.327	1.244	1.307
1948	4.065	1.191	5.223	3.031	2.528	1.340	1.254	1.343
1949	4.829	1.313	6.254	3.132	2.691	1.395	1.268	1.318
1950	6.360	1.600	8.677	3.198	2.692	1.366	1.283	1.395
1951	7.888	1.863	9.355	3.112	2.586	1.281	1.302	1.477

Year								
1952	9.336	2.082	9.638	3.221	2.616	1.262	1.324	1.490
1953	9.244	1.944	9.013	3.331	2.711	1.270	1.348	1.499
1954	14.108	2.820	14.473	3.511	2.906	1.325	1.360	1.492
1955	18.561	3.564	17.431	3.527	2.868	1.271	1.381	1.497
1956	19.778	3.658	18.177	3.287	2.708	1.164	1.415	1.540
1957	17.646	3.134	15.529	3.573	2.910	1.208	1.459	1.587
1958	25.298	4.327	25.605	3.494	2.733	1.097	1.482	1.615
1959	28.322	4.694	29.804	3.460	2.671	1.029	1.526	1.639
1960	28.455	4.554	28.823	3.774	3.039	1.124	1.566	1.663
1961	36.106	5.607	38.072	3.956	3.068	1.092	1.600	1.674
1962	32.955	4.945	33.504	4.270	3.280	1.122	1.643	1.695
1963	40.469	5.879	41.444	4.364	3.319	1.092	1.695	1.723
1964	47.139	6.642	51.193	4.572	3.436	1.984	1.754	1.743
1965	53.008	7.244	72.567	4.552	3.460	1.047	1.823	1.777
1966	47.674	6.295	67.479	4.560	3.586	1.036	1.910	1.836
1967	59.104	7.560	123.870	4.335	3.257	0.895	1.991	1.892
1968	65.642	8.140	168.428	4.446	3.248	0.846	2.094	1.981
1969	60.059	7.210	126.233	4.086	3.038	0.754	2.232	2.102
1970	62.465	7.222	104.226	4.837	3.457	0.791	2.378	2.218
1971	71.406	8.001	121.423	5.370	3.914	0.843	2.482	2.292
1972	84.956	9.252	126.807	5.760	4.136	0.840	2.577	2.371
1973	72.500	7.645	87.618	5.825	4.090	0.775	2.756	2.579
1974	53.311	5.373	70.142	5.647	4.268	0.748	2.976	2.894
1975	73.144	7.068	107.189	6.474	4.661	0.754	3.149	3.097
1976	90.584	8.422	168.691	7.681	5.441	0.815	3.309	3.246
1977	84.076	7.453	211.500	7.813	5.405	0.750	3.479	3.466
1978	89.592	7.532	261.120	7.807	5.342	0.682	3.728	3.778
1979	106.112	8.459	374.614	7.481	5.277	0.615	4.115	4.281
1980	140.513	10.639	523.992	7.285	5.069	0.530	4.578	4.812
1981	133.615	9.605	596.717	7.215	5.162	0.475	5.251	5.242
1982	162.221	11.023	763.829	10.374	7.245	0.589	5.805	5.445
1983	198.744	12.926	1066.828	10.862	7.294	0.530	6.315	5.652
1984	211.198	13.106	995.681	12.642	8.420	0.542	6.937	5.875
1985	279.115	16.558	1241.235	16.549	11.027	0.639	7.473	6.097

Source: Roger G. Ibbotson and Rex A. Sinquefield, *Stocks, Bonds, Bills, and Inflation*, 1982 edition (Institute for Chartered Financial Analysts, Charlottesville, Va., updated in *Stocks, Bonds, Bills, and Inflation: 1987 Yearbook* (Ibbotson Associates, Chicago).

Table 12.5
Basic Series: Year-by-Year Total Returns, 1926–1985

Year	Common Stocks	Small Stocks	Long-Term Corporate Bonds	Long-Term Government Bonds	U.S. Treasury Bills	Consumer Price Index
1926	0.1162	0.0028	0.0737	0.0777	0.0327	-0.0149
1927	0.3749	0.2210	0.0744	0.0893	0.0312	-0.0208
1928	0.4361	0.3969	0.0284	0.0010	0.0324	-0.0097
1929	-0.0842	-0.5136	0.0327	0.0342	0.0475	0.0019
1930	-0.2490	-0.3815	0.0798	0.0466	0.0241	-0.0603
1931	-0.4334	-0.4975	-0.0185	-0.0531	0.0107	-0.0952
1932	-0.0819	-0.0539	0.1082	0.1684	0.0096	-0.1030
1933	0.5399	1.4287	0.1038	-0.0008	0.0030	0.0051
1934	-0.0144	0.2422	0.1384	0.1002	0.0016	0.0203
1935	0.4767	0.4019	0.0961	0.0498	0.0017	0.0299
1936	0.3392	0.6480	0.0674	0.0751	0.0018	0.0121
1937	-0.3503	-0.5801	0.0275	0.0023	0.0031	0.0310
1938	0.3112	0.3280	0.0613	0.0553	-0.0002	-0.0278
1939	-0.0041	0.0035	0.0397	0.0594	0.0002	-0.0048
1940	-0.0978	-0.0516	0.0339	0.0609	0.0000	0.0096
1941	-0.1159	-0.0900	0.0273	0.0093	0.0006	0.0972
1942	0.2034	0.4451	0.0206	0.0322	0.0027	0.0929
1943	0.2590	0.8837	0.0283	0.0208	0.0035	0.0316
1944	0.1975	0.5372	0.0473	0.0281	0.0033	0.0211
1945	0.3644	0.7361	0.0408	0.1073	0.0033	0.0225
1946	-0.0807	-0.1163	0.0172	-0.0010	0.0035	0.1817
1947	0.0571	0.0092	-0.0234	-0.0263	0.0050	0.0901
1948	0.0550	-0.0211	0.0414	0.0340	0.0081	0.0271
1949	0.1879	0.1975	0.0331	0.0645	0.0110	-0.0180
1950	0.3171	0.3875	0.0212	0.0006	0.0120	0.0579
1951	0.2402	0.0780	-0.0269	-0.0394	0.0149	0.0587
1952	0.1837	0.0303	0.0352	0.0116	0.0166	0.0088
1953	-0.0099	0.0649	0.0341	0.0363	0.0182	0.0062
1954	0.5262	0.6058	0.0539	0.0719	0.0086	-0.0050

1955	0.3156	0.2044	0.0048	-0.0130	0.0157	0.0037
1956	0.0656	0.0428	-0.0681	-0.0559	0.0246	0.0286
1957	-0.1078	-0.1457	0.0871	0.0745	0.0314	0.0302
1958	0.4336	0.6489	-0.0222	-0.0610	0.0154	0.0176
1959	0.1195	0.1640	-0.0097	-0.0226	0.0295	0.0150
1960	0.0047	-0.0329	0.0907	0.1378	0.0266	0.0148
1961	0.2689	0.3209	0.0482	0.0097	0.0213	0.0067
1962	-0.0873	-0.1190	0.0795	0.0689	0.0273	0.0122
1963	0.2280	0.2357	0.0219	0.0121	0.0312	0.0165
1964	0.1648	0.2352	0.0477	0.0351	0.0354	0.0119
1965	0.1245	0.4175	-0.0046	0.0071	0.0393	0.0192
1966	-0.1006	-0.0701	0.0020	0.0365	0.0476	0.0335
1967	0.2398	0.8357	-0.0495	-0.0919	0.0421	0.0304
1968	0.1106	0.3597	0.0257	-0.0026	0.0521	0.0472
1969	-0.0850	-0.2505	-0.0809	-0.0508	0.0658	0.0611
1970	0.0401	-0.1743	0.1837	0.1210	0.0653	0.0549
1971	0.1431	0.1650	0.1101	0.1323	0.0439	0.0336
1972	0.1898	0.0443	0.0726	0.0568	0.0384	0.0341
1973	-0.1466	-0.3090	0.0114	-0.0111	0.0693	0.0880
1974	-0.2647	-0.1995	-0.0306	0.0435	0.0800	0.1220
1975	0.3720	0.5282	0.1464	0.0919	0.0580	0.0701
1976	0.2384	0.5738	0.1865	0.1675	0.0508	0.0481
1977	-0.0718	0.2538	0.0171	-0.0067	0.0512	0.0677
1978	0.0656	0.2346	-0.0007	-0.0116	0.0718	0.0903
1979	0.1844	0.4346	-0.0418	-0.0122	0.1038	0.1331
1980	0.3242	0.3988	-0.0262	-0.0395	0.1124	0.1240
1981	-0.0491	0.1388	-0.0096	0.0185	0.1471	0.0894
1982	0.2141	0.2801	0.4379	0.4035	0.1054	0.0387
1983	0.2251	0.3967	0.0470	0.0068	0.0880	0.0380
1984	0.0627	-0.0667	0.1639	0.1543	0.0985	0.0395
1985	0.3216	0.2466	0.3090	0.3087	0.0772	0.0377

Source: Roger G. Ibbotson and Rex A. Sinquefield, *Stocks, Bonds, Bills, and Inflation,* 1982 edition (Institute for Chartered Financial Analysts, Charlottesville, Va., updated in *Stocks, Bonds, Bills, and Inflation: 1987 Yearbook* (Ibbotson Associates, Chicago).

Table 12.6
Basic Series: Total Annual Returns, 1926–1985

SERIES	GEOMETRIC MEAN	ARITHMETIC MEAN	STANDARD DEVIATION
COMMON STOCKS	9.8%	12.0%	21.2%
SMALL STOCKS	12.6	18.3	36.0
LONG TERM CORPORATE BONDS	4.8	5.1	8.3
U.S. TREASURY BILLS	3.4	3.5	3.4
LONG TERM GOVERNMENT BONDS	4.1	4.4	8.2
INFLATION	3.1	3.2	4.9

Source: Roger G. Ibbotson and Rex A. Sinquefield, *Stocks, Bonds, Bills, and Inflation,* 1982 edition (Institute for Chartered Financial Analysts, Charlottesville, Va., updated in *Stocks, Bonds, Bills, and Inflation: 1987 Yearbook* (Ibbotson Associates, Chicago).

standard deviations or risk measures for these instruments were highest for small stocks, followed by common stocks, followed by corporate bonds, long-term Treasury bonds, and Treasury bills. The highest returns were associated with the highest risks.

There are of course other investments that can be made in real assets such as oil, U.S. coins, U.S. stamps, gold, silver, Chinese ceramics, diamonds, and farm land. All had annual rates of return in excess of 10 percent, compared to Treasury bill average returns of 8.8 percent, long-term bond returns of 6.4 percent, and stock returns of 5.7 percent. Over the period 1973–1983, U.S. coins, oil, U.S. stamps, silver, and gold all had an average return in excess of 13 percent compared to a Treasury bill rate of return of 10.1 percent, an average bond return of 6.6 percent, and a stock market return of 7.5 percent. During the period 1978–1983, U.S. stamps, gold, oil, and stocks all had annual average yields over 14.8 percent, while Treasury bills had an average annual return of 12.8 percent and long-term bonds had an annual average return of 7.2 percent. It is interesting to note that investments in oil and stamps, which ranked first and third in the 1968–1983 period overall, ranked last and next to last in 1983 when inflation slowed (see Table 12.7). Investments in oil and farm land would have shown substantial negative returns during 1984 and 1985 as oil and farm prices collapsed, while the stock market had a return of over 32 percent in 1985 and 16.3 percent in 1984. The long-term government and corporate bond markets had annual returns of 30.9 percent in 1985 and close to 16 percent in 1984.

Table 12.7
Annual Rates of Return on Major Investments, 1968–1983

	15 Years	Rank	10 Years	Rank	5 Years	Rank	1 Year	Rank
Oil	20.4%	1	25.4%	2	16.2%	4	-14.7%	15
U.S. coins	17.9	2	25.7	1	13.2	6	16.8	5
U.S. stamps	16.8	3	19.2	3	21.8	1	-6.2	14
Gold	16.6	4	15.5	5	17.5	3	28.6	4
Chinese ceramics	14.2	5	4.0	14	13.1	7	0.0	11
Silver	12.6	6	17.3	4	19.7	2	109.5	1
Diamonds	10.1	7	10.3	7	5.4	13	0.0	10
Farmland	10.0	8	11.7	6	7.0	12	-5.7	13
Treasury bills	8.8	9	10.1	8	12.8	8	10.8	6
Housing	8.6	10	9.2	9	7.4	10	2.1	8
Old Masters	7.8	11	8.4	10	4.1	14	1.7	9
CPI	7.3	12	8.5	11	9.1	9	3.9	7
Bonds	6.4	13	6.6	13	7.2	11	39.0	3
Stocks	5.7	14	7.5	12	14.8	5	51.8	2
Foreign exchange	3.1	15	1.4	15	-2.8	15	-4.3	12

Note: All returns are for the period ended June 1, 1983.

Source: R. S. Salomon, Jr., "Financial Assets—Return to Favor," *Investment Policy: Stock Research*, Salomon Brothers Inc. (June 10, 1983): p. 1. Reprinted by permission.

SUMMARY

Equity means an ownership claim; equity securities are certificates of ownership of a corporation—the residual claim on the assets of a firm after all liabilities are paid. The principal types of equity securities are common and preferred stock; there are also a variety of securities that are convertible into common stock. Households are the largest investors in common stock, followed by pension funds, mutual funds, and life insurance companies. The trust departments of commercial banks also own large amounts of common stock in a fiduciary capacity for their trust accounts and pension fund investments managed for individuals.

Three basic approaches are used to select securities: technical, fundamental, and efficient market selection. Proponents of technical selection believe that security prices often move in identifiable patterns and rely heavily on charts of historical prices and volumes in an effort to extrapolate any apparent trends. Although the securities picked via technical analysis often earn positive rates of return over the long run, the procedures that technicians use have been almost totally discredited by extensive academic research. In contrast to technical analysts, fundamentalists try to forecast future cash flow from a security. The discounted present value of the expected cash flow represents the fundamental analyst's opinion about the intrinsic value of the security. If the actual price at which the security is trading differs from the fundamental analyst's intrinsic value, the security should be bought or sold, as appropriate. The efficient market theory suggests that all information is already reflected in existing security prices and that consequently securities will never be mispriced. Actual trading prices will always be identical to properly calculated fundamental intrinsic values. Research shows that while efficient market theory is an overstatement of reality, the security markets are considerably more price efficient than people believe.

The efficient market hypothesis can be described in three forms: weak, semistrong, and strong. The weak form extends the random walk theory, which implies that technical trading strategies based on the history of prices are not of value in investment decision making. The semistrong form implies that all public information is fully reflected in stock prices, that stock prices incorporate new information in a prompt and unbiased manner, and that for most investors fundamental analysis is of limited value. The strong form suggests that even inside information cannot be used to capture above normal trading profits.

Numerous attempts are made to explain the causes of price fluctuations in stocks. Investor perceptions of the economic situation, the level and outlook for interest rates, the outlook for the dollar vis-à-vis other currencies, the industry relative to the economy, the performance of the company relative to the industry, the expected dividend, the growth rate anticipated in earnings, relative P/e ratios, and the quality of management are all considered to be relevant variables that help explain market prices.

NOTES

1. Marchese, J., "The Major Approaches to the Question of Valuation," *AAII Journal* (October 1985): 31–34.
2. R. J. Doyle, Jr., "Modern Capital Market Theory: The Random Walk and Efficient Markets," *Investments*, HS 328 Study Guide (Bryn Mawr, Penn.: American College, 1984), pp. R7.1–7.2.
3. Doyle, "Modern Capital Market Theory," p. R7.5.
4. J. B. Cohen, E. D. Zinbarg, and A. Zeikel, "Business Cycles and Investment Strategy," *Selected Topics in Investment Management for Financial Planning*, F. G. Fabozzi and S. Kole, eds. (Homewood, Ill.: Dow Jones Irwin, 1985), pp. 148–51.
5. B. G. King, "Market and Industry Factors in Stock Price Behavior," *Journal of Business* (January 1960): 139–90.
6. F. G. Fabozzi and S. Kole, *Selected Topics in Investment Management for Financial Planning* (Homewood, Ill.: Dow Jones Irwin, 1985), pp. 169–78.
7. Ibid., pp. 145–49.
8. J. C. Ritchie, "Convertible Securities," in Fabozzi and Kole, *Selected Topics in Investment Management*, pp. 277–90.
9. Ibid.
10. F. J. Fabozzi and F. G. Zarb, eds., *Handbook of Financial Markets* (Homewood, Ill.: Dow Jones Irwin, 1981), pp. 269–71.

SELECTED BIBLIOGRAPHY

Ahearn, D. S. "The Strategic Role of Fixed Income Securities" *Journal of Portfolio Management* (Spring 1975): 12–16.

Baker, H. Kent, G. E. Farrelly, and R. B. Edelman. "A Survey of Management Views on Dividend Policy." *Financial Management* (Autumn 1985): 78–84.

Baloy, James, "Market Reaction to Merger Announcements." *Financial Analyst Journal* (January–February 1973): 24–27.

Beckman, Neil G. "A Primer on Random Walks in the Stock Market." Federal Reserve Bank of Boston, *New England Economic Review* (September–October 1978): 32–50.

Chen, C. R. "Time Series Analysis of Beta Stationarity and Its Determinants: A Case of Public Utilities." *Financial Management* (Autumn 1982): 64–70.

Cooley, P. L. "A Review of the Use of Beta in Regulatory Proceedings." *Financial Management* (Winter 1981): 75–81.

Enmett, Robert. "How to Value a Potential Acquisition." *Financial Executive* 50 (February 1982): 16–19.

Fisher, L., and J. H. Lorie. "Rates of Return on Investments in Common Stock: The Year-by-Year Record, 1927–1965." *Journal of Business* (July 1968): 291–316.

Flannery, M. J., and C. M. James. "The Effect of Interest Rate Changes on the Common Stock Returns of Financial Institutions." *Journal of Finance* (September 1984): 1141–53.

Hickman, W. B. *Corporate Bond Quality and Investor Experience*. National Bureau of Economic Research, 1958.

Lintner, J. "Distribution of Income of Corporations Among Dividends, Retained Earnings and Taxes." *American Economic Review* (May 1956): 97–113.

Malkiel, Burton G. *A Random Walk Down Wall Street.* 4th ed. New York: Norton, 1985.

Melton, William C. "Corporate Equities and the National Market System." Federal Reserve Bank of New York, *Quarterly Review* (Winter 1978–1979): 13–25.

New York Stock Exchange, *Fact Book.* New York. Published Annually.

Pearce, Douglas K. "The Impact of Inflation on Stock Prices." Federal Reserve Bank of Kansas City, *Economic Review* (March 1982): 3–18.

Piper, Thomas R., and William E. Fruhan. "Is Your Stock Worth Its Market Price?" *Harvard Business Review* 59 (May–June 1981): 124–32.

Richardson, L. K. "Do High Market Risks Lead to High Returns?" *Financial Analyst Journal* 26 (March–April 1970): 124–32.

Robichek, Alexander, H. "Risk and the Value of Securities." *Journal of Financial and Quantitative Analysis* 4 (December 1969): 513–38.

Seligman, Daniel. "Can You Beat the Stock Market?" *Fortune* (December 26, 1983): 82–84.

Simmonds, Richard R. "Modern Financial Theory." *MSU Business Topics* vol. 26, no. 1 (Winter 1978): 54–63.

Soter, Dennis S. "The Dividend Controversy—What It Means for Corporate Policy." *Financial Executive* 47 (May 1979): 38–43.

Index

About the Author

ALAN GART, Professor of Finance at Lehman College of the City University of New York and a Visiting Professor at the Graduate School of Business at Columbia University, received his B.A., M.A., and Ph.D. degrees from the University of Pennsylvania. He is the author of *An Insider's Guide to the Financial Services Revolution, Banks, Thrifts and Insurance companies: Survival in the 1980's,* and *Insurance Company Finance* (with D. Nye) as well as numerous journal and magazine articles. He is a former senior vice president of a family of mutual funds, senior vice president of the Girard Bank, vice president of Manufacturers Hanover and chief economist of INA. Currently, Dr. Gart is on the board of directors of Copenhagen Reinsurance Company of America and The Market Street Fund.

About the Contributors

JERRY BELLOIT, Associate Professor of Real Estate at the University of North Florida, is the co-author of *Real Estate Appraisal,* as well as numerous other publications. He is president of Investor Realty Resources Inc., a corporation specializing in consulting with institutional clients. Dr. Belloit received his Ph.D. from the University of Florida.

JOHN GUERARD, JR., Assistant Professor of Finance at Lehigh University, is a graduate of Duke University and earned his Ph.D. at the University of Texas at Austin. He is the author of scholarly publications in the *European Journal of Operational Research, Communications in Statistics, IEEE Transactions on Engineering Management, Journal of Forecasting, Journal of the Operational Research Society, Financial Analysts Journal,* and a contributor to volumes on robust regression techniques, strategic planning, management of research and development, and mergers and acquisitions. His forthcoming books include *Foreign Currency Options, Forecasting Methods and Applications,* and *Handbook of Financial Decision Making.* Mr. Guerard is a frequent consultant to industry and government.